W9-DAU-552

Wissenschaftliche Untersuchungen
zum Neuen Testament · 2. Reihe

Herausgeber/Editor
Jörg Frey

Mitherausgeber / Associate Editors
Friedrich Avemarie · Judith Gundry-Volf
Martin Hengel · Otfried Hofius · Hans-Josef Klauck

167

Loren L. Johns

The Lamb Christology
of the Apocalypse of John

An Investigation into Its Origins
and Rhetorical Force

Mohr Siebeck

LOREN L. JOHNS, born 1955; 1977–85 Pastor; 1985–88 Theology Book Editor; 1993–2000 Assistant and Associate Professor of Religion, Bluffton College, Ohio; 1998 Ph.D.; Currently Academic Dean and Associate Professor of New Testament, Associated Mennonite Biblical Seminary, Elkhart, Indiana.

ISBN 3-16-148164-X
ISSN 0340-9570 (Wissenschaftliche Untersuchungen zum Neuen Testament 2. Reihe)

Die Deutsche Bibliothek lists this publication in the Deutsche Nationalbibliographie; detailed bibliographic data is available in the Internet at *http://dnb.ddb.de*.

© 2003 by J. C. B. Mohr (Paul Siebeck), P.O. Box 2040, D-72010 Tübingen.

This book may not be reproduced, in whole or in part, in any form (beyond that permitted by copyright law) without the publisher's written permission. This applies particularly to reproductions, translations, microfilms and storage and processing in electronic systems.

The book was printed by Druckpartner Rübelmann GmbH in Hemsbach on non-aging paper and bound by Buchbinderei Schaumann in Darmstadt.

Printed in Germany.

To Rachel,
with love and gratitude

Preface

This book represents a slightly revised version of my doctoral dissertation in New Testament Studies, which I completed at Princeton Theological Seminary in Princeton, New Jersey, under the title, *The Origins and Rhetorical Force of the Lamb Christology of the Apocalypse of John*.

Having come to this point in my journey with this research project, I am quite aware of the ways in which I have benefited from the communities of which I have been a part and from individuals who have read and critiqued what I have written here. This project would not have been possible without the benefits I have reaped from the work of many other people.

Three people whose work in the Apocalypse of John were formative for me early on were Howard Charles, Ted Grimsrud, and William Klassen. I took an undergraduate course in the Apocalypse of John with Dr. Charles at Goshen College. He taught me to be honest with the text within the confines of the subjectivity with which we all must work—to work inductively without forcing preconceived ideas on the text or predetermining a hermeneutical outcome. His deliberate and thoughtful approach also lessened my fear of this book. Later, as theology book editor for Herald Press, I edited Ted Grimsrud's book, *Triumph of the Lamb* (1987), a helpful study guide intended for laypersons and church groups. His study excited me about this book and convinced me that there was potential in reading the Apocalypse ethically. Finally, I found several conversations with William Klassen to be helpful as I began to work with this project. Dr. Klassen provided key bibliographical help and pointed me in helpful directions.

The late Dr. J. Christiaan Beker pressed me early in this project to pay attention to the overall structure and design of this dissertation in order to maintain a healthy sense of the parts within the whole and the flow of the argument. I hope the results meet his high standards in this regard.

My family has been helpful and supportive in various ways. My father, Galen Johns, graciously read part or all of several drafts of this dissertation, catching errors, providing helpful feedback, and asking for clarification. Thank you. My wife Rachel and my daughters, Kendra and Jessica, have been patiently supportive all along the way.

My small group at West Philadelphia Mennonite Fellowship was gracious enough to participate enthusiastically in an extended study I led in the late 1980s on the relevance of the Apocalypse for life in modern Philadelphia. Bluffton College supported my research along the way and helped me to persevere as I completed my dissertation while teaching there. I would especially like to thank my colleague, Dr. J. Denny Weaver, who has been a good conversation partner and whose own work on the Apocalypse has emphasized the theological significance of a preterist reading of the Apocalypse—especially for a Christus Victor Christology.

I would like to thank Princeton Theological Seminary for making this research project possible. Its heritage of serious theological inquiry informed by careful historical-critical methods is as critically valuable to Christ's church today as it has ever been. I would like to thank Dr. Beverly Gaventa, whose careful and thoughtful reading of this dissertation went beyond the call of duty and helped me to avoid some misperceptions.

I would especially like to thank my dissertation committee for the careful reading and helpful suggestions they have given me along the way: Dr. Brian K. Blount, Dr. Ulrich Mauser, and my adviser, Dr. James H. Charlesworth. Each of them read carefully and offered me valuable counsel.

I am grateful to Dr. Charlesworth for his guidance of this project. His important essay, "The Apocalypse of John: Its Theology and Impact on Subsequent Apocalypses," was seminal in my own early reflection on the rhetorical significance of the Lamb Christology and the nature of the redefinitions of power it entailed. I have benefited greatly from his knowledge of the history and literature of Second Temple Judaism. On the more personal level, I found Dr. Charlesworth always to be available, eager and willing to discuss my research and to encourage me along the way. Thank you.

Finally, I would like to express my sincere thanks to Prof. Dr. Jörg Frey of the Evangelisch-Theologische Fakultät, University of Munich, who expressed interest in my work and recommended its publication in the WUNT 2 series.

In light of the valuable help I received from these communities and individuals, I take responsibility for whatever flaws remain in this study. Despite the long labor I endured in giving birth to this work, I was encouraged by the vision of the end and a conviction that the study was both worthwhile and valid in its findings. May the reader conclude in agreement ... or at least be blessed along the way (cf. Rev 1:3).

Vicit agnus noster.

Elkhart, Indiana, July 2003

Loren L. Johns

Table of Contents

Chapter I

Introduction

1. Introductory Observations

Religion is dangerous business. Arguably, more people have been murdered in the name of religion than for any other reason in the history of humanity. Religion has inspired humanity's most profound acts of benevolence *and* its most horrifying acts of violence.

Historically, religion has been capable of inspiring the sort of imagination that motivates people on the deepest level—perhaps uniquely so. When Pontius Pilate first became prefect of Judea around 26 CE, he publicly displayed in Jerusalem several military standards bearing medallions of the emperor. The Jews of Jerusalem saw this display as a wanton disregard of the command against "graven images." When the Jews of the city staged a protest at his residence in Caesarea Maritima, Pilate ordered his troops to provide a display of force, drawing their swords and threatening to kill them if they continued to protest.

However, the protestors' deep commitment to the Law of Moses inspired them to bare their necks, showing that they were prepared to die rather than to tolerate such a violation of the Decalogue. Their religious zeal ran so deep that they even offered the necks of their wives and children to the sword rather than wink at this display of blasphemy. It was a powerful and effective demonstration of nonviolent resistance, motivated by religious zeal. In this case, Pilate backed off, though in others he did not.[1]

Many sources of power lie latent within religion. The key to religion's power lies in its ability to excite the imagination. Some religions do this through scriptural interpretation, preaching, teaching, and liturgies, while others excite the imagination in other ways. Ultimately, it is not religion itself, but religious *labels*, or the personal and corporate *interpretations* of religion that are most dangerous. For instance, during the Crusades the crusaders la-

---

[1] See Josephus, *War* 2.9, 2–3 §169–174; *Ant* 18.3, 1 §53–59; Philo *Embassy* 38 §299ff.; see also 3Mac 1:1–2:24. Examples of heroic and/or foolish self-sacrifice abound in the history and literature of Early Judaism and in subsequent history.

beled another ethnic group as "the Infidel" and associated eternal salvation with whole-hearted participation in a "Holy Crusade" against a foreign land and people. Pope Urban II and others were able to create an interpretation of the spiritual meaning of the Crusades that was powerful enough to motivate tens of thousands of people to leave home and family and to slaughter innocent men, women, and children in the name of Christ—even though such activity was personally painful, costly, and ultimately anti-Christian from the perspective of many Christians today. The power of the Crusaders' vision and the labeling power of words that promised eternal salvation were enough to lead them into their despicable repudiation of the gospel at a high cost to themselves and to others.

More specifically, the power and influence of the New Testament Revelation to John (Apocalypse of John) on the life of the church in the last two millennia have been extensive. The influence of the Apocalypse on the history of Christian art is unparalleled. Marcion rejected the Apocalypse because it was too Jewish.[2] The first three centuries of interpretation saw a polarization on the issue of its millenarianism: some rejected it because of its millenarian theology;[3] some accepted and gladly proclaimed it because of its millenarianism;[4] and still others made peace with its millenarianism by spiritualizing its message.[5]

Personal reactions to the Apocalypse have varied wildly. Augustine found in the Apocalypse's vision of future punishment and reward significant support for his theology.[6] But Augustine also admitted discomfort with the book:

---

[2] See Tertullian, *Against Marcion* III.14 and IV.5. Alexander Roberts and James Donaldson, eds., *The Ante-Nicene Fathers*, Vol. 3. New York: Charles Scribner's Sons (1925), 333, 350.

[3] E.g., Gaius (early 3rd cent.), Dionysius of Alexandria (d. c. 264), and Eusebius (c. 260–c. 340).

[4] E.g., Justin Martyr (c. 100–c. 165); Irenaeus (c. 130–c. 200), although his views on this matter are mixed; Hippolytus (c. 170–c. 236); Victorinus (d. c. 304).

[5] Origen (c. 185–c. 254), Methodius (d. c. 311), Tyconius (d. c. 400), and Augustine (354–430) were among the church fathers who "saved" John's Apocalypse for the church through an allegorizing interpretation, even though Origen and Methodius, and Tyconius and Augustine, respectively, were opponents on most other issues. Although Tertullian (c. 160–c. 225) said little about the Apocalypse, he too "spiritualized" its millenarianism.

[6] Cf. his *De Civitate Dei*, esp. Books 20–22. Nevertheless, one must admit that the Apocalypse was not as significant in his theology as has sometimes been supposed. His inspiration for the theologically programmatic concept of "the city of God" does not come from the Apocalypse's vision of the New Jerusalem. Augustine identifies Ps. 87:3 as the immediate inspiration for his identification of this city with the church: "Glorious things are spoken of thee, O city of God" (11.1). His development of the paradigm of the city of God as a way to understand and organize Christian theology

Though this book is called the Apocalypse, there are in it many obscure passages to exercise the mind of the reader, and there are few passages so plain as to assist us in the interpretation of the others, even though we take pains; and this difficulty is increased by the repetition of the same things, in forms so different, that the things referred to seem to be different, although in fact they are only differently stated.[7]

The Apocalypse was not quickly or easily canonized. Although it enjoyed canonical status earlier in the West, it remained suspect throughout the first millennium in Eastern Christianity. In the West, the Apocalypse was treated with suspicion by many people at different times. Today, despite its official canonical status, it continues to be regarded with suspicion. It is the only major book of the New Testament on which John Calvin wrote no commentary.[8] Martin Luther said, "My spirit cannot accommodate itself to this book. There is one sufficient reason for the small esteem in which I hold it—that Christ is neither taught in it nor recognized."[9]

In 1887, Friedrich Nietzsche called Revelation "jenen wüstesten aller geschriebenen Ausbrüche, welche die Rache auf dem Gewissen hat" [the wildest of written outbursts, which wreaks vengeance on the conscience].[10] He saw the book as an expression of the repressed hatred that pious weaklings often have toward the powerful. In his 1898 Jowett lectures on eschatology, R. H. Charles referred to the thought of the Apocalypse as "unadulterated Judaism." In his

---

depends on a merging or harmonizing of diverse biblical concepts and literatures, including the Psalms of Zion, Jesus' teaching of the kingdom of God, and Paul's dualisms of flesh vs. spirit and chosen people (children of the promise) vs. unchosen people (children of the flesh). When he does discuss the New Jerusalem that comes down out of heaven and the blessings that are associated with it, he concludes that it cannot be speaking figuratively of the church in the present age, but of some future blessing (20.17). Quotations and allusions to the Apocalypse play a minor role, overall, in his theology.

[7] Augustine, *The City of God*, translated by Marcus Dods, with an introduction by Thomas Merton, The Modern Library (New York: The Modern Library, 1950), 32.

[8] Calvin wrote commentaries on 24 of the 27 books of the New Testament. The three on which he wrote none are 2 and 3 John and the Apocalypse.

[9] Martin Luther, in the preface to his 1522 translation of the Bible. For more on Luther's approach to the Apocalypse, see Winfried Vogel, "The Eschatological Theology of Martin Luther; Part II: Luther's Exposition of Daniel and Revelation," *Andrews University Seminary Studies* 25 (Summer): 183–99; Rodney L. Petersen, *Preaching in the Last Days: The Theme of "Two Witnesses" in the Sixteenth and Seventeenth Centuries* (Oxford: Oxford University Press, 1993); H.-U. Hofmann, *Luther und die Johannes Apokalypse* (Tübingen: Mohr-Siebeck, 1982); Gottfried Seebass, "The Importance of Apocalyptic for the History of Protestantism," *Colloquium* 13 (October 1980), 24–35.

[10] Friedrich Nietzsche, *Zur Genealogie der Moral*, Nietzsches Werke (Alfred Kröner Verlag, 1919), 7:331.

historical and theological context, this statement was not considered a compliment. However, the views and attitude of Charles regarding the Apocalypse changed dramatically over his course of study. This negative remark was printed in the 1898 first edition of his *Studies in the Apocalypse*,[11] but it was removed in the 1913 second edition of that book.[12] George Bernard Shaw called the Apocalypse the "curious record of the visions of a drug addict which was absurdly admitted to the canon under the title of Revelation."[13]

D. H. Lawrence expressed "dislike" and "resentment" at the Apocalypse of John and found it "annoying" and "ugly." In fact, Lawrence judged the Apocalypse to be "the most detestable of all [the] books of the Bible."[14] In his 1936 *The Apostolic Preaching and Its Developments*, C. H. Dodd spoke harshly about the theology of the Apocalypse. It reflects, he thought, "a relapse into a pre-Christian eschatology."[15] "The God of the Apocalypse can hardly be recognized as the Father of our Lord Jesus Christ,"[16] nor does its fierce messiah reflect the early kerygma. Dodd advised his readers to have done with such "eschatological fanaticism."[17]

In the introduction to his modern "literary-critical interpretation" of the Apocalypse, Harold Bloom says, "The influence of Revelation is out of all proportion to its literary strength or spiritual value."[18] In Bloom's words,

---

[11] R. H. Charles, *Studies in the Apocalypse* (Edinburgh: T. & T. Clark [1899], 347).

[12] R. H. Charles, *Studies in the Apocalypse*, 347. By the time he finished writing his International Critical Commentary on the Apocalypse in 1920, he considered its theology among the best in the New Testament. He defends the book against those who regarded it as somehow sub-Christian. For instance, he says, "Nowhere in the N.T. is the glory of the exalted Christ so emphasized" (see Charles, *A Critical and Exegetical Commentary on the Revelation of St. John*, Vol. 1. The International Critical Commentary. Edinburgh: T. & T. Clark [1920], cxi; see also cix–cx). I am indebted to G. R. Beasley-Murray for pointing out this shift in Charles' thought; see G. R. Beasley-Murray, "How Christian is the Book of Revelation?" in *Reconciliation and Hope: Essays Presented to L. L. Morris*, R. J. Banks, ed. Grand Rapids: William B. Eerdmans Publishing Company, 276.

[13] George Bernard Shaw, *The Adventures of the Black Girl in Her Search for God* (New York: Dodd, Mead & Company, 1933), 73.

[14] *Apocalypse*, by D. H. Lawrence. Penguin Twentieth-Century Classics (Harmondsworth: Penguin Books, 1974 [originally published 1931]). See esp. 5–9.

[15] C. H. Dodd, *The Apostolic Preaching and Its Developments*, 2d ed., reprint, 1936 (London: Hodder and Stoughton, 1944), 40.

[16] C. H. Dodd, *Apostolic Preaching*, 41.

[17] C. H. Dodd, *Apostolic Preaching*, 41. Dodd later reiterated this judgment, calling the Apocalypse "only superficially Christian" (C. H. Dodd, *The Authority of the Bible* [London, 1960], 180).

[18] "Introduction," *The Revelation of St. John the Divine*, ed. Harold Bloom. Modern Critical Interpretations (New York: Chelsea House Publications, 1988), 1–2.

Resentment and not love is the teaching of the Revelation of St. John the Divine. It is a book without wisdom, goodness, kindness, or affection of any kind. Perhaps it is appropriate that a celebration of the end of the world should be not only barbaric but scarcely literate. Where the substance is so inhumane, who would wish the rhetoric to be more persuasive, or the vision to be more vividly realized?[19]

The rhetorical power of the Apocalypse historically to inspire and motivate interpreters of every kind make it nearly unique as a study in reader-response criticism and in the ethics of interpretation. G. K. Chesterton was certainly correct when he said that "though St. John the Evangelist saw many strange monsters in his vision, he saw no creature so wild as one of his own commentators."[20] The evocative power of the Apocalypse is never more pronounced— for better or for worse—than when the book captures the imagination of a whole community.

The 1993 tragedy experienced near Waco, Texas, with the Branch Davidians led by David Koresh has only confirmed in the minds of some the strange and negative influence of John's Apocalypse. Koresh's fascination with the Apocalypse is well-documented.[21] Appeals to the Old Testament conquest narratives and to the Apocalypse have been used to incite numerous wars and "resistance movements" such as the one led by David Koresh.[22]

The Apocalypse of John is arguably the most dangerous book in the history of Christendom in terms of the history of its effects. It has been used to inspire and mobilize countless Christian communities over the centuries, from Montanism to David Koresh's Branch Davidians.[23] The movements inspired by

---

[19] Bloom, "Introduction," 4–5.

[20] G. K. Chesterton, *Orthodoxy* (New York: John Lane Co., 1908), 29.

[21] See, for instance, Peter Steinfels, "Bible's Book of Revelation Was Key to Waco Cult," *New York Times* 142 (1993): 16; cf. also James D. Tabor, *Why Waco?: Cults and the Battle for Religious Freedom in America*, coauthor Eugene V. Gallagher (Berkeley: University of California Press, 1995), 8–9, 53–55, 191–203.

[22] Koresh himself found the Apocalypse to be the key to the interpretation of the entire Bible. He said, "Every book of the Bible meets and ends in the book of Revelation" (David Koresh, "The Decoded Message of the Seven Seals of the Book of Revelation," unpublished paper, with a preface by J. Phillip Arnold, compiled by James D. Tabor (Houston: Reunion Institute, 1994), 7. Koresh specifically claimed that the Branch Davidians were the beneficiaries of the Apocalypse and that the original readers of the Apocalypse were simply a part of the grace the Davidians were about to receive (cf. p. 8). Furthermore, Koresh claimed that he himself was the Lamb who was worthy to open the sealed scroll (Rev 5) as well as the rider on the white horse (Rev 19; cf. "Comments and Clarifications," James D. Tabor and J. Phillip Arnold, p. A, attached as an appendix to *The Decoded Message*).

[23] For historical surveys of millennialism in the Middle Ages and in the Reformation, see Norman Cohn, *The Pursuit of the Millennium: Revolutionary Millenarians*

apocalyptic literature in general and the Apocalypse of John in particular have
been multifarious.[24] Some groups, such as the medieval monastic orders of the

and Mystical Anarchists of the Middle Ages, 2d ed. (New York: Oxford University Press, 1970); Richard Kenneth Emmerson, *Antichrist in the Middle Ages: A Study of Medieval Apocalypticism, Art, and Literature* (Seattle, Wash.: University of Washington Press, 1981); Thomas Arthur Dughi, *The Breath of Christ's Mouth: Apocalypse and Prophecy in Early Reformation Ideology*. Ph.D. Dissertation (Johns Hopkins University, 1990); Richard Kenneth Emmerson and Bernard McGinn, eds. *The Apocalypse in the Middle Ages* (Ithaca and London: Cornell University Press, 1992); G. Kretschmar, *Die Offenbarung des Johannes: die Geschichte ihrer Auslegung im 1. Jahrtausend* (Calwer Theologische Monographien, Band 9; Stuttgart: Calwer Verlag, 1985); Bernard McGinn, *Visions of the End: Apocalyptic Traditions in the Middle Ages* (New York: Columbia University Press, 1979); F. Rapp, "Apocalypse et mouvements populaires au Moyen Age," *L'Apocalyptique*, ed. by F. Raphaël, Études d'Histoire des Religions, no. 3 (Paris: Librairie Orientaliste Paul Geuthner); Pierre Prigent, *L'Apocalyptique*, ed. by F. Raphaël, Études d'Histoire des Religions, no. 3 (Paris: Librairie Orientaliste Paul Geuthner); and Ned Bernard Stonehouse, *The Apocalypse in the Ancient Church: A Study in the History of the New Testament Canon* (Goes, Netherlands: Oosterbaan & Le Cointre, 1929).

For a helpful overview of the influence of the apocalypse in the Middle Ages, see "The Exegesis of the Apocalypse in Latin Christianity," chapter two of *The Calabrian Abbot: Joachim of Fiore in the History of Western Thought*, by Bernard McGinn (New York and London: Macmillan and Collier Macmillan, 1985), 74–97. For the influence of the Apocalypse on the English renaissance and post-renaissance Victorian literature, see C. A. Patrides and Joseph Wittreich, eds., *The Apocalypse in English Renaissance Thought and Literature* (Ithaca, N.Y.: Cornell University Press, 1984). James H. Moorhead pursues some of the same issues in his survey of the influence of apocalyptic thought during the American civil war; see *American Apocalypse: Yankee Protestants and the Civil War, 1860–1869* (New Haven: Yale University Press, 1978).

[24] The identification of the social location of the communities that have produced and valued apocalyptic writings is a point of debate. Norman Cohn has confidently generalized that the Jewish apocalypses "were directed to the lower strata of the Jewish population as a form of nationalist propaganda" (*Pursuit*, 20). Paul Hanson has argued that apocalypticism had its origins in a shared sociological status: "one of disenfranchisement and alienation from the institutional structures of the community" (*The Dawn of Apocalyptic: The Historical and Sociological Roots of Jewish Apocalyptic Eschatology*, 2d ed. (Philadelphia: Fortress Press, 1979), e.g., 409. In contrast, Leonard Thompson denies that one can speak of a "genre-specific social, historical setting" of apocalypses. He argues that apocalypticists shared a *perception* of crisis, but that "*any social situation can be perceived as one of crisis*" (*The Book of Revelation: Apocalypse and Empire* [New York: Oxford, 1990], 25, 28; emphasis mine). At least one phenomenological study of apocalyptic movements throughout history has tended to confirm Thompson's theory: see Stephen L. Cook, "Millennial Groups in Power: Toward a New Basis for Studying Biblical Apocalyptic Groups," presentation at Society of Biblical Literature annual meeting, 1992, in San Francisco.

late Middle Ages and the nineteenth-century Millerites, found in the Apocalypse a rationale for nonparticipation in society and thus withdrew from society to await the return of Christ.[25] Other groups, such as the violent, revolutionary Münster Anabaptists, found in the Apocalypse a rationale for why they should take up the sword to help God bring in the kingdom.

Interestingly, although the Apocalypse has inspired in some readers much chaos and violence, it has provided for other readers significant hope, peace, and comfort. In his fascinating book, *Irenic Apocalypse: Some Uses of Apocalyptic in Dante, Petrarch and Rabelais*, Dennis Costa argues that modern characterizations of the Apocalypse that are univocally violent are essentially "misappropriations" of the text. While the images of the Apocalypse are surely violent, the book aims to liberate a people and leave them at peace. It is this "irenic" function that is often missed in today's discourse. Even such an author as Dante, often associated with the most violent of images, found in apocalyptic language a means of resolving nonviolently his own political and spiritual aspirations.[26]

Although readings of the Apocalypse in some contexts have inspired Christians to withdraw from society and "wait," readings of the Apocalypse in other contexts have inspired Christians to become more engaged in society. In his compelling little study of the Apocalypse, Allen Boesak says that it should be no surprise that the Apocalypse is a source of encouragement and hope for an oppressed people. He sees in the book a "sharp, critical commentary on contemporary historical events."[27] Apocalyptic literature "always appears against a background of persecution and suffering ... [and] is ... meant as

---

[25] The increasing influence of the Apocalypse in the late Middle Ages is due primarily to the influence of Joachim of Fiore. Umberto Eco's fascinating *The Name of the Rose* recounts part of this story (William Weaver, trans. [New York: Warner Books, 1984]). See also Bernard McGinn, *The Calabrian Abbot: Joachim of Fiore in the History of Western Thought* (New York: Macmillan, 1985). The systems of thought articulated by William Miller (early to mid-nineteenth century) and the works of Hal Lindsey (late twentieth century) provide the focus for Stephen O'Leary's attempt to articulate a theory of millennial rhetoric in Stephen D. O'Leary, *Arguing the Apocalypse: A Theory of Millennial Rhetoric* (New York: Oxford University Press, 1994).

[26] Cf. Dennis Costa, *Irenic Apocalypse: Some Uses of Apocalyptic in Dante, Petrarch and Rabelais* (Saratoga: Cal.: Anma Libri, 1981), 1–3, 44–45; cf. also R. E. Kaske, "Dante's DXV," in *Dante*, John Freccero, ed. (Englewood Cliffs: Prentice-Hall, 1965), 122–140. Costa does not go so far as to suggest that the Apocalypse articulates a nonviolent *ethic*. Rather, his point is that the vision is essential irenic—that whatever the means to the goal, the goal actually is an irenic Paradise, not cataclysmic destruction or violence for its own sake.

[27] Allan Boesak, *Comfort and Protest: Reflections on the Apocalypse of John of Patmos* (Philadelphia: Westminster Press, 1987), 16.

comfort, encouragement, and inspiration for people in times of dire stress and great difficulties."[28] The Apocalypse is "protest literature" because it is inherently subversive. It shows little respect for the *status quo*.

In the Quaker tradition, the Apocalypse of John has shaped and empowered a tradition of prophetic engagement with the world that is unique among the Protestant churches.[29] Friends have often understood social engagement in the world as an expression of the "apocalyptic battle" reflected in John's Apocalypse. Because this engagement is filled with conflict, "battle" imagery and terminology are appropriate even though the tactics themselves are those of nonviolence. George Fox and the early Quakers referred to this radical engagement with the world as "the Lamb's war," drawing on imagery from the Apocalypse. This "Lamb's war" is in one sense political, but one waged through the prophetic power of the word, not through the traditional tactics of violence or power politics. Among the three historic peace churches,[30] the Friends have articulated the clearest vision of engagement with the world, with the powers of darkness. Arguably, it was George Fox's reading of the Apocalypse and his Apocalypse-inspired language that most directly effected this difference.[31]

One recent study of the Apocalypse offers a thorough-going political reading. Wes Howard-Brook and Anthony Gwyther's *Unveiling Empire: Reading Revelation Then and Now* sees in Revelation a consistent critique of the Roman Empire and of any government that, like the Roman imperial cult, demands the allegiance that belongs to Jesus alone.[32] Throughout this book the

---

[28] *Comfort and Protest*, 15.

[29] For a compelling exposition of the influence of the Apocalypse on the life and thought of both George Fox personally and the larger Quaker tradition, see Douglas Gwyn, *Apocalypse of the Word: The Life and Message of George Fox (1624–1691)* (Richmond, Ind.: Friends United Press, 1986).

[30] The historic peace churches in the United States consist of the Mennonites, the Friends (Quakers), and the Church of the Brethren.

[31] Note the judgment of Douglas Gwyn, one of the leading contemporary interpreters of Fox: "Though Fox clearly has a singular grasp of scripture as a whole, Revelation is the only text for which he particularly notes a breakthrough in interpretation. It is also the only book of the Bible to receive an extended, point-by-point interpretation in his writings. But its significance to him is best revealed by the way its language infuses and informs page after page, volume after volume of his works" (Douglas Gwyn, *Apocalypse of the Word*, 186). Gwyn's interpretation of Fox emphasizes Fox's indebtedness to apocalyptic thought in contrast to the mystical interpretation of Rufus M. Jones and the "Protestant" interpretation of Geoffrey Nuttall and Hugh Barbour (cf. Douglas Gwyn, *Apocalypse of the Word*, xiii–xxiii, 213–18).

[32] Wes Howard-Brook and Anthony Gwyther, *Unveiling Empire: Reading Revelation Then and Now*, foreword by Elizabeth McAlister (Orbis Books, 1999).

authors mine the Apocalypse for lessons for today's Christians seeking to understand how to follow Jesus on the way of discipleship. For them, such practical discipleship entails a critique of empire conjoined with real engagement with the poor and disenfranchised.

Howard-Brook and Gwyther say, for instance:

> Despite the spiritualized and politically disengaged interpretations of scripture that have become the norm in our churches, seminaries, and Bible study groups, it is clear to us that Revelation, like all the other biblical texts, was involved in a pitched battle over issues of spirit such as economics and politics.... Because Revelation took seriously the world of the Roman Empire—and declared it a blasphemous caricature of God's sovereignty over the world—we can take our own world no less seriously.[33]

Thus, for some readers, the message of the Apocalypse is not a message of "escape" from this world, but a celebration that the domination system of this world has been defeated in the death and resurrection of Jesus and that Christians must resist the seductive power of that domination system. Its message is a message of nonviolent resistance and its power lies in its unmasking of the present order.[34] As Richard Bauckham has said, "Those who imagine early Christianity as a quietist and apolitical movement should study the book of Revelation."[35] And as Bauckham has said elsewhere, the message of the Apocalypse "is not that the here-and-now are left behind in an escape into heaven or the eschatological future, but that the here-and-now look quite different when they are opened to transcendence."[36] The Apocalypse is, in fact, "the most powerful piece of political resistance literature from the period of the early Empire.[37]

No confessional stance or religious commitment is required to recognize the subversive power and this-worldly potential of the Apocalypse. In the Japanese occupation of Korea during the Second World War, the Japanese were wary of the subversive power of preaching from the Apocalypse. As a result, they prohibited Korean preachers from preaching from the Apocalypse.[38]

---

[33] Howard-Brook and Gwyther, *Unveiling Empire*, xxiv.

[34] Cf. Walter Wink, *Engaging the Powers: Discernment and Resistance in a World of Domination*, The Powers, vol. 3 (Philadelphia: Fortress, 1992), 324.

[35] Richard Bauckham, "The Fallen City: Revelation 18," chapt. 6 in *The Bible in Politics: How to Read the Bible Politically*, by Richard Bauckham (Louisville, Ky.: Westminster/John Knox Press, 1989), 101.

[36] Richard Bauckham, *The Theology of the Book of Revelation*, New Testament Theology (Cambridge and New York: Cambridge University Press, 1993), 7–8.

[37] Bauckham, *The Theology of the Book of Revelation*, 38.

[38] *Comfort and Protest*, 17.

The idea that the Apocalypse is "resistance literature" is not new. Already in 1920, R. H. Charles wrote:

> *The object of the Apocalypse was to encourage the faithful to resist* even to death the blasphemous claims of the State, and to proclaim the coming victory of the cause of God and of His Christ not only in the individual Christian, and the corporate body of such individuals, but also in the nations as such in their national and international life and relations. It lays down the only true basis for national ethics and international law. Hence the Seer claims not only the after-world for God and for His people, but also this world.[39]

But "resistance literature" does not say enough, since there are many conceptions of resistance and as many corresponding political perspectives.[40] For many scholars, "apocalyptic" is nearly synonymous with "other-worldly" and escapist. This questionable association derives in part from German scholarship's dislike of any works which "breathe anything but the clarity of a timeless and logical terminology."[41]

---

[39] R. H. Charles, *A Critical and Exegetical Commentary on the Revelation of St. John*, Vol. 1, The International Critical Commentary (Edinburgh: T. & T. Clark, 1920), xxii; emphasis mine. Although Charles's claim that the Apocalypse "lays down the only true basis for national ethics and international law" is probably too bold, he is correct in seeing the ethic of the Apocalypse as a politically engaged, practical ethic.

[40] For a helpful delineation of the various "political perspectives" reflected in the literature of Early Judaism and a discussion of how the Apocalypse fits within that literature, see Adela Yarbro Collins, "The Political Perspective of the Revelation to John," *Journal of Biblical Literature* 96 (1977): 241–56. Cf. also Klaus Wengst, "Babylon the Great and the New Jerusalem: The Visionary View of Political Reality in the Revelation of John," in *Politics and Theopolitics in the Bible and Postbiblical Literature*, edited by Henning Graf Reventlow, Yair Hoffman, and Benjamin Uffenheimer, *Journal for the Study of the Old Testament* Supplement Series, no. 171 (Sheffield: JSOT Press, 1994), 189–202; Bauckham, "Fallen City"; Oliver O'Donovan, "The Political Thought of the Book of Revelation," *Tyndale Bulletin* 37 (1986): 61–94; Walter Dietrich, "Gott als König: Zur Frage nach der theologischen und politischen Legitimät religiöser Begriffsbildung," *Zeitschrift für Theologie und Kirche* 77 (1980): 251–68; Elisabeth Schüssler Fiorenza, "Visionary Rhetoric and Social-Political Situation," chapt. 7 in *The Book of Revelation: Justice and Judgment* (Philadelphia: Fortress Press, 1985), 181–203; Thomas Harding, "Take Back the Apocalypse," *Touchstone* 3, no. 1 (January 1985): 29–35; Elemer Kocsis, "Apokalyptik und politisches Interesse im Spätjudentum," *Judaica* 27 (1971): 71–89; J. A. du Rand, "An Apocalyptic Text, Different Contexts and an Applicable Ethos," *Journal of Theology in South Africa* 78 (1992): 75–83; and Heinz Schürmann, *Studien zur neutestamentlichen Ethik*, in collaboration with Thomas Söding, *Stuttgarter biblische Aufsatzbände* (Stuttgart: Verlag Katholisches Bibelwerk, 1990); see esp. 269–286, 307–378.

[41] Klaus Koch, *The Rediscovery of Apocalyptic: A Polemical Work on a Neglected Area of Biblical Studies and Its Damaging Effects on Theology and Philosophy*, trans-

One expression of the tendency to criticize apocalypticism as such is Philip Vielhauer's influential but unfortunate "Introduction to Apocalypses and Related Subjects" in Hennecke-Schneemelcher's *New Testament Apocrypha*.[42] In this seminal essay, Vielhauer develops a questionable dichotomy between the this-worldly, national eschatology found in rabbinic texts and the other-worldly eschatology found in the apocalypses[43]—questionable because apocalypticism in the Second Temple period was concerned with ethical issues, and strong links exist between the "testament" and the "apocalypse" as genres.[44]

2. "Apocalypse" in Popular Discourse

The negative assessment of "apocalypse" is not unique to scholarly circles. In popular discourse today, *apocalypse* is often associated with the idea of the violent, cataclysmic end of the world. It carries connotations of chaos, alienation, gruesome horror, awful violence, and an unhealthy interest in the macabre. The movie *Apocalypse Now!* has little to do with hope or with the joyful expectation of God's intervention in history. The very idea of "apocalyptic hope" is considered an oxymoron, appropriate only for those groups that withdraw from society in order to await Christ's return. Thus, the concept of "apocalypse" is generally considered to be both psychologically and socially dysfunctional. This has significant implications for how modern people can or should read the Apocalypse of John today.

---

lated by Margaret Kohl, Studies in Biblical Theology (London: S.C.M. Press, 1972), 113. The negative evaluation of apocalyptic thought, based in part on the tendency of some German scholarship to treat "Judaism" as a foil for "Christianity," is criticized by Koch in his book, originally titled, *Ratlos vor der Apokalyptik*.

[42] Philip Vielhauer, "Apocalypses and Related Subjects: Introduction," rev. Georg Strecker, in *New Testament Apocrypha*, ed. Wilhelm Schneemelcher and Edgar Hennecke, trans. Robert McL. Wilson, reprint, 1965 (Louisville, Ky.: Westminster/John Knox Press, 1992), 542–602.

[43] We will not pause here to challenge directly this false dichotomization between the so-called ethical eschatology of Hebrew prophecy and the escapist eschatology of apocalypticism. For compelling arguments that the Apocalypse is a call to active nonviolent engagement with the world rather than escapist withdrawal from the world, see Klaus Wengst, *The Pax Romana and the Peace of Jesus Christ*, trans. John Bowden (Philadelphia: Fortress Press, 1987), 118–135. See also Christopher Rowland, "The Apocalypse: Hope, Resistance and the Revelation of Reality," *Ex Auditu* 6 (1990): 129–44.

[44] For an insightful investigation of the ethical interests of Jewish apocalypticism, see Christoph Münchow, *Ethik und Eschatologie: Ein Beitrag zum Verständnis der frühjüdischen Apokalyptik mit einem Ausblick auf das Neue Testament* (Vandenhoeck & Ruprecht, 1981).

Because reading the Apocalypse has given rise to such a sobering history of effects over the last 1900 years, today's readers are divided about the ethical value of reading it at all. On the popular level, some embrace the Apocalypse seemingly because they *celebrate* its vision of the future as violent and macabre,[45] while others reject it because they *abhor* its vision of the future as violent and macabre.[46] Both of these responses to the Apocalypse are based on the conclusion—however carefully or carelessly it is considered—that violence lies at the very heart of the rhetoric of the Apocalypse and that its message is primarily predictive.[47]

A spate of recent books has drawn on this popular view of "apocalyptic" with its negative violent connotations. In 1957 Norman Cohn published his influential book, *The Pursuit of the Millennium: Revolutionary Millenarians and Mystical Anarchists of the Middle Ages*.[48] In his first chapter, Cohn identified two major traditions of Jewish prophecy, one of which he calls "ethical" and

---

[45] One example of this celebration that appears to be based on the rejection of a certain form of Christology in favor of another is that expressed by Hal Lindsey. In his book, *There's a New World Coming*, he says, "When Jesus came to earth the first time He came in humility to offer Himself as the Lamb of God to die for the sins of men. But when He comes again He'll return in the strength and supremacy of a lion. His previous lamblike meekness and gentleness will give way to regal power. The first time Christ came as a Savior, offering pardon and cleansing from sin and its consequences; when He comes the second time, He will wield a rod of iron as the Judge of all men. ... With a sword coming out of His mouth, He'll destroy all His enemies and deliver the Tribulation believers who are still living. God will at last send His Messiah to earth as King. Millions of people have said that they could never accept a suffering servant as their Messiah. So here He comes as a conquering King, and it's too late to fall at His feet and call Him Lord! Oh, the blindness of men who *will* not see!" (Hal Lindsey, *There's a New World Coming: A Prophetic Odyssey* [Santa Ana, Cal.: Vision House Publishers, 1973], 94, 262).

[46] Cf. D. H. Lawrence and Harold Bloom, above.

[47] For a further discussion on this matter, see the section, "But Is the Vision Really Ethical?" in the last chapter of this monograph.

[48] Norman Cohn, *The Pursuit of the Millennium: Revolutionary Millenarians and Mystical Anarchists of the Middle Ages*, 2d ed., reprint, 1957 (New York: Oxford University Press, 1970), 1. In his more recent book (Norman Cohn, *Cosmos, Chaos, and the World to Come: The Ancient Roots of Apocalyptic Faith* [New Haven and London: Yale University Press, 1993]), Cohn shows greater sensitivity to the origins and varieties of apocalyptic thought. Although he holds that the Apocalypse is "a profoundly Christian work throughout" (213), and that the ancient combat myth is "radically reinterpreted" in it (219), that reinterpretation lies in its transformation of the ancient myth from an ongoing cycle of cosmic upheavals to a decisive, soon-to-appear kingdom of God—a forecast that proved mistaken. Cohn thus shows his continued acceptance of his older dichotomized view of eschatology and of its relationship with ethics.

the other dominated by "phantasy," war, and revolutionary militance. Adopting Cohn's understanding of an "apocalyptic myth" that "proposes a salvation that is collective, terrestrial, imminent, total, and miraculous," Stephen D. O'Leary attempts to articulate a coherent rhetorical approach to the problems posed by apocalyptic discourse itself in *Arguing the Apocalypse: A Theory of Millennial Rhetoric*.[49] In a similar manner, Arthur P. Mendel treats "apocalyptic" as a synonym for what is "hopelessly utopian, visionary, and unrealistic" and sees John's Apocalypse as the archetypal apocalypse in this sense.

> Virtually the whole of that text is an account of the violence, devastation, suffering, and death necessary to purge the world and clear the way for the pure and perfect Kingdom. Wave after wave of horrendous suffering cascade down on the sinful world as the seals of secret scrolls are broken.... The masses of sinners ... must be annihilated.... Still, the well of suffering and vengeance is not empty: there is yet the Final Judgment.[50]

Common to these popular conceptions of "apocalyptic" is the view that the apocalyptic vision is inherently future-oriented, violent, and pessimistic, and that, unchecked, it leads toward both self- and world destruction.[51] And there lies the crux of the matter! Just how deeply writ in the rhetoric of the Apocalypse are its visions of violence? Traditional interpretations of the Apocalypse fail in part because of the interpreters' lack of attention to the sociocultural environment that provided meaning for the text—or perhaps more accurately, because of the interpreters' uncritical transference of one particular sociocultural environment (their own) onto the text of the Apocalypse. The key is not to isolate cultural context as a variable that can be dispensed with; rather, the key is to be aware of the various cultural contexts of writer, text, and reader in such a way that the integrity of readings can be judged on an ethical basis.[52]

Many authors have rightly seen that John's use of traditional images is both extensive and complex. Sophie Laws' *In the Light of the Lamb* plays on "imagery, parody, and theology in the Apocalypse of John."[53] Jan Fekkes' *Isaiah and Prophetic Traditions in the Book of Revelation: Visionary Antecedents*

---

[49] Stephen D. O'Leary, *Arguing the Apocalypse: A Theory of Millennial Rhetoric* (New York: Oxford University Press, 1994), 6.

[50] Arthur Mendel, *Vision and Violence* (Ann Arbor, Mich.: University of Michigan Press, 1992), 39.

[51] Cf. Mendel, *Vision*, 310.

[52] For a compelling argument about the importance of considering the sociocultural context of a text as a primary variable in interpretation, see Brian K. Blount, *Cultural Interpretation; Reorienting New Testament Criticism* (Minneapolis: Fortress Press, 1995), viii, 8.

[53] Sophie Laws, *In the Light of the Lamb: Imagery, Parody, and Theology in the Apocalypse of John* (Wilmington, Del.: M. Glazier, 1988), 3.

and Their Development[54] is a good example of careful attention to the complexity of allusions to the Old Testament. Nevertheless, as Steve Moyise points out, Fekkes's program of categorizing allusions to Isaiah as "Certain/Virtually Certain," "Probable/Possible," or "Unlikely/Doubtful" occasionally results in an unnecessary ignoring or glossing over of the subtle nuances in John's recasting of traditional images.

Although identifying the *source* of a traditional image is an important part of the analysis of any image in the Apocalypse, it is identifying the rhetorical *force* of that image that is ultimately decisive for authentic exegesis and hermeneutics. As James H. Charlesworth has noted, at the heart of the Apocalypse's power to "transfer" the reader into a new world created by that book's vision lies its ability to "redefine" reality for those readers.[55]

The challenge for modern readers is that these "redefinitions" of reality are painted large on an impressionistic canvas of images, not argued with the precision of propositional language. As a creative artist in his own right, John "interprets" the traditions with which he works as he molds them into a new creation.

3. Methodology and Reading Strategies

Difficult as it is, the modern reader must therefore understand the rhetorical force of a traditional image as experienced by John's original readers so that he or she can hope to appreciate the force of John's *employment* of that tradition. In other words, the modern reader must determine whether the rhetorical force of a traditional image lies in John's *dependence* upon or *reiteration* of that image, along with its traditional world view, or whether it lies in John's particular *use* of and *redefinition* of that image—or even in his repudiation of its traditional world view.

---

[54] Jan Fekkes III, *Isaiah and Prophetic Traditions in the Book of Revelation: Visionary Antecedents and their Development*, JSNTSS 93 (Sheffield: JSOT Press, 1994), 32–44.

[55] James H. Charlesworth, "The Apocalypse of John: Its Theology and Impact on Subsequent Apocalypses," pt. 2 in *The New Testament Apocrypha and Pseudepigrapha: A Guide to Publications, with Excursuses on Apocalypses*, edited by James H. Charlesworth (Metuchen and London: The American Theological Library Association and Scarecrow Press, 1987), 28–30. It is also at this point that David Barr's "The Apocalypse as a Symbolic Transformation of the World: A Literary Analysis," *Interpretation* 38 (January 1984): 39–50, is most helpful. Barr indicates that at the heart of the Apocalypse's rhetorical power is its "symbolic transformations" or "reversals of value."

Attempting to make such a determination is admittedly difficult, but the attempt is important; the stakes are high. If modern readers have never heard of an ancient combat myth, the Gestalt created by the act of reading the Apocalypse is more likely to emphasize the violence of the images. However, if the violent images are recognized as a standard part of the combat myth tradition, the reader will likely be more alert to the manner in which the combat myth is being reshaped and redefined in John's creative use of them.

The proliferation of methodologies and reading styles within the discipline of biblical studies goes on unchecked. Stephen Moore aptly and playfully refers to exegetes peering over the disciplinary fences of their neighbors—even having the audacity to climb over them—while others shake their heads in amusement or outright disapproval.[56] In this environment it seems useful to attempt to explicate my own reading style and methodology—not primarily to *argue* for my methodology, though I do defend it, but to place myself in relation to recognizable landmarks in the landscape of methodologies.

Readings and reading strategies have been remarkably diverse throughout the history of religious communities reading "scriptural" texts. The Western world has for the last 250 years, through the influence of the Enlightenment, enjoyed an illusion of objectivity, an immunity from the vicissitudes of slippery subjectivism. However, even "scientific" Western biblical exegesis has had trouble keeping a firm grip on John's Apocalypse—perhaps *especially* "scientific" Western biblical exegesis. As M. H. Abrams has pointed out, "the symbolic and typological mode in which it is set forth has made Revelation a very flexible text for historical application." To make matters worse for the scientific purist, "the freedom of interpretive maneuver was greatly increased by the early application to Revelation of an allegorical mode of reading."[57]

Recent philosophical discussions about the nature of reading and interpretation have seriously undermined old paradigms of understanding. Many biblical scholars today are aware that like any text, the Apocalypse has no inherent "Meaning" within itself, even if "Meaning," especially in regard to the Apocalypse, has been slippery all along.[58] Meanings are *provided* by readers—constructed in the process of a multi-faceted dialogue with the text and with other readers. The primary dialogue is between the reader and the text. Most readers are also in dialogue with other readers; some readers also attempt to read the text in dialogue with God. All readers are in some ways in dialogue with themselves as they unconsciously offer to the reading process the learned conventions of language, vocabulary, and rhetoric.

---

[56] Stephen D. Moore, *Literary Criticism and the Gospels: The Theoretical Challenge* (New Haven and London: Yale University Press, 1989), xiii.

[57] Abrams, "Apocalypse," 20.

[58] See, e.g., Blount, *Cultural Interpretation*, viii.

Some readers conceptualize an idealized "authorial intent"—the "original meaning" in the mind of the author. Although "authorial intent" remains an important and useful *heuristic* device in interpretation, the receiver of communication simply does not have access to the author's intent; she has access only to the text, the *means* of communication. This is true whether the "author" and "reader" are communicating in the same room or whether they are separated by 2,000 years of historical and cultural distance. Furthermore, the author's intent can never be fully determinative for the meaning of any ancient writing. This is especially true for communities of faith that read a text like the Apocalypse as canonical literature. Interpretation and understanding always involve judgment, commitment, and investment on the part of the reader.

This brief foray into the nature of interpretation and reading may appear to lead one to the brink of chaos, subjectivism, and relativism, as if we are experiencing a broad-based revolution or paradigm shift from modernism to postmodernism. In some ways, it does. Such an understanding of the task of reading lacks objective controls and concrete limits for how one reads and interprets a text. Historical-critical readings carry weight only in communities that understand and value such readings—in communities that share the assumptions and the social locations that lie behind the historical-critical method and are thus persuaded by or through the rhetoric of the historical-critical method.

The lack of objective controls may seem especially pernicious for communities of faith that want the Bible to function in some way as a grounding authority or arbiter of faith. But pernicious or not, authority, like meaning, is always *invested* by both individuals and communities. The "authority" of the Bible is ultimately meaningless and nonexistent apart from flesh-and-blood individuals and communities that ascribe authority to it. Christians gain nothing by pretending that it is otherwise.

So if no independent text exists to serve as an objective arbiter over readings, why has this not led to unbridled chaos in the reading of texts? As Stanley Fish has observed, this is due primarily to the stability of interpretive communities themselves.[59] The task of the reader-critic is ultimately ethical and political: it is not primarily to uncover or construct some unchanging, objective Truth, but to form, reform, and meet the needs of the critic and his or her community. Although this can lead to a kind of hermeneutical opportunism, it need not; one need not be cynical about the value of this task.

Nevertheless, whatever the excesses of practitioners of the historical-critical method, objectivity and historical plausibility remain valuable goals. To be sure, they are elusive. To be sure, there is no final, objective arbiter,

---

[59] Cf. Stanley Fish, *Is There a Text in This Class?* (Cambridge: Harvard University Press, 1980), esp. 171–72. Cf. also the helpful discussion of Stephen Moore in chapter seven (108–30) of his *Literary Criticism*.

whether person or "text," that can finally determine a reading as "better" or "worse." What does remain are communities that, through their own process of valuing, determine which readings are to be valued highly and which are not.[60] The integrity of any given reading cannot therefore be determined apart from the ethics of the reading process itself as expressed in the reading community's exercise of power.[61]

I read as one who has been trained to appreciate and employ the disciplines of the historical-critical method. I also read as one who has been chastened but not fully converted by the philosophical challenges of deconstruction. I readily acknowledge and embrace the communities of interpreters that have most affected my own reading style. Properly speaking, my acknowledgement of these communities does not belong primarily to a preface or a special acknowledgments section; it belongs to the very explication of my rationale and methodology.

I aim in this dissertation at a "faithful" reading of the text—faithful in both the historical and the ethical sense. In using the concept of "historical faithfulness" I mean to imply that I tend to value readings that conform, more or less, to the historical probabilities surrounding the original social and historical context of the author and original readers of the text. I thus argue for a reading of the text of the Apocalypse that tries to take seriously what is in the text itself, occasionally even appealing heuristically to the concept of authorial intent. Having acknowledged already that "historical faithfulness" cannot exist as an independent arbiter, I wish only to argue that such considerations can serve as trans-subjective heuristic devices in developing a persuasive reading of the text and that the actual persuasiveness of this evidence and argument will vary, depending on the cultural context of whatever community happens to read this monograph.

By "ethical faithfulness" I mean to imply that the value and truthfulness of any reading of the Apocalypse depend ultimately on the result of that reading for the community of faith that defines itself in some sense by the Apocalypse. In arguing for the reading of the Apocalypse that follows, I do not mean to imply that my reading is the only good way of reading the Apocalypse. Rather, I offer it to the scholarly community as a contribution to a conversation, as *a* reading of the Apocalypse, with the hope that it will prove both attractive and convincing among the plurality of readings that have been offered.

---

[60] For a discussion of both the limits and the indispensability of the historical-critical method for biblical theology, see Ulrich Mauser, "Historical Criticism: Liberator or Foe of Biblical Theology?" chapt. 5 in *The Promise and Practice of Biblical Theology*, edited by John H. P. Reumann, with a preface by John W. Vannorsdall (Minneapolis: Fortress, 1991), 99–113.

[61] Cf. Blount, *Cultural Interpretation*, 16.

I write as a member of two overlapping communities: the community of scholars and the community of faith. As a member of those communities, I want to read the Apocalypse of John in such a way that my reading captures as accurately as can be captured from this distance the origins and force of John's Lamb Christology within the author's cultural, political, and religious milieu. Whether my reading is compelling will be determined by the scholarly community on the basis of the plausibility of its argument within the text's historical and cultural context.

I also want to read the Apocalypse in a way that illuminates the text for people of faith today, whether that illumination comes by way of appreciation or criticism. I want to be honest with the text; I want also to show how the Apocalypse of John can serve to empower believers today to resist the seductive idolatry of the "domination system" of violence through the blood of the Lamb.

I understand my reading strategy to be similar to that of Elisabeth Schüssler Fiorenza. Fiorenza has admitted that her aim in reading the Apocalypse is to "analyze how biblical texts and interpretations participate in creating or sustaining oppressive or liberating theo-ethical values and sociopolitical practices."[62] She specifically characterizes her reading program as "rhetorical," but her explanation above makes clear that her rhetorical program is broad enough to encompass sociocultural perspectives:

> The reconceptualization of biblical studies in rhetorical rather than just hermeneutical terms provides a research framework not only for integrating historical, archaeological, sociological, literary, and theological approaches as perspectival readings of Revelation but also for raising sociopolitical and theo-ethical questions as constitutive questions for the interpretive process. Rhetorical interpretation does not assume that the text of Revelation is a window to historical reality ... but sees it as a perspectival discourse constructing its own worlds and symbolic universe.[63]

Tina Pippin has recently expressed great boldness in owning her strategy of reading the Apocalypse. In her provocative book, *Death and Desire: The Rhetoric of Gender in the Apocalypse of John*,[64] Pippin acknowledges openly and often her "desires" in reading the Apocalypse. Her explanation of her own readings strategies, interestingly enough, is couched in the language of desire. For instance,

---

[62] Elisabeth Schüssler Fiorenza, *Revelation: Vision of a Just World*, Proclamation Commentaries (Minneapolis: Fortress, 1991), 3.

[63] Fiorenza, *Revelation: Vision*, 3.

[64] *Literary Currents in Biblical Interpretation* (Louisville: Westminster/John Knox Press, 1992).

I want to play with the polyvalence of the symbols.... *I want* to take a post-modern turn.... *I want* to feel and see and hear and touch my way through the narrative.... *I want* to expose the tension between death and desire in the Apocalypse.... *I want* to push against the boundaries (visible and invisible) in Apocalypse studies.... *I want* to push against the old boundaries of interpreting genre/form.... *I want* to enter into the subversive action of being one reading of the Apocalypse.... *I want* to play with the theory that this text is an open text. *I want* to play with a deconstructive reading.[65]

This is only a sampling of many such statements. Pippin acknowledges that some of her readings entail "risky and uncertain hermeneutical leaps."[66]

The risk as well as the greatest benefit in openly acknowledging our respective desires in reading the text lie in opening explicitly to our own readers the "angles" we are pursuing. All writers pursue angles and distort the evidence—however intentionally or innocently—in keeping with the "angles," biases, and interests that derive from their respective cultural contexts. The present writer suspects that Pippin's interpretations finally reflect her own desires as much as they do of John's desires and thus do more to disclose her own context as a sensitive feminist than they do the context of the writer. The present reader must judge for himself or herself whether, where, and how the present writing does so as well.

4. Problems Central to this Dissertation

Interest in the Apocalypse has focused mostly on its eschatology—or at least on a particular "timetables" form of eschatology—but only a few have asked how its eschatology supports its ethical vision[67] or how its Christology relates to its ethics. The focus of the present study is on the relationship of Christology and ethics in the figure of the Lamb.

Even apart from the questions of eschatology many questions remain about the nature and origins of the symbols employed in the Apocalypse. A recent dictionary article on "lamb" begins by noting that "there is much uncertainty and debate about the religio-historical background of the image of Christ as a lamb."[68] After examining the religio-historical background of the image of

---

[65] *Death and Desire*, 16, 22, 23, 25, 46, 88; emphasis mine.

[66] *Death and Desire*, 11.

[67] Cf. Christoph Münchow, *Ethik und Eschatologie: Ein Beitrag zum Verständnis der frühjüdischen Apokalyptik mit einem Ausblick auf das Neue Testament* (Göttingen: Vandenhoeck & Ruprecht, 1981). Cf. also Rowland, "The Apocalypse."

[68] Pieter W. van der Horst, "Lamb," in *Dictionary of Deities and Demons in the Bible*, edited by Karel van der Toorn, Bob Becking, and Pieter W. van der Horst (Leiden/New York/Köln: E.J. Brill, 1995), 938.

Christ as lamb in the first part of this study, I will attempt to explicate the shape of its rhetorical force in the Apocalypse.

Some have denied the relevance and importance of the analysis of the religio-historical background of the image of Christ as lamb. In his otherwise wonderful commentary on the Apocalypse, G. B. Caird says, "We need not waste time searching through the Old Testament and other Jewish literature to find the meaning of this symbol [i.e., the symbol of the Lamb], for John has told us what he means by it."[69] I cannot agree with this statement. If we are to understand what John does with this symbol, we must first understand what associations or traditions it may have evoked in the mind of his readers. Even if the Lamb were not the crucial symbol in the Apocalypse, the author's use of Old Testament images is so pervasive that understanding the Apocalypse is impossible without constant reference to the Old Testament and its images.[70] And since contradictory understandings of the origins of the Lamb image have led to contradictory understandings of its rhetorical force within the Apocalypse, it is important to analyze this background at the start.

The thesis of this dissertation is that the Lamb Christology of the Apocalypse has an ethical force: the Seer sees in the death and resurrection of Jesus Christ both the decisive victory over evil in history and the pattern for Christians' nonviolent resistance to evil. John's readers are to "overcome" in the same way that the Lamb overcame, making Jesus' death and resurrection ethically paradigmatic for the readers. The ethics of the Apocalypse are indissolubly connected to its theology and Christology.

The author communicates his ethic/theology of nonviolent resistance to evil in a variety of ways. In spite of the prevalence of martial metaphors and violence in the book, the believers are not invited to join in any literal battle; the only battle enjoined upon the believers is the battle won at the cross. Rather, the author uses the "divine warrior" tradition to underscore that humans have only a marginal role in the battle with evil: the decisive role is God's through Christ.

In light of all the "holy war" allusions in the book, it is significant that no extended conflict or battle is narrated in the book—not even one between the Lamb and the dragon or beasts. The only conflict portrayed as decisive in the Apocalypse is that which occurred in the death and resurrection of Christ. The death and resurrection of Christ are intimately connected in the Apocalypse; neither has a function apart from the other. Jesus' death is the inevitable consequence of and ultimate proof of his faithful witness, while the resurrection is the demonstration of the ultimate triumph of that witness. Where one expects a massive battle scene (chap. 19), one finds the rider approaching the battle

---

[69] Caird, *Revelation of St. John*, 74.

[70] For a similar judgment, see Fekkes, *Isaiah*, 155n47.

dressed in a robe dipped in blood (i.e., his own blood). No real battle takes place here because the decisive battle is already over. That is also why he can already ride the white horse. His victory is consistently portrayed in terms of his death and resurrection. The blood that flows in the Apocalypse is primarily the blood of the "martyrs"—those who have maintained a faithful witness.

5. Procedure and Outline

In the chapters that follow, I will first examine the terms the author used of Christ in the Apocalypse, concentrating on the single most important image of the Lamb (τὸ ἀρνίον; chapter 2). Second, I will survey various possible points of origin for that figure in Graeco-Roman sources predating the Apocalypse (chapter 3), in extracanonical Jewish sources (chapter 4), and in the Hebrew Bible (chapter 5). Finally, I will examine more carefully the specific ethical-rhetorical force of the lamb Christology within the text of the Apocalypse (chapter 6).

Chapter II

What Is τὸ ἀρνίον?

1. Lamb Lexicography and Statistics

The word ἀρνίον ("lamb") occurs 30 times in the New Testament: once in John 21:15 and 29 times in the Apocalypse.[1] Not limited to one or two scenes, the term appears in fully half of the 22 chapters of the Apocalypse.[2] In the Apocalypse, ἀρνίον refers once to a "counter figure" of Christ in 13:11 and the other 28 times as a title for Christ.

᾽Αρνίον is by far the most frequent designation for Christ in the Apocalypse. It appears more than twice as often as any other name or image for Christ—even more than the simple name ᾽Ιησοῦς, the title Χριστός, or variations thereof.[3] The Apocalypse is the only book in the New Testament that applies the word as a title for Christ.[4]

2. Questions about Translation

All occurrences of the word ἀρνίον in biblical and classical Greek refer to a young sheep or lamb. Nowhere does it refer to an adult ram in literature that predates the Apocalypse. That ἀρνίον nowhere refers to an adult ram in the extant literature has actually been a matter of dispute in modern lexicography.

---

[1] At Rev 5:6, 8, 12, 13; 6:1, 16; 7:9, 10, 14, 17; 12:11; 13:8, 11; 14:1, 4[bis], 10; 15:3; 17:14[bis]; 19:7, 9; 21:9, 14, 22, 23, 27; 22:1, 3.

[2] The word itself does not occur in chaps. 1–4; 8–11; 16; 18; or 20, although an occasional pronoun referring to the Lamb does appear (e.g., 8:1). Besides the explicit references to ἀρνίον, the concept is implied elsewhere, as Hohnjec has rightly noted. See Nikola Hohnjec, "Das Lamm, τὸ ἀρνίον" in der Offenbarung des Johannes: Eine exegetisch-theologische Untersuchung (Rome: Herder, 1980) 11.

[3] Jesus is referred to by the full title Jesus Christ (᾽Ιησοῦ Χριστοῦ) only at the beginning of the Apocalypse (1:1, 2, 5). "Jesus" alone (᾽Ιησοῦς) appears at 1:9 [bis]; 12:17; 14:12; 17:6; 19:10 [bis]; 20:4; and 22:16.

[4] For titles used of Christ in the Apocalypse, including substantival participial phrases, see Appendix II.

For instance, the Louw and Nida *Greek-English Lexicon of the New Testament Based on Semantic Domains* lists ἀρνίον as "a sheep of any age—'lamb, sheep, ram.'"[5] In the *Theologisches Wörterbuch zum neuen Testament*, Gustav Stählin notes that "ἀρνίον auch das Bild des jungen, starken Widders verbindet, aber zweitens und vor allem, daß es derselbe Christus ist, der einst wehrlos wie ein Lamm dem Gericht der Menschen verfiel, aber dann selber als zürnender Richter an den Menschen schrecklich Gericht halten wird."[6] Whether ἀρνίον can mean either lamb or ram will be a central issue in this chapter.

Rabbinic literature defines a lamb impressively and precisely.[7] For the purposes of proper sacrifice, definitions were developed to distinguish between a lamb and a ram. According to the Mishnah,[8] lambs must not be more than one year old and rams not more than two years old to be acceptable as offerings. Rams must be at least one year, one month, and one day old. Sheep that fall between the age of one year and the age of one year, one month, and one day are called פַּלְגָּס—likely a loan-word taken by analogy from the Greek πάλλαξ, which means (early) adolescent (before the age of 18).[9] Such animals could not be offered as a sacrifice. Danby's translation reads:

> Lambs [כְּבָשׂ] must be [not more than] one year old, and rams [אֵיל] [not more than] two years old; and always the year is reckoned from day to day. What is

---

[5] Johannes P. Louw and Eugene A. Nida, eds., *Greek-English Lexicon of the New Testament Based on Semantic Domains; Volume 1: Introductions & Domains*, in collaboration with Rondal B. Smith and Karen A. Munson (United Bible Societies, 1988), s.v. ἀρνίον.

[6] Note that Stählin here is appealing to the supposedly ambiguous meaning of ἀρνίον in explicating ὀργή, and did not extensively research ἀρνίον as Joachim Jeremias did in his article. Stählin is doubtlessly dependent upon Spitta at this point and Jeremias would deny Stählin's claim. See Gerhard Kittel, ed. *Theologisches Wörterbuch zum neuen Testament* (Stuttgart: W. Kohlhammer, 1949–1979), s.v. ὀργή, 5:430.

[7] Rabbinic literature is marked by an approach to theological truths that is more synthetic than it is diachronic. This has also been true historically of the study of rabbinic literature itself. In recent years scholars have begun to treat rabbinic literature in more intentionally historical ways. The challenge for New Testament studies is that few rabbinic traditions can clearly be shown to date from the New Testament era. However, given the social function of the *halaka* on the categorization of lambs by age, it is plausible that this tradition was already in place in the New Testament era.

[8] m.Par 1.3.

[9] See m.Par 1.3; Herbert Danby, ed., *The Mishnah* (Oxford: Clarendon, 1933), 698n4; and Adin Steinsaltz, *The Talmud: The Steinsaltz Edition, A Reference Guide* (New York: Random House, 1989, 245, s.v. פַּלְגָּס. See also Henry George Liddell, comp., *A Greek-English Lexicon: With a Supplement*, A new ed., rev. and augm. throughout by Henry Stuart Jones, with the assistance of Roderick McKenzie, and with the cooperation of many scholars, in collaboration with Robert Scott and Henry Stuart Jones, reprint, 1951 (Oxford: Clarendon Press, 1968), s.v. πάλλαξ and ἔφηβος.

thirteen months old is not valid whether as a ram or as a lamb. R. Tarfon calls such a one a *pallax*; Ben Azzai calls it a *noked*; R. Ishmael calls it a *parakhadeigma*. If a man offered it he must bring for it the Drink-offerings of a ram, but it is not accounted to his credit as his prescribed animal-offering. If it was thirteen months old and a day it counts as a ram.[10]

The problem long noted in the Apocalypse is that the word *lamb* does not seem to fit well the context. For instance, the ἀρνίον of the Apocalypse has horns (cf. Rev. 5:6; 13:11); some lambs had horns, but most did not.[11] The lamb of the Apocalypse is a vigorous and majestic image; no sense of weakness or powerlessness on the part of the Lamb is implied. On the contrary, the Lamb is praised as being worthy of "power" (δύναμις, Rev. 5:12) and "might" (κράτος, Rev. 5:13). Furthermore, in Rev. 6:16-17, people scramble in terror to the caves and the mountains and cry out, "Fall on us and hide us from the face of the one seated on the throne and from the wrath of the Lamb; for the great day of their wrath has come, and who can stand?" Finally, in 17:14, ten kings make war on the Lamb and the Lamb conquers them. This hardly sounds like a lamb!

The above considerations have led numerous commentators to search for alternative translations of the word ἀρνίον and for alternative origins of this image. The Animal Apocalypse of the Enochic literature treats the kings of Israel as "rams" who lead the sheep (the people of Israel).[12] In light of this analogy and of the considerations above, some have suggested that "ram" is a more appropriate translation for ἀρνίον than is "lamb."

The suggestion that "ram" is the preferred translation was made popular by Friedrich Spitta in an essay entitled, "Christus das Lamm."[13] Some commentators have followed him in this suggestion.[14] Pieter W. van der Horst claims that ἀρνίον "originally meant 'ram,'" but the basis for this is weak. ἀρνίον is etymologically related to ἀρνειός, a word used for rams in early classical Greek literature, but etymological appeals unsupported by contextual linguistic

---

[10] Danby, *Mishnah*, 698 (m.Par 1.3).

[11] Cf. R. H. Charles, *A Critical and Exegetical Commentary on the Revelation of St. John*, Vol. 2. The International Critical Commentary (Edinburgh: T. & T. Clark, 1920), 452. In any case, the idea that lambs could have horns was not unknown in the ancient world. According to one tradition, some lambs immediately begin to develop horns at birth (cf. Homer, *Odyssey* 4.85; Aristotle, *Historia Animalium* 7.19).

[12] Cf. esp. 1En 89:41-50; 90:38.

[13] Friedrich Spitta, "Christus das Lamm," in *Streitfragen der Geschichte Jesu* (Göttingen: Vandenhoeck und Ruprecht, 1907) 172–223.

[14] Even Josephine Massyngberde-Ford, who says that the character of the animal in the Apocalypse best matches that of the ram, ends up translating ἀρνίον as "little lamb," since linguistic evidence for ἀρνίον as ram is lacking: "Linguistically the only possible translations are 'little lamb' or 'lamb'"; cf. Ford, *Revelation*, 83, 86.

evidence are insufficient. Liddell-Scott suggest that ἀρνειός itself derives from ἄρσην (male). But nowhere in the literature does ἀρνίον refer to an adult male ram. Thus, while most commentators have agreed that no linguistic evidence exists for such a translation, they have nevertheless appealed to the contextual evidence noted above. More recently, however, Otfried Hofius has impressively demonstrated in his exhaustive search of ancient Greek literature that there is simply no evidence to support the claim that ἀρνίον and κριός can be considered synonyms.[15]

3. The Semantic Domain of "Lamb" in the New Testament

The Apocalypse is unique in calling Christ ἀρνίον. Three other words for lamb appear in the New Testament, two of which are applied to Christ. Paul refers to Christ as our πάσχα (Paschal Lamb) in 1 Cor. 5:7.[16] In the Fourth Gospel, John the Baptist introduces Jesus as ὁ ἀμνὸς τοῦ θεοῦ ὁ αἴρων τὴν ἁμαρτίαν τοῦ κόσμου ("the Lamb of God who takes away the sin of the world") in 1:29. The Fourth Evangelist has John repeat the title itself (ὁ ἀμνὸς τοῦ θεοῦ) without the participial modifier in John 1:36. In John 21:15, Jesus says to Peter, "Feed my lambs (ἀρνία)," but there ἀρνία (the only place it appears in the plural in the New Testament) refers to those who believe in Jesus. The second and third responses to Peter's "yes" are, "Shepherd (or feed) my sheep (πρόβατα)" (21:16, 17). Hence, ἀρνίον in the singular is found only in the Apocalypse, where it clearly denotes Jesus.

The word used of Christ in John 1:29, 36 (ἀμνός; lamb) also appears in Acts 8:32, where Philip quotes Isaiah 53:7-8 according to the Septuagint: "As a sheep (πρόβατον) is brought to the slaughterhouse, and as a lamb (ἀμνός) be-

---

[15] See Otfried Hofius, "'Ἀρνίον – Widder oder Lamm? Erwägungen zur Bedeutung des Wortes in der Johannesapokalypse," *ZNW* 89 (1998): 272–281. When Hofius looks for an alternative explanation about why the author would have used ἀρνίον, he concludes that the author must have used ἀρνίον to express his theological understanding of the atonement. I would argue that the Apocalypse itself suggests otherwise: John used ἀρνίον to convey the vulnerability of one who resists evil consistently and nonviolently. I would suggest that the pervasive political language, the language of violence and nonviolence, and the near-absence of traditional atonement language in the Apocalypse supports my reading.

[16] The word πάσχα also appears in Mt 26:2, 17, 18, 19; Mk 14:1, 12[*bis*], 14, 16; Lk 2:41; 22:1, 7, 8, 11, 13, 15; Jn 2:13, 23; 6:4; 11:55[*bis*]; 12:1; 13:1; 18:28, 39; 19:14; Acts 12:4; and Heb 11:28, where it refers to the Passover Festival and/or Passover victim. Despite chronological differences between the Synoptics and the Fourth Gospel regarding the events of Jesus' last week, all four Gospels develop a link between Jesus' death and death of the Passover victim.

fore its shearer is silent, thus did he not open his mouth." 1 Peter 1:18-19 says, "Knowing that you have been set free from the vanity of the lifestyle of your ancestors, not by means of things that deteriorate, like gold or silver, but by means of the valuable blood of Christ, like that of a lamb (ἀμνός) without defect or blemish." In both Acts and 1 Peter, the sacrificial burnt offering is in view, and in each instance, ἀμνός is the word used to refer to Jesus.

In Luke 10:3, Jesus sends out the 70 (or 72) two-by-two, saying to them, "Go! Behold, I am sending you out like lambs (ἄρνας, from ἀρήν) in the midst of wolves."[17] The parallel in Matthew 10:16 has πρόβατα (sheep) for Luke's ἄρνας (lambs). Technically, ἀρήν is the noun of which ἀρνίον is the diminutive, though these forms had lost their diminutive force by the time the New Testament was written.[18] Although diminutives normally express either smallness ("small lamb") or endearment ("Lämmlein," "lambkin," or "lamby"), the historical linguistic evidence suggests that neither of these can be pressed in New Testament times apart from corroborating contextual evidence, which is certainly lacking in this case. However, questions about whether the diminutive was still in force by the New Testament times are a bit beside the point with reference to lamb, since ἀρήν itself means a little (i.e., young) sheep. This is the only place that ἀρήν appears in the New Testament.[19]

In the Hatch and Redpath concordance, the occurrences of ἀρήν in the LXX are listed under ἀρνός even though ἀρνός is the genitive singular form of

---

[17] It is interesting that the word for lamb in Lk 10:3 (ἀρήν) in the context of sending out the 70 or 72 apostles is the same word that is used in 1Esd 8:66 (63) to describe the 72 lambs of the thanksgiving sacrifice offered by Ezra and his company when they arrived in Jerusalem from exile.

[18] The word θήριον clearly does not mean "little beast" (communicating size) or "beastie" (communicating endearment); one should thus be cautious of attributing the same value on ἀρνίον. On the -ιον ending no longer expressing a diminutive force in biblical Greek, see P. Walters, *The Text of the Septuagint: Its Corruptions and Their Emendation* (Cambridge: Cambridge University Press, 1973), 46. See also Joachim Jeremias, "ἀμνός, ἀρήν, ἀρνίον," *Theologische Wörterbuch zum neuen Testament*, Gerhard Kittel, ed. (Stuttgart: W. Kohlhammer, 1949–1979), 1.344; Bauer-Arndt-Gingrich, *A Greek-English Lexicon*, s.v. ἀρνίον; Colin Brown, gen. ed., *The New International Dictionary of New Testament Theology* (Grand Rapids, Mich.: Zondervan Publishing House, 1976), s.v. "Lamb" (410): "In the LXX both ἀμνός and ἀρήν are used, while ἀρνίον is no longer felt to be a diminutive, either in the LXX or in the NT."

[19] There is simply no linguistic evidence for the definition of ἀρνίον in the Louw-Nida lexicon as "lamb or sheep of any age" or as "ram." Cf. Johannes P. Louw and Eugene A. Nida, eds., *Greek-English Lexicon of the New Testament Based on Semantic Domains; Volume 1: Introductions & Domains*, in collaboration with Rondal B. Smith and Karen A. Munson (New York: United Bible Societies, 1988), 42.

ἀρήν, which is a minor consonant (nasal) stem third declension noun.[20] They list it so because the nominative singular form appears only in early inscriptions.[21]

Commentators sometimes find it significant that the Fourth Gospel and the Apocalypse both refer to Christ as a lamb. For Josephine Massyngberde Ford, the lamb Christologies of the Fourth Gospel and of the Apocalypse provide a point of contact between both of these works and John the Baptist traditions.[22] Identifying the origin of the lamb Christology of the Fourth Gospel is itself a complex issue outside the scope of our study.[23] As we will see in the succeeding chapters, the rhetorical force of ἀρνίον in the Apocalypse is more perspicuous than is the rhetorical force of ἀμνός in the Fourth Gospel.

Despite occasional protests to the contrary,[24] the differences between the Lamb Christology of the Fourth Gospel and that of the Apocalypse are great. First, the words for lamb are different (ἀμνός in the Fourth Gospel; ἀρνίον in the Apocalypse). Second, although the Gospel of John is the only other New Testament writing to use the word ἀρνίον, it does not apply it to Christ, but to believers. Third, in its only appearance in the Fourth Gospel, ἀρνίον appears in the plural, whereas in the Apocalypse it always appears in the singular. Fourth, besides the use of a different word for lamb in the Apocalypse, neither of the modifiers found in the Fourth Gospel (τοῦ θεοῦ ["of God"] and ὁ αἴρων τὴν ἁμαρτίαν τοῦ κόσμου ["the one who takes away the sin of the world"]) ap-

---

[20] Edwin Hatch, *A Concordance to the Septuagint and the Other Greek Versions of the Old Testament (Including the Apocryphal Books)*, by Henry A[deney] Redpath, reprint, 1897–1906 (Baker Book House: Grand Rapids, Mich., 1983).

[21] Walter Bauer, *A Greek-English Lexicon of the New Testament and Other Early Christian Literature: A Translation and Adaptation of Walter Bauer's Griechisch-Deutsches Wörterbuch zu den Schriften des neuen Testaments und der übrigen urchristlichen Literatur*, 2d ed., trans. and ed. William F. Arndt and F. Wilbur Gingrich, ed. Frederick W. Danker, reprint, 1957 (Chicago: University of Chicago, 1979).

[22] See J. Massyngberde Ford, *Revelation*. The Anchor Bible, vol. 38 (Garden City, N.Y.: Doubleday & Company, 1975), 30–31.

[23] For a helpful discussion of the three main theories that have been proposed for the origin of the lamb image in John 1:29, 36, see Raymond E. Brown, *The Gospel According to John, I–XII: A New Translation with Introduction and Commentary*, 2d ed., reprint, 1966. The Anchor Bible, vol. 29 (Garden City, New York: Doubleday & Co., 1981), 58–63. I would hold that Brown rightly accepts Dodd's rejection of the argument made by C. J. Ball and expanded by C. F. Burney that ἀμνός in the Fourth Gospel represents a misunderstanding of טליא (boy or servant, as with παῖς) as טליא (lamb). Cf. Charles Fox Burney, *The Aramaic Origin of the Fourth Gospel* (Oxford: Clarendon Press, 1922), 104–08; see also Joachim Jeremias, "ἀμνός, ἀρήν, ἀρνίον," 1:343.

[24] See esp. Peter Whale, "The Lamb of John: Some Myths About the Vocabulary of the Johannine Literature," *Journal of Biblical Literature* 106 (1987) 289–95.

pears in the Apocalypse. The title "Lamb of God" (or *agnus Dei*) is unique to the Fourth Gospel, appearing in the entire Bible only in John 1:29, 36. Finally, most commentators see John 21 as redactional. Thus, if there is any connection to be made between the two, it is surely not to be made with John the Baptist or the Fourth Evangelist, but with later "Johannine" traditions.

If the lamb Christology of the Apocalypse has little to do with that of the Fourth Gospel, on what does it draw? To answer this question, we must take a step back and survey the features and parameters of this semantic domain in the Hebrew Bible and the literature of Early Judaism. Our focus here will be more narrowly semantic and lexical; discussion of the relevance of the Hebrew Bible and Septuagint for understanding the rhetorical force of the lamb figure must await chapter 5.

4. "Lamb" in the Hebrew Bible and the Septuagint

The symbolic/semantic domain of sheep is broad and deep in biblical traditions. According to Roy Pinney, sheep are directly referred to 742 times in the Bible.[25] "The [sheep] assumed a vital role in Hebrew culture, bound up indivisibly with the religious, civil, and domestic life of the Israelites."[26] A smaller, but still significant part of this broader domain is the more limited semantic domain of young sheep, or lambs, of one kind or another. Though smaller in scope, this domain is still broad and complex, as the chart in Appendix I indicates.

By far the most common word for lamb in the Hebrew Bible is כֶּבֶשׂ, from an unused verbal root meaning to tread down, dominate, or subdue.[27] It is

---

[25] Roy Pinney, *The Animals in the Bible: The Identity and Natural History of All the Animals Mentioned in the Bible* (Chilton Books: Philadelphia and New York, 1964), 108.

[26] Roy Pinney, *Animals in the Bible*, 108.

[27] Francis Brown, ed., *The New Brown, Driver, and Briggs Hebrew and English Lexicon of the Old Testament*, by William Gesenius, translated by Edward Robinson, in collaboration with S[amuel] R[olles] Driver and Charles A[ugustus] Briggs, reprint, 1907 (Associated Publishers and Authors: Lafayette, Ind., 1981), 461. C. Dohmen suggests that "Heb. *kebeś* is related to the common Semitic verb *kbš*, 'overthrow,' and *kbs*, 'roll,' derived from Akk. *kabāsu*, 'tread (down).' The semantics of *kabsu* may be explained by the early use of sheep to tread seed into the ground or to tread out grain on the threshing floor; this etymology is supported by the Egyptian parallels *sḫ* and *sḫ.t*" (*Theological Dictionary of the Old Testament*, vol. 7, G. Johannes Botterweck, ed. [Grand Rapids, Mich.: Eerdmans, 1995], 43).
According to Pesikta de-Rab Kahana 6.4, there was a controversy between the school of Hillel and the School of Shammai over the etymology of the word: The disciples of Shammai read kebasim as though written kabbasim, 'they that put out of sight.'

usually translated in the LXX with the word ἀμνός.[28] Although שֶׂה/πρόβατον is a common combination, these words are more general. שֶׂה can refer to any single animal out of the flock, whether that flock is made up of goats or sheep.[29] πρόβατον usually refers to the adult "sheep." The צֹאן/πρόβατον combination is also common, צֹאן being so general as to refer to a broad spectrum of small, four-footed cattle, including sheep, lambs, and goats.

Appendix I represents in chart form the lamb domain in the Hebrew Bible and the Greek Septuagint. The broader or more general words for sheep, like שֶׂה and צֹאן in the Hebrew Bible and πρόβατον in the Septuagint, are cited in Appendix I only when the corresponding word in the other language is a more restrictive one for lamb or where the context seems to demand a young sheep or "lamb."

The chart reveals that the semantic field is complex, with at least 25 different Hebrew-Greek combinations accounting for the 196 or so appearances of the concept of "lamb" in the Hebrew Bible and the Septuagint. Approximately two-thirds of those 196 appearances are from the Pentateuch, all of which refer to literal lambs.

In his article on כֶּבֶשׂ in the *Theologisches Wörterbuch des alten Testaments*, Dohmen notes that of the 130 occurrences of כֶּבֶשׂ in the Hebrew Bible, 112 are in "sacrificial" contexts and 18 are in "secular" contexts. But some further distinctions may be helpful: Of the 112 "sacrificial" contexts, only one refers to the paschal lamb (Exod 12:5), which is not really sacrificial. One refers to the "unredeemable" status of lambs (Num 18:17), while the other 110 refer to the lamb as a burnt offering. Similarly, of the 18 "secular" uses of lamb, ten refer to the utilitarian use of lambs as a source of food and clothing (Gen 21:28, 29, 30; 30:32, 33, 35, 40; Deut 14:4; Job 31:20; and Prov 27:26), and eight use כֶּבֶשׂ symbolically (2Sam 12:3, 4, 6; Isa 5:17; 11:6; Jer 11:19; Hos 4:16; and Sir 13:17). Although it is impossible to state propositionally what the symbolism of each of these occurrences communicates, most if not all of these occurrences communicate the vulnerability of the lamb, either in the presence of a potential enemy or as a symbol of eschatological peace.

That is, the daily offering of the lambs brings it about that God puts Israel's iniquities out of sight, as the verse tells us, *He will turn again and have compassion upon us; He will put our iniquities out of sight (yikbos)* (Micah 7:19). But the disciples of Hillel said: The phrase *kebasim bene sanah*, 'he-lambs of the first year' (Num 28:3), is to be understood as though written *kabbasim bene sanah*, 'they that cleanse the things which are of many a year.' That is the daily offerings cleanse the sins of Israel, as is said *Though your sins be as of many a year, they shall be as white as snow* (Isa 1:18).

[28] ἀμνός also appears in 2Chr 35:8, where כֶּבֶשׂ is assumed.

[29] Cf. on this point and more broadly, Dohmen, "כֶּבֶשׂ [Kebes]," in *Theological Dictionary of the Old Testament* (Grand Rapids, Mich.: Eerdmans), 43–52, esp. 44.

The semantic force of the lamb domain varies outside the Pentateuch. The handful of occurrences in the Former Prophets are divided equally between the literal[30] and symbolic senses.[31] In the Writings, the literal sense predominates.[32] In the book of Ezekiel, dominated as it is with the priestly perspective, the word *lamb* appears only in the literal sense.[33] With the exception of Ezekiel and Isaiah 1:11, the lambs in the Latter Prophets are all symbolic.[34]

Although ἀμνός and ἀμνάς *can* be used symbolically,[35] ἀμνός is the favored word when speaking of lambs as burnt offerings. Within the sacrificial system, lambs were not the primary animal associated with the purification offering[36]; rather, bulls and goats were. The bull was normally required for the purification offering (see Lev 4:1-21). Alternatively, in certain contexts a goat (Lev. 4:22-31), a ram (Lev 5:14-19), a sheep (Lev 4:32-35), or birds or grain (Lev 1:14–2:16; 5:7-13; 9:3; 14:21) could also be used. In some settings the lamb was used for the reparation offering (cf. Num 6:14). Over time, the whole burnt offering lost its expiatory sense when offered by individuals.[37]

As Dodd noted already in 1960, according to the Hebrew Bible, the lamb is not the characteristic purification offering; it was "the blood of bulls and goats."[38] Lambs also played no role in atonement for sin. However, although the phrase "bulls and goats" can serve as a shorthand expression for the

---

[30] 1Sam 7:9; 17:34; 2Kgs 3:4.

[31] 2Sam 12:3, 4, 6. No sharp distinction between *literal* and *symbolic* can be legitimate. Our aim is simply to distinguish between those contexts in which the symbolic force predominates ("symbolic") and those in which it does not ("literal").

[32] But cf. Ps 114:4, 6.

[33] In Ezek 27:21 the reference is to the utilitarian value of lambs; in 45:15; 46:4, 5, 6, 7, 11, 13, 15 lambs of the sacrificial cult are in view.

[34] Isa 5:17; 11:6; 34:6; 40:11; 53:7; 65:25; Jer 11:19; 50:45; 51:40; Hos 4:16; Mic 5:7).

[35] Cf. 2Sam 12:3, 4, 6; Isa 53:7; Hos 4:16; Wisd 19:9; Sir 13:17.

[36] In using the language of "purification" instead of "sin"; and "reparation" instead of "guilt," I am following the suggestion of Jacob Milgrom. See Jacob Milgrom, *Studies in Cultic Theology and Terminology*. Studies in Judaism in Late Antiquity, vol. 36 (E. J. Brill: Leiden, 1983). See also Jacob Milgrom, *Leviticus 1–16: A New Translation with Introduction and Commentary*. Anchor Bible, vol. 3 (Doubleday: New York, 1991). For a helpful summary, see Gary A. Anderson, "Sacrifice and Sacrificial Offerings (OT)," David Noel Freedman, editor-in-chief, *Anchor Bible Dictionary*, associate editors Gary A. Herion, David F. Graf, and John David Pleins, managing editor Astrid B. Beck (Doubleday: New York, N.Y., 1992), 5:870–86.

[37] See Jacob Milgrom, "Further on the expiatory sacrifices," *Journal of Biblical Literature* 115, no. 3 (Fall 1996): 513n21.

[38] Cf., e.g., Heb 9:13; 10:4.

sacrificial system in the Old Testament, lambs are sometimes also mentioned in the same context.[39]

There is no strong correlation between the individual Hebrew words for lamb and the way in which those lambs function. It is clearly true that כֶּבֶשׂ is the most common word for lamb and that it appears primarily in Pentateuchal passages describing the sacrificial cult. However, כֶּבֶשׂ can also be used symbolically.[40] It can refer both to the paschal lamb[41] and lambs used for clothing.[42] Similarly, כִּבְשָׂה (or כַּבְשָׂה or כִּשְׂבָּה) can be used in sacrificial contexts,[43] symbolic contexts,[44] or to the inherent value of lambs as a source of food.[45] פֶּסַח is used exclusively of the Passover victim. Although כַּר, צְעִירֵי הַצֹּאן, and רָחֵל are not used in sacrificial contexts, they apparently apply equally well to lambs whose utilitarian value is in view and to lambs as a symbol for vulnerability.[46]

Identifiable correspondences appear to be stronger in the Greek, however. The chart in Appendix I confirms the suggestion by Lothar Coenen, Erich Beyreuther, and Hans Bietenhard in the *Theologisches Begriffslexikon zum neuen Testament* that "ἀμνός bezeichnete von vornherein das junge, häufig einjährige Schaf, das *Lamm*, insbesondere als Opfertier bei zahlreichen kultischen Anlässen. Tritt der kultische Bezug zurück, so wird das Lamm als Schlachttier ἀρήν genannt."[47] Although several other Greek words for lamb

---

[39] See, e.g., Num 7:87-88; Deut 32:14; 2Chron 29:21; Ezra 8:35; Isa 1:11. All of these mention bulls, goats, *and* lambs; but cf. also Lev 16:15, 18, 27; Num 15:24; Ps 50:9, 13, Heb 9:13; 10:4; where bulls and goats are mentioned, but not lambs or rams.

[40] Isa 5:17; 11:6; Jer 11:19; Hos 4:16; Sir 13:17; cf. 2Sam 12:3, 4, 6 for כִּבְשָׂה/כַּבְשָׂה.

[41] Ex 12:5.

[42] Job 31:20; Prov 27:26.

[43] Lev 5:6; 14:10; Num 6:14.

[44] 2Sam 12:3, 4, 6.

[45] Gen 21:28, 29, 30.

[46] For the former, see Gen 31:38; 32:14(15); Deut 32:14; 2Kgs 3:4; Pss 65(64):13(14); Isa 53:7; Jer 50(27):45; and Ezek 27:21.

[47] *Theologisches Begriffslexikon zum neuen Testament*, ed. Lothar Coenen, mit Erich Beyreuther und Hans Bietenhard, Band II/1 (Wuppertal: Theologischer Verlag Rolf Brockhaus) s.v. Lamm. "ἀμνός denoted from the outset a young sheep, frequently a one-year-old lamb, especially as used for sacrifice on numerous cultic occasions. In non-sacrificial contexts, the lamb as an animal for slaughter was called ἀρήν." Quoted from the English edition: Colin Brown, gen. ed., *The New International Dictionary of New Testament Theology* (Grand Rapids, Mich.: Zondervan Publishing House, 1976), s.v. "lamb" (2:410). A further distinction suggested by Paul Harlé is compatible with the above distinction: namely, that ἀρήν/ἀρνός designates a sheep that is less than a year old, ἀμνός a year-old lamb/sheep, and κριός a ram (i.e., a male sheep more than a year old). See P[aul] Harlé, *Le Lévitique*, vol. 3 of *La Bible d'Alexandrie*, D[idier] Pralon (Paris: Cerf, 1988), 44; cf. also José Berenguer Sánchez, "ἀρνόν en PGurob 22 y el Empleo del Término ἀρνίον en los Papiros Documentales," *Emerita: Revista (Boletin) de Lingüística y Filología Clásica* 57, no. 2 (1989): 277–88.

are occasionally used to symbolize some aspect of tenderness or vulnerability,[48] the majority of the times the image of the lamb appears in symbolic contexts, the words ἀρήν[49] and its diminutive, ἀρνίον,[50] are used. Furthermore, although the word ἀρνίον corresponds to at least three or four different Hebrew words or word pairs, it is used exclusively in nonsacrificial contexts in which it symbolizes vulnerability of some kind. This concept of vulnerability will become a major dimension of our study of the Lamb Christology of the Apocalypse.

5. The Lamb Domain in Josephus and Philo

5.1 In Josephus

Josephus rarely uses the same word for lamb that the Septuagint does when a biblical parallel is present. Unlike the Septuagint, which uses ἀμνός more than any other word to describe the sacrificial lamb, Josephus uses ἀμνός only once, according to Rengstorf, compared to 31 uses of ἀρήν/ἀρνός.[51] The single time Josephus uses ἀμνός is in *Antiquities* 7.382 where he is describing the feast held in honor of Solomon's accession to the throne.[52] Like the Septuagint, Josephus uses ἀμνάς to relate Nathan's parable of the ewe-lamb that represented the possession of Uriah the Hittite, where the Hebrew has כִּבְשָׂה.[53] Josephus's only other use of ἀμνάς comes in a section that has no biblical parallel, where he is describing the means of purification available when one exceeds the maximum allowed time of defilement.[54] Such a person "is required to sacrifice two lambs [ἀμνάς], of which one must be devoted to the flames and the other is taken by the priests."[55]

According to Rengstorf, Josephus uses ἀρνίον only two or three times: in *Ant* 3.221(?); 3.226; and 3.251. In two of these three instances, he adds the

---

[48] ἀμνός in Isa 53:7; Hos 4:16; Sir 13:17; and Wisd 19:9; ἀμνάς in 2Sam 12:3, 4, 6; and possibly πρόβατον in Isa 53:7.

[49] In Isa 5:17; 11:6; 34:6; 40:11; 65:25; Jer 51(28):40; Mic 5:7(6); 1Esd 47:3.

[50] Ps 114:4, 6; Isa 40:11[Aq]; Jer 11:19; 50(27):45; and PsSol 8:23.

[51] References to Rengstorf are to Karl Heinrich Rengstorf, *A Complete Concordance to Flavius Josephus* (Leiden: Brill, 1973–1983), vol. 1, s.v. ἀμνός, ἀμνάς, ἀρνίον, and ἀρήν.

[52] The biblical parallel is in 1Chr 29:21, where the Hebrew has כֶּבֶשׂ and the LXX, ἀρήν.

[53] Compare 2Sam 12:1–6 with *Ant* 7.148–150.

[54] Cf. Num 19:10b-22; 31:19-20.

[55] *Ant* 3.262.

modifier "one-year-old" (*Ant* 3.221: ἀρνίον τῶν ἐτησίων;[56] and *Ant* 3.226: ἀρνίον καὶ ἔριφον· ταῦτα μὲν ἐπέτεια ...).[57] Josephus's intent in using the "one-year-old" modifier was very likely to communicate that the lamb was to be close to a year old, but no *more* than a year old, since the logic of the sacrificial cult seems to require it and a similar shorthand way of describing an upper limit is also common in the Mishnah.[58] Furthermore, the presence of the modifier would seem to support the consensus that the diminutive force was no longer in force by the end of the first century CE. In his third use of ἀρνίον, in *Ant* 3.251, Josephus uses the word without modifier in parallel with Leviticus 23:12, which has the modifiers "without blemish" and "one-year-old" in both the Hebrew (כֶּבֶשׂ תָּמִים בֶּן־שְׁנָתוֹ) and the Greek (πρόβατον ἄμωμον ἐνιαύσιον). In all three of these cases, Josephus uses ἀρνίον to speak of the burnt offering of the sacrificial cult.

In describing the razing of the Antonia fortress in August of 70 in the *Jewish War*, Josephus says the daily sacrifice (the *Tamid*) ceased to be offered on the 17th of Panemus (i.e., the 17th of Tammuz, or August 6) "for lack of men" (ἀνδρῶν ἀπορίᾳ). Although the manuscript evidence for this reading is unanimous, most scholars have emended the text to read ἀρνῶν ἀπορίᾳ (for lack of lambs). In the aftermath of the destruction, Josephus recounts several fantastic portents that, in retrospect, forewarned of the tragedies that were to come. In one such story, at a Feast of Unleavened Bread "before the war," "a cow that had been brought by some one for sacrifice gave birth to a lamb (ἄρνα, from ἀρήν/ἀρνός) in the midst of the court of the temple" (*War* 6.292).

Josephus uses ἀρήν/ἀρνός 29 times in his *Antiquities*, according to Rengstorf. In 3.222 it parallels ἀμνάς (and כֶּבֶשׂ) in Num 7:17, 23, 29, 35, 41, 47, 53, 59, 65, 71, 77, 83, and 88. In 3.228 it apparently parallels ἀρήν/ἀρνός (and כֶּבֶשׂ) in Lev. 3:7. In 3.231 it parallels πρόβατον (and כֶּשֶׂב) in Lev. 4:32. In 3.233 and 234, ἀρήν/ἀρνός parallels ἀμνός (and כֶּבֶשׂ) in Num 15:5, 11. In 3.237 Josephus uses ἀρήν/ἀρνός to speak of the *Tamid*, paralleled in Numbers 28:1-8 by ἀμνός and כֶּבֶשׂ. Josephus also uses ἀρήν/ἀρνός to speak of the New Moon sacrifice, again paralleled in Exod 29:38-41 by ἀμνός and כֶּבֶשׂ. The same combination is found in speaking of the Rosh HaShanah sacrifices

---

[56] Codices R (Regius Parisinus) and O (Oxoniensis [Bodleianus]) have ἀρνίῳ (or ἀρνείῳ; see further below) ἐτείῳ.

[57] This reading is questionable, however, since Codex M (Marcianae Venetae) has ἀρνί (from ἀρήν/ἀρνός), Codex R has ἀρνείω (from the adjective ἄρνειος, Codex S (Caesareae Vindobonensis) has ἀρνειῶ (from the noun ἀρνειός), and Codex P (Parisinus) has ἀρνιῶ (an unknown accentuation). The textual evidence cited here is from *Flavii Iosephi Opera*, Benedictus Niese, ed. (Berlin: Apud Weidmannos, 1887), ix–xviii, 202.

[58] See also Dohmen, "כֶּבֶשׂ [Kebes]," in *Theological Dictionary of the Old Testament* (Grand Rapids, Mich.: Eerdmans), 51.

(ἀρήν/ἀρνός in *Ant* 3.239, ἀμνός and כֶּבֶשׂ in Num 29:1-6), the Yom Kippur sacrifices (ἀρήν/ἀρνός in *Ant* 3.240, ἀμνός and כֶּבֶשׂ in Num 29:7–11), the Sukkoth sacrifices (ἀρήν/ἀρνός in *Ant* 3.246 and 247, ἀμνός and כֶּבֶשׂ in Num 29:12-40), the Passover sacrifices (ἀρήν/ἀρνός in *Ant* 3.249, ἀμνός and כֶּבֶשׂ in Num 28:16-25), and the Shavuoth (Festival of Weeks) sacrifices (ἀρήν/ἀρνός in *Ant* 3.252 and 253, ἀμνός and כֶּבֶשׂ in Num 28:26-31).

In describing Hezekiah's celebration of the Passover after his cleansing of the Temple, Josephus uses ἀρήν/ἀρνός in *Ant* 9.268 and 270 to parallel the biblical ἀμνός and כֶּבֶשׂ (cf. 2Chron 29:20-24). The same is true of Josephus's account later of Josiah's celebration of the Passover at the time of his reform: Josephus uses ἀρήν/ἀρνός in *Ant* 10.70 and 71 [*bis*] in parallel with the biblical ἀμνός and כֶּבֶשׂ in 2Chron 35:7.

In recounting Darius's official decree that Israel's neighbors subsidize the cost of the sacrifices in Jerusalem, Josephus uses ἀρήν/ἀρνός (*Ant* 11.102) in parallel with the ἀρήν/ἀρνός in 1 Esdras 6:29(28) and ἀμνός in 2 Esdras 6:9 (אִמַּר in Ezra 6:9). The same combination (ἀρήν/ἀρνός in *Ant* 11.107 and 1 Esdras 7:7; ἀμνός in 2 Esdras 6:17; and אִמַּר in Ezra 6:17) occurs a few lines later. Yet again we have the ἀρήν-ἀρνός/ἀμνός/כֶּבֶשׂ combination in *Ant* 11.137 and 1 Esdras 8:63; 2 Esdras 8:35; and Ezra 8:35; respectively.

Josephus also uses ἀρήν/ἀρνός in places where the LXX has ἀρήν/ἀρνός, such as *Ant* 6.25 (cf. 1 Sam. 7:9, where the BHS has טָלֶה). In Ant. 6.182 [*bis*], ἀρήν/ἀρνός parallels πρόβατον and שֶׂה in the story of David's rescue of a lamb from the mouth of a lion (1Sam 17:34-37). In recounting the extensive provisions required by King Solomon, Josephus reports that he required 100 lambs (ἀρήν/ἀρνός) daily (*Ant* 8.40), where the biblical account is more general: 100 πρόβατα (or צֹאן; 1Kgs 4:23; 5:3 in BHS and LXX). Second Chronicles 17:11 reports that the "Arabs" brought Jehoshaphat 7,700 rams (אַיִל) and 7,700 male goats (תַּיִשׁ; the LXX has simply 7,700 κριοὺς προβάτων). However, in *Ant* 8.396, Josephus reports that the Arabs supplied Jehoshaphat with 360 lambs (ἀρήν/ἀρνός) and goats (ἔριφος) every year (κατ᾽ ἔτος). In a passage with no biblical parallel, Josephus recounts the story of Bagōsēs, one of the generals of Artaxerxes II, who imposed an exorbitant tax of 50 drachmas for every lamb (ἀρήν/ἀρνός) sacrificed in the *Tamid* (*Ant* 11.297).

In conclusion, Josephus never uses ἀμνός where the LXX has ἀμνός. The only time Josephus uses ἀμνός the LXX has ἀρήν/ἀρνός. The only times Josephus uses ἀμνάς is in reference to the Nathan/Bathsheba story (three times), where the LXX also has ἀμνάς. Josephus uses ἀρνίον where the LXX has three other words (ἀμνός, ἀρήν/ἀρνός, and πρόβατον), and Josephus's favorite word, ἀρήν/ἀρνός, is paralleled in the LXX by four words: ἀρήν/ἀρνός, πρόβατον, ἀμνός, and ἀμνάς. In other words, Josephus uses the same Greek word for lamb only 7 of the 47 times in which a biblical parallel exists among the extant LXX manuscripts (15% of the time).

5.2 In Philo

The case is somewhat different in Philo. Philo uses ἀρήν/ἀρνός and ἀμνός in nearly equal portion. He uses ἀρνίον just once. In Gaius's interview with the Embassy, he asks them about the Jewish dietary laws. When questioned about the Jewish abstinence from pork, one of Gaius's attendants points out that many people don't offer up [in sacrifice and then eat] (προσφέρω) lambs (ἀρνία), which are readily available (*Embassy to Gaius* 362).

The LXX uses ἀμνός to speak of the Sabbath offering in Num 28:9-10; Philo has ἀμνός as well (*Special Laws* 1.169). The Tamid is called an ἀμνός in *Special Laws* 1.170 and in *Who Is the Heir* 174, in parallel with the ἀμνός in Num 28:3-8; likewise the New Moon ἀμνός in *Special Laws* 1.177–178 parallels Num 28:11-14. The first-fruits offering also reflects the common use of ἀμνός (Lev. 23:18-20 and Philo, *Special Laws* 1.184). Both the LXX and Philo use ἀμνός to identify animals that are clean (Deut. 14:4 and *Special Laws* 4.105).

However, Philo uses ἀρήν/ἀρνός of the Yom Kippur sacrifices (*Special Laws* 1.188) where the LXX has ἀμνός (Num 29:8-10). At the Feast of Tabernacles, the LXX speaks of offering 14 ἀμνοί per day (Num 29:12-40) and Philo of 98 ἄρνες for the week (*Special Laws* 1.189). Besides the calf or the goat, Philo specifies the lamb (ἀμνός in Special Laws 1.198; ἀρήν/ἀρνός in *Embassy to Gaius* 317) as the proper burnt offering where the LXX does not specify (Lev. 1:3-13). In speaking of the sin offering, Philo speaks of an αμνάς (*Special Laws* 1.226, 233) where the LXX has προβάτον (Lev. 4:32-35). Where the LXX uses ἀμνός and ἀμνάς to speak of the male and female lambs to be offered for the Nazirite vow (Num 6:12, 14), Philo uses ἀρήν/ἀρνός and ἀμνάς respectively (*Special Laws* 1.251). In that context Philo pauses to point out that the three animals to be brought for these sacrifices—the ram (κριός), the male lamb (ἀρήν/ἀρνός), and the female lamb (ἀμνάς)—all belong to the same species (*Special Laws* 1.253).

Philo speaks at some length about the philosophical and moral insight behind various obscure and apparently idiosyncratic Mosaic laws, such as the proscription about boiling a kid in its mother's milk (Exod 23:19). Both the LXX and Philo (*Virtues* 133; 142–144) use ἀρήν/ἀρνός in this context, where the BHS has גדי. In most cases Philo uses ἀμνός in sacrificial contexts, though he is capable of using it outside the contexts as well (*Change of Names* 159). We have no instance of Philo using a word to parallel ἀρήν/ἀρνός in the LXX, but we do apparently see the beginning of a shift away from ἀμνός and toward ἀρήν/ἀρνός. In summary, Philo uses the same word for lamb 10 of the 14 times in which a biblical parallel exists (70% of the time).

5.3 The Josephus and Philo Evidence Interpreted

How is one to account for the fact that while Philo's choice of words for lamb usually matches that of the Septuagint, Josephus's choice *differs* from the LXX most of the time? Philo probably used the "Septuagint," though the term itself is quite imprecise. That is, although Philo used a Greek translation of the Bible, several manuscript traditions were in existence. Furthermore, there is the real possibility that in the transmission of Philo's own corpus, adjustments were made to bring his work into conformity with the Septuagintal traditions of the day.[59]

The question is not easily answered for Josephus, either, since the issue of what sort of biblical text Josephus used is even more complex. The most reliable interpretive statement is that Josephus did not use a Greek text for his biblical material that is identical with the text we have today. But that is not saying much; how much further can we go?[60]

Making such a judgment will require one to balance several issues, each of which is complex in itself. First, to what extent were Josephus's word choices due to his dependence on the Greek stylists he admits using?[61] It may well be that Josephus's own word choices were revised by stylists who either ignored or did not understand the nuances inherent in the Hebrew Bible or the Greek of the Septuagint.

Second, Josephus may intentionally have leveled the linguistic nuances in his choice of words for lamb. His Roman audience likely was not interested in the technical aspects of lamb terminology nor would they have been in a position to pick up on the finer linguistic nuances had they been present. Josephus may have used ἀρήν/ἀρνός 85% of the time to simplify the complex semantic domain in the Hebrew Bible.

The most likely consideration is that the Greek language itself was changing from the fourth century BCE to the end of the first century CE. Evidence within the Septuagint itself could support the idea that ἀρήν/ἀρνός was grad-

---

[59] See, e.g., Peter Katz, *Philo's Bible: The Aberrant Text of Bible Quotations in Some Philonic Writings and Its Place in the Textual History of the Greek Bible* (Cambridge: Cambridge University Press, 1950) 3–4, 103.

[60] For a marvelous overview of attempts to determine the nature of the Hebrew and Greek texts on which Josephus depended, see Louis H. Feldman, *Josephus and Modern Scholarship (1937–1980)* (Berlin and New York: Walter de Gruyter, 1984), 121–34. See also Michael A. Stone, ed., *Jewish Writings of the Second Temple Period: Apocrypha, Pseudepigrapha, Qumran Sectarian Writings, Philo, Josephus*, in *The literature of the Jewish people in the period of the second temple and the Talmud*, Compendia Rerum Iudaicarum ad Novum Testamentum (Assen and Philadelphia: Van Gorcum and Fortress Press, 1984), 211.

[61] Cf. *Apion* 1.50.

ually coming to replace ἀμνός by the third century BCE. Such a hypothetical trend may have continued in the succeeding centuries, with Josephus representing a stage advanced beyond that of Philo. Although the data necessary for developing and sustaining such a judgment are inconclusive, the documentary papyri tend to support this conclusion. The evidence suggests that ἀμνός had begun to fall out of use by the first century BCE in favor of ἀρήν/ἀρνός.[62] If this is correct, then the uses of ἀμνός as a christological term in the New Testament would have had a distinctly archaic, biblical ring to them.

It is impossible to suggest a biblical *Vorlage* for Josephus's comments on lambs based on the small body of evidence we have examined. Though the evidence suggests that Josephus did not use a biblical text close to our Septuagint, the data resist further conclusions regarding Josephus's use of biblical materials. However, the three appearances of ἀρνίον in Josephus in contexts where the Septuagint has ἀμνός,[63] ἀρήν/ἀρνός,[64] and πρόβατον[65]—all of which refer to literal lambs used in the sacrificial cult—provide some caution about overinterpreting the unanimous witness of the Septuagint to ἀρνίον exlusively as a symbol of vulnerability.

The semantic domain of "lamb" has been investigated by José A. Berenguer Sánchez in *Emerita*.[66] In this article Berenguer Sánchez investigates the unusual form ἀρνόν, which appears several times in PGurob 22, a papyrus of the third century BCE. In contrast to Petrie and others, including the compilers and editors of the Liddell-Scott-Jones-Mackenzie Greek-English lexicon, who see ἀρνόν as a variant of ἀρήν/ἀρνός, Berenguer Sánchez argues successfully that ἀρνόν there is really a variant of ἀρνίον. Furthermore, Berenguer Sánchez concludes that the word ἀμνός was gradually dying out in use toward the end of the first millennium BCE and that ἀρήν/ἀρνός was coming to replace it. ἀρνίον occasionally still carried the force of a diminutive when used in conjunction with ἀρήν/ἀρνός. Its use as a term of endearment—especially in informal, popular documents—outlasted its strictly diminutive use, but even that sense gave way over time. Thus, ἀρνίον gradually came to be the term of choice for lambs broadly conceived, taking the place of all previous terms.

[62] José Berenguer Sánchez, "ἀρνόν en PGurob 22 y el Empleo del Término ἀρνίον en los Papiros Documentales," *Emerita: Revista (Boletin) de Linguistica y Filología Clasica* 57, no. 2 (1989): 277–88.
[63] *Ant* 3.221//Lev 7:15.
[64] *Ant* 3.226//Lev 1:10.
[65] *Ant* 3.251//Lev 23:12.
[66] José Berenguer Sánchez, "ἀρνόν en PGurob 22 y el Empleo del Término ἀρνίον en los Papiros Documentales," *Emerita: Revista (Boletin) de Linguistica y Filología Clásica* 57, no. 2 (1989): 277–88.

6. ἀρνίον as a Cryptogram

In *Nelson's Bible Commentary*, Frederick C. Grant suggested that APNION is really "a cryptogram for αὐτὸς ῥάβδῳ νικησεῖ Ἰησοῦς ὁ Ναζαρῆνος ('Jesus the Nazarene will conquer with a rod') in fulfillment of Psalm 2:9, one of John's favorite texts."[67] Though imaginative, this suggestion has little to commend it. While it is true that Psalm 2:9 is a favorite of the author's, all three of the texts that quote it or allude to it state that he will "rule" (ποιμαίνω is the verb in each case, not νικάω) with a rod *of iron* (ῥάβδῳ σιδηρᾷ), not that he will "conquer" with simply "a rod" (ῥάβδῳ; cf. 2:27; 12:5; 19:15). Without spelling out the cryptogram in some way, it is difficult to see how the hearers of the Apocalypse would have made the leap to this odd expression when they heard ἀρνίον. Furthermore, it is unclear what significance "Nazarene" had in the province of Asia in the first century.[68] The word *Nazarene* does not occur in the Apocalypse. Most importantly, the suggestion seems to assume wrongly that the Apocalypse is code language designed to obscure to outsiders the political critique of the empire going on in the book.

7. Conclusion

The image of a victorious slain lamb is anomalous indeed. There is something about this picture that just does not fit common understandings about how life works. However, as readers we must be open to the possibility that the anomaly of this image lies at the very heart of the revelation represented by this book. If the image seems strange, that may be because it requires prophetic insight to see it and to hear what the Spirit is saying to the churches.

Within the New Testament, there is little connection between the Fourth Gospel and the Apocalypse in terms of the lamb images. New Testament references to Christ as ἀμνός depend heavily on the Septuagint and emphasize atonement for sin. References to Christ in the Apocalypse as ἀρνίον seem not to depend on the Septuagint and emphasize the vulnerability of the Lamb to slaughter. Given the relative disuse of ἀμνός by the first century CE, it would have had a peculiarly biblical or archaic ring to it, and was limited by this time almost exclusively to the sacrificial system.

The closest parallel to ἀρνίον *rhetorically* in the New Testament is also a close parallel *linguistically*. The reference to the disciples as "lambs in the

---

[67] Cf. also Robert H. Mounce, "Christology of the Apocalypse," *Foundations* 11 (1968) 43.

[68] Cf. the attempt to explain significance and distinctions between "Jesus," "Christ," "Messiah," and "Nazarene" in Gospel of Philip 19 and 47.

midst of wolves" in Luke 10:3 uses *lamb* as a symbol of vulnerability in a way similar to the rhetorical force of *lamb* in the Apocalypse. Furthermore, the word for lamb there is ἀρήν, the noun most closely related to the ἀρνίον of the Apocalypse.

In conclusion, the semantic domain of *lamb* in the Hebrew Bible, the Septuagint, and the New Testament is a complex one. The particular word for lamb used in the Apocalypse suggests a nonsacrificial lamb. The few times ἀρνίον occurs in the LXX it has a symbolic value expressing vulnerability. This makes a *prima facie* case that in the Apocalypse its symbolic value communicates vulnerability in some way, though it is not yet clear whether the rhetoric of the Apocalypse can support such an identification. Furthermore, the historical shift taking place in the choice of words for lamb in this period cautions us against treating this as more than a *prima facie* case at this point. To this issue we will return in chapter five.

Chapter III

Lambs in the Ancient Near East and
the Graeco-Roman Environment

Analysis of the role played by animal symbolism must be attuned both to the direct correspondences provided by ancient mythologies[1] and to the semantic value, or the overall cultural Gestalt of the various animals used as symbols. This Gestalt refers to the sum total intellectual and emotional associations or messages connected with a given animal symbol in a particular time period, place, and culture. To rely exclusively on logocentric explanations of the semantic value of the lamb in the Hellenistic world, for instance, would be to ignore the richer associations communicated in ritual, myth, art, and daily routine. The recovery of such a Gestalt, while essential to understanding ancient theriomorphic mythologies and the texts that relate to them, is necessarily difficult, approximate, and incomplete, given our historical and cultural distance and the fragmentary nature of our sources.

According to Jean-Pierre Darmon, the symbolism of animals in classical Greek thought has not yet been studied as a whole nor have many individual spieces been subjected to systematic study.[2] In a similar vein, Professor Phillipe Derchain of the University of Cologne says that "the meanings of the Egyptian bestiary ... still remain poorly known."[3]

We have no intent of remedying this need here, since a proper study would entail volumes. Furthermore, the data are no longer available that would be necessary in order to trace the original motivation behind the association of

---

[1] For instance, as a symbol of the divine, the bull would immediately be identified in Egypt with Apis, the bull god of Memphis; in the East with El, the bull god of Ugaritic mythology.

[2] Jean-Pierre Darmon, "The Semantic Value of Animals in Greek Mythology," *Greek and Egyptian Mythologies*, Yves Bonnefoy, comp., Wendy Doniger, ed. (Chicago: University of Chicago Press, 1992), 128–133; see esp. 128, 131.

[3] Phillipe Derchain, "The Divine and the Gods in Ancient Egypt," David White, trans., *Greek and Egyptian Mythologies*, Yves Bonnefoy, comp., Wendy Doniger, ed. (Chicago: University of Chicago Press, 1992), 224–229; see esp. 229.

certain animals with certain gods.[4] Nevertheless, that animals had semantic value in the mythological discourse of both the Egyptians and the Greeks is without doubt. Given the importance of animal symbolism in Egyptian and Greek mythology and the apparent potential of this symbolism for the origins and function of the Lamb Christology in the Apocalypse, a general delineation of the parameters of this symbolism in the Graeco-Roman world seems useful.

The warrant for such an investigation is clear enough. Animals in the Graeco-Roman world functioned as symbols, not just as signs. They therefore had "a semantic value of their own, sometimes very rich, that can be discovered by tracing the appearances of each animal, both in mythical sequences ... and in innumerable pictorial representations."[5]

Occasionally the semantic value of an animal is explicitly explored in the ancient literature. Thus, Philo of Alexandria says, "The ram (*aries*) is connected with the air, as being a very violent and vivacious animal. ... The ram is akin to the word, or to reason ... because it is a male animal ... because it is a working animal, and ... because it is the cause of the world."[6]

The study of animals was considered a basic part of education in the Graeco-Roman world. The ancients seemed captivated with them. Aristotle wrote a multi-volume work, *On the History of Animals* and was quite fascinated with his dissection and study of animals. Based on his study, he could describe at length the body parts of many species, their mode of procreation, and their characteristics. Pliny the Elder's *Natural History* depends on and extends Aristotle's work. In the second century CE, Aelian also wrote a multi-volume work entitled, *On the Characteristics of Animals*, drawing on numerous sources dating from earlier centuries, including Alcman, Herodotus, and Manetho.

Interest in animals spanned a broad range of interests, from scientific analysis to the telling of fables and stories about mythological beasts. In totemistic religion, animals often functioned as the central emblem, symbol, or sacred being for a family, clan, or larger group. As such, they took on political importance as people identified themselves "in" or "out" in relation to the totem.[7]

---

[4] Cf. K. Smelik and E. Hemelrijk, "'Who Knows Not What Monsters Demented Egypt Worships': Opinions on Egyptian Animal Worship in Antiquity as Part of the Ancient Conception of Egypt," in *Principat 17-4: Heidentum: Römische Götterkulte, orientalische Kulte in der römischen Welt*, vol. 8 of *Aufstieg und Niedergang der römischen Welt, 2*, edited by Wolfgang Haase (Berlin: Walter de Gruyter, 1984), 1862.

[5] Jean-Pierre Darmon, "The Semantic Value," 128.

[6] Philo, *The Works of Philo: Complete and Unabridged*, translated by C. D. Yonge, with an introduction by David M. Scholer (Peabody, Mass.: Hendrickson Publishers, 1993), 842–43. This particular work, "Questions and Answers on Genesis," is not extant in Greek and thus does not appear in the Loeb editions.

[7] Cf. note 20 below.

The ancient world was also fascinated with the metamorphoses of animals and the mixture and nonmixture of animal species. Ovid was fascinated with the metamorphoses that take place in the animal world, both natural and mythological. He scarcely mentions lambs without reference to wolves, their traditional adversary. He knows the myth of Medea's transformation of an old ram into a young lamb and recounts it with additional imaginative details. [8] Several of the "endangered species" of ancient mythology have barely survived to today, such as the phoenix, the griffin, the centaur, the minotaur, the unicorn, the dragon, and others. Sometimes ancient authors were not sure what was mythological and what was historical. Sometimes it mattered; sometimes it did not.[9]

1. Prehistoric Animal Mythologies

The important role of animals in prehistoric mythologies is suggested by their frequent appearance in the wall paintings of early Paleolithic art. Although the importance of animals may be due to their use as a source of meat for simple survival, the apparent lack of correspondence between the fauna depicted and what Paleolithic humans hunted suggests that the animals played some sort of nonfood role in that society. Nevertheless, the data are scarce enough to warrant caution in such a judgment.[10]

Sheep apparently played a small role in early Paleolithic art. Historians of Paleolithic art analyze the groupings of animal figures using four major categories of animals: A (horse), B (bovid), C (stag, mammoth, and occasionally the chamois and reindeer), and D (fierce animals, such as the rhinoceros, the bear, and the big cats). According to Leroi-Gourhan, although the AB group

---

[8] See p. 61 below.

[9] Cf. Herodotus (2.73) and Pliny the Elder (*Nat. Hist.* 10.2) on the phoenix. Ovid and Tacitus also knew of it. Clement appeals to the phoenix as a sign of the resurrection (1Clem 25–26). The phoenix tradition is also reflected in Eusebius (Life of Constantine 4.72) and the Apostolic Constitutions; cf. also Job 29:18 in the NRSV.

In reporting on the Egyptian tradition about the lamb in Bocchorus's reign having two heads, two tails, four horns, and eight feet, Aelian says, "The Egyptians assert (though they are far from convincing me), ... How can one pay any regard to Egyptians who exaggerate like this? However, fabulous though they be, I have related the peculiarities of this lamb"; Claudius Aelian, *On the Characteristics of Animals*, Alwyn Faber Scholfield, Loeb Classical Library (Cambridge, Mass.: Harvard University Press, 1958–59), 12.3.

[10] Cf. "Prehistoric Religion," by André Leroi-Gourhan, Gerald Honigsblum, trans. *Greek and Egyptian Mythologies*, Yves Bonnefoy, comp., Wendy Doniger, ed. (Chicago: University of Chicago Press, 1992), 14.

rarely appears alone, "the AB group is always present and dominates the groupings both numerically and topographically."[11] The C group often appears on the periphery of the paintings, which can be represented by an AB + C formula—a pattern which is among the most frequently attested. However, the chamois, which is most closely related to the sheep, is among the least-represented in the C group.[12]

The presence of wounds on approximately 4% of the animals in Paleolithic art could seem suggestive for the Apocalypse. These wounds might testify, for instance, to the exercise of magic spells or other cultic rituals, such as animal sacrifice. However, the plurality of animals showing wounds are the bison (8%) and then the horse (2.5%), with the chamois representing less than 1% of animals with wounds.[13] Furthermore, some evidence supports the suggestion that the wounds have the value of a female symbol.[14]

For all of the suggestiveness of Paleolithic animal art, there is far too little evidence to support a coherent development of the role of the animal within prehistoric religion, let alone anything that could be tied to the Apocalypse. We can say, however, that rams were objects of worship from prehistoric times. Rock engravings at Djebel Bes Seba in the Saharah-Atlas range (Algeria) dating from the Bubalus Period (c. 7000 to 4500 BCE) show a man worshiping a ram crowned with the solar disk.[15] As early as 9000 BCE the sheep is attested as the earliest of the domesticated animals.[16]

2. Egyptian Religion

According to the Palermo Stone, which was discovered in 1866 and dates from the 5th dynasty (mid-3rd millennium BCE), the ram god Heryshef was worshiped at Herakleopolis Magna from at least as early as the 1st dynasty (3100–

---

[11] André Leroi-Gourhan, "Prehistoric Religion," 15.

[12] According to B. A. Litvinskii, "in Upper Paleolithic art ... 7 percent of the animal representations consist of images of Revelation" (B. Litvinskii, "Sheep and goats," in *The Encyclopedia of Religion*, vol. 13, edited by Mircea Eliade [Macmillan: New York, 1987], 233).

[13] André Leroi-Gourhan, "Prehistoric Religion," 18.

[14] See Leroi-Gourhan, "Prehistoric Religion," 15, for a discussion of these phenomena.

[15] Joseph Campbell, *The Way of the Animal Powers*. Historical Atlas of World Mythology, vol. 1 (Harper & Row: San Francisco, 1983), 82. See also Joseph Campbell, *The Mythic Image*, M. J. Abadie, coll. (Princeton, N.J.: Princeton University Press, 1984), 209. Campbell suggests that the solar disk may have been added later.

[16] James Mellaart, *Catal Huyuk: A Neolithic Town in Anatolia* (McGraw-Hill: New York, 1967), 19.

2890 BCE).[17] The ram god Banebdjedet was worshiped at Mendes (a Delta town) from at least the second dynasty. According to Herodotus, despite Banebdjedet's being a ram god, goats at Mendes were held as sacred and sheep were offered in sacrifice.[18]

Compared to Greek mythology, the analysis of the semantic value of the lamb in Egyptian religion is even more complex, given the chronological and geographical relativity of animal symbolism there and the more important role animals played in Egyptian society.[19] Gods were considered powerful or successful not on the basis of the inherent characteristics of the animal associated with that god; rather, their reputation depended on the political power of the region that was at the center of that particular animal's cult. Nicolas Grimal suggests that Egypt's political development stems directly from the totemic origins of its religion as groupings of people developed around the various animal symbols.[20] While this is probably the case, a bit of the reverse is also true: the character of an animal's semantic Gestalt in Egypt derived in part from the political character of the regions that came to be defined by that animal.

In Egypt, rams tended to represent protection. The Temples at Meroe, Naga, and Soba were all guarded by rams at their entrances.[21] Magnificent statues of rams have been found in other temples in Egypt. These rams are manifestations of Amun protecting the pharaohs. Nearly identical statues from different millennia depict Amun as a huge ram, kneeling as he protects the pharaoh from harm. The pharaoh is depicted as much smaller and stands between the ram's front two legs and under his chin. One statue protects Pharaoh Amenhotep III in the 14th century BCE,[22] while the other protects Pharaoh Taharqo in the 7th century BCE.[23] Along with several other gods, Amun was considered to be the father of the gods, or the creator of the gods. Throughout

---

[17] Ian Shaw, ed., *British Museum Dictionary of Ancient Egypt*, coedited by Paul Nicholson (The British Museum: London, 1995), 126, 218, 240.

[18] Cf. Herodotus 242. Ian Shaw and Paul Nicholson suggest, however, that Herodotus may have mistaken the sacred ram of Mendes for a goat (Shaw, *British Museum Dictionary*, 126).

[19] Cf. Arielle P. Kozloff, ed., *Animals in Ancient Art from the Leo Mildenberg Collection* (Cleveland: Cleveland Museum of Art and Indiana University Press, 1981), 56. In some cases, even the accidental killing of certain species was considered a capital offense in Egypt.

[20] Nicolas-Christophe Grimal, *A History of Ancient Egypt*, translated by Ian Shaw (Oxford and Cambridge, Mass.: Blackwell, 1994), 40.

[21] Yves Bonnefoy, comp., *Greek and Egyptian Mythologies*, edited by Wendy Doniger (Chicago: University of Chicago Press, 1992), 240.

[22] See Campbell, *Mythic Image*, 209.

[23] Shaw, *British Museum*, 31.

most of the second millennium BCE, he was considered the highest of the gods and was often called "king of the gods."[24]

The pluralism of Egypt's theriomorphic religions[25] was broad and occasionally the scorn of outside observers.[26] Each culture had its own way of understanding an animal's natural characteristics and its "personality." In Satire 15, written around 127 CE,[27] the Roman Juvenal bitterly castigates Egyptian religion for both its theriomorphism and its regionalism:

> Who knows not, O Bithynian Volusius, what monsters demented Egypt worships? One district adores the crocodile, another venerates the ibis that gorges itself with snakes. ... No animal that grows wool may appear upon the dinnertable; it is forbidden there to slay the young of the goat; but it is lawful to feed on the flesh of man![28]

Sometimes the regionalism of Egyptian religion even led to long-standing feuds between towns.[29]

2.1 Ram Deities

The worship of the ram in the prehistoric era continued into the early periods in the history of Egypt. In the south, at Elephantine, the ram god Khnum was the major deity. According to Phillipe Derchain, the ram was a peaceful herbivore who became aggressive only where females are concerned. The earliest ram-gods were apparently based on the *Ovis longipes palaeoaegyptiaca* species. This species had long, wavy horns.[30] The Nubians, who lived just to the south of the Aswan, were known as a people of peace, and in this locality, the semantic value of the ram was related more to fertility than to aggression.

---

[24] Erik Hornung, *Conceptions of God in Ancient Egypt: The One and the Many*, translated by John Baines (Ithaca, N.Y.: Cornell University Press, 1982), 231.

[25] I use the word *theriomorphic* here in the broad sense: As Smelik and Hemelrijk have pointed out, the true nature of the Egyptian gods was considered hidden. Theriomorphic, anthropomorphic, and hybrid representations "are merely a form of iconographic signs and can be compared to hieroglyphics"; Smelik and Hemelrijk, "Who Knows Not," 1861.

[26] For an excellent analysis of Egyptian animal worship in the understandings of Greece and Rome, see Smelik and Hemelrijk, "Who Knows Not."

[27] Decimus Junius Juvenalis, *Juvenal and Persius*, English translation by G. G. Ramsay (Harvard University Press: London, 1971), xii.

[28] Juvenal, *Satire* 15.1–3, 11–13; cf. Tacitus *Histories* 5.5. The regionalism of Egyptian religion is also witnessed to by Herodotus: "No gods are worshipped in common by the whole of Egypt save only Isis and Osiris" (Herodotus 2.42).

[29] Juvenal, *Satire* 15.33–38.

[30] Shaw, *British Museum*, s.v. ram.

"Everything that comes from the south is therefore a blessing, which a ram god, a sign of fertilizing virility, clearly symbolizes."[31]

In Thebes, Amun was the chief god. In contrast to the long, wavy horns of the Elephantine *Ovis longipes palaeoaegyptiaca* species, the *Ovis aries platyra aegyptiaca*, associated with Amun, had horns that curved around next to the head. In the New Kingdom, the cult of Amun began to absorb and supercede that of Khnum. Amun was associated primarily with the adult, horned ram. The Amun of the African Meroitic Empire was often represented with a ram's head, whereas representation of the Egyptian Amun tended to be more anthropomorphic. In some localities and periods, the association of Amum with Re led to a combining of their image as Ammon-Re.

The use of combined names for deities in Egypt is a complex subject. It was not merely a matter of translation nor was it a matter of equating or substituting one god for another. While such a combining of names has often been treated in the past as an example of syncretism, recent scholarship has suggested that the combining or association of names represents instead the juxtaposition of person and function or the inhabitation of one god by another. Sometimes the one name or identity designates the person, or the local presence of the deity, while the other designates the function the deity fulfills at a given time.[32] According to Phillipe Derchain, this relationship is typically a vertical relationship of dependence rather than a horizontal one in which the two identities are equivalent but from differing origins. Although such words as *syncretism* and *identification* have been used to describe the phenomenon of the associating[33] of divine identities, they can be used only with caution and with the recognition that such divinities were not horizontal equivalences nor were they entirely subsumed into each other.[34]

---

[31] Derchain, "The Divine and the Gods," 226. According to Ariel Golan, the association of the ram with vegetation and fertility was not unique to Upper Egypt. Hacilar pottery from Asia Minor dating from as early as the sixth and fifth millennia BCE indicate that ram horns there symbolized vegetation. See Ariel Golan, "The Sacred Ram," in *Myth and Symbol: Symbolism in Prehistoric Religions*, translated by Rita Schneider-Teteruk (Jerusalem: Ariel Golan, 1991), 84.

[32] Derchain, "The Divine and the Gods," 228.

[33] We will use the verb *associate* to speak of the complex ways in which deities were related to each other, without implying any particular concept of syncretism or full identification.

[34] For a discussion of the problem of how to articulate the "combining" or "associating" of gods in Egypt, see the excellent discussion in Erik Hornung, "Names and Combinations of Gods," chapt. 3 in *Conceptions of God in Ancient Egypt: The One and the Many*, translated by John Baines (Ithaca, N.Y.: Cornell University Press, 1982), 66–99, esp. 91–99.

At least by the fifth century BCE, Ammon was associated with Zeus and was considered a hypostasis of Zeus.[35] Both Ammon and Zeus were considered "father of the gods" in their respective regions. Apparently because of Amun's association with the ram, Thebans avoided the sacrifice of sheep, substituting goats in their stead. Once a year, however, at the festival of Zeus, one and only one ram was killed. It was then flayed and its fleece was ceremoniously placed on the image of Zeus (or Amun) and the image of Heracles (or Shu) was brought before it. Then the entire assembly would beat their breasts in mourning for the ram and, according to Herodotus, they would bury him in a "holy sepulchre."[36] This ceremony was apparently an annual symbolic reenactment of the legend that after finally capitulating to Heracles's long desire to see him, Zeus had shown himself to Heracles wearing the fleece of a ram. Ovid knows this tradition, saying, "Jove [Zeus] ... changed into a ram, from whence the horns of Libyan Ammon came."[37]

Despite the fact that Egypt had a long history of ram worship, sheep were considered unclean and therefore inappropriate as food for purified persons.[38] Lambs apparently had little or no symbolic value in Egypt apart from their association with grown ewes and rams.

2.2 The Lamb to Bocchoris

In his *Aegyptiaca* (The History of Egypt), the famous chronographer Manetho reports that in the reign of King Bocchoris[39] of the twenty-fourth dynasty of Egypt,[40] "a lamb spoke" (ἀρνίον ἐφθέγξατο).[41] We know more about the reign

---

[35] J. Leclant, "The Cults of Isis Among the Greeks and in the Roman Empire," translated by Danielle Beauvais, in *Greek and Egyptian Mythologies*, edited by Wendy Doniger, compiled by Yves Bonnefoy (Chicago: University of Chicago Press, 1992), 250. The association of Ammon with Zeus was known already by Herodotus (cf. 1.46; 2.32, 55).

[36] Herodotus 2.42.

[37] Ovid, *Metamorphoses* 5.327.

[38] Shaw, *British Museum*, 240.

[39] Bocchoris is variously spelled Bochchoris, Bokchoris, Bokkhoris, and Bocchorus in the secondary literature. The fragments from Syncellus spell it βόχχωρις. The king in question is also known as Bakenranef (or Bekenranef), which is the monument form of the name. Although the dates given for Bocchoris's six-year reign vary considerably within about a five-year range, K. A. Kitchen's judgment is that he reigned about 720–715 BCE. He was king when the forces of Sargon II approached Egypt after defeating Israel (K. A. Kitchen, *The Third Intermediate Period in Egypt [1100–650 B.C.]* [Warminster, England: Aris and Phillips, Ltd., 1973], 175§142). He was deposed by Shabako in 715 BCE. (Kitchen, *Third Intermediate Period*, 379§340).

[40] Tacitus, relying on "most authors," considers Bocchoris the reigning Pharaoh during the Exodus (*Histories* 5.3).

[41] Access to the quotation in question comes via fragments of a manuscript contain-

of Bocchoris from other sources, so it is interesting that Maneto or his epitom-
ist chose to characterize Bocchoris by the legend that it was in his reign that a
lamb spoke. Aelian in his *On Animals* XII.3 also reports this legend. He says:

> The Egyptians assert (though they are far from convincing me), they assert, I
> say, that in the days of the far-famed Bocchoris a Lamb was born with eight
> feet and two tails, and that it spoke. They say also that this Lamb had two
> heads and four horns.[42]

In the late nineteenth century a damaged and fragmented papyrus, now in
Vienna, was found in the ruins of Sokhnopaiou Nesos near Birket Karun,
north of the Farum.[43] It is internally dated to 7 CE and describes the prophecy

---

ing a history of the world prepared around 800 CE by George the Monk, otherwise
known as Syncellus. Syncellus's work, Ἐκλογὴ Χρονογραφίας, is a history of the world
from Adam to Diocletian. For this particular reference to Bocchoris, Syncellus himself
relied on quotations of Manetho found in Sextus Julius Africanus, whose *Chronicle*
dates from 217–221 CE, and quotations of Manetho found in Eusebius, who wrote in
the early fourth century CE. Africanus and Eusebius apparently worked from an
epitome made of Manetho's *History* not long after its appearance (cf. *Manetho*, ed. W.
G. Waddell [Loeb Classical Library; Cambridge, Mass.: Harvard University Press,
1940], xv–xvii).

[42] The key sentences in this quote in Greek are: λέγουσι δ' οὖν ἄρνα καὶ ὀκτάπουν
καὶ δίκερκον κατὰ τὸν Βοκχοριν τὸν ᾀδόμενον ἐκεῖνον γενέσθαι, καὶ ῥῆξαι φωνήν. καὶ
δύο κεφαλὰς ᾄδουσι τῆς ἀρνός, καὶ τετράκερω γενέσθαι φασὶ τὴν αὐτήν (Aelian, *On
Animals* 12.3 [LCL; Cambridge, Mass.: Harvard University Press, 1958–59], 10–11).
Aelian was born c. 170 CE and was likely dependent upon the first-century CE *Aegyp-
tiaka* of Apion of Alexandria for much of his Egyptian material. See, e.g., A. F. Scholfield, "Introduction," *De Natura Animalium*, by Claudius Aelianus, vol. 3 (Loeb Classical Library; Harvard, Mass.: Harvard University Press, 1959), xix; C. C. McCown,
"Hebrew and Egyptian Apocalyptic Literature," *Harvard Theological Review* (1925)
357–411; esp. 394–95. In his article, "Ein neues Bruchstück Manethos über das Lamm
des Bokchoris," Eduard Meyer argues that the Manetho tradition is authentic (i.e., goes
back to Manetho), while the details from Aelian about the eight feet, two tails, two
heads, and four horns represent typical Greek coloration (*Zeitschrift für Ägyptische
Sprache und Altertumskunde* 46 [1909–10], 135–136).

[43] For text and German translation, see J. Krall, "Vom König Bokchoris," in *Fest-
gaben zu Ehren Max Büdingers* (Innsbruck, 1898), 3–11. A more recent translation into Dutch was prepared by Jozef M. A. Janssen in 1954: Jozef M. A. Janssen, "Over
Farao Bokchoris," in *Varia Historica, Aangeboden Aan Professor Doctor A. W. Byvanck ter Gelegenheid van Zijn Zeventigste Verjaardag* (Assen: Van Gorcum, 1954),
17–29. For discussion of this demotic "apocalypse," see C. C. McCown, "Hebrew and
Egyptian Apocalyptic Literature," *Harvard Theological Review* (1925) 357–411, esp.
392–395; see also J. Gwyn Griffiths, "Apocalyptic in the Hellenistic Era," in David
Hellholm, *Apocalypticism in the Mediterranean World and the Near East: Proceedings
of the International Colloquium on Apocalypticism [Uppsala, Aug. 12–17, 1979]* (Tü-

and subsequent death of a lamb in the reign of Bocchoris.[44] Although the lamb is nowhere identified within the papyrus (or in later tradition) in terms of other known deities, it is possible that this lamb was a manifestation of Khnum.[45] According to the demotic papyrus, this lamb prophesied a catastrophe that was about to happen to Egypt, followed by a restoration. Like the angel in Rev 18 that announced the imminent fall of Babylon (Rome), this lamb pronounced woes on the cities of Egypt:

The Imprecations on Egypt

According to Griffiths/Janssen[46]	*According to McCown/Krall*[47]
14　There is much malediction against it (Egypt). Heliopolis weeps in the East, for it is vanquished ..., Bubastis weeps, ...; one makes the streets of Sebennytus into a vineyard.	The misfortune of Egypt is great. Let Heliopolis mourn in the East, ... let Hermopolis mourn ... they make the roads from Hebit (?) ... let Thebes mourn.
19　The lamb finished its curses against all these (places). Pshenḥor spoke to him: 'Shall this happen (before we have?) observed it?'	The Lamb ended its curses. Psenyris said to him: 'What ... ?'
20　He said to him: 'It shall happen, when I ... upon the head of the King, which shall be after the end of 900 years,	The Lamb said: '... for full [or, at the end of] nine hundred years ...'
21　while I have power in Egypt, yet .... He turned his face to Egypt while he withdrew	'I will smite Egypt. ... He (some deity) turns his face toward Egypt. He departs
22　from the ... they shall go out ... the injustice shall go to ruin, right and law shall exist in	from the strange warriors. ... Lies, the destruction of justice and law, as it has [existed?] in
23　Egypt. And they shall ... the precious shrines of the Egyptian gods before them to Nineveh in the land	Egypt. ... They will take ... the shrines of the gods of Egypt with them to Nineveh, to the land

---

bingen, J. C. B. Mohr [Siebeck], 1983), 273–293, esp. 285–287 (reprinted in *Atlantis and Egypt: with other Selected Essays* [Cardiff: University of Wales Press, 1991], 185–207, esp. 195–197).

[44] "[10] This is the end of the book, written in the 33rd year, on the 8th of Mesore, [11] of Caesar [i.e., Augustus]" (III.10–11, translation by Griffiths, "Apocalyptic in the Hellenistic Era," 286).

[45] This opinion is offered without discussion by J. G. Griffiths in Griffiths, "Apocalyptic in the Hellenistic Era," 287) and L. Kákosy (L. Kákosy, "Prophecies of Ram Gods," *Acta Orientalia [Hungary]* 19, no. 3 [1966]: 344).

[46] Griffiths, "Apocalyptic," 285–286. This is Gwyn Griffiths's translation into English of Jozef Janssen's fresh translation of the Demotic into Dutch.

[47] This is C. McCown's translation into English of J. Krall's translation of the Demotic into German.

24 of Assyria, and it shall happen that the Egyptians will go to the land of Syria and will make themselves master of its provinces and will find

3.1 the shrines of the gods of Egypt. They ... can speak on account of the well-being which shall happen to Egypt

2 ... the infertile shall

3 exult, and she who has borne (children) shall rejoice because of the good events which shall happen; and Egypt and the generation (?) of men that shall be in Egypt

4 shall say, "O now, would that my father and my grandfather were here with me," in the good time

5 that shall come.' The lamb finished ...

of Amor [Syria], he .... The men of Egypt go into the land of Charu, they conquer the districts, they recover

the [stolen] shrines of the gods of Egypt.'

... The lamb finished his words and made his purification [i.e., died].
Psenyris had it [the Lamb] put upon a new ... ship and he delayed not to go to the place where King Bocchoris was. They read the papyrus roll in the king's presence, that is, concerning all the misfortune that was to befall Egypt. ... The king said, 'Psenyris, look after the Lamb, let it be put into a shrine [?], let it be buried like a god, let it remain on earth as is the custom with every noble person.'

10 This is the end of the book, written in the 33rd year, on the 8th of Mesore,

11 of Caesar (= Augustus) ...

(Vienna P. Dem. D. 10.000.)

In his essay entitled, "Apocalyptic in the Hellenistic Era," J. Gwyn Griffiths discusses this papyrus in his aim to illustrate manifestations of "apocalyptic" in the Hellenistic era outside of Jewish circles.[48]

Several points of contact with the Apocalypse make this a particularly interesting possibility as a source for the Lamb Christology of the Apocalypse.

---

[48] Griffiths does not define apocalyptic as he uses it and the existence of apocalypses outside of pre-Christian Judaism is debated; see, for instance, J. H. Charlesworth, "Folk Traditions," 93n2. As John J. Collins notes, access to Persian apocalypses is highly fragmentary and based on late manuscripts. Thus, "any reconstruction of a literary form of 'apocalypse' must be extremely tentative and hypothetical" ("Persian Apocalypses," *Semeia* 14 (1979): 207–217 [207], "Apocalypse: The Morphology of a Genre."

Some have judged these points of contact to be significant enough to conclude that Egyptian religion has directly influenced the Apocalypse.[49] First, we have a prophecy concerning judgment on a land, including a period of persecution, following by a period of prosperity. The judgment-restoration theme is common in Jewish apocalyptic literature, including the Apocalypse. Second, the tradition reflects interest in periodization, another common theme. Third, the judgment is given as a mediated revelation, another constituent element of Jewish apocalyptic literature. Fourth, in both the Apocalypse of John and the Lamb papyrus, we have a lamb as the central figure, who died and was then revered and worshiped.[50] Fifth, in both the Apocalypse of John and in traditions about the Lamb to Bocchorus, the image of the lamb is grotesque with its multiple body parts.[51] Sixth, in both the Apocalypse of John and the Lamb to Bocchorus a scroll is opened in the presence of the king that reveals what is about to take place in the land. Seventh, the presence of weeping adds pathos to the drama being played out in the narrative. Finally, both works seem designed to offer hope through the promise of the demise of a hated foreign power; in the case of the lamb to Bocchoris, Greece's occupation of Egypt;[52] for the Apocalypse, Rome's blasphemous claim to sovereignty.

---

[49] Note, e.g., Hugo Gressmann, *Der Messias*, Forschungen zur Religion und Literature des Alten und Neuen Testaments, vol. 26 (Göttingen: Vandenhoeck & Ruprecht, 1929), 426; Siegfried Morenz, "Ägypten und die Bibel," in *Die Religion in Geschichte und Gegenwart*, vol. 1, Kurt Galling, gen. ed., edited by Hans Freiherr von Campenhausen (Tübingen: J.C.B. Mohr, 1957), 120.

[50] This must be interpreted, however, within the context of Egypt's sacred animal cults, in which various animals, including ibises, falcons, baboons, bulls, cows, lions, jackals, rams, and crocodiles were cared for by priests, who venerated, mummified, and buried them underground in extensive complexes; cf. Shaw, *British Museum Dictionary*, s.v. sacred animals. Egyptians spent enormous sums of money and expended considerable labor in their worship of sacred animals; cf. Smelik and Hemelrijk, "Who Knows Not," 1892.

[51] Nothing of the sort is reported in the demotic papyrus. However, according to Aelian, the lamb to Bocchoris had two heads, two tails, four horns, and eight feet (Aelian, *On Animals*, 12.3). The antiquity of Aelian's multiple-body-parts tradition is doubted by some (see note 42 above; cf. also Kákosy, "Prophecies of Ram Gods," 345). In Rev 5:6 we read that the Lamb had seven horns and seven eyes. The multiplicity of body parts is a common feature in prophetic and apocalyptic literature (cf. Ezek 1:6,8,10; Dan 7:6-8; 4Ezra 11:1; Rev 12:3; 13:1), as well as in classical Greek mythology (e.g., Euripides, *Pheonician Women* 1116). Four-headed deities were common in Egyptian tradition; cf. Kákosy, "Prophecies of Ram Gods," 351.

[52] Cf. the analysis of Harold W. Attridge, who calls this oracle "eschatologically oriented, yet politically based" (168). Although the oracle itself identifies Syria as the invader of Egypt, the oracle may have been used later as resistance literature in the Ptolemaic period; cf. Harold W. Attridge, "Greek and Latin Apocalypses," *Semeia*, no. 14 (1979): 168–69; cf. also L. Kákosy, "Prophecies of Ram Gods," 355.

While these parallels may seem suggestive, several important differences must be noted. First, although the lamb of the demotic papyrus is the *mediator* of the revelation in that story, in John's Apocalypse, the Lamb is at least in part the *object* of the revelation and an angel or angels are used as mediators of the revelation and dialogue with the recipient of the revelation. Second, although it is *the lamb's* prophecy that is written down in the demotic papyrus, it is *John's* prophecy that is written down in the Apocalypse. In fact, the Lamb does not speak at all in the Apocalypse, even though his name is the Word of God (19:13). Finally, and more importantly, the death of the lamb of the demotic papyrus does not have any saving effect on the Egyptians, and in the Apocalypse it is the key to the Lamb's "worthiness" and enables him to open the scroll (Rev 5:9b).

3. Aesopic Fable Traditions

Unfortunately, recent study of Jewish apocalyptic literature has paid little attention to potential sources of apocalyptic imagery in non-Jewish texts. It is not unreasonable to surmise that some of the bizarre images and theriomorphic symbolism used and developed by the writers of Jewish apocalypses had precursors in the folk traditions, tales, and iconography of Egypt, Greece, and Rome.[53]

Fables were a popular form of folklore in the ancient Near East. Although fables are frequently associated with Aesop—who was born in Thrace in the 6th century BCE and who may have lived in Asia Minor—Sumerian fables predated the Greek ones by several hundred years. Some of the classical Aesopic fables have even been traced back to earlier Mesopotamian sources.[54]

The sheep and the lamb are frequently associated with vulnerability in the classical era. Like the fables attributed to Aesop, in the Sumerian fables, animals speak, interact, attack, eat, and sometimes attempt to outwit each other. Occasionally an animal successfully censures a human.[55] Even outside of the

---

[53] See James H. Charlesworth, "Folk Traditions in Jewish Apocalyptic Literature," in *Mysteries and Revelations: Apocalyptic Studies Since the Uppsala Colloquium*, edited by John J. Collins and James H. Charlesworth, Journal for the Study of the Pseudepigrapha Supplement Series, no. 9 (Sheffield: JSOT Press, 1991), 93.

[54] Cf. Gordon, "Sumerian Animal Proverbs," 1. Ben Edwin Perry has confidently concluded that we now have "the final answer" regarding the origin of the Aesopic fables: They came to the Greeks "from the Sumerians by way of the neo-Babylonian and Assyrian wisdom literature" (*American Journal of Archaeology* 66 [1962] 206).

[55] Cf. *Babrius* 51, an example of a sheep that was *not* dumb before its shearer! (cf. Isa 53:7). The references to Phaedrus and Babrius in this section are to Ben Edwin Perry, ed. and trans., *Babrius and Phaedrus*, Loeb Classical Library (Cambridge,

fable literature, the idea of vulnerability and the juxtaposition of wolf and lamb in eschatological contexts are seen in the old Sumerian paradise myth of Enki and Ninhursag: "The lion kills not, the wolf snatches not the lamb." [56]

One of the common themes in the Aesopic fable is the foolishness of trying to trick nature.[57] In short, the wolf cannot lie down with the lamb: it just will not work in the long run. Although surface peace can be established on the basis of illusion for a while, a twist of fate or a trick will eventually cause the ruse to break down and the expected violence will result. The illustration of such foolishness often takes the form of stories about inferior species tricking a superior species for a while, but then being found out. A variation is that a human wrongly figures that he or she can outwit nature, but is eventually proved wrong. Thus although the "moral" is sometimes that one should be truthful and do what is right or honorable,[58] it is just as often the message that truthfulness will not succeed in subverting natural animosities.[59]

The near inevitability of the domination of the stronger over the weaker is shown in fables that illustrate (1) the laughable but dangerous irrelevance of a rationalization that opposes nature;[60] (2) the false offering of peace when the

---

Mass.: Harvard University Press, 1965). Babrius, who wrote in Greek, wrote at the end of the first century CE; Phaedrus, who wrote in Latin, wrote at the beginning of the first century CE.

[56] Benjamin Mazar, ed., *Views of the Biblical World*, translated by M. Dagut, in collaboration with Michael Avi-Yonah and Abraham Malamat (Chicago: Jordan Publications, 1959), 3.36.

[57] Lane C. McGaughy maintains that "the narrative fables of Babrius are frequently of the anti-actantial variety in which the failure of the hero is caused by a twist of fate or trick. The failure ... serves as the basis for the fable's lesson" (Lane C. McGaughy, "Pagan Hellenistic Literature: The Babrian Fables," in *Society of Biblical Literature 1977 Seminar Papers*, Society of Biblical Literature Seminar Papers Series (Missoula, Mont.: Scholars Press, 1978), 211). However, the categories of hero and anti-hero do not adequately reflect the fables, which ironically use the element of surprise to support the inviolability of conventional wisdom.

[58] Cf. *Phaedrus* 1.17.

[59] *Babrius* 89; cf. *Phaedrus* 1.1.

[60] *Babrius* 89; cf. *Phaedrus* 1.1; 1.5; cf. also Ahiqar 120–123. A good example of this type of rationalization is found in the first fable in Phaedrus's collection, a variation of Fable 89 in Babrius's collection. Upon encountering a lamb, a wolf accuses the lamb falsely of several transgressions in order to justify his desire to attack and eat the lamb. The lamb successfully repudiates each of the charges. The wolf finally gives up his accusing and says, "You're not going to rob the wolf of his dinner even though you do find it easy to refute all my charges" (*Babrius* 89). In a slight variation on this fable, the nineteenth-century Russian writer Ivan Andrevick Krylov added the epimythium, "Hungry nations, like wolves, want to eat of Israel"; Shlomo Pesach Toperoff, *The Animal Kingdom in Jewish Thought* (Northvale, N.J.: J. Aronson, 1995), 240.

true intent is evil;[61] (3) the revelation of a supposedly friendly association as truly violence-prone;[62] and (4) the need for third-party protection.[63] In one instance a sheep (οἴς) explains to a wolf that it would rather be sacrificed to a god than eaten by a wolf.[64]

Nevertheless, occasionally the hope for an "unnatural" peace surfaces, such as in Babrius's Fable 102, which is reminiscent of Isa 65:25. In the reign of a particularly peaceful lion, all of the animals come together and live at peace. All of the animals are called to account for their deeds by other animals, including the wolf by the lamb. Finally a fearful rabbit says, "This is the day for which I have long prayed, a day that would make the weak creatures feared even by the strong."[65]

The symbolism most consistently associated with lambs in these fables revolves around the vulnerability of the lambs.[66] In some of these cases the vulnerability of the sheep is not the fable's main concern, but is part of the fable's set-up for another point, revealing that the vulnerability of the sheep or lamb is part of the deep structure of the symbolic language in the Aesopic tradition.

It is impossible to say what role Aesop had in the creation or development of the lamb as a symbol of vulnerability, but we do know that his fables were well-known and broadly influential in the classical world.[67] According to John

---

[61] *Babrius* 93; cf. *Iliad* 22, which says that "there can be no covenants between men and lions, wolves and lambs can never be of one mind, but hate each other out and out and through." The same image is at work in Jub 37:21, where Esau is addressing Jacob: "And if the wolves make peace with lambs so as not to eat them or assault them, and if their hearts are (set) upon them to do good, then peace will be in my heart for you"; cf. James H. Charlesworth, ed., *The Old Testament Pseudepigrapha: Expansions of the "Old Testament" and Legends, Wisdom and Philosophical Literature, Prayers, Psalms, and Odes, Fragments of Lost Judeo-Hellenistic Works*, 2 (Garden City: Doubleday & Company, Inc., 1985), 127. Esau's speech is meant as a rebuff of Jacob.

[62] *Babrius* 113.

[63] Dogs often play this role with respect to sheep and wolves. See, e.g., *Babrius* 93; 113; 128; Fables from Recension Ia 342 (in Perry, *Babrius and Phaedrus*); 705; cf. also *Siphre* 157 on Numbers 31:2, where a wolf talks a dog into colluding against a lamb.

[64] *Babrius* 132.

[65] Perry, *Babrius and Phaedrus*, fable 102; cf. EcclR 9:1: "A time will come when the wolf will have fleece of fine wool and the dog a coat of ermine"; Toperoff, *The Animal Kingdom*, 241.

[66] Cf. *Babrius* 51; 89; 93; 113; 128; 132; *Phaedrus* 1.1; 1.17; Perotti's Appendix, Fable 26; Other Aesopic Fables, nos. 160, 209, 234, 342, 366, 451, 595, 596, 636, 655, and 705.

[67] See, e.g., Aristophanes' *The Wasps* 568–575 (fifth century). According to Plato, Socrates knew of Aesop's fables (*Phaedo* 59e–61b) as did Diogenes Laertius (cf. Diogenes Laertius, *Diogenes Laertius I*, translated and edited by R. D. Hicks, Loeb Classical Library [Cambridge, Mass.: Harvard University Press, 1925], 530–35).

Priest, Aesopic collections were available in Greek and probably also in Semitic translation hundreds of years before the beginning of the common era.[68] David Flusser has argued that Jesus knew the Aesopic fables, since on three different occasions he used Aesopic associations in connection with Herod Antipas.[69] Although proverb and fable traditions were quite fluid, the evidence suggests that the fable, either in its Sumerian form or its later Aesopic (Greek) form, was one of the *Gattungen* that eventuated in the rabbinic parable. The influence of Aesopic fable traditions on later rabbinic literature is extensive.[70]

Thus, quite apart from the issue of whether John drew inspiration from Aesop's fables for his portrayal of the Lamb in the Apocalypse, it is clear that the lamb attested in the fable tradition was broadly associated with vulnerability. Like Aesop, Philo considered it nearly impossible for the wolf to lie down with the lamb. The natural animosity between human and beast was created by God; it was ingrained and inviolable: "Just as it is with wolves (λύκοι) toward lambs (ἄρνες), so also is it with all animals toward all humans."[71]

4. Greek and Roman Mythology and Religion

In the Mycenaean period of Greek mythology (1600–1100 BCE) there were five gods of war, according to Tn 316, a clay tablet from the palace of Pylos: Ares,

---

[68] E.g., Syriac translations were known to have existed (cf. John Priest, "Thomas and Aesop," chapt. 8 in *Religion, Literature, and Society in Ancient Israel, Formative Christianity and Judaism*, vol. 2 of *New Perspectives on Ancient Judaism*, edited by Jacob Neusner, et al., Studies in Judaism [Lanham, Md.: University Press of America, 1987], 127–128).

[69] See David Flusser, "Ursprung und Vorgeschichte der Jüdischen Gleichnisse," chapt. 6 in *Die rabbinischen Gleichnisse und der Gleichniserzähler Jesus*, Judaica et Christiana (Bern: Peter Lang), 153. Cf. also David Flusser, "Aesop's Miser and the Parable of the Talents," in *Parable and Story in Judaism and Christianity*, edited by Clemens Thoma and Michael Wyschogrod, Studies in Judaism and Christianity: Exploration of Issues in the Contemporary Dialogue Between Christians and Jews (New York: Paulist Press, 1989), 9–25. David Daube points out that in its narrow definition (a short narrative in which an animal, plant, or object behaves like a human), the fable is avoided in the New Testament, though it appears in the Old Testament (David Daube, *Ancient Hebrew Fables: The Inaugural Lecture of the Oxford Centre for Postgraduate Hebrew Studies* [Oxford: Oxford Centre for Postgraduate Hebrew Studies, 1973], 7).

[70] See, e.g., Haim Schwarzbaum, "Talmudic-Midrashic Affinities of Some Aesopic Fables," in *Essays in Graeco-Roman and Related Talmudic Literature*, edited by Henry A. Fischel, The Library of Biblical Studies (New York: KTAV Publishing House, 1977), 425–42.

[71] Philo, *On Rewards and Punishments*, 8.

Peresa, Ipemedeya, Diwya, and the triple Heros.[72] Although the name Ares probably derived etymologically from ἀρήν, the Greek word for lamb, this association was not developed in the mythology. In the later classical Greek mythology, Ares and Athena become the two great gods of war.[73] Ares is the male power; Athena the female. However, these two gods have clearly contrasting roles. Athena is the warrior god who exhibits cunning, wisdom, and strategy. She is respected universally. Ares is the warrior god of brute force, the murdering fool, "the god of warrior fury that runs riot"; and Ares is hated by all the gods.[74] In the Iliad, "Ares always loses: Athena wins and imposes her will each time."[75] In other words, Ares represents the uncontrolled, chaotic, hated, and ultimately unsuccessful side of warfare in Greek mythology, while Athena the controlled, shrewd, respected, and effective side of warfare.

4.1 Lions and Lambs in Homer's Epics

In the Classical Greek world, the lion was a symbol of bravery, ferocity, and majesty.[76] The lion was a central character in the Homeric epic and the archetypal symbol of the hero, expressed especially as the warrior in combat.[77] With it are associated the virtues of ἀλκή and μένος, both of which communicate something of the prowess or courage exhibited in war. According to Jean-Pierre Darmon, the symbolic value of the lion is so advanced in the Homeric epic that the lion becomes "a pure ideological construction, a cultural archetype which has broken its ties with the naturalistic universe."[78]

Although Homer often uses animals to exemplify this or that human quality in his epics,[79] he uses some animals more often than others. As a result, the

---

[72] Paul Faure, "Crete and Mycenae: Problems of Mythology and Religious History," translated by David White, in *Greek and Egyptian Mythologies*, edited by Wendy Doniger, compiled by Yves Bonnefoy (Chicago: University of Chicago Press, 1992), 31–32.

[73] Cf. Homer, *The Iliad*, edited and translated by A. T. Murray, Loeb Classical Library (Cambridge, Mass.: Harvard University Press, 1978), 5.430.

[74] Jean-Pierre Darmon, "The Powers of War: Ares and Athena in Greek Mythology," translated by Danielle Beauvais, in *Greek and Egyptian Mythologies*, edited by Wendy Doniger, compiled by Yves Bonnefoy (Chicago: University of Chicago Press, 1992), 114–15; see esp. 114.

[75] Darmon, "Powers of War," 114, citing Homer, *Iliad* 5.765 and 824–864; 15.121–142; 21.391–415.

[76] Kozloff, *Animals in Ancient Art*, 80.

[77] Darmon, "Semantic Value," 128.

[78] Annie Schnapp-Gourbeillon, "The Heroic Bestiary," in *Greek and Egyptian Mythologies*, edited by Wendy Doniger, compiled by Yves Bonnefoy (Chicago: University of Chicago Press, 1992), 129.

[79] According to Annie Schnapp-Gourbeillon, "The Heroic Bestiary," in *Greek and Egyptian Mythologies*, edited by Wendy Doniger, compiled by Yves Bonnefoy (Chi-

semantic value of some animals was more developed than that of others. For instance, in contrast to the lion, the sheep plays a minor role in the Homeric epic. Nevertheless, three important elements emerge in the semantic value of the sheep. The first, identified by Annie Schnapp-Gourbeillon, has to do with the place of mutton in a strict hierarchy of meat values developed in Homer's epics. The meat of the fatted sheep was near the top of this hierarchy, with castrated male or female bovines and fatted sheep at the top and pigs and goats at the bottom.[80]

Second, the sheep often appears as a symbol of vulnerability in the Homeric epic.[81] At one point in recounting the Trojan War, Homer says, "They had been penned in Ilios like lambs (ἀρήν/ἀρνός)."[82] One difference between the animal symbolism of Homer and what we see in the rest of Greek literature is noteworthy. Where the wolf is usually portrayed as the natural enemy of the sheep and lambs in Greek mythology, the lion typically plays that role in Homer's work.[83] However, the victims of Homer's lions were many: stags, goats, deer, dogs, and wolves. Thus while the lion was the archetypical *adversary* in Homer's epics,[84] the lion had many *victims*. In any case, the lion is a fierce warrior, a strong and savage hunter who attacks without mercy. Finally, the sheep or the lamb is often associated with sacrifice in Homer.[85]

4.2 Oracular Deities and Deities Associated with the Ram

The Greek god Ammon derived from the Egyptian god Amun. These gods shared a close relationship with the ram iconographically. Both were oracular deities. In Greece, Apollo was the prime oracular god, but a shrine of Ammon in Athens existed by 337 BCE[86] and the Athenians consulted him frequently.

---

cago: University of Chicago Press, 1992), 128, there are more than 100 animal similes in the *Iliad* alone.

[80] Annie Schnapp-Gourbeillon, "The Animal as Agent," in *Greek and Egyptian Mythologies*, edited by Wendy Doniger, compiled by Yves Bonnefoy (Chicago: University of Chicago Press, 1992), 130.

[81] E.g., "All around me my comrades were slain like sheep or pigs for the wedding breakfast, or picnic, or gorgeous banquet of some great nobleman" (*Odyssey* 11).

[82] *Iliad*, 8.131.

[83] For the lion/sheep combination, see *Odyssey* 6; 9; *Iliad* 5; 10; 11; 24. But see *Iliad* 16.352; 22.261–64: "Achilles glared at him and answered, 'Fool, Don't talk to me about covenants. There can be no covenants between men and lions, wolves and lambs can never be of one mind, but hate each other out and out and through.'"

[84] Occasionally an eagle also plays the role of the enemy of the lamb or hare (*Iliad* 22.308–310). For a parallel in Hellenistic Jewish literature, see LetAris 146.

[85] For sacrifice in Homer, see p. 64 below.

[86] Lily Ross Taylor, *The Divinity of the Roman Emperor*, American Philological Association Monograph Series, no. 1 (Atlanta: Scholars Press, 1975 [1931]), 15n38.

When Alexander conquered Egypt in 331 BCE, he traveled out of his way to consult the oracle of Zeus Ammon in the Libyan desert, at the sanctuary of the Oasis. (Alexander's side trip to the Oasis was not all that rare: extant Greek literature reveals several occasions on which residents of Greece and Anatolia traveled to Libya to consult this oracle.) When he arrived, the priests there greeted him with the title, "Son of Zeus." Thereafter, Alexander embraced his "divine ancestry" and remained a devotee of Zeus-Ammon.[87] His coinage represented Alexander as Zeus-Ammon, or Ammon-Re, as do marble busts.[88]

Alexander's devotion to Zeus-Ammon, which was influenced by Egyptian traditions, coincides with the rise of the emperor cult in Asia Minor. Though the emperor cult existed in Greece prior to Alexander's reign, with Alexander emperor worship developed into a Hellenistic tradition.[89] While Roman deification had Greek antecedents, Greek deification had Egyptian and Persian ones.[90]

The oracle of Apollo at Delphi was the most important Greek oracle. Even when the oracle at Delphi began to lose its attraction in the first century CE, the oracles of Apollo in Asia Minor were going strong. Apollo had oracles at Didyma near Miletus and at Clarus near Colophon, near Ephesus.[91]

Though an oracular god, Apollo was not usually associated with the ram. At Argos, Apollo was worshiped as λύκειος (wolf-like) or, according to Sophocles, as λυκοκτόνος (wolf-killer or wolf-like killer), though he was never

---

[87] J. Leclant, "Cults of Isis," 245–51; see esp. 249–51 on Ammon.

[88] See, e.g., Helmut Koester, author & trans, *History, Culture, and Religion of the Hellenistic Age*, vol. 1 of *Introduction to the New Testament*, Hermeneia: Foundations and Facets (Philadelphia: Fortress Press, 1982), 7.

[89] See Simon R. F. Price, *Rituals and Power: The Roman Imperial Cult in Asia Minor* (New York and Cambridge: Cambridge University Press, 1984), 25–27; and Lily Ross Taylor, *The Divinity of the Roman Emperor*, reprint, 1931, American Philological Association Monograph Series, no. 1 (Atlanta: Scholars Press, 1975), 1–34. See also Everett Ferguson, *Backgrounds of Early Christianity* (Grand Rapids, Mich.: William B. Eerdmans Publishing Company, 1987), 158: "The cult given after [Alexander's] death was the beginning of divine monarchy in the western world."

[90] For the importance of Persia's influence on Alexander and the emperor cult, see Taylor, *Divinity of the Roman Emperor*, 1–8.

[91] Molly Whittaker, *Jews and Christians: Graeco-Roman Views* (Cambridge: Cambridge University Press, 1984), 215–16. In light of the centrality of the throne in the Apocalypse, it is interesting that the oracular seat of Apollo was called a θρόνος. See Henry George Liddell, comp., *A Greek-English Lexicon: With a Supplement*, (Oxford: Clarendon Press, 1968), s.v. θρόνος. But many of Domitian's coins represent him on a throne; A. Abaecherli, "Imperial Symbols on Certain Flavian Coins," *Classical Philology* 30 (1935): 131–40. Furthermore, the symbolism may well come from Ezek 1.

actually *portrayed* as a wolf. Homer calls him Λυκηγενέϊ (wolf-born, or son of a wolf).[92] Perhaps because of his λύκειος character, the sacrifice of lambs often accompanied consultation of Apollo.[93] In any case, the divining of oracles was associated with the blood of a sacrificial animal and with the interpretation of entrails.[94] According to Pausanias, no entrails were as valuable as those of the ram for divining.[95] Sleeping on the fleece of a sacrificed ram was also helpful for divining.[96] Occasionally the blood of a lamb was used, though the blood of rams and of other animals is also attested.[97] Lambs were sacrificed as part of solemn oath-making rituals.[98] The powers of divination and prophecy were not associated only with the sheep family, however; prophecy was generally associated with Egypt's gods, including Apis the Bull and the crocodile gods.

The gods of Dionysos, Pan, and Hermes [Mercury], were sometimes associated with the ram or the goat in the Graeco-Roman world.[99] Dionysos placed a ram in heaven as the constellation Aries.[100] He was a fertility god associated with "female followers [who] wore deerskins, carried the thyrsus, suckled fawns, tore to pieces and ate wild beasts, and allegedly indulged in sexual promiscuity."[101] Although the figure of Hermes was complex and his symbolic

---

[92] *Iliad* 4.101, 119.

[93] See, e.g., Homer, *Iliad* 1.58–67; 23.864, 873.

[94] See, e.g., Pausanias, *Description of Greece*, 1.34.4; 2.24.1.

[95] Pausanias, *Description of Greece*, 9.39.6.

[96] Pausanias, *Description of Greece* 1.34.5.

[97] The association of sheep and sheep livers with divining is ancient. See, e.g., Edmund I. Gordon, "Sumerian Animal Proverbs and Fables: 'Collection Five' (Conclusion)," *Journal of Cuneiform Studies* 12, no. 2 (1958): 5.46. Pausanias, writing in the second century CE, knows of divination by kids, lambs, or calves as an ancient tradition; cf. Pausanias, *Description of Greece*, translated by W.H.S. Jones (Cambridge, Mass.: Harvard University Press, 1918), 6.2.5.

[98] See, e.g., Homer, *Iliad* 3.97–120; 4.155–163.

[99] The association of Dionysos with the ram may be significant for the Apocalypse, since Dionysos may have been of Phrygian origin; see Michael Grant and John Hazel, *Who's Who in Classical Mythology* (New York: Oxford University Press, 1993), 112. Grant calls him "the greatest deity of the later Greek (Hellenistic) world" (112). Pan was the pastoral god, especially the god of sheep and goats (Grant and Hazel, *Who's Who*, 254). The ram, a favorite sacrificial animal, is often associated with Hermes, the patron deity of shepherds, travelers, and tradesmen. However, too little is known about the range of associations and metaphorical import of rams in late Archaic and early Classical Greek art and religion to know whether or how ram figurines played a part in the cult of Hermes; see Kozloff, *Animals in Ancient Art*, 129, 162, 199. Some of these figurines may have been used purely for decorative or aesthetic reasons. However, the religious or apotropaic and the aesthetic functions need not be mutually exclusive (see Kozloff, *Animals in Ancient Art*, 115).

[100] Grant and Hazel, *Who's Who*, 115.

[101] Grant and Hazel, *Who's Who*, 115.

role developed over time, in the Mycenaean period, Hermes was the fertility god who was worshiped by shepherds and who ruled over animal breeding.[102]

Deities that required ram sacrifices included Athena, Cybele,[103] Dionysos, Eros, Heracles, Helios, Jupiter, Pan, Pelops, and Priapus. According to Robert Bell, those who wished to consult the oracle Trophonius were required to offer a ram.[104] Along with other animals, lambs were offered in sacrifice to Hecate (black lambs only), Helios, Heracles, Hermes, Juno, Pan, and the Nymphs.[105]

4.3 The Golden Fleece

One famous legend in Greek mythology is that of the Golden Fleece. According to this tradition, Ino, Athamas's second wife, schemed to get rid of the children to his first wife, Nephele, by attempting to have them sacrificed to Zeus. She explained that doing so would avert a famine—one she had helped create. When Nephele learned of this scheme, she provided Phrixus and his sister Helle a way of escape via a flying ram or lamb.

Some sources talk of the Golden Ram, some of the Golden Lamb. Pseudo-Apollodorus speaks of the "Golden Ram" (κριός) of Jason and the Argonauts,[106] as does Pausanias[107] and Pindar.[108] However, when speaking of the Golden Fleece of Atreus and Arestes, Pseudo-Apollodorus uses the word for lamb, ἀρνός.[109] Euripides speaks of the "Golden *Lamb*,"[110] as does Plato.[111] That the difference between ram and lamb was not considered important is clear from the following quotation from Pausanias: "Advancing a little way in the Argive territory from this hero-shrine one sees on the right the grave of Thyestes. On it is a stone ram (κριός), because Thyestes obtained the golden lamb (ἀρήν/ἀρνός) after debauching his brother's wife."[112]

Hermes, god of the sheep, had made this ram with a golden fleece for Poseidon, Zeus's brother. The children fled on the back of this golden ram. Al-

---

[102] Faure, "Crete and Mycenae," 30–40; cf. also Laurence Kahn-Lyotard, "Hermes," translated by Danielle Beauvais, in *Greek and Egyptian Mythologies*, edited by Wendy Doniger, compiled by Yves Bonnefoy (Chicago: University of Chicago Press, 1992), 185–89.

[103] For the Cybelene cult, see below, p. 66.

[104] Robert E. Bell, *Dictionary of Classical Mythology: Symbols, Attributes, and Associations* (Oxford and Santa Barbara, Cal.: ABC CLIO, 1982), 197.

[105] Bell, *Dictionary of Classical Mythology*, 145.

[106] Pseudo-Apollodorus, *The Library* 1.9.1.

[107] Pausanias, *Description of Greece* 1.24.2; 9.34.5.

[108] Pindar, *Pythian* 4.68.

[109] Pseudo-Apollodorus, *The Library* e.2.10–11 [2.165]; e.3.21 [2.191].

[110] ἀρνός; *Electra* 705, 719; *Iphigeneia in Taurica* 197, 813; *Orestes* 810; 998.

[111] Plato, *The Statesman* 268.

[112] Pausanias, *Description of Greece* 2.18.1.

though Helle sadly fell into the sea, thus giving the sea its name—Helles-pont—Phrixus made it safely to Colchis on the East side of the Black Sea. Phrixus then sacrificed the animal in gratitude to Zeus and the fleece was hung in a garden to be guarded by a dragon.[113]

When Pelias, king of Iolcus, began to fear Jason, one of his subjects, he decided to give Jason an impossible task to accomplish: to bring back the Golden Fleece from Colchis. Jason gathered a fleet of noble and powerful men and sailed off. Overcoming many obstacles in this adventuresome tale, Jason and the Argonauts—so named after their ship, Argo—finally arrived at Colchis. There the king of Colchis, Aeëtes, set up another series of impossible tasks for Jason to accomplish in order to gain access to the Golden Fleece. Against all odds, Jason accomplished these tasks and demanded the fleece. However, Aeëtes reneged on his promise. Fortunately, Hera intervened and made Aeëtes' daughter, Medea, fall in love with Jason. With Medea's help, Jason stole the Golden Fleece and fled Colchis.

Back in Iolchus, Medea convinced Pelias's daughters that they could make their old, frail father young again. She did this by killing an old ram (κρι-ός),[114] dismembering it, and boiling it in a pot.[115] Sure enough, a young lamb (ἀρνός) sprang from the pot! Delighted with these results, Pelias's daughters[116] did the same with their father, but with sadder results.

In other versions of this legend, the brothers Atreus and Thyestes quarrel over a lamb that was found to have golden fleece.[117] According to Euripides' *Orestes* scholia, the epic *Alkmaionis* reported that Hermes had sent a golden lamb to Atreus in anger via the shepherd Antiochos.[118] According to Pseudo-Apollodoros and the *Iliad* scholia, however, the legend goes that Atreus had promised to sacrifice to Artemis the most beautiful animal from his flocks. When he discovers a golden lamb among them, he decides to kill it and hide it (or at least its fleece) in a chest rather than offer it to Artemis.[119] In both versions, Atreus and Thyestes agree that the lamb symbolizes kingship and the right to hold the throne of Mycenae.[120] When Thyestes seduces Aerope to get the lamb, she gives it to him and Thyestes becomes king in place of Atreus.

---

[113] For Pseudo-Apollodorus's version of this tale, see *The Library*, 1.9.

[114] The Greek here is from pseudo-Apollodorus, *The Library* 1.9.27. Pausanias, *Description of Greece* 8.11.2, uses the same words.

[115] Two vases commemorating this metamorphosis have been found.

[116] Or perhaps Medea herself (Pausanias, *Description of Greece* 8.11.3).

[117] For a succinct summary of the evidence and the sources for this legend with regard to Atreus and Thyestes, see Timothy Gantz, *Early Greek Myth: A Guide to Literary and Artistic Sources*, 2 volume set (John Hopkins), 545–50.

[118] *Orestes* 990.

[119] *Orestes* 811; Pseudo-Apollodorus *Library* e.2.10.

[120] *Orestes* 995; 998; *Electra* 699–726.

The legends of the Golden Fleece were well-known in Classical Greece. The Perseus web site at Tufts University lists quite a number of vases and votive offerings that depict scenes from the legends of the Golden Fleece, including pictures of Phrixus sacrificing the ram with the Golden Fleece as an adult with horns (Harvard 1960.367) and a Lucanian Red Figure vase from the fourth century.[121] Harvard 1960.315, an Attic black figure vase dating from the end of the sixth century BCE, shows Medea demonstrating to the daughters of Pelias how to change a ram into a lamb.[122]

The semantic value of the ram or lamb in the Golden Fleece legends developed over time. The semantic value of gold in the Greek myths is extensive and well-developed. Literally dozens of golden objects dot the pages of these myths, so the semantic value of "Golden Fleece" probably derives as much from the adjective as from the noun. The legend may well draw on the value of ram as protector, but this is not developed. The fleece was certainly something of great value and its possession was simultaneously desired, elusive, and dangerous. In the Atreus and Thyestes version, it came to symbolize the right to reign as king, but as the myth progressed, its association with danger and disaster tarnished its image and the desirability of the fleece. Later tradition suggests that for all its value, the Golden Lamb brought nothing but woe, heartache, and murderous vengeance.[123]

4.4 Sacrifice Traditions

Ritual sacrifice was widespread in the ancient world. In Greece it was as common in the ancient period as it was in the Hellenistic and Roman eras. In the Archaic and Classical periods it was not considered proper to consult or petition a deity without bringing a sacrifice.[124] Sacrifice was "one of the three principal acts of worship"[125] in the ancient world and was perhaps even the most important form of action in Greek religion.[126]

Near the end of Virgil's *Aeneid*, when Turnus challenges Aeneas to combat, Aeneas accepts and prepares for the battle. Before the combat is to begin,

---

[121] See also its treatment of Naples 2858, a hydria with nearly the same scene (cf. also Berlin F 3144; Naples 1988).

[122] Cf. also London B 328; Louvre F 372; Amherst 1950.59. See the additional bibliography provided at the web site: http://www.perseus.tufts.edu.

[123] See Euripides, *Iphigeneia in Taurica* 192–202; *Orestes* 1008–12.

[124] For an excellent analysis of sacrifice traditions in archaic and classical Greece, see F. T. van Straten, *Hiera Kala: Images of Animal Sacrifice in Archaic and Classical Greece*, Religions in the Graeco-Roman world, vol. 127 (Leiden: E.J. Brill, 1995).

[125] Everett Ferguson, *Backgrounds of Early Christianity*, 144.

[126] R. C. T. Parker, "Sacrifice, Greek," in *Oxford Classical Dictionary*, 3d ed., ed. Simon Hornblower and Antony Spawforth (Oxford: Oxford University Press, 1996).

a priest is brought in to perform ritual sacrifice. The priest is dressed in white and brings with him a pig as well as a lamb for sacrifice—a lamb that had never been shorn. With his face toward the rising sun, the priest sprinkles salt and barley meal on the animals, marks their foreheads, and clips some hair from their heads.[127] Then he pours some wine on their heads between their horns and throws more wine on the fire. Similar descriptions of ritual sacrifice appear in the Odyssey, in which the pouring out of milk, honey, and especially wine was part of the ritual of the drink-offering. Often the sprinkling of ground barley accompanied the burnt offering in ritual sacrifice.[128]

Although in Egypt, sacrifices were carried out daily, monthly rituals were most common in early Greece.[129] Sacrifice was considered primarily a community responsibility, with less interest in or opportunity for individual sacrifice, except on special occasions. Thus sacrifice was often associated with occasions of entertainment, processions, or special community events. Usually the financial burden of a sacrifice was accepted by the community as a public expense. Since eating a portion of the sacrificed animal was usually a constituent component of the ritual, public banquets were often part of the event. Persons in positions of power in the community were allowed and expected to take a central role in the sacrificial ritual, though the νεόκοροι, the temple wardens, also had a central role. In the late classical era, daily sacrifice occurred in the Asclepius cult and in the ruler cult.[130] Typically, a portion of the sacrificed animal would be dedicated to the god, a leg would go to the νεόκορος, and the rest of the animal would be eaten by the person or community offering the sacrifice.[131] However, a second type of sacrifice existed—comparable to the holocaust in the Hebrew Bible—in which none of the animal was eaten.[132]

The use of lambs in sacrifice is well-attested in classical Greek and early Latin literature, both in regular worship and for special occasions.[133] Black

---

[127] For the clipping of hair as part of the pre-sacrifice ritual at the altar, see also *Iliad* 3.273.

[128] For a description of the sacrificial ritual as typically practiced, see Thomas R. Martin, *Ancient Greece: From Prehistoric to Hellenistic Times* (New Haven, Conn., and London: Yale University Press, 1996), 128.

[129] Everett Ferguson, *Backgrounds of Early Christianity*, 145; cf. Virgil, Eclogues 1.6–10 and 1.40–45; Duncan Fishwick, *The Imperial Cult in the Latin West: Studies in the Ruler Cult of the Western Provinces of the Roman Empire*, Etudes preliminaires aux religions orientales dans l'Empire romain, no. 108 (Leiden and New York: E. J. Brill, 1987–92), 531.

[130] Everett Ferguson, *Backgrounds of Early Christianity*, 145.

[131] Everett Ferguson, *Backgrounds of Early Christianity*, 145.

[132] Straten, *Hiera Kala*, 3.

[133] See, e.g., Virgil, *Eclogues* 1.

lambs were occasionally sacrificed to avert the coming of a storm.[134] The three most common types of animal used in sacrifice in Greece were the pig, the cow (or bull), and the sheep.[135] Occasionally goats were sacrificed.

The choice of animal for these sacrifices depended in part on the particular god to whom the animal was to be sacrificed and in part on the financers of the sacrifice, whether individual, family, polis, or league. According to van Straten, however, the former limitation was rare, and in most cases the cost of the animal—as appropriate to the wealth of the person, clan, polis, or league offering the sacrifice—was the more important consideration. In general, the cost of sacrificial victims ascended a scale from pigs to sheeps to cattle, and within those categories, the younger the animal, the less expensive it was. Thus, young lambs cost a fraction of what a ram did. Municipalities could, of course, afford larger-scale sacrifices with more expensive victims.[136]

Sacrifices were offered both to the gods and to the heroes, though the meanings associated with the acts apparently differed.[137] Herodotus even made a distinction between the two in his terminology for the act of offering (θύω for the gods and ἐναγίζω for the heroes).[138]

In the Homeric literature we see a keen interest in sacrifice and in its proper practice. In the fifth century BCE critique of the sacrificial cult by the philosophers centered on the proper attitude in sacrifice and criticized mechanistic understandings of its efficacy. In this sense, the Greek philosophers were not unlike the classical prophets of the Hebrew Bible, who attacked not the cult itself but the unethical practice of it. Over the next several centuries, sacrifice in Greek religion waned somewhat as "rational" religion came to be emphasized. Seldom do we find explicit reflection on the meaning or significance of sacrifice. Nevertheless, sacrifice was still important in the public ceremonies and in the various cults practiced by municipalities.

---

[134] See Aristophanes, *The Frogs* 847; cf. Virgil, *Aeneid* 3.120.

[135] According to van Straten, the proportion of sheep sacrifices varied, depending on the type of evidence used and the scope of evidence allowed for comparative purposes: "In the sacrificial calendars sheep are clearly predominant [with over 50% of sacrifices being of sheep], in votive reliefs pigs, and in vase paintings cows and bulls"; van Straten, *Hiera Kala*, 175. This difference may at first seem puzzling, but van Straten successfully demonstrates that the differences derive from the different venues or occasions for sacrifice associated with each medium.

[136] At the sacrifice at the Greater Panathenaia of 410/409 BCE, several municipalities naturally supplied funds for the sacrifice. The funds from Athena alone amounted to 5114 drachmae, already enough to purchase a hecatomb of cows; van Straten, *Hiera Kala*, 178. The recent study by Vincent J. Rosivach, *The System of Public Sacrifice in Fourth-Century Athens* (Atlanta: Scholars Press, 1994), appears to confirm most of the conclusions of van Straten.

[137] Cf. Pausanias, *Description of Greece* 2.10.1.

[138] Parker, "Sacrifice, Greek," 1344.

Even apart from cult settings, sacrifice was common. It was common for a family to offer sacrifice to the *genius* of a person on his or her birthday. When Augustus embarked on his program to revitalize religious life among his subjects, he asked that localities offer sacrifice to the *genius* of the emperor as part of the ceremonies.[139] Purification of both the participants and the victims was considered important. Both before and during the sacrifice the victim had to be inspected to ensure that it was without defect. A monthly sacrifice of a lamb at the temple of Apollo Diradiotes at Argos is associated with prophecy. Once a month a woman who had refrained from sexual intercourse with a man would receive inspiration to prophesy after drinking the blood of a lamb.[140]

According to another tradition, Hermes once averted a plague from the city of Tanagra by carrying a ram on his shoulders. To commemorate this heroic deed, Calamis made an image of Hermes with a ram (κριός) draped across his shoulders. Thereafter, at the annual feast of Hermes, the youth who was judged most handsome was permitted to walk around the walls of Tanagra carrying a lamb (ἀρήν/ἀρνός) on his shoulders.[141]

4.5 Rams and Lambs in Greek Art

Strictly speaking, the lamb was not very important in the animal symbolism of the ancient Near East as witnessed to by the archaeological evidence. However, the ram played an influential role. Excavations at Sardis have unearthed several decorative animal pins, apparently worn as jewelry. Examples include several lions as well as a ram, dating from the eight century BCE.[142]

> Rams—victims of sacrifice, companions of Hermes—occur almost as widely in Archaic Greek art as do lions. Their sturdy belligerence and steadfast resistance to the foe made them popular shield devices. ... Rams as guardians or as sacrificial victims recur too frequently in Greek art not to have evoked multiple associations, allusions, meanings in their viewers and users.[143]

---

[139] Everett Ferguson, *Backgrounds of Early Christianity*, 162.

[140] See, e.g., Pausanias 2.24.1. Elsewhere Pausanias notes that persons who consulted the oracle of Amphiaraus had to sleep on the skin of a sacrificed ram (1.34.5).

[141] Pausanias 9.22.1. See Boston 04.6 (Boston Museum of Fine Arts), for a sixth-century miniature bronze votive offering that depicts Hermes carrying a ram. Boston 99.489 is another miniature bronze votive offering from slightly later, also showing Hermes carrying a ram. Hermes is often known as the ram-bearer (κριόφορος; e.g., Pausanias, *Description of Greece* 9.22.1; cf. 2.3.4; 4.33.4; 5.27.8).

[142] For a photograph of the ram pin and a brief description, see Kozloff, *Animals in Ancient Art*, no. 24, pp. 37–38.

[143] Kozloff, *Animals in Ancient Art*, 81; for ram sacrifices, see Gloria Ferrari Pinney and Brunilde Sismondo Ridgway, eds., *Aspects of Ancient Greece* (Allentown, Pa.: Allentown Art Museum, 1979), 76–77.

Figures of rams, lying down or standing, were used in the mid-first millennium BCE in classical Greece as decorative jar lids (119),[144] decorative vases (96), decorative bowl handles (168), or as appliques for household vessels (167). Some were used as votive offerings (107–109). Ram heads were often used as architectural ornaments (110). Minitiature models served as pin terminals for earrings, clasps (*fibulae*), armbands, and pendants (24, 142).

4.6 Roman Religion and the Magna Mater

One of the great religious traditions in Roman religion was worship of the Great Mother. In 1935, P. Touilleux argued that the Lamb Christology of the Apocalypse is intended as a direct challenge to the cult of Cybele and Attis.[145] According to Touilleux, the Apocalypse encourages resistance to local pressures to participate in both this cult and the imperial cult.

The Great Mother was associated with Isis in Egypt, with Rhea in Rome, with Artemis in Asia, and with Cybele in Phrygia. The Megalensia, annual festival held in Rome from April 4 to April 10 was established in 191 BCE to honor the Magna Mater, specifically Cybele.[146] The center of worship of Cybele was located on Mt. Dindymus at Pessinus, in Phrygia, where she was known as Agdistis. The center of worship of Artemis was the great temple in Ephesus, which ranked among the seven wonders of the world.[147]

Several of the cities of Asia sported temples to the Great Mother, including Pergamum and Smyrna, where Cybele was the leading deity.[148] Many of the priests of Cybele, whether in Asia or in Rome, came from Phrygia. Greece and Rome both recognized and accepted Cybele, except that Rome consistently banned ritual self-castration, part of the cult.[149] Montanus had been a priest of

---

[144] Numbers in parenthesis in this paragraph refer to the entry number in Kozloff, *Animals in Ancient Art.*

[145] Paul Touilleux, *L'Apocalypse et les Cultes de Domitien et de Cybele* (Paris: Libraire Orientaliste Paul Geunther, 1935).

[146] Lesley Adkins and Roy A. Adkins, *Dictionary of Roman Religion* (New York: Facts on File, Inc., 1996), s.v. Megalensia.

[147] John Ferguson, *The Religions of the Roman Empire*, Aspects of Greek and Roman Life (Ithaca, N.Y.: Cornell University Press, 1970), 21.

[148] John Ferguson, *The Religions of the Roman Empire*, 23; Koester, *History, Culture, and Religion of the Hellenistic Age*, 1.192. See Ferguson, chapt. 1, "The Great Mother," 13–31, esp. 26–31, for a helpful overview of the Cybelene cult.

[149] The Cybelene cult was actually the first eastern religion formally accepted in Rome—in 204 BCE; Helmut Koester, author & trans, *History, Culture, and Religion of the Hellenistic Age*, vol. 1 of *Introduction to the New Testament*, Hermeneia: Foundations and Facets (Philadelphia: Fortress Press, 1982), 364.

Cybele (or possibly Apollo) before becoming a Christian,[150] and the Cybelen cult was quite popular in Asia, surviving until at least Eusebius's day.[151]

Cybele symbolized fertility. Like Rhea, she personified Mother Earth ($\dot{\eta}$ $\gamma\dot{\eta}$). She was associated most directly with the lion,[152] and also with healing and the giving of oracles. The central mystery rite of the Cybelene cult was the *taurobolium*, first attested in Pergamum around 105 CE.[153] In this rite, a pit was dug and the high priest crawled into it. Above the pit, planks were laid on which a bull was placed. After consecrating a spear, the bull was speared and the blood ran down through the cracks onto the priest, who caught as much of the blood as possible until his face and entire body were covered and his robes saturated. When the bull's carcas was drug off and the priest emerged, the priest, covered from head to toe in blood, was held in awe and worshiped.[154]

A less expensive variant of the *taurobolium* was the *criobolium*, in which a ram would be used instead of a bull. It appears that the taurobolium was also practiced in Mithraism, a sister mystery religion to the Cybelene cult.[155] The symbolic significance of the rite was that it granted expiation of sin through the act of the high priest, for 20 years or eternally. In some cases the rite was performed "for the well-being of the Emperor" or to consecrate a priest.[156] According to Koester, "the moral demands of the religion of the Great Mother were severe and rigorous," with awareness of sin and guilt being central to the cult.[157]

---

[150] John Ferguson, *The Religions of the Roman Empire*, 184.

[151] Eusebius, *Preparatio Evangelica* 2.2.24. Firmicus Maternus, writing in 347 CE, describes the Cybele cult as part of his appeal to Emperor Constans to suppress the cult (*On the Error of Pagan Religions* 18.1; 22.1), demonstrating its continuing popularity.

[152] David R. West cites 24 examples of iconography depicting Cybele with lions; see David R. West, *Some Cults of Greek Goddesses and Female Daemons of Oriental Origin*. Alter Orient und Altes Testament, Band 233 (Kevelaer/Neukirchen-Vluyn: Butzon & Bercker/Neukirchener Verlag, 1995).

[153] John Ferguson, *The Religions of the Roman Empire*, 29. This was probably not the actual initiation rite, which may have involved self-castration and the offering of one's testicles to the goddess in the temple, though this is disputed; cf. Koester, author and trans, *History, Culture, and Religion of the Hellenistic Age*, 1.193.

[154] For several quotations from Roman sources on the Cybele cult, including the rite of the taurobolium, see Whittaker, *Jews and Christians*, 228–36.

[155] John Ferguson, *The Religions of the Roman Empire*, 112.

[156] Molly Whittaker, *Jews and Christians*, 234. See also C[harles] K[ingsley] Barrett, *The New Testament Background: Writings from Ancient Greece and the Roman Empire That Illuminate Christian Origins*, rev. ed. (San Francisco: HarperSanFrancisco, 1995), 125.

[157] Helmut Koester, author & trans, *History, Culture, and Religion of the Hellenistic Age*, vol. 1 of *Introduction to the New Testament*, Hermeneia: Foundations and Facets (Philadelphia: Fortress Press, 1982), 194.

Attis, Cybele's consort, was originally a minor part of Cybele's cult. Claudius reorganized the cult in the first century CE, lifting some of the restrictions
on it, though retaining the prohibition of castration. In this reorganization,
Attis gained official status. Thereafter, the Cybelene cult was an official state
religion.

Touilleux showed how knowledge of this Cybelene cult could clarify the
symbolism of the Apocalypse, which he saw as a direct answer to the cult:

> instead of the ram of the Cybele cult, it depicts Christ as the triumphant Lamb,
> and instead of the mother-goddess Cybele, it presents the church as both
> mother and bride (Rev 12:1-2; 19:7-8). In place of the initiation rite, it con-
> centrates on the participation of Christians in the blood of the Lamb and their
> marriage to the Lamb, and it replaces the great processions of the Cybele cult
> with visions of the celestial liturgy before God's throne.[158]

It would be difficult to demonstrate that the original hearers of the Apocalypse would not have made any such connections in their minds as they heard
it read, given the popularity of the Cybele cult in Asia at the end of the first
century CE. Nevertheless, Touilleux's thesis is problematic. The church in the
Apocalypse is associated primarily with stars on the local level and with the
bride on the corporate level, not with a "mother." In Revelation 12, the church
is most clearly associated with τῶν λοιπῶν τοῦ σπέρματος αὐτῆς (the rest of
her offspring; 12:17). Furthermore, the central mystery rite of the Cybele cult
was the *taurobolium*, not the *criobolium* or even the *arniobolium*. It was the
former that was more widely practiced and which was most often associated
with the cult. If challenge of the Cybele cult had been central in the purposes
of the author, he would more effectively have elicited the proper associations
by depicting Christ as a slain bull.

4.7 Aries: Lamb of the Zodiac

Bruce Malina maintains that characterizations of Christ as Lamb in the Apocalypse have to do with the constellation Aries. Ancient representations normally picture it with its head turned back, giving the appearance of having a
broken neck, "thus [it] was 'slaughtered,' yet standing."[159] According to Ma-

---

[158] This quotation is from the helpful summary of Arthur W. Wainwright, *Mysterious Apocalypse*, 147.

[159] Bruce J. Malina, *On the Genre and Message of Revelation: Star Visions and Sky
Journeys* (Peabody, Mass: Hendrickson Publishers, 1995), 53. Malina suggests that it
is turned back toward Taurus, but in *The Odyssey* (10), Circe tells Ulysses that in order
to avoid disaster, he must sacrifice a ram and a black ewe, "bending their heads towards Erebus," while his own was turned in the opposite direction. Erebus personified
darkness and the place of the dead in Greek mythology (cf. also *Odyssey* 11).

lina, astrology is the key to understanding the book of Revelation and its Lamb Christology.

Malina's approach is not new. Already in the eighteenth century Charles-François Dupuis had maintained that Christianity was but a variant of an ancient solar myth that lay at the root not only of Christianity, but also of Zoroastrianism, Judaism, Etruscan religion, and the mystery cults.[160] To demonstrate his thesis, he interpreted the Apocalypse as "a Phrygian manual of instruction for initiates into the mysteries of the light and the sun."[161] He supposed that it had been used at the spring equinox under the symbol of Aries, the lamb. In 1914 Franz Boll developed the "astral mythology" reading of the Apocalypse at some length in his commentary.[162]

Although archaeological evidence clearly shows that Jews living in Palestine dating from the 4th to 6th centuries used zodiacs as decorative devices in the floors of of their synagogues, scholars have traditionally held that the knowledge and use of astrology was either limited or nonexistent in the Judaisms of the first century CE. It is true that Jewish sensibilities to iconographic representation were changing quickly in the first few centuries of the Common Era. For instance, sometime around 6–5 BCE Herod erected an eagle over the entrance to the temple. Outraged by this blasphemous act, several sages orchestrated a protest that resulted in a riot and the subsequent execution of the instigators. "Yet, by the fourth century CE the eagle had become one of the most ubiquitous symbols gracing the synagogues of Galilee!"[163] The aniconic concern was probably relaxed in the Diaspora. For instance, the massive table in the large synagogue at Sardis, built in the second century CE, is supported by two eagles.[164]

Today, however, continuing analysis of the synagogue zodiacs and of the astral allusions in the Enochic traditions and new evidence emerging from the Dead Sea Scrolls and elsewhere have revealed that astrological ideas played a larger role than previously thought in Second Temple Judaisms.[165] James H.

---

[160] Charles-François Dupuis, *The Origin of All Religious Worship*, reprint, 1795, 1872 (New York: Garland Publishing, 1984).

[161] Wainwright, *Mysterious Apocalypse*, 136.

[162] Franz Boll, *Aus der Offenbarung Johannis: Hellenistische Studien zum Weltbild der Apokalypse*, Stoicheia: Studien zur Geschichte des antiken Weltbildes und der griechischen Wissenschaft, vol. 1 (Leipzig/Berlin: B.G. Teubner, 1914).

[163] Levine, *Ancient Synagogues*, 7; cf. Josephus *War* 1.33.2–4 [1.648–655].

[164] Koester, *History, Culture, and Religion*, 1.221.

[165] See, e.g., Michael Owen Wise, *Thunder in Gemini: And Other Essays on the History, Language and Literature of Second Temple Palestine*, Journal for the Study of the Pseudepigrapha Supplement Series, no. 15 (Sheffield: JSOT Press, 1994), 14; James H. Charlesworth, "Jewish Interest in Astrology During the Hellenistic and Roman Period," *Aufstieg und Niedergang der Römischen Welt: II, Principat* 20.2 (1987): 926–56; Lester John Ness, "Astrology and Judaism in Late Antiquity," Miami Univer-

Charlesworth says, "We now possess undeniable evidence of Jewish interest in astrology by at least the first century B.C."[166] Beyond just interest in the stars or the constellations, the Dead Sea Scrolls reflect a belief that the sign under which a person is born determines that person's character.[167] Regardless of whether this belief was a majority or minority viewpoint at Qumran or in Israel generally, its presence is significant.

So is it now credible that Christian Jews living in Asia Minor at the end of the first century would have had the necessary astrological background to make the Apocalypse understandable as an astral document? In short, the answer is, "Probably so." Josephus says that although the term zodiac (ζῷδιον) comes from the Greeks, the phenomenon was long known to the Hebrews.[168] The recent manuscript discoveries at Qumran have further substantiated not only that the zodiac was known among conservative Jews of the first century, but also that there was an interest in astrology.

In most cases, the zodiacs on the synagogue floors are represented both pictorially and in writing. Interestingly, the signs of the zodiac on the synagogue floors are often the only words in Hebrew, while the other inscriptions are written in Aramaic, with the donor blessings in Greek. This may suggest the antiquity of the designations. Wherever the sign for Aries has been found in Hebrew, it is written טלה.[169] The טלה is not the powerful aggressive ram of Daniel 8, but the young, suckling lamb of Isa 40:11 and 65:25. Only in the Hammat Tiberias synagogue is the animal clearly *pictured* as a ram; in most cases it is a lamb.

The sun at the vernal equinox passed from the sign of Taurus to that of Aries, the ram, or lamb, somewhere around 2,400 BCE. The rise in veneration of the Ram, especially in Amun, seems to correspond with Aries now being the first constellation in the zodiac,[170] though admittedly this transition pro-

---

sity (Ohio) Ph.D. Diss., reprint, 1990, University Microfilms International (Ann Arbor, Mich., 1997); Lee I. Levine, *Ancient Synagogues Revealed* (Jerusalem and Detroit: The Israel Exploration Society and Wayne State University Press, 1982). Charlesworth's amassing of evidence for Jewish interest in astrology during the Hellenistic and Roman period is particularly impressive.

[166] Charlesworth, "Jewish Interest in Astrology," 927.

[167] See esp. 4Q186.

[168] Josephus, *War* 5.217 and *Antiquities* 3.186.

[169] The tradition of referring to the sign of Aries in terms that mean "baby lamb" continues in the present day. In Hebrew, the sign continues to be טלה, while in Classical Arabic, it is *Hamal* (cf. also Malina, *Genre and Message*, 79); in spoken Arabic, *Tali*.

[170] Hornung states that Amun "was the chief god through the Middle and New kingdoms, until he was displaced by Osiris at the beginning of the late period"; (Hornung, *Conceptions of God*, 231).

ceeded at different rates in different localities. In 1811 the comparative lin-
guist Sir William Drummond suggested that פסח probably means "transit" and
that the Passover Festival may have been instituted "as a memorial of the transit of the equinoctial Sun from the sign of the *Bull* to that of the *Ram*, or
Lamb."[171] He further suggested that the paschal lamb was a "type of the *Astro-
nomical Lamb*."[172] The zodiac in some form predated Moses in Egypt, Mesopotamia, and India, coming to Palestine from Mesopotamia via Egypt.[173] According to Drummond, the sign of Aries was called *Emro* by the Syrians and
Bara by the Persians, both of which mean *lamb*.[174] The tradition of designat-
ing Aries as lamb in Palestine probably derives from ancient Persian or Phoenician practice, which also designated Aries as a lamb.[175]

Drummond suggests that the worship of the golden calf derived from the
honored position of Taurus in most regions of Egypt outside of Thebes. In any
case, the Jewish tradition that the Egyptians worshiped lambs derives from a
midrash on the passage in Exodus 32 where Israel worships the golden calf.
The midrash reads,

THAT THOU HAST BROUGHT FORTH OUT OF THE LAND OF EGYPT (ib.). What was
his idea in mentioning here the going out of Egypt? Because it was thus that
Moses pleaded: 'Lord of the Universe, see from which place Thou hast
brought them out—from Egypt where everyone worships lambs.' ... Lord of
the Universe! Thou didst ignore the entire world and hast caused Thy children
to be enslaved only in Egypt, where all worshipped lambs, and from whom
Thy children have learnt [to do corruptly]. It is for this reason that they also
have made a Calf,' and for this reason does it say, THAT THOU HAST BROUGHT
FORTH OUT OF THE LAND OF EGYPT, as if to say: 'Bear in mind whence Thou
hast brought them forth.'"[176]

---

[171] Sir William Drummond, *The Oedipus Judaicus* (Kent: Research Into Lost
Knowledge Organisation, 1986 [orig. pub. 1811]), 368.

[172] Drummond, *Oedipus Judaicus*, 193.

[173] Michael Owen Wise, *Thunder in Gemini: And Other Essays on the History,
Language and Literature of Second Temple Palestine*, Journal for the Study of the
Pseudepigrapha Supplement Series, no. 15 (Sheffield: JSOT Press, 1994), 48.

[174] Drummond, *Oedipus Judaicus*, 191.

[175] J. M. Robertson, ed., *Religious Systems of the World: A Contribution to the
Study of Comparative Religion, a Collection of Addresses Delivered at South Place
Institute, Now Revised and in Some Cases Rewritten by the Authors, Together with
Some Others Specially Written for This Volume*, 10th ed. (London: G. Allen, 1911),
202. Cf. also Robert Brown, who claims to have traced the use of the Phoenician word
Teleh (lamb) as a designation of Aries back to around 1200 BCE; Robert Brown, Jr.,
*Researches into the Origin of the Primitive Constellations of the Greeks, Phoenicians
and Babylonians* (London: Williams and Norgate, 1899–1900), 1.119.

[176] *Exodus*, trans. and ed. S. M. Lehrman (Midrash Rabbah; London and New York:
Soncino Press, 1983), 502–503.

According to this interpretation, the inauguration of the Passover was designed specifically to replace the honored position of the bull (in Egyptian religion) with that of the lamb (in Hebrew religion).[177]

Goodenough maintained that the figure crowning the large open gate in
the zodiac in the synagogue at Dura-Europos is Aries supervising the Exodus
from Egypt.[178] However, his identification of the figure with Aries has been
challenged. André Grabar identified the statue as Baal Zephon.[179] Kraeling,
followed by Kurt Weitzmann and Herbert L. Kessler, all maintain that the
statue is a statue of a Pharaoh.[180]

The significance of the presence of zodiacs in ancient Jewish synagogues of
the fourth to sixth centuries has been widely debated.[181] In most Palestinian
synagogues, inscriptions accompany pictorial representations of the zodiac. In
the "more conservative" synagogue found at En Gedi, the *names* of the twelve
signs of the zodiac are inscribed in the mosaic floor without the usual pictorial
representations.[182] Some suggest that the zodiacs were just a decorative motif,
while others claim that the zodiac communicated the importance of the Jewish
calendar or the power of God in creating the cosmos or that it had some other
religious significance. Still others, drawing on praises of Helios in Sefer Ha-
Razim, which dates from the fifth century CE, have suggested that Helios represents Yahweh. Pierre Prigent suggests that the zodiacs were more than aesthetic—that they played the role of a confession of faith in image form.[183]

In the brontological text found in Cave 4 at Qumran (4Q318), דכרא ("ram,"
for Aries) is clearly readable in Fragment II, 2.1 and 2.6. Jonas Greenfield and

---

[177] This interpretation was also known in Philo, who frequently criticized the Egyptians for their godlessness and the foolishness of their worshiping animals; cf. Embassy
to Gaius 163; and other citations in Philo, *Philo*, in *Loeb Classical Library*, translated
by J. W. Earp, 10 (Cambridge and London: Harvard University Press and William
Heinemann Ltd, 1921), 304–05.

[178] Erwin Ramsdell Goodenough, *Jewish Symbols in the Greco-Roman Period*,
edited and compiled by Jacob Neusner, Bollingen Series (Princeton, N.J.: Princeton
University Press, 1988), 180.

[179] Carl H. Kraeling, *The Synagogue*, reprint, 1956, Excavations at Dura-Europos:
Final Report, vol. 8 (New York: KTAV Publishing House, 1979), 77–80, fig. 16.

[180] Kurt Weitzmann, *The Frescoes of the Dura Synagogue and Christian Art*,
coauthor Herbert L. Kessler (Washington, D.C.: Dumbarton Oaks Research Library
and Collection, 1990), 39.

[181] Cf. Goodenough, *Jewish Symbols*, 1:248–51, 10:190–97; R. Wischnitzer, "The
Beth Alpha Mosaic: A New Interpretation," *Jewish Social Studies* 17 (1955): 133–44;
Levine, *Ancient Synagogues*, 9; compare also 2En 14–15; SibOr 5.512–31.

[182] Levine, *Ancient Synagogues*, 118.

[183] Pierre Prigent, *L'Image dans le Judaisme: du IIe au VIe siècle*. Le Monde de la
Bible, no. 24 (Geneva: Labor et Fides, 1991).

Michael Sokoloff have suggested that דכרא, which clearly means "ram," was the original Aramaic designation for "Aries"—one that later was replaced by אימר, which, in Palestinian Aramaic, is capable of meaning either ram or lamb.[184] Because "lamb" is the more common meaning for אימר, it was misunderstood in this way and this is the sense it came to have in Palestine. Although this interpretation is one possibility, it remains more likely that although the Aries-as-lamb tradition elsewhere derives from the older Persian practice, it did not influence the Qumran community at this point.

In some quarters the lamb/ram of Aries was connected to the lamb/ram with the Golden Fleece. For instance, Manilius (early first century CE) said, "Resplendent in his golden fleece, first place holder Aries look backward admiringly at Taurus rising."[185] And Lucian wrote, "Thyestes then indicated and explained to them the Ram (κριός) in the sky, because of which they mythologize that Thyestes had a gold Lamb (ἀρήν)."[186]

Given the antiquity of the zodiac and the relative familiarity of first-century Jews with it and with astronomy, are we now in a position to accept Malina's analysis of the Apocalypse as an astral document? Malina is certainly right in his plea that interpreters of the Apocalypse take into consideration the possibility that extra-canonical traditions lie behind the symbolism of the Apocalypse. Furthermore, contra de Silva,[187] he is probably right that the author of the Apocalypse was not interested in "the future"—at least as defined by Malina. The Apocalypse has much more to say about the readers' past and present than it does about the distant future.[188]

However, Malina's book raises more questions than firm conclusions. In the first place, despite Malina's expert sociological analyses of New Testament texts in the past, this reader is not convinced that in this book he has built a plausible case for why or how his "astral" interpretation of the Apocalypse speaks to the social situation of its original readers. Malina rightly rejects the

---

[184] See Jonas C. Greenfield, "An Astrological Text from Qumran (4Q318) and Reflections on Some Zodiacal Names," coauthor Michael Sokoloff, *Revue de Qumran* 16, no. 64 (December 1995): 507–25.

[185] Cf. Marcus Manilius, *Astronomica*, trans. and ed. G. P. Goold, Loeb Classical Library, no. 469 (Cambridge, Mass.: Harvard University Press, 1977), 1.263–64.

[186] Lucian, *On Astrology* 12.

[187] David A. de Silva, review of "On the Genre and Message of Revelation: Star Visions and Sky Journeys," by Bruce J. Malina, *Journal of Biblical Literature* 116, no. 3 (Fall 1997).

[188] Malina goes a bit too far when he says, "There is nothing in the book of Revelation that refers to the future" (Malina, *Genre and Message*, 266). Malina can say this only because he uses the word *forthcoming* to speak of the immediate future, relegating the word *future* to the more distant future.

old "comfort for a persecuted community" thesis, but he does not replace it
with a compelling alternative scenario.

Second, Malina's book is filled with questionable assertions and supposi-
tions. He suggests, for instance, that the reason John was exiled to Patmos was
because he was practicing astral prophecy, even though the author says he was
there "on account of the word of God and the testimony of Jesus."[189] Malina
does not bother to demonstrate how or why we should read διὰ τὸν λόγον τοῦ
θεοῦ καὶ τὴν μαρτυρίαν Ἰησοῦ as a reference to his astral involvements.

Finally, I find Jacques M. Chevalier's recent critique of Malina compelling.[190] Chevalier argues that Malina has failed to take into account "the functions of John's metaphorical rhetoric." Many of the images in the Apocalypse
are treated as symbols whose rhetorical value lies in their *character*, their cultural Gestalt, not in some referent literally conceived. Words like ὡς and ὅμοιος serve as a signal that this type of rhetorical strategy is in force.[191] As Chevalier says,

> Unlike identity attributions, metaphors have two interrelated effects: they
> establish a relationship of similarity between one thing and another, but they
> also maintain the distance required to distinguish the two things compared,
> thereby eschewing a relationship of full identity. While it is easy to recognize
> the first effect, which tends to be more explicit, the implications of the second
> effect are less obvious. ... From an exegetic perspective, the implications of
> the language of approximation is that a perfect match between one dominant
> mythology (logocentrism) and another subserving it (astralism) can never be
> firmly established.[192]

In short, it appears that in writing this book, Malina has attempted to
"push the stars" for all they are worth—and maybe more—without attempting
to consider whether in this or that instance a different tradition more adequately explains a passage or an allusion in the Apocalypse. Like Goodenough's
Jewish Symbols in the Greco-Roman Period, Malina's *On the Genre and Message of Revelation: Star Visions and Sky Journeys* may be more valuable as a
source book for data than it is as an interpretation of that data.

---

[189] Malina, *Genre and Message*, 259.

[190] Jacques M. Chevalier, *A Postmodern Revelation: Signs of Astrology and the
Apocalypse* (Toronto: University of Toronto Press, 1997).

[191] The word ὡς appears 60 times in the Apocalypse, nearly twice as often as in any
other book of the New Testament. And nearly half of the occurences of ὅμοιος in the
New Testament are in the Apocalypse (21/45).

[192] Chevalier, *A Postmodern Revelation.*

5. Summary and Conclusion

The above evidence shows that the semantic value or cultural Gestalt attributed to animals in the Graeco-Roman world was significant. The semantic
value of the ram differed from century to century and from region to region.
Even within fifth-century Egypt, the cultural and semantic value of the ram
differed regionally. Despite the diversity of expression, a few generalizations
seem warranted and defensible.

First, rams were generally considered more valuable than lambs in sacrifice. With few exceptions, lambs were not considered valuable or desirable as
sacrificial victims. In Egypt, rams were associated with creation, an association that Philo knew.[193] In some localities rams symbolized fertility, while in
others, protection. While the lion was the preminent symbol of *aggressive* violence in sculpture, iconography, and the Homeric epic, the wolf was the preeminent symbol of aggressive violence in most Classical Greek literature. The
ram was the preeminent symbol of *defensive* violence in Egypt. Although the
association of the ram with fertility and violence did not extend to the lamb,
both rams and lambs were widely associated with divination and the consultation of oracles in Greece, though rams predominated in Egypt.

Second, the symbolic values reflected in the Aesopic traditions clearly attribute to sheep—and especially to lambs—the value of vulnerability. This
does not mean that they were necessarily *victims*, but they were *vulnerable*. In
the Aesopic traditions, lambs often appear in relation to wolves, their mortal
enemy. The vulnerability of the lamb is also central to the animal's semantic
value in Homer, though its archetypal enemy there seems to be the lion.

Finally, although the Lamb to Bocchoris papyrus chronicles a most interesting legend in the mythology of Egypt, it should not be over-interpreted as a
candidate either as a source for the Lamb Christology of the Apocalypse or as
a contributor to the cultural Gestalt of the lamb figure generally. Besides the
significant differences noted above, there is not enough evidence to make a
pronouncement on how widely known this tradition was in the Graeco-Roman
world. At best it witnesses in a general way to the currency of apocalyptic-like
notions in Egypt, the association of lambs with divination, and the presence of
multifarious animal cults in Egypt.

What emerges most significantly in relation to the Apocalypse is that
lambs in the Graeco-Roman world were often associated with divination, with
the consulting and interpretation of oracles, and with vulnerability. It is to
these latter associations that we will return in chapter six.

---

[193] Philo, *Works*, 843.

Chapter IV

Lambs in Early Judaism

1. Introduction

Much attention has been given to locating the possible origins of the lamb Christology in extrabiblical traditions within Early Judaism. Was there a tradition in Early Judaism about a lamb who would redeem Israel? If so, might this not be the first place to look for traditions to explicate the Lamb Christology in the Apocalypse? Some specialists have said there simply is no precedent for the lamb redeemer figure in Early Judaism. Joachim Jeremias has written emphatically about this in the *Theologische Wörterbuch zum neuen Testament*: "Dem Spätjudentum ist die Bezeichnung des Erlösers als Lamm unbekannt; die einzige Stelle, die man anführen könnte, Test Jos 19, steht in dem Verdacht, christliche Interpolation zu sein."[1] Joining Jeremias in this opinion is, *inter alia*, Sophie Laws, who rejects the idea that the lamb was established in Jewish apocalyptic literature as a messianic figure.[2]

Other commentators, however, speak confidently about the warrior lamb figure in Early Judaism and appeal to traditions about that figure in explaining the origins and function of John's Lamb Christology. In his 1978 commentary, Beasley-Murray says,

> We have in this image [of Christ as lamb] a coalescence of the apocalyptic tradition of the Warrior-Lamb and the Christian understanding of the death of Christ as a fulfilment of the passover-Lamb typology. ...

> Despite protestations to the contrary, there seems to be no doubt that this figure [of the lamb] is derived from Jewish apocalyptic imagery, which repre-

---

[1] "The description of the Redeemer as a lamb is unknown to later Judaism; the only possible occurrence (TJos 19) falls under the suspicion of being a Christian interpolation." See Joachim Jeremias, "ἀμνός, ἀρήν, ἀρνίον," in *Theologische Wörterbuch zum neuen Testament*, edited by Gerhard Kittel (Stuttgart: W. Kohlhammer, 1949–1979) 1.342.

[2] Sophie Laws, *In the Light of the Lamb: Imagery, Parody, and Theology in the Apocalypse of John* (Wilmington, Del.: M. Glazier, 1988), 27–28.

sented the people of God as the flock of God out of which arises a deliverer who rescues them from their foes.[3]

In a recent dictionary article, Pieter Willem van der Horst acknowledges "uncertainty and debate about the religio-historical background of the image of Christ as a lamb."[4] Nevertheless, he says, "It is very likely that ... Jewish apocalyptic imagery forms the prototype of many lamb passages in Revelation."[5] Scholars who appeal to some version of the Lamb-Redeemer figure in Early Judaism as a key to understanding the symbolism of the lamb in the Apocalypse include Raymond Brown,[6] George Wesley Buchanan,[7] R. H. Charles,[8] C. H. Dodd,[9] Ernst Lohmeyer,[10] Josephine Massyngberde-Ford,[11] Leon Morris,[12] Robert H. Mounce,[13] Charles H. Talbert,[14] and Etienne Trocmé.[15]

---

[3] G. R. Beasley-Murray, *The Book of Revelation*, 2d ed. (New Century Bible Commentary; Grand Rapids, Mich., Wm. B. Eerdmans Publishing Co., 1978), 28, 124–125. For a discussion about the appropriateness of identifying the passover victim as a lamb, see chapt. 5 below.

[4] Pieter W. van der Horst, "Lamb," in *Dictionary of Deities and Demons in the Bible*, edited by Karel van der Toorn, Bob Becking, and Pieter W. van der Horst (E.J. Brill: Leiden/New York/Köln, 1995), 938.

[5] Van der Horst, "Lamb," 940.

[6] Raymond E. Brown, *The Gospel According to John, I–XII: A New Translation with Introduction and Commentary*, 2d ed., reprint, 1966, The Anchor Bible, vol. 29 (Garden City, New York: Doubleday & Co., 1981), 58–60.

[7] George Wesley Buchanan, *The Book of Revelation: Its Introduction and Prophecy*, New Testament Series, vol. 22 (Lewston/Queenston/Lampeter: Mellen Biblical Press, 1993), 149–50.

[8] R. H. Charles, *A Critical and Exegetical Commentary on the Revelation of St. John*, Vol. 1, The International Critical Commentary (Edinburgh: T. & T. Clark, 1920), 141.

[9] C. H. Dodd, *The Interpretation of the Fourth Gospel* (Cambridge, England: Cambridge University Press, 1953), 236.

[10] Ernst Lohmeyer, *Die Offenbarung des Johannes*, 6th ed., reprint, 1926, Handbuch zum Neuen Testament, no. 16 (Tübingen: J.C.B. Mohr, 1953), 51–55.

[11] J. Massyngberde Ford, *Revelation*, The Anchor Bible, vol. 38 (Garden City, N.Y.: Doubleday & Company, 1975), 88–89.

[12] Leon Morris, *The Gospel According to John*, 2d ed. (Grand Rapids, Mich.: Eerdmans, 1995), 129.

[13] Robert H. Mounce, *The Book of Revelation*, New International Commentary on the New Testament (Grand Rapids: Eerdmans, 1977), 145; Robert H. Mounce, "Christology of the Apocalypse," *Foundations* 11 (January–March 1968): 42–51.

[14] Charles H. Talbert, *The Apocalypse: A Reading of the Revelation of John* (Louisville: Westminster John Knox Press, 1994), 29.

[15] Etienne Trocmé, "Lamb of God," in *The Oxford Companion to the Bible*, edited by Bruce M. Metzger and Michael D. Coogan (New York and Oxford: Oxford University Press, 1993), 418–19.

According to these scholars, the presence of a traditional Lamb-Redeemer figure in Early Judaism clarifies how and why John chose to portray Christ as a Lamb (ἀρνίον). At stake in this issue is whether the image is a continuation or extension of military might suggested in the titles ὁ λέων ὁ ἐκ τῆς φυλῆς Ἰούδα (the lion from the tribe of Judah), ἡ ῥίζα Δαυίδ (the root [or shoot] of David) from Rev 5:5 or whether the image turns the old ideas of power upside down.

It is the *character* of the animal that is at stake here. Although some commentators have followed Spitta in suggesting that ἀρνίον should be translated as "ram" or "Widder," most of the scholars mentioned above would agree that the *character* of the ἀρνίον is that of a ram, not a lamb. The question is whether the radical reinterpretation of traditional images known in the Apocalypse extends to the Lamb, or whether that image is continuous with something already known in Early Judaism. George Wesley Buchanan's position is clear. The portrayal of Christ as ἀρνίον in the Apocalypse is in keeping with the messianic expectations of the Jews in New Testament times. He says, "In New Testament times a messiah was expected to overthrow all ruling forces by his military strength and take control of the promised land, ruling there as king."[16]

The person primarily responsible for influencing the scholarly world regarding the alleged existence of an established tradition of a lamb-redeemer figure in Early Judaism is Friedrich Spitta. His ideas are built in part on Bousset's commentaries of 1896 and 1906, which claimed that the figure of the lamb was a messianic symbol. Nevertheless, Spitta is the one who developed the concept and first suggested that "ram" (*Widder*) is the better translation of ἀρνίον in the Apocalypse. In 1907, Spitta claimed that we have in the Apocalypse a unique convergence of two separate lamb traditions, both of which derive from Jewish traditions. One is the lamb as sacrificial victim and the other is the powerful ram.[17]

Spitta's intriguing suggestion was then picked up by R. H. Charles and C. H. Dodd. In his 1920 commentary on the Apocalypse, R. H. Charles appealed to 1 Enoch 90 and Testament of Joseph 19 to suggest that the figure of the Lamb is best understood against the backdrop of "apocalyptic tradition," which expected the Jewish Messiah to emerge as "warrior and king."[18] In his

---

[16] Buchanan, *The Book of Revelation*, 149.

[17] Friedrich Spitta, "Christus das Lamm," Vierter Abschnitt, *Streitfragen der Geschichte Jesu* (Göttingen: Vandenhoeck und Ruprecht, 1907) 172–224; esp. 176, 194. As far as I can tell, Spitta was the first to muster the Animal Apocalypse of 1 Enoch, Testament of Benjamin 3, and Testament of Joseph 19 in the attempt to demonstrate a militaristic ram tradition in Early Judaism.

[18] Charles, *Commentary on Revelation*, 1.141.

book, *Interpretation of the Fourth Gospel*, C. H. Dodd devoted a chapter to "the messiah" as a leading idea in the Fourth Gospel. Much of it is on the "lamb of God" as a title peculiar to the Fourth Gospel. He notes that "in the LXX ἀμνὸς ἄμωμος is never applied to the paschal victim, nor indeed is the term ἀμνός so applied at all, except in a variant" reading on Ex 7:5. [19] Dodd thinks it more probable that the reference is to Isa 53:7: ὡς ἀμνὸς ἐναντίον τοῦ κείροντος ἄφωνος. The "association of these ideas of violence and power with the figure of a lamb is at first sight paradoxical. But an explanation is found in the Jewish apocalyptic tradition." [20]

Unfortunately for Dodd, he cannot find a term for lamb in the Greek literature of Early Judaism that consistently expresses this militaristic redeemer-lamb figure. He admits that "Enoch has ἀρήν, *Apoc. Joh.* ἀρνίον, *Test. Jos.* ἀμνός. In the LXX all three are used to translate כֶּבֶשׂ, ἀρήν and ἀμνός also for טָלֶה. If there is any such connection as I here postulate, it must have been established in the pre-Greek stage of these writings or of the tradition behind them." [21]

Dodd does not mention that ἀρνίον in the LXX is always used metaphorically and that it signals vulnerability. Nor does he mention that only once does it translate כֶּבֶשׂ (Jer 11:19), where it is modified by the adjective אַלּוּף, "docile" or "gentle." Dodd does admit that ἀρνίον never appears in the Jewish apocalypses. Rather,

> ἀμνός, as well as ἀρήν, κριός and πρόβατον, is used of the bell-wether of the flock. While the author of the Apocalypse of John chose the term ἀρνίον, other Greek-speaking Christians who thought of the Messiah in apocalyptic terms may well have selected ἀμνός, which is in fact better suited than ἀρνίον to describe a young horned ram, since ἀρνίον, to Greeks for whom the diminutive form still had force, might suggest an infant sheep, while ἀμνός is the regular equivalent of כֶּבֶשׂ, which denotes the young adult animal. [22]

These are damaging concessions by Dodd. He as much as admits that the author could not have chosen in ἀρνίον a more ill-suited word within the semantic domain. There is a long tradition of using animal metaphors to speak of leaders or rulers in Israel and in the ancient Near East generally. As Patrick Miller has shown, אַיִל (ram) is the word most commonly used "to designate leaders, princes, nobles, and similar personnel." [23] We see this, for instance, in

---

[19] *The Interpretation of the Fourth Gospel* (Cambridge: Cambridge University Press, 1953), 231.

[20] Dodd, *Interpretation*, 231.

[21] Dodd, *Interpretation*, 232n2.

[22] Dodd, *Interpretation*, 236.

[23] Patrick D. Miller, "Animal Names as Designations in Ugaritic and Hebrew," *Ugarit-Forschung* 2 (1970): 181.

Ex 15:15; 2Kgs 24:15; Jer 4:22 [emendation based on LXX]; Ezek 17:13; 30:13; 31:11, 14; 32:21; 39:18; and Dan 8. This particular metaphorical tradition appears to be tied to the Hebrew. The Septuagint never uses κριός metaphorically and instead substitutes ἄρχοντες (rulers), ἰσχυροί (strong ones), or ἡγούμενοι (leaders), thus unpacking the animal symbolism for the reader.

Nevertheless, had John wanted to symbolize a "bell-wether of the flock," he could have used κριός, the most natural "translation" of the Hebrew metaphor, or even χιμάραρχος, the technical term for "bell-wether of the [goat-] flock."[24] And there were many other, more appropriate words at his disposal, such as τράγος or χίμαρος or αἴξ ["goat"], common translations of עַתּוּד, which is used metaphorically of leaders in Isa 14:9 and Jer 50:8. Nevertheless, John chose ἀρνίον, one of the more inappropriate words to speak of a leader of Israel, given the animal metaphors attested in the literature.

2. The Literature Examined

2.1 Testament of Joseph 19:8

If this redeemer lamb figure existed in the traditions and literature of Early Judaism, where do we find evidence of it? In the Testament of Joseph 19, Joseph sees a vision of Israel's future restoration. The twelve stags, divided into groups of nine and three, represent the twelve tribes of Israel.[25] As the three stags cry out to the Lord, they become lambs and "the nine stags were gathered to him, and they all became like twelve sheep" (TJos 19:4). Then in the vision, Joseph sees twelve bulls, representing also the twelve patriarchs of Israel. "The horns of the fourth bull [i.e., the fourth patriarch, Judah] ascended to heaven and became as a rampart for the herds" (TJos 19:6).

---

[24] Henry George Liddell, comp., *A Greek-English Lexicon: With a Supplement*, A new ed., rev. and augm. throughout by Henry Stuart Jones, with the assistance of Roderick McKenzie, and with the cooperation of many scholars, in collaboration with Robert Scott and Henry Stuart Jones, reprint, 1951 (Oxford: Clarendon Press, 1968), s.v. χιμάραρχος.

[25] According to Howard C. Kee, the division of the tribes of Israel into nine and three instead of ten and two (with Levi being numbered with the house of Judah instead of the house of Israel) was not otherwise unknown in the literature of Early Judaism (see James H. Charlesworth, ed., *The Old Testament Pseudepigrapha: Apocalyptic Literature and Testaments*, 1 (Garden City: Doubleday & Company, Inc., 1983), 824n19a; 1En 89:72; 1QM 1.2). The stag was an important sculptural symbol during the Hittite Empire Period (1400–1200 BCE) as well as later among the Luristan tribes of the Iranian mountains in the early first millennium BCE; see Arielle P. Kozloff, ed., *Animals in Ancient Art from the Leo Mildenberg Collection* (Cleveland: Cleveland Museum of Art and Indiana University Press, 1981), 6–7.

Verses 3-7 of chapter 19 are extant only in Armenian. Parallel Greek and Armenian versions exist from 19:8 to 19:12, though the readings differ significantly. Kee's judgment is that the 45 Armenian manuscripts now known of the Testaments of the Twelve Patriarchs are translations of the Greek; none represents an independent testimony to a hypothetical Semitic original.[26] The Greek textual basis for the translation that follows is the 13th-century Greek Codex 731 and the so-called β recension of manuscripts, regarded by R. H. Charles as containing more late Christian interpolation than the α recension upon which he based his critical edition. M. de Jonge's conviction that the readings of the β recension are closer to the original is related to his position that the Testaments of the Twelve Patriarchs as a whole were written by a Christian, not a Jew—a theory Kee rightly rejects as "both unwarranted and unnecessary."[27]

The translations by Kee in the *Old Testament Pseudepigrapha* follow:[28]

[8]And I saw that a virgin was born from Judah, wearing a linen stole; and from her was born a spotless lamb (ἀμνὸς ἄμωμος). At his left there was something like a lion, and all the wild animals (τὰ θηρία) rushed against him, but the lamb conquered (ἐνίκησεν) them, and destroyed (ἀπώλεσεν) them, trampling them underfoot.	[8]And I saw in the midst of the horns a certain virgin wearing a multicolored stole; from her came forth a lamb. Rushing from the left were all sorts of wild animals and reptiles, and the lamb conquered them.
[9]And the angels and mankind and all the earth rejoiced over him.	[9]Because of him the bull rejoiced and the cow and the stags were also glad with them.
[10]These things will take place in their time, in the last days.	[10]These things must take place in their appropriate time.

---

[26] See Howard C. Kee in James H. Charlesworth, ed., *The Old Testament Pseudepigrapha: Apocalyptic Literature and Testaments*, 1 (Garden City: Doubleday & Company, Inc., 1983), 775–76. Kee rightly agrees with Jeremias that the arguments of R. H. Charles and others for a Semitic *Vorlage* have been found wanting. Although the Testaments had loose Semitic *models*, they were written in Greek. In addition to Kee, see Joachim Jeremias, "Das Lamm, das aus der Jungfrau hervorging (Test. Jos. 19,8)," *Zeitschrift für die neutestamentliche Wissenschaft* 57 (1966) 216–219. J. H. Charlesworth notes that 51 Armenian manuscripts are now known; see *The Old Testament Pseudepigrapha and the New Testament: Prolegomena for the Study of Christian Origins* (Society for New Testament Studies Monograph Series, no. 54; Cambridge: Cambridge University Press, 1985), 95.

[27] Kee, *OTP* 1.777.

[28] The exception to this is v. 10, which I translated myself from de Jonge's Greek text. The apparent clarification, "in the last days," is probably the extent of the Christian interpolation in this verse.

[11]You, therefore, my children, keep the Lord's commandments; honor Levi and Judah, because from their seed will arise the Lamb of God who will take away the sin of the world, and will save all the nations, as well as Israel.

[12]For his kingdom is an everlasting kingdom which will not pass away. But my kingdom will come to an end among you, like a guard in an orchard who disappears at the end of the summer.

[11]And you, my children, honor Levi and Judah, because from them shall arise the salvation of Israel.

[12]For my kingdom shall have an end among you, like an orchard guard who disappears after the summer.

Speaking of this passage, C. H. Dodd says, "There can be little doubt that in this tradition of apocalyptic symbolism we must find the origin of the 'Lamb' of the Apocalypse of John. The 'Lamb' is the Messiah, and primarily the militant and conquering Messiah."[29]

But note the convergence of several elements common to the development of early christological traditions: (1) a virgin (2) from the tribe of Judah (3) gives birth to (4) a spotless lamb, (5) who is then attacked by wild beasts[30] (6) but who conquers them and thus (7) secures the joyful redemption of creation. The convergence here of early christological traditions developing within Christianity is simply too extensive to be fortuitous, especially when one notes the linguistic connections with the New Testament.[31] The additional comment, "the Lamb of God who will take away the sin of the world" seems to clinch the conclusion that we have here either a Christian document based on Jewish sources or extensive Christian interpolations supplied by someone familiar with the traditions reflected in the Fourth Gospel and the Apocalypse of John, and with traditions reflected in other portions of the New Testament.[32]

However, before we agree too readily with Jeremias that these *apparently* christological elements derive from a Christian interpolator, we should consider two further arguments by Murmelstein and O'Neill that a pre-Christian

---

[29] Dodd, *Interpretation*, 232.

[30] The wild beasts *could* reflect knowledge of the two beasts in the Apocalypse, but they may just as easily reflect awareness of the beasts in Dan 8:4.

[31] See the Greek supplied in the quotations above. Joachim Jeremias sees in παρθένος awareness of Mt 1:23 (and Isa 7:14); in ἐκ τοῦ Ἰούδα, Heb 7:14; in ἔχουσα στολὴν βυσσίνην, Rev 12:1; in ἀμνὸς ἄμωμος, 1Pet 1:19; in θηρία, Rev 17:3-18; in ἐνίκησεν, Rev 17:14; in ἀνατελεῖ [TJos 19:11], Heb 7:14 [cf. also ἀνατολή in Lk 1:78]; in ὁ ἀμνὸς τοῦ θεοῦ, Jn 1:29,36; and in χάριτι σώζων πάντα τὰ ἔθνη καὶ τὸν Ἰσραήλ, Mt 1:21. See Jeremias, "Das Lamm, das aus der Jungfrau hervorging," 218–19.

[32] The labels "Christian" and "Jewish" are, of course, anachronistic when applied to the first century. The crucial issue here is whether one can sort out messianic traditions in the Testaments that were *not* influenced by the early Jesus movement.

lamb tradition can be recovered from these texts. Murmelstein argued that what appear to be christological elements imported from early Christian tradition, derive, in fact, from Egyptian religion. Murmelstein points to a hieroglyphic text that speaks about a dead king, whose resurrection (i.e., birth) is being anticipated: "You have no father among men and no mother; your father is the great bull and your mother the virgin."[33] This divine being is clearly portrayed "in the middle of the horns" in an ancient Egyptian illustration showing the mythical ox with the sun god sitting on its head and the sun disk (with uraeus) above its head.[34] This shows, according to Murmelstein, that the idea of the bull, the virgin, and the conception of "the middle of the horns" are of Egyptian origin.

Murmelstein suggests that the sun god sitting between the horns of a cow represents a later variety of the bull with the solar disk, a motif common in Egypt.[35] And since according to the Egyptian zodiac, the era of the bull passed to the era of the ram somewhere around 2400 BCE, we begin to see the representation of the zodiac as a ram with the sun disc between its horns, then a sun god with the head of a ram, and finally the ram as the sun god.[36] According to Murmelstein, the Testament of Joseph bears witness to this transition:

> The sun still stands 'in the middle of the bull's horns,' but the lamb—in Hebrew טלה—can be treated as a representation of the ram of the zodiac: It has already been born and is about to assume its triumphal procession.[37]

According to Murmelstein, ἔχουσα στολὴν βυσσίνην (TJos 19:8) comes not from Rev 12:1, as Jeremias maintained, or from priestly garb, as K. Koch maintained, but from the important role played by linen in the Egyptian cult. According to Plutarch, in the Osiris mystery religions, the priest wrapped a

---

[33] B. Murmelstein, "Das Lamm in Test. Jos. 19:8," *Zeitschrift für die neutestamentliche Wissenschaft* 59 (1968) 273–74.

[34] Published by R. V. Lanzone in *Dizionario di mitologia egizia*, 2nd ed., vol. II.2 (pp. cxxxi and clxxxvii); see Murmelstein, "Das Lamm," 274n9.

[35] A beautiful bronze cast of Apis, the bull god of Memphis, likely dating from the sixth century BCE, is held in the Leo Mildenberg collection of animals in ancient art at the Cleveland Museum of Art. For a color reproduction, see Kozloff, *Animals in Ancient Art*, 67; cf. also 73–74.

[36] One might also note that knowledge of this tradition may be reflected in the otherwise strange saying in the Babylonian Talmud, "Do not stand in front of a bull when he comes up from the meadow, because Satan dances between his horns. Samuel said: This applies only to a black bull, and only in the month of Nisan" (b.Pes 112b; b.Ber 33a).

[37] Murmelstein, 279: "Noch steht die Sonne »in der Mitte der Stierhörner«, aber das Lamm—hebräisch *ṭāleh*—als Bezeichnung des Tierkreiswidders bekannt, ist bereits geboren und im Begriff, seinen Triumphzug anzutreten."

golden cow with a linen stole because they viewed the cow as an image of Isis
and the earth.[38] Isis herself appeared in a "multi-colored tunic, made of fine
linen," according to Apuleius's *Metamorphosis* 11:3.

Murmelstein admits that the Greek version reflects extensive Christian interpolation. He also suggests that the Egyptian motifs were intentionally destroyed by the Christian interpolator, since they clearly reflected pagan motifs.
Verse 9 universalizes the rejoicing of the Armenian version in keeping with
the universalism of the Apocalypse. The interpolator's knowledge of the Apocalypse is probably what allowed him to expand the rejoicing to include all of
creation.[39] This universalization is also evident in v. 11, where "Israel" is expanded to "all the nations, as well as Israel." Verse 10 makes explicit that the
time for these things is "in the last days." Verse 11 adds the Johannine "the
Lamb of God who will take away the sin of the world." And v. 12 contrasts the
eternal messianic kingdom with the temporal kingdom of Joseph.

There is nothing novel here in the likening of Israel to lambs.[40] In fact, if
Murmelstein is right in tracing the origins of the bull, the virgin, and the lamb
to Egyptian mythology, there may be no Christian interpolation at all in the
Armenian version of TJos 19.[41] Certainly nothing is startling about the idea
that the salvation of Israel will come from Levi and Judah (19:11). The idea of
two messiahs, or one messiah with two roles—one priestly and one royal—was
common in certain parts of Early Judaism.[42]

But Murmelstein's argumentation is problematic on several grounds. First,
the transition from Apis, the bull god worshiped at Memphis, to a virgin between the horns of the bull from Judah, who gives birth to a lamb, is not as

---

[38] Plutarch, *Isis and Osiris* 39.

[39] Compare the gradual expansion of praise in Rev 5:8-14.

[40] See, e.g., Pss 23; 100:3; Isa 40:11; Hos 4:16. This is, of course, related to the
even more common metaphor of Israel as sheep; see Pss 78:52; 80:1; Jer 50:6-7; Ezek
34; Zech 9:16; 10:2-3; 1En 89–90.

[41] Although Murmelstein assumed a Semitic *Vorlage* for the Testaments, the pre-
sumed existence of such a *Vorlage* is irrelevant to the issue at hand. The relative ori-
ginality of the Armenian version could simply imply that the Armenian represents a
translation from the Greek at an earlier stage in the accretion of Christian interpolation, which may have taken place over several hundred years. More extensive testing in
the rest of the Testaments is required in order to confirm or deny this implication.

[42] Cf. TestDan 5:10; TestGad 8:1; 1QS 9.11; CD 12.23; 14.19; 19.10–11; 20.1;
Zech 4:14; cf. J. Liver, "The Doctrine of the Two Messiahs in Sectarian Literature in
the Time of the Second Commonwealth," *Harvard Theological Review* 52 (1959) 156–
163; R. B. Laurin, "The Problem of Two Messiahs in the Qumran Scrolls," *Revue de
Qumran* 4 (1963–64) 39–52; John J. Collins, *The Scepter and the Star: The Messiahs
of the Dead Sea Scrolls and Other Ancient Literature* (New York: Doubleday, 1995),
74–77.

clear or as smooth as Murmelstein implies. Second, the picture Murmelstein reproduced from Lanzone's dictionary clearly shows an udder with two teats: this is a cow, not a bull. His suggestion that the cow simply represents a later version of the bull requires further verification to be considered tenable. Furthermore, the being portrayed between the horns is likely the sun god, not the virgin mentioned in the hieroglyphic text. If so, this breaks the connection between the bull and the virgin. Third, nothing from Egyptian mythology suggests as neatly as does the Apocalypse the idea of a "conquering lamb" (TJos 19:8, in both Greek and Armenian). Only by subtly substituting the virgin from the hieroglyphic text for the sun god in the illustration from Lanzone can Murmelstein avoid the conclusion that the Armenian version of TJos is also indebted to some Christian interpolation. Even if one were to grant plausibility to Murmelstein's argument, one is still a great distance from postulating the existence of a redeemer-lamb tradition in Early Judaism on this basis.

There is yet an alternative reading of the *Testaments* that may be significant. J. C. O'Neill has argued that somewhere between the beginning and end of the composition history of the Testaments of the Twelve Patriarchs, we can discern a stage that contained pre-Christian references to a "Lamb of God."[43] If this is the case, then the Testaments may indeed be significant for the Lamb Christology of the Apocalypse *despite* the acknowledged later Christian redaction. O'Neill claims that in his reading, "the difficulties lift like mist in the morning."[44] Furthermore, on the basis of his reading, O'Neill can say that "it is almost certain ... that Jews before Jesus Christ looked for the Messiah who would be called the Lamb of God."[45]

O'Neill's reading is problematic on several grounds. First, even if the Testaments as we have them represent a Christian redaction of an originally Jewish work, the sort of precision at which O'Neill aims in terms of the composition history of the document is elusive at best. O'Neill continually argues that while a Christian would never have written this or that, a Christian would have let it go (redactionally) if someone else had written it. Although he admits that this appears to be a weakness in his approach, he denies that it is.[46]

Second, O'Neill bases his reconstruction of the history of composition in part on questionable emendations of the text. For instance, he argues that καὶ

---

[43] John C. O'Neill, "The Lamb of God in the Testaments of the Twelve Patriarchs," in *New Testament Backgrounds: A Sheffield Reader*, edited by Craig A. Evans and Stanley E. Porter, The Biblical Seminar, vol. 43 (Sheffield: Sheffield Academic Press, 1997), 46–66. This is a reprint of the article by the same title in *Journal for the Study of the New Testament* 2 (1979): 2–30.

[44] O'Neill, "The Lamb of God," 46.

[45] O'Neill, "The Lamb of God," 64.

[46] O'Neill, "The Lamb of God," 52.

ἐξ ἀριστερῶν αὐτοῦ ὡς λέων ("and on his left there was one like a lion") in TJos 19:8 is a scribal mistake for καὶ ἐξ ἀριστερῶν αὐτός ὡς λέων (and he was at her [i.e., the virgin's] left hand like a lion"). The only warrant for this is O'Neill's own imagination about how a Christian scribe would or would not have redacted and the presence of an erasure in one of the manuscripts. Third, most of O'Neill's argumentation is based on his own confidence that he can tell the difference between what is simply a textual corruption and what represents distinct layers in the tradition. Such confidence has rarely been seen since the days of R. H. Charles. Fourth, the Apocalypse nowhere refers to Christ as the "Lamb of God" (ἀρνίον τοῦ θεοῦ); such a designation can only come from the Fourth Gospel, thereby weakening the link between the alleged militant redeemer lamb of Early Judaism and the Lamb of the Apocalypse. Finally, O'Neill's argument fails the test of simplicity. I hold that what can plausibly be argued on the basis of a simple reconstruction is preferable to what can plausibly be argued on the basis of a complex reconstruction.

This brings us back to the question of what may have been original to the *Testament of Joseph*. I take a "conservative" view on the origin of the Testaments of the Twelve Patriarchs. It is clear that the Testaments have a strong Jewish-Christian character to them. It may be that the "Christian interpolations" can indeed be identified and separated out from an alleged Jewish Vorlage, as R. H. Charles thought.[47] It may also be that the entire work is the work of a Christian who was steeped in his Jewish traditions, as de Jonge and Bryan have more recently claimed.[48] In either case we are talking about sources that were at one stage (non-Christian) Jewish and which were eventually redacted from a Christian point of view into what can now be called a (Jewish) Christian construct. Whether that "redaction" came in the pre-authorship, authorship, or post-authorship stage in the composition history of the document may not be that significant.[49] What is important for the present study is the recognition that Christian elements do exist in the Testaments, that the precise details in the history of their composition can no longer be recovered, and that the text as it now stands cannot be appealed to in order to demon-

---

[47] R. H. Charles, ed., *The Greek Versions of the Testaments of the Twelve Patriarchs: Edited from Nine MSS. Together with the Variants of the Armenian and Slavonic Versions and Some Hebrew Fragments* (Oxford: Clarendon Press, 1908).

[48] Martinus de Jonge, *The Testaments of the Twelve Patriarchs: A Study of Their Text, Composition, and Origin* (Leiden: Brill, 1953); David Bryan, *Cosmos, Chaos and Kosher Mentality*, Journal for the Study of the Pseudepigrapha Supplement Series, no. 12 (England: Sheffield Academic Press, 1995), 263–72.

[49] Cf. H. Dixon Slingerland, *The Testaments of the Twelve Patriarchs: A Critical History of Research*, Society of Biblical Literature Monograph Series, vol. 21 (Missoula, Montana: Scholars Press, 1977), who helpfully points Testaments scholarship in a new direction.

strate a pre-Christian redeemer lamb tradition as a basis for understanding the Apocalypse.

The simplest and most compelling argument is that verses 7-8 in the Armenian represent Christian interpolation as well as all of the Greek additions of 19:8-12. This adjudication of the issue has the advantage both of showing which elements were original to the Testaments and of demonstrating how that original may reasonably have given rise to the later Christian interpolations. That is, a Christian, reading the rather vague, generalized messianic prophecy of Joseph, connected the idea of lambs in v. 3 with the messianic (?) horn of v. 6, which was born of the tribe of Judah. This, in turn, reminded him of John 1:36, "Behold, the lamb of God," and 1:29, "... who takes away the sin of the world." This led him to insert the reference to the virgin birth, derived from elsewhere in the tradition,[50] and the combat myth, derived from the Apocalypse or readily available elsewhere. Careful analysis of these versions thus indicates that the Armenian version, while clearly containing Christian interpolations, is closer to the original than the extant Greek.[51]

The result of this analysis for our own investigation is mostly negative. Nothing in the original Jewish version of the Testament of Joseph 19 could have served as a model or forerunner to the lamb figure of the Apocalypse of John. We thus agree completely with Jeremias' conclusion of 1966 (against Koch): "Ergebnis: Test. Jos. 19,8 ist christlich und kein Zeugnis dafür, daß das antike Judentum die Bezeichnung des Erlösers als Lamm gekannt habe. Für diese Bezeichnung gibt es bis jetzt keinen antiken jüdischen Beleg."[52]

2.2 Testament of Benjamin 3:8

The same sort of Christian interpolation is evident in Testament of Benjamin 3:8, where, according to Howard Clark Kee, "the major text traditions include a Christian interpolation."[53] Certainly the majority of the Greek manuscripts betray this interpolation:

---

[50] Cf., e.g., Mt 1:23; Lk 1:27, 34–35; James Hamilton Charlesworth, *The Odes of Solomon*, Pseudepigrapha Series, vol. 7 (Chico: Scholars Press, 1977), Ode 19.

[51] Precision is important here. We do not claim, as Klaus Koch did, that the Armenian version is *free* of Christian interpolation. See K. Koch, "Das Lamm, das Ägypten vernichtet. Ein Fragment aus Jannes und Jambres und sein geschichtlicher Hintergrund," *Zeitschrift für die neutestamentliche Wissenschaft* 57 (1966) 79–93. Furthermore, one need not deny that the Armenian itself was translated from the Greek (i.e., an earlier Greek recension) to make the case that it is closer to the original.

[52] "Testament of Joseph 19:8 is Christian and thus offers no evidence that ancient Judaism had a conception of the redeemer as a lamb. For this understanding there is so far no ancient Jewish evidence." Jeremias, "Das Lamm," 219.

[53] Howard C. Kee, *OTP* 1.826n3b.

> [Jacob speaking:] Through you [Joseph] will be fulfilled the heavenly prophecy
> concerning the Lamb of God, the Savior of the world, because the unspotted
> one will be handed over by lawless men, and the sinless one will die for impi-
> ous men by the blood of the covenant for the salvation of the gentiles and of
> Israel and the destruction of Beliar and his servants.

By way of comparison, the Armenian version reads:

> In you will be fulfilled the heavenly prophecy which says that the spotless one
> will be defiled by lawless men and the sinless one will die for the sake of im-
> pious men.[54]

Here again we see in the Greek the convergence of several early christological themes, such as (1) the fulfilling of prophecy, (2) reference to "the Lamb
of God," (3) the Savior of the world, (4) the "unspotted" and "sinless" one,
(5) who will be "betrayed" by lawless men and (6) whose death can be referred
to as "the blood of the covenant," and (7) whose death will result in the salvation of the gentiles and of Israel. This is clearly Christian.

Whether the Armenian version is closer to the original is again a difficult
question. Is it possible that a Jew could have talked about prophecy being ful-
filled in the Testament of Joseph, a prophecy that spoke of a "spotless" and
"sinless" one who would die for the sake of impious men? Joseph is called a
υἱὸς τοῦ θεοῦ in Joseph and Aseneth 6:3 and 5 (cf. 13:13; 18:11; 21:4; 23:10).
However, C. Burchard's judgment is probably correct that this epithet means
that "Joseph is an example of the just man in whom God can be recognized,"
not that he was a prototypical redeemer figure.[55]

It is more likely that the reference to the spotlessness of the descendent of
Joseph led the Christian interpolater to think of 1 Peter 1:19, which speaks of
"the precious blood of Christ, like that of a lamb without defect or blemish"
(τιμίῳ αἵματι ὡς ἀμνοῦ ἀμώμου καὶ ἀσπίλου Χριστοῦ).

2.3 1 Enoch 89–90

When we come to the Dream Visions of 1 Enoch, we are on entirely different
ground, since the Dream Visions of 1 Enoch are clearly pre-Christian. Largely

---

[54] Both translations here are by Howard C. Kee, *OTP* 1.826.

[55] See C. Burchard, "Joseph and Aseneth," *The Old Testament Pseudepigrapha:
Expansions of the "Old Testament" and Legends, Wisdom and Philosophical Litera-
ture, Prayers, Psalms, and Odes, Fragments of Lost Judeo-Hellenistic Works*, vol. 2,
James H. Charlesworth, ed. (Garden City: Doubleday & Company, Inc., 1985), 191–
92. Burchard also points out that Aseneth is called "a daughter of the Most High" in
21:4 and that although Joseph and Aseneth assume the necessity of salvation for non-
Jews, this redemption "was not wrought by a redeemer (let alone a dying one like
Christ)" (Burchard, "Joseph and Aseneth," 192).

because of the transparent references to the Maccabeans in the work, most scholars date this work to the fourth decade of the second century BCE—that is, in the 160s—making it 250 years older than the Apocalypse of John.[56]

The Animal Apocalypse, part of the Dream Visions (Book Four: chapters 83–90), contains a rehearsal of Israel's history in which the main characters are presented as various animals. The twelve patriarchs—as well as their descendants, the Israelites—are presented as sheep. The Egyptians are portrayed as wolves. In 89:45 Samuel is portrayed as a sheep or lamb (ἀρήν in the Vatican Greek MS 1809) who promotes another sheep or lamb (also ἀρήν in the Vatican Greek MS 1809)—i.e., David—to become a ram in place of the sheep (so Ethiopic MS Kebrān 9/II) or ram (so Ethiopic MS EMML 2080) that represents Saul. The kings of Israel are then portrayed as rams, leaders among the sheep, while the prophets are simply called sheep. In 1 Enoch 89:45-46, David is a lamb (ἀρήν), "which becomes a ram, a ruler and leader of the sheep (εἰς κριὸν καὶ εἰς ἄρχοντα καὶ εἰς ἡγούμενον τῶν προβάτων).

The later (seventy) Israelite kings are called shepherds. Israel's enemies are first called dogs [Philistines],[57] foxes [Ammonites and perhaps also the Moabites], and wild boars [Edomites] (89:42-43,46-47,49), and later, lions [Babylonians], leopards (or tigers) [Syrians], wolves (or bears) [Egyptians], hyenas [Assyrians], foxes [Ammonites and Moabites], and wild beasts [all of Israel's enemies?] (89:55-58, 65-66, 68).

When the writer gets to the Maccabean revolt, he portrays the Maccabeans as lambs (90:6-9) who grew horns (i.e., became powerful) and entered into conflict with the ravens (i.e., the Seleucids). Numerous commentators on the Apocalypse have pointed out that the Maccabeans are represented as horned lambs in this passage.[58] This statement, however, is misleading at best, since the lambs must become something else, like rams, in order to function as leaders and rulers. The bleating lambs whose cries are not heard (1 Enoch 90:6-12) probably refer to the Maccabeans (and other faithful Jews) who experienced the violent persecution of Antiochus Epiphanes *before* the one lamb grew

---

[56] See James C. VanderKam, *Enoch and the Growth of an Apocalyptic Tradition* (The Catholic Biblical Quarterly Monograph Series, 16; Washington, D.C.: The Catholic Biblical Association of America, 1984), 161–163; cf. also Patrick A. Tiller, *A Commentary on the Animal Apocalypse of I Enoch* (Early Judaism and Its Literature, no. 4; Atlanta, Ga.: Scholars Press, 1993), 61–63, 78–79. Despite lack of consensus with regard to the *precise* dating of the Animal Apocalypse, there is a broad consensus that it was written between 167 and 164 BCE; cf. Bryan, *Cosmos, Chaos*, 38–39.

[57] Identified by Tiller, *Animal Apocalypse*, 32–36, 320. The additional identifications that follow are also by Tiller.

[58] See, e.g., Robert Mounce: "In I Enoch 90:9 the Maccabees are symbolized as 'horned lambs'"; Mounce, *The Book of Revelation*, 145.

a great horns and became a ram (i.e., before Judas Maccabeus began to exercise his leadership).

Several scholars have attempted to identify these lambs more precisely. R. H. Charles,[59] J. T. Milik,[60] and James VanderKam[61] have identified these lambs as the early Hasidim. David Bryan is more cautious, content to identify them as "a group of priests who opposed the policy of Hellenization supported by the priestly leaders in Jerusalem."[62] Bryan's caution is judicious, though we should also see in the lamb symbolism a reference to the early persecutions mentioned in 1 Maccabees 1–2. While the persecution theme is central to the lamb symbolism here, their Jewish identity is also a part of the semantic value of the lambs.

The image of one animal "becoming" another animal is not just a passing observation. The Animal Apocalypse reflects interest in a strict hierarchy of beings, with each metamorphosis significant.[63] The lamb who grew "one great horn" (90:9; Judas Maccabeus)[64] is, from 90:13 on, called a "ram." Thus, the text itself implies that *lamb* is not an appropriate symbol for a leader or a ruler, unless it be for a ruler who is suffering persecution. The rams in this section represent "royal leadership,"[65] the great warriors and leaders of the people, while Israel's enemies are represented as eagles [Macedonians], vultures [not original to the Aramaic],[66] ravens [Seleucids], and kites [the Ptolemies] (90:11-12).

The Animal Apocalypse divides history into three separate periods or ages: the past, the present, and the ideal future. Each age begins with a single patriarch pictured as a white bull. Bulls are reserved primarily for the antediluvian period. After the figure of Isaac, they do not appear again until the very brief description of the coming ideal age in 90:37-38. The color white represents the righteous; black the sinners; while the semantic value of red is puzzling.[67] As

---

[59] R. H. Charles, *The Book of Enoch*, 2d ed., reprint, 1893 (Oxford: Clarendon Press, 1912), 207.

[60] J. T. Milik, *The Books of Enoch*, M. Black (Oxford: Oxford University Press, 1976), 43.

[61] VanderKam, *Enoch*, 161n56.

[62] Bryan, *Cosmos, Chaos*, 72.

[63] For discussion of metamorphoses through various levels in the Animal Apocalypse, see Bryan, *Cosmos, Chaos*, 47–52.

[64] Cf. the discussion of VanderKam on the identity of the "one great horn," *Enoch*, 161–162; and that of Tiller, *Animal Apocalypse*, 62–63.

[65] Bryan, *Cosmos, Chaos*, 69.

[66] See Tiller's comments, *Animal Apocalypse*, 36.

[67] For discussions of the symbolic value of the colors in the Animal Apocalypse, see Bryan, *Cosmos, Chaos*, 74–79; and Ida Fröhlich, "The Symbolical Language of the Animal Apocalypse of Enoch (1 Enoch 85–90)," *Revue de Qumran* 14 (April 1990): 630.

David Bryan has shown, the Israelites are symbolized only by animals that are ritually clean, whereas their Gentile enemies are symbolized only by various *unclean* animals.[68]

The coming ideal age is described briefly in chapter 90:

> [37]Then I saw that a snow-white cow was born, with huge horns; all the beasts of the field and all the birds of the sky feared him and made petition to him all the time. [38]I went on seeing until all their kindred were transformed, and became snow-white cows; and the first among them became something, and that something became a great beast with huge black horns on its head. The Lord of the sheep rejoiced over it and over all the cows. [39]I myself became satiated in their midst. Then I woke up and saw everything.[69]

The identity of the "something" of v. 38 (Ethiopic, *nägär*) is a problem not easily solved. Much like the Hebrew דָּבָר, *nägär* can mean "word" or "thing" or "something" or "matter," hence Isaac's translation. Most commentators have concluded that the text is corrupt here and have thus emended the reading in some way. Several solutions have been proposed for the problem.[70] First, R. H. Charles, following Dillmann, suggested that the Hebrew underlying this may have been ראם (buffalo or wild ox), which was transliterated ρημ, which was then mistaken by the Ethiopic translators as ῥῆμα.[71] Although at this time Charles thought Enoch was originally written in Hebrew, the Aramaic for buffalo or wild ox (ראמא or רימא) works as well or even better for his theory. The major problem with this view is that there is no obvious reason why the translators should have resorted to transliteration at this point. David

---

[68] Bryan, *Cosmos, Chaos, passim.*

[69] Ephraim Isaac, trans. and ed., "1 (Ethiopic Apocalypse of) Enoch," in *Old Testament Pseudepigrapha*, vol. 1, edited by James H. Charlesworth (Garden City, N.Y.: Doubleday, 1983), 5–89.

[70] The following summary depends largely on Patrick Tiller's helpful analysis of the problem, *Animal Apocalypse*, 386–89.

[71] R. H. Charles, *The Book of Enoch* (1893), 258–59. Most scholars have since accepted and followed this explanation of the matter; see VanderKam, *Enoch*, 168. Michael A. Knibb also adheres to this view, and so translates *nägär* as "wild ox"; see Knibb, *The Ethiopic Book of Enoch: A New Edition in the Light of the Aramaic Dead Sea Fragments* (Oxford and New York: Clarendon Press and Oxford University Press, 1978), 2.216; cf. also Knibb's translation in H. F. D. Sparks, ed., *The Apocryphal Old Testament* (Oxford: Oxford University Press, 1984), 216; M. Black in *The Book of Enoch or I Enoch: A New English Edition with Commentary and Textual Notes* (Studia in Veteris Testamenti Pseudepigrapha, no. 7; Leiden: Brill, 1985), 83; S. Uhlig in *Apokalypsen: Das äthiopische Henochbuch* (Jüdische Schriften aus hellenistisch-römischer Zeit, 5.6; Gütersloh, 1984), 704; F. Corriente and A. Piñero in A. Diez Macho, *Apócrifos del Antiguo Testamento* (Madrid, 1984), 4.123.

Bryan accepts Dillmann's proposal, suggesting that the motive for the Greek transliteration "was to signify that this eschatological figure was Jesus Christ (cf. Jn 1.1)."[72] Bryan does not emend the text, however, and translates *nägär* as "word," despite its corruption.

Second, in 1912, Charles, following Goldschmidt, suggested that *nägär* is from מלה (Hebrew and Aramaic, meaning "word," "thing"), which was a corruption of an original תלה (Hebrew, but which could also be spelled this way defectively in Aramaic, for תליה, meaning "lamb").

Third, in his 1920 commentary on the Apocalypse, Charles says, "I now regard 83–90 as derived from an Aramaic original, and explain the meaningless term 'word' in 90[38] as a rendering of אֵימַר which was a corruption of אִמַר = 'lamb.'"[73] In his 1976 article, "A Bull, a Lamb and a Word: 1 Enoch 90:38,"[74] Barnabas Lindars also concluded that the original text had read אמר, although on a slightly different basis. He suggested that the Greek translators deliberately mistranslated the original אִמַר as if it were אֵימַר (= λόγος) in order to make the vision a prophecy of Christ.[75] Dillmann was aware of this possibility and objected that when λόγος is used in this sense it is always represented by *qāl* in the Ethiopic. To meet this objection, Lindars countered that the Ethiopic translators did not catch the intent of the Christian Greek translators.

Fourth, in his Hermeneia commentary on 1 Enoch, George W. E. Nickelsburg suggests that the Aramaic דבר (or "leader") was vocalized as דָּבָר and read as "word," as if it had been in Hebrew. The main problem with this proposal is that the proposed word is not well attested.[76]

There are, however, those who resist the temptation to emend the text. Although David Bryan agrees in part with Dillmann that the Aramaic for ox was transliterated as ῥῆμα, he hesitates to emend the text on that basis and translates it "word."[77] Ephraim Isaac also refrains from emendation, preferring to render *nägär* in its most natural sense as "something."[78] In light of the lack of a compelling case for any of these emendations, it seems best to avoid such speculation and translate *nägär* as "something," while noting the difficulties involved.

---

[72] Bryan, *Cosmos, Chaos*, 63; cf. also Barnabas Lindars below.

[73] Charles, *Commentary on Revelation*, 2.452.

[74] *New Testament Studies* 22 (1975–1976): 483–86.

[75] Lindars, "A Bull," 485.

[76] Cf. 4QEn^e 4 2.16; George W. E. Nickelsburg, *1 Enoch 1: A Commentary on the Book of 1 Enoch, Chapters 1–36, 81–108*. Hermeneia Commentaries (Minneapolis: Fortress Press, 2001), 403. See also Tiller, *Animal Apocalypse*, 387–88, who also offers the critique repeated here.

[77] Bryan, *Cosmos, Chaos*, 63.

[78] Isaac, "1 Enoch," in *OTP* 1:71.

There is, moreover, a serious question whether the distinction between sheep and lambs existed in the original Aramaic. Tiller comments:

> Although the Ethiopic text distinguishes only between sheep and rams, the Greek text has another category: lamb (cf. the 'little sheep' of vs. 48b). Unfortunately the Greek text is not necessarily a reliable indicator of the specific term used in Aramaic, and the Ethiopic is certainly not a reliable indicator of the Greek term used. In every place where the Aramaic text is extant, the Ethiopic *bagᶜ* ('sheep,' sg.) represents אמר ('lamb') and *'abāgeᶜ* ('sheep,' pl.) represents אמרין ('lambs') or ען ('flock') (see table 6). אמר may be the only Aramaic word used, and there may be no distinction between different kinds of sheep, except for the distinction between normal sheep and rams that wield political or military power. The distinction in Greek between πρόβατον ('sheep') and ἀρήν ('lamb') is a false one since πρόβατα is used to translate ען ('flock') and ἀρήν is used to translate אמר ('lamb'). ... [Footnote 19:] It is likely that 90.6,8,9, where the Ethiopic uses the term *maḥseʾt* ('lambs'), the Greek had ἀρνές ('lambs'). Aramaic may have read טליין ('lambs') but more likely simply had אמרין ('lambs').[79]

Patrick Tiller has provided a helpful chart listing the translation equivalences for sheep in the Animal Apocalypse:

Translation Equivalences for Sheep in the Animal Apocalypse

ARAMAIC	GREEK	ETHIOPIC	ENGLISH	REFERENCES
דכר	κριός	*ḥargē*	ram	89.(14) 44
דכר די ען	?	*bagᶜ*	sheep (sg.)	89.12
אמר	πρόβατον?	*bagᶜ*	sheep (sg.)	89.16,32,35,36,37
אמרין	πρόβατα?	*'abāgeᶜ*	sheep (pl.)	89.12,14
ען	πρόβατα	*'abāgeᶜ*	sheep (pl.)	89.27,28,32,33,35,44
?	ἀρήν	*bagᶜ*	sheep (sg.)	89.45
?	ἀρήν?	*maḥāseᶜ*	lambs	90.6,8,9
צפירינ/אילין	τράγοι/κριοί?	*dābēlāt*	he-goats, rams	90.10
עפיר/איל	τράγος/κριός?	*dābēlā*	he-goat, ram	90.11,13,16,31

NOTE: The English column translates the words in the Ethiopic column. For *ḥargē, bagᶜ,* and *'abāgeᶜ* the Aramaic equivalences are attested in the fragments. The Greek equivalences are attested only for דכר = κριός and ען = πρόβατα (89.44). See the note on 90.31 for the use of *dābēlā* as distinct from *ḥargē*.[80]

---

[79] Tiller, *Animal Apocalypse*, 310.
[80] Table 6 from Tiller, *Animal Apocalypse*, 275.

What evidence do we have that John knew portions of the traditions that eventually came to be known as 1 Enoch?[81] Although this complex and difficult question goes beyond the parameters of the present study, some preliminary observations may be in order. First, the vision of the throne room in Rev 4 and 5 may well depend in part upon the vision of the throne room in 1En 14:18-25 (Book One: The Parable of Enoch):

> And I observed and saw inside it a lofty throne—its appearance was like crystal and its wheels like the shining sun; and (I heard?) the voice of the cherubim; and from beneath the throne were issuing streams of flaming fire. It was difficult to look at it. And the Great Glory was sitting upon it—as for his gown, which was shining more brightly than the sun, it was whiter than any snow. None of the angels was able to come in and see the face of the Excellent and the Glorious One; and no one of the flesh can see him—the flaming fire was round about him, and a great fire stood before him. No one could come near unto him from among those that surrounded the tens of millions (that stood) before him. He needed no council, but the most holy ones who are near to him neither go far away at night nor move away from him. Until then I was prostrate on my face covered and trembling. And the Lord called me with his own mouth and said to me, 'Come near to me, Enoch, and to my holy Word.' And he lifted me up and brought me near to the gate, but I (continued) to look down with my face.[82]

Second, John's many references to myriads of myriads[83] could derive from 1En 40:1 (Book Two: The Similitudes): "And after that, I saw a hundred thousand times a hundred thousand, ten million times ten million, an innumerable and uncountable (multitude) who stand before the glory of the Lord of the Spirits." Third, John's vision of eschatological blessing, experienced in part as eating from the tree of life planted in the holy city, may derive from Enoch's description of the same in 25:1-7 (Book One: The Parable of Enoch).[84]

---

[81] Charles lists as parallels: (1) Rev 4:1 // 1En 14:15; (2) Rev 6:11 // 1En 47:3-4; (3) Rev 8:8 // 1En 18:13; 21:3; (4) Rev 9:1 // 1En 86:1; (5) Rev 9:20 // 1En 99:7; (6) Rev 14:10 // 1En 48:9; (7) Rev 1:13 and 14:14 // 1En 46:1; (8) Rev 17:14 // 1En 9:4; (9) 20:8 // [1En 56:5-8, conceptually]; (10) Rev 20:13 // 1En 51:1; (11) Rev 22:2 // 1En 62:3,5; see R. H. Charles, *Revelation*, 1.lxxxii–lxxxiii.

[82] Translation by Ephraim Isaac, *OTP* 1:21. As David Aune has pointed out, "the related motifs of the heavenly door, the invitation to enter, and a vision of the throne room of God constitute a commonplace in ancient revelatory literature" (David E. Aune, "Revelation," *Harper's Bible Commentary*, James L. Mays, gen. ed. (San Francisco: Harper & Row, 1988), 1309.

[83] Cf. Rev. 5:11; 1En 14:22; but cf. also Dan. 7:10.

[84] Note that the tree of life is associated both with the throne of God and the holy city—in the context of eschatological blessing—both in 1 Enoch 25 and Revelation 22 (cf. also 4Ezra 8:52; Rev. 2:7; 22:14).

Fourth, John's vision of four living creatures ceaselessly worshiping God and saying, "Holy, holy, holy," (Rev 4:8) bears strong resemblance to Enoch's vision of all of creation not sleeping, but [ceaselessly] standing before the glory of God, blessing, praising, and saying, "Holy, holy, holy" (1En 39:12 [Book Two: The Similitudes]). Fifth, John's warning not to add or subtract anything from this book (Rev 22:18-19) may derive from a similar warning in Enoch not to "alter nor take away from my words, all of which I testify to them from the beginning!" (1 Enoch 104:11 [Book Five: Epistle of Enoch]; cf. 104:10-13).[85]

Sixth, the idea of the prayers of the righteous martyrs ascending to heaven (Rev 5:8; 6:10; 8:3-4) may well derive from 1 Enoch 47:1-4:

> In those days, the prayers of the righteous ascended into heaven, and the blood of the righteous from the earth before the Lord of the Spirits. ... Their prayers shall not stop from exhaustion before the Lord of the Spirits—neither will they relax forever—(until) judgment is executed for them.[86]

The martyr's death was thus seen as a sign of the end, as part of the eschatological labor pains.[87] Seventh, the association of the final judgment with opening books containing the names and/or the deeds of the righteous, is common to both works.

These parallels are suggestive at best. None of these parallels by itself nor the sum of them proves that John was aware of 1 Enoch or that his apocalypse is directly dependent literarily on it. Nevertheless, the numerous points of contact between 1 Enoch and the Apocalypse—and the secure dating of 1 Enoch 100 years or more before the Apocalypse[88]—make it likely that the author of the Apocalypse was aware of and used concepts from 1 Enoch in the throne vision of his Apocalypse.[89]

---

[85] The idea of not adding or subtracting anything from what has been written is, however, a τύπος in ancient historiography; see Josephus, *Antiquities* 1.17; *Thucydides*, History 5.29; Plato, *Phaedo* 95e; cf. Isocrates *Panathenaicus* 264 [Isocrates 12.264].

[86] Cf. also Ps. 141:2.

[87] Cf. TMos 9:6-7, which also treats the martyr death as a sign of the eschaton. See Adela Yarbro Collins, "The Political Perspective of the Revelation to John," *Journal of Biblical Literature* 96 (1977): 241–56, for a helpful comparison of the role martyrdom had in the various resistance strategies reflected in the literature of Early Judaism.

[88] Aside from the Similitudes.

[89] Ephraim Isaac says, "There is little doubt that 1 Enoch was influential in molding New Testament doctrines." "It influenced Matthew, Luke, John, Acts, Romans, 1 and 2 Corinthians, Ephesians, Colossians, 1 and 2 Thessalonians, 1 Timothy, Hebrews, 1 John, Jude (which quotes it directly), and Revelation (with numerous points of contact)"; Ephraim Isaac, trans. and ed., "1 (Ethiopic Apocalypse of) Enoch," in *OTP* 1.10. Milik also is quite confident. He sees this direct influence primarily in 1En 22:12 // Rev 6:9-10; 1En 86:1 // Rev 9:1, 11; 8:10; 1En 91:16 // Rev. 21:1. On the basis of these

What implications does the foregoing analysis have for our question about the possible sources of the Lamb Christology within Early Judaism? It is important to recognize what is *not* in the Animal Apocalypse. First, although many commentators have spoken readily of the "messianic" figure of 1En 90:38,[90] it should be noted that there is simply no mention of the Messiah in the Animal Apocalypse nor is it said anywhere that this figure is Davidic.[91] Given the already questionable grounds upon which to speculate about messianic expectations as such within Early Judaism, one must conclude with Sophie Laws that the evidence for the idea that the term *lamb* was itself already established as a messianic image or title "is very shaky."[92]

Second, apart from the questionable emending of the text by Dillmann, Charles, and those who have followed in their wake, neither sheep nor lambs appear in the eschatological vision of 90:37-39. That is, we have no eschatological sheep or lamb figures at all in 1 Enoch; sheep, including rams, serve only as allegorical representations of the people of Israel and their royal leadership in the history of Israel.

---

and other parallels, he says it is "clear that the Christian writer [of the Apocalypse] had first-hand knowledge of the Book of Enoch"; J. T. Milik, *The Books of Enoch*, M. Black (Oxford: Oxford University Press, 1976), 199.

[90] As an example, see the comments of Barnabas Lindars: The Animal Apocalypse "consists of a complete history of the world from Adam to the setting up of the Messianic Kingdom. ... The text then describes the arrival of the Messiah and the conversion of the Gentiles. ... The Messiah begins by being a bull because he is a member of the human race"; Barnabas Lindars, "A Bull, a Lamb and a Word: 1 Enoch 90:38," *New Testament Studies* 22 (1976-1976): 484-85. Examples from other commentators could be multiplied; for a partial listing, see James H. Charlesworth, "From Messianology to Christology: Problems and Prospects," chapt. 1 in *The Messiah: Developments in Earliest Judaism and Christianity*, edited by James H. Charlesworth, in collaboration with J. Brownson, M. T. Davis, S. J. Kraftchick, and A. F. Segal (Minneapolis: Fortress Press, 1992), 18-19 and 19n50.

[91] Cf. VanderKam, *Enoch*, 168. Cf. also the cautions of M. de Jonge in Charlesworth, *The Old Testament Pseudepigrapha and the New Testament*, 111; and more recently the salutary comments of J. H. Charlesworth, "From Messianology to Christology," 3-35; see esp. 16-19. Unfortunately, the subhead, "From the Maccabean revolt to the establishment of the messianic [*sic*] kingdom," in Isaac's translation (Ephraim Isaac, trans. and ed., "1 [Ethiopic Apocalypse of] Enoch," in *Old Testament Pseudepigrapha*, vol. 1, edited by James H. Charlesworth [Garden City, N.Y.: Doubleday, 1983], 69) will contribute to the tendancy to read messianism into texts where it is not explicitly present.

[92] Sophie Laws, *In the Light of the Lamb: Imagery, Parody, and Theology in the Apocalypse of John* (Wilmington, Del.: M. Glazier, 1988), 27. Laws concludes that the lamb imagery is John's own creation.

Third, it is not clear that lambs appear at all in the Animal Apocalypse, since the distinction between lambs and sheep that appears in the Greek may not be original to the Aramaic.

Finally, even if we were to grant the possibility that lambs did appear in the Aramaic original of the book, it is significant that David as "lamb" (ἀρήν) became a "ram" (κριός) when he became ruler of Israel.[93] And even if the "something" or the "word" of 1En 90 *was* a lamb at an intermediate stage, it, too, had to become something else (a great beast with huge black horns) before the Lord of the sheep rejoiced over it. It is the *bull* that represents for the author the prime symbol of strength and power, not the ram, let alone the lamb.[94]

Lambs consistently represent vulnerable characters in the Animal Apocalypse. Some of these vulnerable characters turn out to be victims. It is in the changing of these characters from lambs to rams or bulls that their status is shifted from one of vulnerability and/or victimization to powerful figures of resistance—to victimizers in their own right. Thus, despite repeated appeals to the Animal Apocalypse as the source for the Lamb Christology of the Apocalypse, the text itself reveals that "lamb" was not used for or even considered appropriate as a symbol for a ruler or a powerful leader—whether eschatological or otherwise.

2.4 Psalms of Solomon 8

PsSol 8 is one of the three Psalms that allude most directly to Pompey's capture of Jerusalem in 63 BCE.[95] Pompey laid siege to the city and captured it, slaughtering many. In PsSol 8 the Psalmist rehearses the terrifying events, prayerfully laments the slaughter, and ponders the justice of God in it. Verses 1–22 consist of the Psalmist's rehearsal of the events. With v. 23, the Psalmist turns to lament, reflection, and supplication. Verse 23 reads:

> God was proven right in his condemnation of the nations of the earth,
> and the devout of God are like innocent lambs [ὡς ἀρνία ἐν ἀκακίᾳ] among
> them.

As this is one of only five places where ἀρνίον appears in certain Septuagintal traditions (apart from Isa. 40:11[Aq]), it is worthy of note. The phrase ἐν ἀκακίᾳ suggests a parallel with Jer 11:19, where Jeremiah says, "I was like a gentle lamb (ἀρνίον ἄκακον)." In both of these instances, the word ἀρνίον communicates vulnerability in the presence of a violent, superior power. In PsSol 8, that vulnerability is experienced as the people of Jerusalem experien-

---

[93] 1 Enoch 89:45-46.

[94] Bryan, *Cosmos, Chaos*, 68.

[95] The other two are 2 and 17.

ced the devastating slaughter of Pompey; in Jer 11:19, the reference is to Jeremiah himself as the undeserving recipient of violence.

3. Lambs in Rabbinic Literature

Haggadic legends about lambs reflect metaphorical traditions quite similar to the ones we find in the Hebrew Bible. We see lambs as (1) sacrifice; (2) as sources of wool for clothing and meat for food; (3) as symbols of humility and meekness; (4) as symbols of vulnerability in the presence of a superior power; and (5) as symbols of the repudiation of pagan idolatry. The last category of symbolism is an additional one that we do not see in the Old Testament.

Although most of the references to lambs as sacrifice are treated in halakic sources, occasionally a reference pops up in the haggadic legends. For instance, in describing the cult of Molech, an order is given of the perceived relative value of various sacrifices. From least to the greatest, they are: (1) fowl; (2) goat; (3) lamb; (4) calf; (5) bullock; (6) ox; and (7) human son.[96] Sometimes these categories are mixed. In several texts, the traditional animals of sacrifice are deemed appropriate for sacrifice specifically *because of their vulnerability:* "R. Judah bar Simon said in the name of R. Yose bar Nehorai: A bullock is pursued by the lion, a lamb by the wolf, a goat by the leopard. But the Holy One said: Bring no offering to Me from those who pursue, only from those who are pursued."[97] The legends also occasionally refer to lambs and goats as sources for food and clothing.[98]

One old legend about Noah appears to be designed to warn about the foolishness of drinking an excessive amount of wine. It appears to treat the lamb as a symbol of humility or meekness, though not in a positive way. According to this legend Satan found Noah planting a vineyard and offered to help. When Noah agreed, Satan slaughtered a ewe lamb, a lion, a monkey, and a pig over the vine and watered it with the blood dripping from the animals, signifying that when one drinks one cup of wine, one acts like a ewe lamb, "humble and meek"; when one drinks two, one becomes mighty as a lion and begins to

[96] Hayim Nahman Bialik, ed., *The Book of Legends [Sefer Ha-Aggadah]: Legends from the Talmud and Midrash*, edited by Yehoshua Hana Ravnitzky, translated by William G. Braude, with an introduction by David Stern (New York: Schocken Books, 1992), 515§95.

[97] Cf. Bialik, *Book of Legends*, 173§59, who cites Tanhuma B, *Emor*, 13; Tanhuma, *Pinhas*, §12; Lev.R. 27:6; cf. also Eccles 3:15. The idea that the persecuted receive the special attention of Yahweh, see b.Hul 89a; Bialik, *Book of Legends*, 335§19.

[98] b.Hul 84a; cf. Bialik, *Book of Legends*, 587§120; 610§395; cf. also Tanhuma B, *Emor*, 13; Tanhuma, *Pinhas*, §12; LevR 27:6.

brag; when one drinks three cups, one becomes like a monkey, hopping around and dancing, giggling, and uttering obscenities in public; finally, when one becomes completely drunk, one acts like a pig, wallowing in mire, and eventually one winds up sitting in garbage.[99]

We also see lambs as symbols of vulnerability in the haggadic legends. In commenting on the complaint of the Israelites against Moses in Exodus 5:21, "You ... have put a sword in their hand to kill us," R. Judah the Levite, son of R. Shallum, taught that the people said to Moses, "To what may we be compared? To a lamb that a wolf has come to snatch. Though the shepherd runs after the lamb to save it from the mouth of the wolf, the lamb, pulled this way by the shepherd and that way by the wolf, is torn apart. So, too, Israel said, 'Moses, between you and Pharaoh, we are being pulled to death.'"[100] In another legend, Israel is portrayed as a defenseless lamb in an allegory about a swineherd who stole a lamb from its owner and refused to give it back. The legend explains that the lamb owner represents "the King of Kings"; the lamb, Israel; and the swineherd, Pharaoh.[101] Similar symbolism is at work in the cemetery of Praetextatus in Rome, where a fresco dating from c. 350 CE portrays Susanna as a lamb and the two elders as wolves.

That Egyptians worshiped lambs is well-represented in rabbinic literature, a tradition known outside of Judaism.[102] We see a reference to this in Exodus 8:26: "But Moses said, 'It would not be right to do so; for the sacrifices that we offer to the LORD our God are offensive to the Egyptians. If we offer in the sight of the Egyptians sacrifices that are offensive to them, will they not stone us?'" Targum Pseudo-Jonathan Exodus 8:22[103] has, "But Moses said, 'It would not be right to do so, for we would take lambs that are idols of the Egyptians and offer (them) before the Lord our God. Behold, if we offer the idols of the Egyptians before them, behold, it would be right (for them) to stone us with stones.'"[104]

---

[99] Bialik, *Book of Legends*, 589§136.

[100] Bialik, *Book of Legends*, 65§44; cf. ExR 5:21.

[101] Bialik, *Book of Legends*, 69–70§67; cf. also ExR 20:1 and Esth.R. to 9:2, where כֶּבֶשׂ is used.

[102] Cf. Rashi on Exod. 8:22; Piska 7.9; PR 17:5; ExR 16:3; cf. also *Wisdom* 11:15-16; 12:27; SibOr 5.275–280; LetAris 135; Philo, *De Decalogo* 76–80; *De Vita Contemplativa* 8–10. For non-Jewish references to this tradition, see Herodotus, *The Persian Wars* 2.43; and Juvenal, *Satires* 15.11–12. These latter sources, however, speak in general about the worship of sheep generally (οἴς and κριός, and *lanatis animalibus*; sheep and ram, and woolly animals; respectively), not about lambs in particular.

[103] = English 8:26.

[104] Michael Maher, "Targum Pseudo-Jonathan: Exodus," in *Targum Neofiti 1: Exodus; and Targum Pseudo-Jonathan: Exodus*, Martin McNamara, gen. ed., The Aramaic Bible: The Targums (Collegeville, Minn.: Liturgical Press, 1987), 182.

Within the Jewish family, this tradition perhaps relies in part on the belief that the choice of the lamb for the Passover Festival was directly related to the Egyptians' idolatry in worshiping the lamb. According to this interpretation, the Passover Festival represents a test of loyalties and a chance to reaffirm one's allegiances: a yes to Yahweh and a no to Egyptian idolatry. [105] In commenting on Exod. 12:21, "Draw out, and take your lambs according to your families, and kill the passover lamb," R. Ḥiyya bar R. Adda of Jaffa commented, "Each of you is to draw out—that is, drag out an Egyptian's [lamb, which is his] god, and kill it before his very eyes, even as the Egyptian, in his anxiety for it, speaks up in protest."[106] Braude and Kapstein suggest that the Passover victim thus became a symbol of daring nonviolent resistance to Egyptian idolatry: "Thus the Passover lamb as well as the two lambs offered daily in the Temple were meant to remind God of an entire people's willingness to risk life for the sake of making its covenant with God, of taking Him unto itself."[107]

In at least one tradition known to Tacitus, the Pharaoh at the time of the Exodus was Bocchoris. Tacitus says, "Most authors agree that once during a plague in Egypt ... King Bocchoris approached the oracle of Ammon and ... was told to purge his kingdom and to transport this race into other lands, since it was hateful to the gods."[108] While this tradition clearly links the Exodus with contention over Egyptian animal worship, a connection between the Exodus traditions and the Lamb to Bocchoris, while intriguing, seems unlikely.

The contempt held by Jews toward Egyptian animal worship is well-attested in the rabbinic literature. There is at least some evidence that the contention went the other way. Smelik and Hemelrijk argue, for instance, that at least one of the reasons why the priests of Khnum at Elephantine collaborated in the destruction of the Jewish temple there at the end of the fifth century BCE was because of the sacrifice of rams there.[109] Tacitus thinks that the Hebrews'

---

[105] Cf. ExR 11:3; 16:3; for a discussion of this tradition, see David Stern, *Parables in Midrash: Narrative and Exegesis in Rabbinic Literature* (Cambridge, Mass., and London: Harvard University Press, 1991), 142.

[106] Pesikta de Rab Kahana 5.17, in William Gershon Zev Braude and Israel J. Kapstein, trans. and ed. *Pěsiḳta dě-Raḇ Kahăna: R. Kahana's Compilation of Discourses for Sabbaths and Festal Days* (Philadelphia: Jewish Publication Society of America, 1975), 118; cf. also Mekhilta Pisḥa 6 and 11 (on Ex 12:7 and 12:22, respectively).

[107] Braude, *Pěsiḳta dě-Raḇ Kahăna*, 119n122.

[108] Tacitus *Histories* 5.3.

[109] K. Smelik and E. Hemelrijk, "'Who Knows not What Monsters Demented Egypt Worships': Opinions on Egyptian Animal Worship in Antiquity as Part of the Ancient Conception of Egypt," in *Principat 17-4: Heidentum: römische Götterkulte, orientalische Kulte in der römischen Welt*, vol. 8 of *Aufstieg und Niedergang der römischen Welt, 2*, edited by Wolfgang Haase (Berlin: Walter de Gruyter, 1984), 1907.

motive for sacrificing rams was to deride Ammon and their motive for sacrificing bulls to deride Apis.[110]

As we have seen, Israel is often portrayed as vulnerable sheep or lambs in
the Old Testament. It is not surprising that the same is true in the rabbinic literature. In ARN 17, Rab. Natan sees Song of Songs 1:8 as suggestive of Moses' charge to Joshua: "The people I am putting in your cave are not yet goats
but only kids, not yet sheep but only lambs."[111]

In a few instances, lambs prove victorious over their more powerful traditional enemies. Although not immediately obvious, this is properly to be seen
as part of the category of vulnerability. In these instances the power of the
legend inheres in the surprise of the reversal of the traditional symbolic roles:
though vulnerable, they were not victimized. For instance, in b.BB 15b we see
the lambs of Job tending the wolves in order to attack them. In EsthR 10:11
we read, "Great is the Lamb that was able to withstand 70 wolves, great is the
shepherd of the 70 wolves before whom a Lamb was allowed to smash them
together." In Tanhuma *Toledot*, §5 we read, "Hadrian said to R. Joshua: The
lamb that stays alive among seventy wolves must be great. R. Joshua: Even
greater is the shepherd who delivers it, protects it, and destroys the wolves
around it. Hence, 'no weapon that is formed against thee shall prosper' (Isa
54:17)." The Isaiah quote shows that the overcoming of the lamb and of the
shepherd symbolizes not only the reversal of traditional fortune, but the pro-
vidence of God in caring for the vulnerable. That is, the promise of salvation
in Isaiah is not portrayed in terms of the display of military power and its
superiority, but rather as the *subversion* of military power. This subversion of
military power is in turn symbolized in rabbinic tradition as the victory of a
lamb in the midst of seventy wolves.[112]

3.1 Moses as Lamb

Traditions similar to these probably also lie behind Targum Pseudo-Jonathan
on Ex 1:15: The little lamb prevailed over an apparently unconquerable super-
power. These hero traditions are attractive not because the lamb or ram heroes

---

[110] Tacitus *Histories* 5.4.

[111] Cf. also ExR 2:2; Bialik, *Book of Legends*, 101§134–35 cf. also Yalkut, Pinhas,
§776; Sif Zuta, Pinhas §16; Yelammedenu.

[112] This legend is based on the more widely known tradition that Israel is surrounded by 70 Gentile nations. b.Yoma 69b and En Yaakov, ad loc.; p.Ber 7:3, 11c,
which attempt to redefine the greatness of God: "The greatness of His might lies precisely in His restraining His wrath and extending patience to the wicked. And these are
His awesome deeds: but for the awe of the Holy One, blessed be He, how could one
nation exist among seventy hostile nations?" Cf. also b.Suk 55b; Tanhuma B. *Pinhas*,
§14–15.

in them represent strength or power, but because they represent apparent
weakness overcoming apparent power. In other words, the power of the
legends themselves inhere in the survival and triumph of the vulnerable
through trust in God, not in the survival and triumph of the vulnerable
through the exercise of superior violent force.[113]

In a 1966 article, Klaus Koch argued that a portion of the lost book, "Jannes and Jambres," was preserved in the Targum of Pseudo-Jonathan on Ex
1:15.[114] He claimed that the tradition in question derived from this lost apocalypse. He connected this tradition with the Lamb to Bocchoris and TJos 19:8
in order to allege the existence of a tradition about a lamb that destroyed
Egypt. The passage in question reads:

> And Pharaoh said that while he was asleep, he had a dream. And in his dream
> he saw that all the land of Egypt was placed in one scale of a balance, and a
> lamb, the son of a sheep [i.e., a young sheep], was in the other scale. And the
> scale with the lamb in it outweighed the other. So he sent and called all the
> magicians of Egypt and told them his dream. Immediately Jannes and Jambres,
> the chief of the magicians, opened their mouth and answered Pharaoh, 'A
> certain child is about to be born in the congregation of Israel by whose hand
> will be the destruction of all the land of Egypt.' Therefore Pharaoh, king of
> Egypt, counseled the Hebrew midwives, the name of one of whom was Shifra,
> and the name of the other, Pu'ah, who is Miriam her daughter.[115]

Koch's article elicited two immediate responses. First, Joachim Jeremias
responded with an article entitled, "Das Lamm, das aus der Jungfrau hervorging (Test. Jos. 19,8)."[116] In this article, Jeremias is concerned neither with

---

[113] See also b.BQ 65b.

[114] Klaus Koch, "Das Lamm, das Ägypten vernichtet. Ein Fragment aus Jannes und
Jambres und sein Geschichtlicher Hintergrund," *Zeitschrift für die Neutestamentliche
Wissenschaft* 57 (1966): 79–93.

[115] Translation adapted from J. W. Etheridge, *The Targums of Onkelos and Jonathan ben Uzziel on the Pentateuch with the fragments of the Jerusalem Targum, from
the Chaldee* (New York, Ktav Publishing House, 1968), 444. The Aramaic reads:

ואמר פרעה דמך הוה חמי בחילמיה והא כל ארעא דמצרים קיימא
בכף מודנא חדא וטלייא בר בכף מודנא חדא והות כרסא כף
מודנא דטלייא בגויה מן יד שדר וקרא לכל חרשי מצרים ותני
להון ית חילמיה מן יד פתחון פוהון יניס וימברס רישי
חרשייא ואמרין לפרעה ביר חד עתיד למיהוי מתיליד
בכנישתהון דישראל דעל ידוי עתידא למחרבא כל ארעא דמצרים
ובגין איתיעט ואמר פרעה מלכא דמצרים לחייתא יהודייתא
דשמא דחדא שפרא היא ושמא דתנייתא פועה היא מרים
ברתה.

[116] Joachim Jeremias, "Das Lamm, das aus der Jungfrau hervorging (Test. Jos. 19,
8)," *Zeitschrift für die neutestamentliche Wissenschaft* 57 (1966): 216–19.

Koch's interpretation of the demotic papyrus about the Lamb to Bocchoris nor with the connection between this papyrus and Targum Pseudo-Jonathan on Ex 1:15. Rather, Jeremias's concern is whether Koch's attempt to reclaim the Testament of Joseph for Early Judaism is legitimate—whether it, in fact, witnesses to a pre-Christian lamb-redeemer tradition. Taking Koch's reading point-by-point, Jeremias argues that Christian influence best accounts for the presence of the lamb traditions found there.

In an article even more devastating for Koch's thesis, Christoph Burchard picked apart most of Koch's major points.[117] Burchard asserts that Jeremias adequately answered Koch's appeal to the Testament of Joseph. Furthermore, the tradition about Moses as a lamb is not apocalyptic nor does it derive from Jannes and Jambres. Rather, it comes from a haggadic legend like those we visited above. And the very designation, "the lamb that destroys Egypt" is an exegetical misunderstanding of the text. In short, Koch's attempts to treat the lamb tradition as apocalpytic, to connect the targum with Jannes and Jambres, and to establish a developed eschatological military Messiah-lamb in Early Judaism are all deemed to have failed.[118]

Moses did not attack Egypt. The very rhetoric of the Targum derives its power from the absurdity of a small lamb outweighing the whole land of Egypt! Thus, the force of the image supports not the existence of an alleged militant lamb-redeemer figure, but rather the irony of God's power at work through the prophetic word (cf. Sir 45:3). The Exodus account of Moses before Pharaoh is full of implications of Moses' vulnerability. It plays an essential role in the author's demonstration of Yahweh's sovereignty. Moses' own career as a warrior is cut short and treated as an embarrassing failure in Ex 2:11-15. Thereafter, it is only by the word of Yahweh that he opposes Pharaoh. Although the Exodus is the paradigmatic event for Israel's "holy war" tradition, Israel did not fight, nor did Moses. Rabbinic tradition treats the Israelites at the edge of the Red Sea as lambs, led by their shepherd Moses, being pursued by a wolf.[119] But Moses is no typical ruler or warrior figure in this role. Later tradition thought of Moses' role here as that of a prophet: "By a prophet the LORD brought Israel up from Egypt, and by a prophet he was guarded"

---

[117] C. Burchard, "Das Lamm in der Waagschale: Herkunft und Hintergrund eines haggadischen Midraschs zu Ex 1:15-22," *Zeitschrift für die neutestamentliche Wissenschaft* 57 (1966): 219–28.

[118] Most scholars have since agreed that Burchard convincingly refuted Koch's ideas; cf., e.g., Alfred Pietersma and R. T. Lutz, trans. and eds., "Jannes and Jambres," in *Old Testament Pseudepigrapha, Volume 2*, James H. Charlesworth, gen. ed. (Garden City, N.Y.: Doubleday, 1983), 432.

[119] ExR 21:8; cf. Bialik, *Book of Legends*, 73, §84. Cf. also 1En 89:21-27, which portrays the Egyptians' pursuit of the Israelites at the Exodus as wolves chasing sheep.

(Hos 12:13). Thus, Moses could hardly be seen as a prototypical warrior in Hebrew tradition.[120]

3.2 David as Lamb

In another attempt to connect a late Targum with an alleged eschatological military Messiah-lamb tradition, J. C. de Moor and E. van Stallduine-Sulman have argued that the Song of the Lamb referred to in Rev 15:2-3 is a pre-Christian tradition reflected in the Tosephta Targum on 1Sam 17:43.[121] Although "no convincing Jewish background for this glorious Lamb has been discovered,"[122] de Moor and van Stallduine-Sulman believe they have now found it in the Tosephta-Targum. In this Targum, Goliath is called a lion and a bear and David is called a lamb. "Because he [David] is a victorious lamb and because the whole poem appears to have had an extra apocalyptical dimension," de Moor and van Stallduine-Sulman claim that "it is warranted to say that this is the background of the messianic title 'Lamb' in the Book of Revelation."[123]

Further additional parallels supposedly help to establish this connection. The authors point out, for instance, that Goliath is called a lion and a bear, and Rev 13:2 says that the beast resembled a lion and a bear. Furthermore, "Goliath, the shameless sinner" (*glyt gly pnym* in Aramaic, a designation known from b.Sota 42b) has the numerical value of 666. Sixteen further considerations seem to solidify the thesis.

De Moor and van Stallduine-Sulman claim that the passage from the Tosephta-Targum, though a complete acrostic in itself, is only a fragment of what was originally a larger piece. This allows de Moor and van Stallduine-Sulman to connect the passage from the Tosephta-Targum with others from Pseudo-Philo and Targum Jonathan treating the same events reported in 1 Samuel 17. The existence of these parallels along with some philological arguments about the alleged antiquity of certain expressions in the Tosephta-Targum allow de Moor and van Stallduine-Sulman to posit a date for the Song of the Lamb early enough to have been known by the author of the Apocalypse.

---

[120] In 3En 15B, Moses, upon ascension into heaven, is threatened with attack by the hosts of heaven, but Moses is not a warrior here: he pleads for mercy. In *Peri Pascha*, Melito reflects knowledge of a tradition about the passover lamb attacking the Egyptians, but saving the Israelites with its own blood. This lamb, however, is not a figure of Moses nor is it an eschatological redeemer.

[121] J. C. de Moor and E. van Staalduine-Sulman, "The Aramaic Song of the Lamb," *Journal for the Study of Judaism* 24, no. 2 (1993): 266–79.

[122] de Moor and van Staalduine-Sulman, "The Aramaic Song of the Lamb," 267.

[123] de Moor and van Staalduine-Sulman, "The Aramaic Song of the Lamb," 273.

The thesis set forth in this article is problematic on several accounts. First, the threads between the Tosephta Targum and other known David and Goliath traditions are quite thin. Even though there are parallels between the Tosephta Targum on 1 Samuel and Pseudo-Philo, David is not treated as a lamb in Pseudo-Philo. The disparate traditions that de Moor and van Stallduine-Sulman try to thread together have little more in common than their relationship to the David and Goliath story as a whole.

Second, the Targum that actually treats David as a lamb is so late that the dating of a tradition preserved in it to a solidly pre-Apocalypse date is speculative in the extreme. Although traditions preserved in these late Targums *may* predate the Targum itself by centuries, establishing such dating requires the sort of strong independent witness that de Moor and van Stallduine-Sulman do not have in this case. The very *lack* of independent verification in this case suggests that the tradition may not be very old.

Third, in the Tosephta Targum itself, David plays quite a passive role in the scene as Yahweh intervenes on Israel's behalf. It is not even David himself who kills Goliath in the Tosephta Targum; rather "it is the word of the Lord that sends the stone of Aaron flying."[124] The depiction of David as lamb in this Targum is more akin to the vulnerability motif than it is the militaristic Messiah motif that many have attempted to recover. Thus, the role of David as lamb in the Tosephta Targum does not mesh well at all with the militant messiah-lamb tradition.

Finally, even though the Targum cannot plausibly witness to a militant messiah-lamb tradition or to a pre-Apocalypse Song of the Lamb tradition, it *does* witness to the existence of the *vulnerable* lamb tradition. Furthermore, the origin of the tradition of David as lamb can easily be explained on other grounds. Though the youngest of the sons of Jesse and busy seeing to the flock of sheep (1Sam 16:11), he is chosen by Yahweh through Samuel to be the next king of Israel and is anointed by Samuel. Though the context is not one of vulnerability in the face of danger, there is a reversal of expectations here as the youngest, the smallest, the most insignificant, הַקָּטָן (1Sam 16:11), is exalted. This theme of reversal later becomes the central theme in Psalm 151.[125]

Later stories about David associate him "with the sheep," tending the sheep (cf. 1Sam 16:19), though typically he plays the role of shepherd, even as ruler

---

[124] J. C. de Moor and E. van Staalduine-Sulman, "The Aramaic Song of the Lamb," *Journal for the Study of Judaism* 24, no. 2 (1993): 273.

[125] On the non-Masoretic psalms of David, see James A. Sanders, "Non-Masoretic Psalms," in *Angelic Liturgy, Prayers, and Psalms*, James H. Charlesworth, gen. ed., edited by Henry W. L. Rietz, The Dead Sea Scrolls: Hebrew, Aramaic and Greek texts with English translations, vol. 4 (Tübingen and Louisville, Ky.: J.C.B. Mohr (Siebeck) and Westminster John Knox Press, 1997).

(2Sam 5:2; Ps 78:70-71). However, in Psalm 23, we see a portrayal of David as a lamb or sheep: "The LORD is my shepherd, I shall not want. ..." This is clearly related to the larger tradition of Israel as sheep (cf. Pss 95:7; 100:3; Isa 40:11; Ezek 34:11-16), but the image within the Psalm is that of David as a lamb or a sheep, being led to green pastures and still waters, and being protected by the rod and staff of his Shepherd.

It is but a small step to connect this picture of David as a tender lamb with the widely known traditions about the lamb as the common victim of wild animals and to apply these images to the story about David and Goliath. We may even see a stage in this development in the supernumerary Psalms of David. The theme of Psalm 151 is the exaltation of David from insignificance among his father's flocks to the role of shepherd (151:1; cf. 1Sam 16:11), ruler (151:1, 7; cf. 2Chr 7:18), and leader (151:7; 2Sam 7:8). Psalm 151 emphasizes the smallness and the youth of David (cf. Sir 47:3-4). It also emphasizes David's former position among the flocks of his father: "I was the smallest ... and the youngest" (151:1). Furthermore, the Psalm emphasizes that David was taken from the sheep: "He ... took me from behind the flock"[126]; "He ... removed me from the sheep of my father."[127] David was a young one, a small one taken from the sheep, a lamb. If any weight at all can be placed on the Greek translation of Ethiopic Enoch, David is known there as a lamb (ἀρνός) in 1 Enoch 89:45 before being promoted as a ram. Thus there are several plausible avenues by which the tradition of David as lamb may have arisen apart from a presumedly lost apocalyptic fragment.

4. Conclusion

The foregoing analysis has yielded some important, if mostly negative, results. First, there is no evidence at this point to establish the existence of anything like a recognizable redeemer-lamb figure in the apocalyptic traditions of Early Judaism. Connection with haggadic legend is possible, though this tends to give credence to the view that the lamb imagery has more to do with the symbolism of vulnerability than to an apocalyptic redeemer figure.

The consequence of this analysis is that we must agree with Joachim Jeremias that there is simply no clear evidence for a Lamb Redeemer figure in

---

[126] According to the Hebrew of 11QPs^a 151; cf. James H. Charlesworth, trans. and ed., "More Psalms of David," in collaboration with James A. Sanders, in *Old Testament Pseudepigrapha, Volume 2*, James H. Charlesworth, gen. ed. (Garden City, N.Y.: Doubleday, 1983), 613; Sanders, "Non-Masoretic Psalms".

[127] According to the Syriac of 5ApocSyrPs 1a; Charlesworth, "More Psalms of David," 614. Cf. also 2Sam 7:8.

Early Judaism. Thus, in so far as the Lamb Christology of the Apocalypse draws upon the traditions of Early Judaism outside of the Old Testament, it does so in a general and inclusive way, rather than in specific dependence on one particular tradition.

Chapter V

Lamb Symbolism in the Old Testament and the Apocalypse

1. The Lamb and the Meaning of Symbols

In chapter two we examined the semantic domain of lamb in the Hebrew and Greek Scriptures. We maintained that the linguistic evidence has not been adequately taken into account in previous analyses of the origins and rhetorical force of the Lamb Christology within the Apocalypse. We observed that ἀρνίον is always used symbolically to communicate vulnerability in the Septuagint and that it never refers to the passover victim, the sacrificial victim, the Suffering Servant of Isaiah, or even to rams in extant Greek literature. This observation suggests that the theme of vulnerability be investigated in the Apocalypse to determine the appropriateness of this symbolic association.

However, while essential, linguistic analysis is only the beginning of the task. Semantics is more than semiotics[1] and symbol analysis more than semantics. In chapter three we suggested that an analysis of the semantic value of the Lamb in the Apocalypse requires a broader awareness of the overall cultural Gestalt of animal symbolism in the Graeco-Roman world generally. After delineating the broad parameters of that Gestalt for the figure of the lamb in chapter three, we considered in chapter four the attempt of several writers to make sense of the Lamb Christology of the Apocalypse in terms of an alleged already-existing apocalyptic militant messianic lamb figure in Early Judaism. While the existence of such a figure would have been quite promising for our understanding of the Lamb symbolism in the Apocalypse, we found that the historical evidence for such a figure in the traditions of pre-Christian Judaism was unfortunately weak to nonexistent.

Since John does not include a dialogue about who the Lamb is, or why Christ is portrayed as a lamb, it would seem that John was drawing on a trea-

---

[1] Cf. Paul Ricoeur, *The Rule of Metaphor: Multi-Disciplinary Studies of the Creation of Meaning in Language*, translated by Robert Czerny, Kathleen McLaughlin, and John Costello, University of Toronto Romance Series, no. 37 (Toronto: University of Toronto Press, 1977), 66.

sury of common understandings and traditions about lambs. As we have already seen, some of these common understandings are discernible in the archaeology, art, and literature of the ancient Near East. Lambs were widely associated with sacrifice outside of Judaism, though their role was minor in comparison to full-grown sheep, rams, and bulls. Along with rams, lambs were also associated with prophecy and with the consultation of oracles. Finally, lambs were paired with lions and especially wolves as symbols of vulnerability to a greater power. Did these associations inform the average Ephesian so that the image of the ἀρνίον in the Apocalypse would be understandable?

2. Method in Symbol Analysis

The Apocalypse of John is full of symbolic language and it uses the vehicles of metaphor, simile, symbolism, and mythological narrative to transmit and empower its rhetoric. No "translation" of the rhetoric in propositional or linear language can ever adequately recover or duplicate the rhetorical force of the book.[2] While the Apocalypse has a rhetorical power unequaled in the New Testament,[3] it also leaves readers with a dizzying array of interpretive options in response to the multivalence of the text itself, as amply witnessed by the multiplicity of readings in the history of its interpretation. If it is true that mythological thinking cannot be superseded, as Northrop Frye asserts,[4] then it would seem that no attempt to translate or limit the mythological representations of the Apocalypse in propositional language is warranted, since such "translation" is neither fully possible nor desirable. Nevertheless, if the author of the Apocalypse were to see all the various interpretations of his work that have been made over the centuries and the uses to which it has been put, I think he would be both surprised and offended.[5]

---

[2] According to Ricoeur, it was, in fact, the study of ancient rhetoric through classification and taxonomy that ironically led to the very disempowerment and subsequent decline of rhetoric. See Paul Ricoeur, "The Decline of Rhetoric: Tropology," chapt. 2 in *The Rule of Metaphor*, by Paul Ricoeur, reprint, 1975 (Toronto: University of Toronto Press, 1977), 44–64.

[3] Northrop Frye's judgment, for instance, is that the central vision of the Apocalypse is "an incredible *tour de force* singlehandedly working out the entire *dianoia* or metaphor-cluster of the Bible along with its demonic parody, an achievement ranking with the dizziest technical flights of literature" (Northrop Frye, *Words with Power: Being a Second Study of "the Bible and Literature"* [San Diego: Harcourt Brace Jovanovich, 1990], 103).

[4] Frye, *Words with Power*, xvi.

[5] For a helpful analysis of method in symbol analysis, see Ian Paul, "The Book of Revelation: Image, Symbol and Metaphor," in *Studies in the Book of Revelation*, edited by Steve Moyise (Edinburgh: T & T Clark, 2001), 131–47; see also the comments of

For all its power, metaphor is slippery. While it is a powerful and indispensable tool in communication, it is elusive and the boundaries between proper and improper associations are indistinct. Thus we may ask what sorts of limits or controls may legitimately be placed on the multivalency of the text, given the imprecision of metaphorical language itself.

Even when perfectly understood, metaphors play a variety of roles. Frye describes the slipperiness of metaphor as follows:

> "Metaphorical" is as treacherous a conception as "truth" or "reality" could ever be. Some metaphors are illuminating; some are merely indispensable; some are misleading or lead only to illusion; some are socially dangerous. ... [Metaphor] is a primitive form of awareness, established long before the distinction of subject and object become normal, but when we try to outgrow it we find that all we can really do is rehabilitate it.[6]

Similes and metaphors abound in the Apocalypse. Recent advances in metaphor theory suggest the distinction between them should not be pressed. The signals of simile—ὡς and ὅμοιος in the Greek—occur quite often.[7] These words probably represent the Semitic -פ in the mind of the author, who wrote in a particularly crude form of "biblical Greek."[8] Sometimes these words signal a simile, as in Revelation 1:10: "I heard behind me a voice, loud (lit., great: μεγάλη) as (ὡς) a trumpet," or as in 1:14: "And his head and hair were white as (ὡς) white wool, like (ὡς) snow," or 4:7: "And the first living creature was like (ὅμοιος) a lion." Sometimes they signal vague indistinction, represented by "something like" or "as if" in the English, as in 4:6: "And in front of the throne was something like (ὡς) a sea of glass, like (ὅμοιος) crystal," or 6:6: "And I heard something like (ὡς) a voice in the midst of the four living creatures," or 1:13: "And in the midst of the lampstands, something like (ὅμοιος) a son of man." Sometimes they signal additional descriptive but paradoxical information, as in Rev 5:6: "And I saw ... a lamb, standing 'as'

David L. Barr in his book, *Tales of the End* (Santa Rosa, Cal.: Polebridge Press, 1998), 6–10.

[6] Frye, *Words with Power,* xxiii.

[7] They occur 71 and 21 times respectively.

[8] See G. Mussies, "The Greek of the Book of Revelation," in *L'Apocalypse Johannique et l'Apocalyptique dans le Nouveau Testament,* edited by Jan Lambrecht, Bibliotheca Ephemeridum Theologicarum Lovaniensium, no. 53 (Leuven: Leuven University Press, 1980), 167–77, for an analysis of the language used by John. R. H. Charles also examined John's use of the Greek, noting that typical Greek constructions for which no parallel exists in the Semitic languages are rare or missing. For instance, there are no genitive absolutes in the Apocalypse (R. H. Charles, *A Critical and Exegetical Commentary on the Revelation of St. John,* Vol. 1, The International Critical Commentary [Edinburgh: T. & T. Clark, 1920], cxxxviii).

slaughtered (ὡς ἐσφαγμένον)."[9] Quite often, however, the language of meta-phor is used: "I saw seven golden lampstands" (1:12) or Rev 5:6: "And I saw ... a lamb."[10]

Occasionally we see the telltale sign of metaphor in the use of the verb "to be": "And the seven lampstands are (εἰσιν) the seven churches" (1:20). Num-erous scholars have pointed out the presence of a subversive rhetoric in the Apocalypse in which there are parodies and reversals. But this sort of rhetori-cal strategy is risky, since it can cut both ways: If apparent defeat is really vic-tory, does that mean that apparent victory is really defeat? The history of the effects of Revelation demonstrates the existence of such ambiguity clearly enough. The rhetorical ambiguity that accompanies a literary strategy charac-terized by parody and reversal can be illustrated in the following question: Does the Lamb Christology effectively subvert the Combat Myth, as Adela Yarbro Collins seemed to suggest in her dissertation,[11] or does the combat myth eventually subvert the Lamb Christology, as Yarbro Collins now sug-gests in her article on Revelation in the *Anchor Bible Dictionary*?[12] It seems to me that the only way to answer this question is through a rhetorical analysis that is sensitive to the historical and social situation, a question treated further below.

Discussions of symbolism in biblical literature have been dominated by the distinction between sign and symbol, or between "tensive" symbols and "steno" symbols. This distinction was made famous by Philip Wheelwright in his influential studies of metaphor.[13] A "steno" symbol is essentially stipula-tive or referential: once the referent is understood (i.e., identified), the "meaning" of the sign or steno symbol is exhausted and the sign itself becomes superfluous. A "tensive" symbol, however, is what Wheelwright called in his

---

[9] This should not be translated "as if," suggesting that the marks of slaughter are ambiguous. The lamb of the Apocalypse is clearly a slain lamb, but it stands, suggest-ing victory and resurrection. See G.K. Beale, *The Book of Revelation: A Commentary on the Greek Text* (New International Greek Testament Commentary; Grand Rapids: Eerdmans, 1999), 352.

[10] I am grateful here for the help provided by Dr. Beverly Gaventa in discussions on metaphor theory.

[11] Adela Yarbro Collins, *The Combat Myth in the Book of Revelation*, Harvard Dissertations in Religion, no. 9 (Missoula, Montana: Scholars Press, 1976).

[12] Adela Yarbro Collins, "Book of Revelation," in *Anchor Bible Dictionary, Volume 5 (O–Sh)*, David Noel Freedman, gen. ed. (New York: Doubleday, 1992), 694–708.

[13] Philip Wheelwright, *The Burning Fountain: A Study in the Language of Sym-bolism*, 2d ed., reprint, 1954 (Bloomington, Ind.: University of Indiana Press, 1968); Philip Wheelwright, *Metaphor and Reality*, 6th ed., reprint, 1962 (Bloomington, Ind.: University of Indiana Press, 1975).

earlier work an "expressive" or "depth symbol."[14] Such symbols are invested with associations and meanings that go beyond the mere referential. With tensive symbols there is a "stored up potential of semantic energy and significance which the symbol, when adroitly used, can tap."[15] Norman Perrin made use of Wheelwright's studies and popularized his distinction between steno and tensive symbols within biblical studies.[16]

Wheelwright's definition of symbol remains valuable. He said, "A symbol owes its symbolic character to the fact that it stands for something other than, or at least more than, what it immediately is."[17] Furthermore, symbols can be distinguished from other semantic vehicles by means of three main characteristics:[18]

[First,] the attitude to which a symbol appeals is contemplative, rather than directive or pragmatic. Thus the red light of traffic lights is not a symbol but a signal. However, it becomes a symbol in the sentence 'the atom bomb is God's red light'.

[Second,] a symbol is not a natural sign, but involves a contributing factor of human choice, whether individual or collective, conscious or unconscious. A stormy sky, therefore, is a sign and not a symbol. But thunder, which can be a natural sign (i.e., that rain shall follow) and a signal (i.e., 'seek shelter'), can be made into a symbol.

[Third,] a symbol has a certain stability which endures beyond one or a few occasions.[19]

The distinction between steno and tensive symbols is common in the literature on symbolism, though the language used varies, as do the nuances. Essentially parallel to Wheelwright's steno/tensive dichotomy is the dichotomy be-

---

[14] Compare *Metaphor and Reality*, 93–94, with *Burning Fountain*, 11–13.

[15] Wheelwright, *Metaphor and Reality*, 94.

[16] See, e.g., Norman Perrin, "Eschatology and Hermeneutics: Reflections on Method in the Interpretation of the New Testament," *Journal of Biblical Literature* 93 (March 1974): 3–14; Perrin, "Wisdom and Apocalyptic in the Message of Jesus," in *Proceedings of the Society of Biblical Literature* (Los Angeles: Society of Biblical Literature, 1972), 543–72; Norman Perrin, "The Interpretation of a Biblical Symbol," *Journal of Religion* 55 (1975): 348–70; Norman Perrin, *Jesus and the Language of the Kingdom: Symbol and Metaphor in New Testament Interpretation* (Philadelphia: Fortress, 1976).

[17] Wheelwright, *The Burning Fountain*, 7.

[18] I am indebted here to David Bryan's treatment of Wheelwright; see David Bryan, *Cosmos, Chaos and Kosher Mentality*, Journal for the Study of the Pseudepigrapha Supplement Series, no. 12 (England: Sheffield Academic Press, 1995), 28–31.

[19] Wheelwright, *The Burning Fountain*, 9–10.

tween sign and symbol that we see in such philosophers as Paul Tillich and Paul Ricoeur.[20] Northrop Frye uses the language of "sign" and "motif" to make essentially the same distinction.[21]

But how precise is this distinction, how obvious are its implications, and how appropriate is it in the analysis of ancient works? As Philip Wheelwright has noted, the primary distinction between steno and tensive symbols lies in the creative imagination invested by the author in the latter.[22] However, what this means in practice is that tensive symbols are those which, in the imagination of the *reader*, the author invested with greater-than-referential meaning. Furthermore, the distinction often entails an implicit value judgment on the creativity of the author as commentators consider whether the sort of symbolism used by this or that author is "only" steno symbolism or whether it is a more imaginative, enduring, invested "tensive" symbolism. These observations suggest that while the distinction between steno and tensive symbols has some heuristic value, how and where one makes the distinction may—and usually does—say as much about the reader as it does about the text or the author.

The imprecision of the "steno" and "tensive" categories can be illustrated by Norman Perrin's use of the distinction and the slight difference of opinion between Patrick Tiller and David Bryan about whether the symbolism of Enoch's Animal Apocalypse is a steno or tensive symbolism. In a 1974 article on the methodology of symbol analysis for the study of the kingdom of God in apocalyptic literature, Perrin[23] painted the symbolism of "Jewish apocalyptic" in broad strokes as flat, referential "steno-symbols" that "bore a one-to-one relationship to that which is depicted."[24] When challenged on his rather facile and flat reading of apocalypses, Perrin was forced to modify his approach. In *Jesus and the Language of the Kingdom*, Perrin says:

> It now seems to me that I have pressed too hard the distinction between a 'steno-' and a 'tensive' symbol in the case of apocalyptic symbols. It is still a

---

[20] Cf. Paul Ricoeur, *The Symbolism of Evil*, translated by Emerson Buchanan (Boston: Beacon Press, 1969), 15; Paul Tillich, *Dynamics of Faith* (New York: Harper & Brothers, 1957), 41–42.

[21] Northrop Frye, *Anatomy of Criticism: Four Essays* (Princeton: Princeton University Press, 1971), 73.

[22] Wheelwright, *The Burning Fountain*, 32.

[23] For an analysis of Perrin's treatment of the literature of Early Judaism, see James H. Charlesworth, "The Historical Jesus in Light of Writings Contemporaneous with Him," edited by W. Haase, *Aufstieg und Niedergang der Römischen Welt:* Principat, no. 25 (1982), 451–76; see also Calvin R. Mercer, *Norman Perrin's Interpretation of the New Testament: From "Exegetical Method" to "Hermeneutical Process,"* Studies in American Biblical Hermeneutics, no. 2 (Macon, Ga.: Mercer University Press, 1986), 83–89.

[24] Perrin, "Eschatology and Hermeneutics," 11.

most important distinction, and it is still true that most apocalyptic symbols are steno-symbols. But it is also true that the distinction is not hard and fast, and that ... some seers no doubt saw the symbols as steno-symbols while others saw them as tensive.[25]

The proper implication of the above, according to Perrin, is that "we have to investigate each case on its merits."[26]

Patrick Tiller's commentary on the Animal Apocalypse is significant for its attention to the referentialism of the text. He calls the Animal Apocalypse an "allegory" and works hard at identifying each of its animal symbols in terms of its referent. He can tell, for instance, that *ravens* in the Animal Apocalypse refers to the Seleucids. Tiller's approach is not narrowly referential; in chapter three Tiller considers the "inner or metaphysical meaning of the history that it represents." However, perhaps because historical interests are central for Tiller, he says that while "the allegorical language of the *Animal Apocalypse* is not strictly steno-language, ... it does seem to lean in that direction."[27] This should not be seen as a negative judgment about the writing. As David Flusser adds, "The allegory [inscribed in the Animal Apocalypse] is mostly external and clumsy, but this is why its content can be easily revealed."[28]

The central contribution of David Bryan's analysis of the Animal Apocalypse lies in his insight that all of the animals in the Animal Apocalypse that symbolize foreign nations are *unclean* animals, whereas the Israelites are always portrayed by way of *clean* animals. This, along with other observations, supports Bryan's thesis that a "kosher mentality" lies behind the symbolism of this Enochic apocalypse. Close analysis demonstrates even further distinctions in the semantic value of the individual animals as well as in their colors.

M. Eugene Boring's discussion of symbolic and mythological language in the Apocalypse is helpful,[29] though like the early Perrin, he presses the distinction too far. He contrasts the "pictorial" language of the Apocalypse, which requires one set of interpreting strategies, with the "propositional" language of the Apocalypse.[30] Admitting that the Apocalypse contains both types of com-

---

[25] Perrin, *Jesus and the Language of the Kingdom*, 31. Perrin clearly saw the steno/tensive categories as an either/or matter.

[26] Perrin, *Jesus and the Language of the Kingdom*, 31.

[27] Patrick A. Tiller, *A Commentary on the Animal Apocalypse of I Enoch*, Early Judaism and Its Literature, no. 4 (Atlanta, Ga.: Scholars Press, 1993), 26.

[28] "Vision of Seventy Shepherds," *Encyclopaedia Judaica* (1971–72) 14:1199.

[29] See M. Eugene Boring, *Revelation*, Interpretation: A Bible Commentary for Teaching and Preaching (Louisville: John Knox, 1989), 51–59.

[30] Adela Yarbro Collins makes a similar distinction, using the categories "informational" vs. "expressive"; see Adela Yarbro Collins, "Reading the Book of Revelation in the Twentieth Century," *Interpretation* 40, no. 3 (July 1986): 234–35. This distinction is simply a variation on "steno" and "tensive" symbols.

munication, he maintains that recognizing the difference is essential to proper interpretation.

> To a degree greater than other apocalyptic texts, the language of Revelation is visionary language that deals in pictures rather than propositions. Pictures themselves are important to John as the vehicle of his message. They are not mere illustrations of something that can be said more directly. A picture makes its own statement, is its own text. ... [Thus,] language about the picture can never replace the message communicated in and through the picture itself.[31]

Unfortunately, in Boring's eagerness to put to rest the reading strategy of American dispensationalists, he goes too far. It is a disservice to the text itself to imply that *all* referential interpretation is a misreading of the Apocalypse, for two reasons. First, not all referential readings claim to exhaust the meaning of the text. That is, identifying a referent does not suggest that the symbol, once "decoded," has lost its potential to communicate and can therefore be discarded.[32] Second, the Apocalypse itself seems to invite some referentialism. Thus, we read that "the seven stars 'are' the angels of the seven churches, and the seven lampstands 'are' the seven churches" (1:20). This explanation serves as a somewhat pedantic, steno-symbol-like decoding of a symbol. And "the lake that burns with fire and sulfur ... 'is' the second death" (21:8).[33] At places the text of the Apocalypse itself even seems to call for some "decoding": "This calls for wisdom: let anyone with understanding calculate the number of the beast, for it is the number of a person. Its number is six hundred sixty-six" (13:18).[34] Such an injunction clearly calls for an interpretation of a symbol that is steno.

Nevertheless, Boring is right to challenge the erroneous assumption that all of Revelation's symbols invite the reader to decode them by identifying the referent. The rhetoric of Revelation's symbolic language is more complex than that. In one sense, the author intended his rhetoric to *resist* full decoding. If, for instance, the central burden of the seer was to challenge the idolatry of the

---

[31] Boring, *Revelation*, 52. See also Jörg Frey, "Die Bildersprache der Johannes-apokalypse," *Zeitschrift für Theologie und Kirche* 98 (2001): 161–85.

[32] See the methodological reflections of Ian Paul for a similar critique of Boring. Ian Paul, "The Book of Revelation."

[33] Other examples include, "[the] seven flaming torches ... are the seven spirits of God" (4:5); the "seven eyes [of the Lamb] ... are the seven spirits of God sent out into all the earth" (5:6); and the "golden bowls full of incense ... are the prayers of the saints" (5:8).

[34] Elisabeth Schüssler Fiorenza denies that this is a call to decode. She says, "The number 666 is a polysemous symbol that defies referential analysis" (*Revelation: Vision of a Just World*, 18). She bases this judgment in part on the lack of consensus scholarship has enjoyed regarding the decoding of this symbol.

seven churches expressed through their assimilation to Graeco-Roman society, then it is indeed ironic that modern readers thoroughly assimilated to what Walter Wink calls the "Domination System"[35] mine the Apocalypse for clues that will allow them to manipulate that system for their own escape.

Thus, even if the seven lampstands "are" the seven churches, simply "identifying" them as such reveals only a part of the image's capacity to communicate. And to say that the Lamb in Revelation "is" Jesus does little justice to *its* capacity to communicate, as it is with identifying the λόγος of the prologue of the Fourth Gospel as Jesus. These "identifications" may be accurate, but they do not fully mine the meaning capacity of the symbols. In other words, symbol analysis must move beyond mere "identification" and/or source criticism to ask about the nature, function, power, imaginative force, and effect of the symbolic system being constructed in the text.[36]

Thus it is not enough simply to identify a symbol's tradition history, nor to define its role within literature by reducing it to an "essence," nor simply to identify its referent. The exegete of the Apocalypse is not one who strives to crack a code. Certain distinctions can actually be quite misleading. As Robert Funk has argued, in interpreting Revelation's symbols, one must be aware that "literal" and "figurative" are false alternatives, since "'figurative' language can be interpreted with a kind of pedestrian literal-mindedness."[37]

Rather, one must, in Elisabeth Schüssler Fiorenza's words,

> trace [a symbol's] position within the overall form-content configuration (*Gestalt*) of Rev. and see its relationships to other images and within the 'strategic' positions of the composition. ... Only a 'proportional' analysis of its images can determine what they are about within the structure of the work determining the phase of action in which they are invoked.[38]

Elisabeth Schüssler Fiorenza describes her rhetorical method further in *Revelation: Vision of a Just World*. Her aim, she says, is "to analyze how biblical texts and interpretations participate in creating or sustaining oppressive or liberating theo-ethical values and sociopolitical practices."[39]

---

[35] Walter Wink, *Engaging the Powers: Discernment and Resistance in a World of Domination*, The Powers, vol. 3 (Philadelphia: Fortress, 1992), 13–104.

[36] See Tiller, *Animal Apocalypse*, 13; Paul A. Porter, *Metaphors and Monsters: A Literary-Critical Study of Daniel 7 and 8*, Coniectanea biblica, Old Testament, no. 20 (Uppsala: Gleerup, 1983), 43–60.

[37] Boring, *Revelation*, 51, and Robert W. Funk, "Myth and Literal Non-Literal," in *Parables and Presence* (Philadelphia: Fortress Press, 1982), 111–38.

[38] Elisabeth Schüssler Fiorenza, *The Book of Revelation: Justice and Judgment* (Philadelphia: Fortress, 1985), 188.

[39] Elisabeth Schüssler Fiorenza, *Revelation: Vision of a Just World*, Proclamation Commentaries (Minneapolis: Fortress, 1991), 3.

> The reconceptualization of biblical studies in rhetorical rather than just her-
> meneutical terms provides a research framework not only for integrating his-
> torical, archaeological, sociological, literary, and theological approaches as
> perspectival readings of Revelation but also for raising sociopolitical and theo-
> ethical questions as constitutive questions for the interpretive process. Rhetori-
> cal interpretation does not assume that the text of Revelation is a window to
> historical reality ... but sees it as a perspectival discourse constructing its own
> worlds and symbolic universe.[40]

The above discussion has several implications. First, some explicit interpretation is necessary. Some of John's images *should* be "decoded" in the
sense of identifying a specific counterpart in the churches' historical framework. John wrote to real churches and real hearers in the province of Asia in
the first century and it should surprise no one that he communicated to and
within his social-historical situation. Second, such identification must not be
seen as exhausting the meaning capacity of a symbol. To identify Babylon as
Rome is not to exhaust the power of the signifier *Babylon*; rather, it points to
three signifiers: to the biblical Babylon, to Rome, and to the history of salvation—indeed, to the relationship among all three. And contra Lohmeyer,
recognizing the power and theological insight of the signifier does not require
denying the historical specificity of its immediate referent.

Third, we should be aware of the implications of the two-millennium distance between the writing and our reading of the Apocalypse. This distance
predisposes those modern readers who are trained in the historical-critical
method to look at the symbol in the text and inquire about the historical referent. Such a procedure requires the reader to see the text as a window to the
world behind the text so that the world *behind* the text can in turn illuminate
the world *within* the text—a procedure that inevitably entails some circularity.
But even beyond the problems of circularity, such a reading strategy distances
the reader from the rhetorical force of the writing. The author of the Apocalypse *assumes* the historical and social knowledge we require for full exegesis;
its rhetorical power lies elsewhere. For example, twentieth-century scholars
have expended enormous energies in trying to match the seven kings of Rev
17:10 with the Roman emperors in the first century CE. The payoff for such a
pursuit is that if we knew for sure who the seventh and eighth kings were, we
could more easily place the Apocalypse in its proper historical setting and understand its rhetoric in light of it. However, the subtle danger of this pursuit is
that the historical pursuit subtly robs the Apocalyspe of its rhetorical power to
communicate. We take our eyes off the text to consider the history behind the
text. As Eugene Boring aptly puts it, John's "hearer-readers needed no help in
identifying *who* the contemporary rulers were; John wanted to expose them for

---

[40] Fiorenza, *Revelation*, 3.

what they were—agents and embodiments of the transcendent powers of evil."[41] Thus, while "identifying" the first beast with the Roman emperor and the second beast with the imperial cult is probably correct, it is incomplete. The more profound claim of the Apocalypse is that the emperor and its imperial cult are really *beasts* opposed to the purposes of God.

Fourth, we should avoid setting up false hermeneutical alternatives: Should Revelation be interpreted as speaking only to the immediate social-historical situation of the churches in the first century (often called the preterist position) or does it speak more broadly in theological terms (sometimes called the idealist approach)?[42] Although a "mixed" historical-theological hermeneutic has long been applied to the Pauline corpus, the fact that historical categories are part of the *content* of the revelatory vision of the Apocalypse make it more difficult to mix these approaches here, though it is legitimate and necessary to do so. Fortunately, recent investigations of the apocalyptic genre that recognize the subcategory of historical apocalypses have helped to liberate scholarship from such false alternatives.

Patrick Tiller's symbol analysis of the Animal Apocalypse reveals some of the problems that can derive from an unwarranted dichotomy between "truth" and historical referentiality. Tiller distinguishes between two levels of the story within the Animal Apocalypse:

> the surface story about cattle, the sheep and their keepers, and the predatory animals; and the real story, the referent of the surface story, which is the history of humanity as seen in the 'true' light of divine and angelic activity. What is said on the surface level is clearly a fiction but can be understood to be true on the referential level.[43]

However, it may be that the truth the author wishes to communicate has more to do with the symbols living in the surface story than with the so-called real story of history. If that is the case, one ought to distinguish *three* levels of meaning: (1) the historical referent behind the surface story, which is history and only history; it can be described in more or less "accurate" ways, but never in a "true" way; (2) the surface story, which is a creation of the writer and the vehicle of communication; and (3) the "meaning" of the story, which is a recreation of the reader within the limits of plausibility provided by the text. It is the task of the interpreter to "re-create" meaning from the story. This "recreation" of meaning—if it is to be "faithful"—cannot be an *ex nihilo* crea-

---

[41] Boring, *Revelation*, 151–52.

[42] Lohmeyer represents, perhaps, the classical example of this approach; see Ernst Lohmeyer, *Die Offenbarung des Johannes*, 6th ed., reprint, 1926, Handbuch zum neuen Testament, no. 16 (Tübingen: J.C.B. Mohr, 1953).

[43] Tiller, *Animal Apocalypse*, 22.

tion; rather it must emerge from the intentionality the author poured into the text. The result is a conversation with the social-historical situations of both the author and the reader.

There are serious problems with the Apocalypse when read retrospectively on the referential level. Jesus did *not* quickly return and the New Jerusalem did *not* soon descend from heaven, as John seems to have expected. This issue of the "delay of the parousia" is interpreted variously by contemporary readers.[44] If it is indeed a misstep, as I think an honest reading suggests, the credibility of the implied author must suffer some damage. Nevertheless, for many readers the Apocalypse has real theological insight and a relevant and welcome power to sustain nonviolent resistance for those who understand human existence in terms of a cosmological conflict. The proof is in the power of the reading for the community of readers. When the Apocalypse reveals the truth of God's involvement in the affairs of humanity in such a way that it rings true in human experience and empowers human faithfulness, its truth needs no further demonstration.

Comparatively speaking, the Apocalypse of John is richer in symbolism than most of the other Jewish and Christian apocalypses. There are signs in the Apocalypse that the author—or perhaps second-century scribes[45]—even obscured the referential in order to create a revelation that speaks more

---

[44] M. Eugene Boring has written an excellent critique of various commentators' attempts to deal with the obvious problem of the error of this expectation. Some try to explain that *end* really does not mean *end*, while others that *soon* really does not mean *soon*; see M. Eugene Boring, "Revelation 19–21: End Without Closure," *Princeton Seminary Bulletin* (1994), Supplementary Issue, no. 3. However, one of the more satisfying arguments that "nearness" is itself part of the author's rhetorical strategy—and is theologically appropriate despite the historical problems—is that of Richard Bauckham, "The Delay of the Parousia," *Tyndale Bulletin* 31 (1980): 3–36; cf. also Richard Bauckham, *The Theology of the Book of Revelation*, New Testament Theology (Cambridge and New York: Cambridge University Press, 1993), 157–59. On a similar note, see David L. Barr, "Waiting for the End that Never Comes: The Narrative Logic of John's Story," in *Studies in the Book of Revelation*, edited by Steve Moyise (Edinburgh: T & T Clark, 2001), 101–12.

[45] Although this phenomenon is notoriously difficult to track, given our lack of evidence, there are signs that scribes were affected by contemporary theological controversies in their transmission of the text; see Bart D. Ehrman, *The Orthodox Corruption of Scripture: The Effect of Early Christological Controversies on the Text of the New Testament* (Oxford: Oxford University Press, 1993). Though not demonstrable, it is reasonable to suggest that the struggles with Marcionism and Montanism in the second and third centuries CE may have affected the transmission of the text of the Apocalypse in ways no longer recoverable. If such tampering with the text occurred, it would most reasonably have been in the direction of softening or removing that which was most clearly referential within first-century history.

broadly and profoundly. He was certainly conscious of recording spiritual insights that spoke both pointedly and generally from the authority of God. The over-used phrase "only symbolic" is nonsensical. Historically, the rhetoric of symbolism has motivated people more powerfully than any other mode of discourse. Even allegories play an important, but often demeaned, role in communication. As Angus Fletcher has said, "Allegories are far less often the dull systems that they are reputed to be than they are symbolic power struggles."[46]

If Schüssler Fiorenza's rhetorical approach is warranted, and I believe it is, the key questions for our study become, What kind of symbolic universe does the Lamb Christology help to construct? What does the Lamb Christology *do* within that symbolic universe? What kind of effects does the discourse of the Apocalypse produce and how does it produce them? What plausibility structures, derived from the literary context as well as the social-historical context, provide the most compelling framework in which to understand the Lamb Christology of the Apocalypse?

3. The Social-Historical Setting of the Apocalypse

Reconstruction of the social-historical context of the seven churches of the Apocalypse is a complex and difficult task. Volumes have been written in the attempt to recover this context and its implications for the interpretation of the Apocalypse. While this topic is not the focus of this research, some understanding of this context is essential for the development of a Gestalt for the Lamb Christology, since the attractiveness of such a construction depends at least in part on how compelling or plausible it is within that historical context. Our discussion will touch on only the highlights in this complicated but fascinating discussion.

In the last fifty years, discussions of the historical situation of the Apocalypse were dominated by the issue of whether there was a Domitianic persecution of the church in last decade of the first century CE.[47] Even as scholars of

---

[46] Angus Fletcher, *Allegory: The Theory of a Symbolic Mode* (Ithaca, N.Y.: Cornell Paperbacks, 1970), 22.

[47] See especially Donald McFayden, "The Occasion of the Domitianic Persecution," *The American Journal of Theology* 24 (1920): 46–66; R. L. P. Milburn, "The Persecution of Domitian," *Church Quarterly Review* 278 (January–March 1945): 154–64; E. Mary Smallwood, "Domitian's Attitude Toward the Jews and Judaism," *Classical Philology* 51 (1956): 1–13; Barclay Newman, "The Fallacy of the Domitian Hypothesis: A Critique of the Irenaeus Source as a Witness for the Contemporary Historical Approach to the Interpretation of the Apocalypse," *New Testament Studies* 10, no. 1 (1963): 133–39; L. W. Barnard, "Clement of Rome and the Persecution of Domitian," *New Testament Studies* 10 (1964): 251–60; Fergus Millar, "The Imperial Cult and the

Roman history had long assumed that there was no massive persecution under Domitian, previous generations of biblical scholars had taken it for granted. In keeping the Domitianic persecution thesis alive, these biblical scholars drew largely on the language of the Apocalypse itself, which is full of allusions to persecution and martyrdom, and partly on fragmentary evidence in the patristics about the cruelty of Domitian.[48] A typical expression of the scholarly consensus is the following quotation from Martin Rist: "It is obvious that Revelation was written in a time when the Christians of Asia Minor ... were being persecuted by Roman officials for their refusal to worship the emperors."[49]

Today, however, it is a commonplace in Revelation scholarship that the Domitianic persecution is a fallacy. The debate is now characterized more by the question about how best to articulate the nature of the rhetoric of the Apocalypse given the *absence* of a Domitianic persecution. We see this debate, for instance, in Leonard Thompson's "no crisis" position[50] vs. Adela Yarbro Collins' "perceived crisis" position,[51] both of whom agree that there was no persecution of the church under Domitian.

Persecutions," in *Le Culte Des Souverains dans l'Empire Romain*, edited by W. den Boer, Foundation Hardt pour l'Étude de l'Antiquité Classique (Geneva: Vandoeuvres, 1972), 145–75; Pierre Prigent, "Au Temps de l'Apocalypse, 1: Domitien (A Suivre)," *Revue d'Histoire et de Philosophie Religieuses* 54, no. 4 (1974): 455–83; Savas Agourides, "The Character of the Early Persecutions of the Church," in *Orthodox Theology and Diakonia*, edited by D. Constantelos (Brookline, Mass.: Hellenic College Press, 1981), 117–43. Of these treatments, the analysis of Prigent seems the most thorough and balanced.

[48] Note especially Eusebius, *The Ecclesiastical History, Volume 1*, translated and edited by Kirsopp Lake, Loeb Classical Library (Cambridge, Mass.: Harvard University Press, 1980), 3.17–20; cf. also Tertullian, *Apology* 5. I quite agree with Milburn that the appeals of Barnard and others to 1 Clement 1.1 and 7.1 as evidence of a Domitianic persecution are misguided (see note 120 above). According to Eusebius, Melito of Sardis, writing around 165 CE, said, "The only emperors who were ever persuaded by malicious men to slander our teaching were Nero and Domitian"; Eusebius, *Ecclesiastical History*, 4.26.9. And while the correspondence between Pliny the Younger and Trajan does not constitute evidence of a Domitianic persecution, it does lend credence to the hypothesis of local episodic persecutions based on allegiance to the imperial cult; see Pliny, *Epistle* 10.96–97.

[49] Martin Rist, "The Revelation of St. John the Divine," in *Interpreter's Bible, Volume 12*, George Arthur Buttrick, gen. ed. (New York: Abingdon Press, 1957), 354.

[50] Leonard L. Thompson, *The Book of Revelation: Apocalypse and Empire* (New York, Oxford: Oxford University Press, 1990).

[51] Adela Yarbro Collins, *Crisis and Catharsis: The Power of the Apocalypse* (Philadelphia: Westminster Press, 1984).

What does the text of the Apocalypse itself say? We have already mentioned its many allusions to persecution and martyrdom. However, a closer examination shows that the evidence is not as clear as one might think. Only a few passages in the Apocalypse refer to a *past* or *present* experience of persecution. Adela Yarbro Collins identifies three:[52] In 1:9 John says, "I, John, your brother and partner in the suffering and kingdom and patient endurance (ὑπομονή) in Jesus, was on the island called Patmos on account of the word of God and the testimony of Jesus." Second, in 2:13 the word to Pergamum is, "I know where you live, where Satan's throne is, and that you are holding on to my name and have not denied your faith in me, even in the days of Antipas, my faithful witness, who was killed among you, where Satan lives." Third, in 6:9-11 the souls under the altar cry out, "How long, O Master, holy and true, will you not judge and avenge our blood on those who dwell on the earth?"

All other references to persecution in the Apocalypse suggest the *expectation* of persecution rather than the present *experience* of persecution (cf. 2:10-11; 7:13-14; 11:7-9; 12:11; 16:6; 17:6; 18:24; 19:2; 20:4-6). Even those passages that have sometimes been seen as clear indications of a present crisis are suspect. For instance, In 2:13 the author says, ἐν ταῖς ἡμέραις Ἀντιπᾶς ... (*in the days* of Antipas ...), suggesting that the martyrdom of Antipas was in the distant past, no longer part of the present reality of the implied audience. And the references in 6:9-11 and 20:4 can as plausibly be explained as visions of anticipated persecution like that in 7:13-14 or as generalized references to the sort of persecutions the faithful have always experienced (cf. 16:6).

Some scholars have attempted to show that the reference in 1:9 is not a reference to persecution. Several have pointed out that no Roman evidence exists to support the idea that Patmos was a penal colony. Although R. H. Charles cited Pliny's *Natural History* 4.12.23 in evidence that it was a penal colony,[53] Pliny's identification is actually of the islands *neighboring* Patmos. Barclay Newman has suggested that John's was not really an exile; it was more like "protective custody."[54] Leonard Thompson has suggested that John was on Patmos simply because he wanted to preach there.[55]

Nevertheless, these attempts to deny that Rev 1:9 refers to a situation of real and present persecution are misguided. Patristic evidence, while admit-

---

[52] Collins, Adela Yarbro, *Crisis and Catharsis*, 70–71.

[53] See R. H. Charles, *A Critical and Exegetical Commentary on the Revelation of St. John*, Vol. 1, The International Critical Commentary (Edinburgh: T. & T. Clark, 1920), 22; cf. also *Natural History* 4.12.69.

[54] Newman, "The Fallacy of the Domitian Hypothesis: A Critique of the Irenaeus Source as a Witness for the Contemporary Historical Approach to the Interpretation of the Apocalypse," 138.

[55] Thompson, *The Book of Revelation*, 173.

tedly of limited value, suggests that John was exiled to Patmos because of his Christian prophetic activities.[56] More importantly, the most natural reading of the language of the text itself, with John's statement that he is the reader/hearers' "brother" and "partner in suffering and consistent resistance" (1:9),[57] is that John was banished to Patmos because of his prophetic activities.[58]

Several scholars have recently renewed an old suggestion that the Apocalypse should be dated a generation earlier.[59] This would presumably allow readers to revive the persecution thesis, applied this time to Nero. However, the arguments advanced by Adela Yarbro Collins for a late (Domitianic) dating are compelling.[60] Furthermore, Nero's persecution, though intense, was localized. It is highly unlikely that it reached to the provinces in Asia Minor. Thus, even if the earlier dating of the Apocalypse were to be accepted, it would do little to clarify the persecution and martyrdom rhetoric of the Apocalypse.

Recent reevaluations of the evidence suggest that the persecution theory should not yet be put to bed. Most discussions of the Domitianic persecution assume that if there was persecution of the church during the reign of Domitian and if it was related to the emperor cult, then it had to have come from the top down. Thus the "Domitian fallacy" consisted at least in part in the faulty assumption that if there was a persecution of the church under Domitian, *he* must have initiated it. But recent dissertations by P. Duane Warden[61] on 1 Peter and Steven J. Friesen[62] on the imperial cult in Ephesus have shown

---

[56] This patristic evidence includes Clement of Alexandria's reference to John's stay on Patmos during the reign of the "tyrant" Domitian in *Who Is the Rich Man that Shall Be Saved?* 42. In *De praescriptione haereticorum* 36, Tertullian says that John was "in insulam relegatur."

[57] "Consistent resistance" is Elisabeth Schüssler Fiorenza's apt translation of ὑπομονή; Fiorenza, *The Book of Revelation: Justice and Judgment*, 4, 182.

[58] See the arguments of Charles, *Commentary on Revelation*, 21–22, which I still find compelling.

[59] See, e.g., Christopher Rowland, *The Open Heaven: A Study of Apocalyptic in Judaism and Early Christianity* (New York: Crossroad, 1982), esp. 413; Gentry, Kenneth L., *Before Jerusalem Fell: Dating the Book of Revelation: An Exegetical and Historical Argument for a Pre-A.D. 70 Composition* (Tyler, Texas: Institute for Christian Economics, 1989); J. Christian Wilson, "The Problem of the Domitianic Date of Revelation," *New Testament Studies* 39 (1993): 587–605.

[60] See Adela Yarbro Collins, "Dating the Apocalypse of John," *Biblical Research* 26 (1981): 33–45. See also Collins, Adela Yarbro, *Crisis and Catharsis*, chapt. 2.

[61] Preston Duane Warden, *Alienation and Community in 1 Peter (Asia Minor, Anatolia)*, Ph.D. dissertation (Duke University, 1986).

[62] Steven J. Friesen, *Twice Neokoros: Ephesus, Asia and the Cult of the Flavian Imperial Family*, Religions in the Graeco-Roman World, vol. 116 (Leiden and New York: E.J. Brill, 1993).

that the impetus for the persecution of Christians came more from local municipalities than from Rome. And while rejecting the traditional "Domitianic persecution" thesis in his dissertation on *Imperial Cult and Commerce in John's Apocalypse*, J. Nelson Kraybill concludes that "it is likely that John wrote Revelation during some episode of *local* persecution."[63]

There is little question that the province of Asia was the world leader in the imperial cult. The imperial cult certainly had precursors in the tradition of the divinity of the pharaohs and spread through Alexander the Great throughout the whole Western world. However, in an important sense, Asia was the initiator and propeller of the imperial cult. Asia was the first province to initiate an emperor cult and the only Roman province at the end of the first century CE to have more than one temple dedicated to the worship of the emperor.

Mark Antony wintered in Ephesus in 32–31 BCE before being defeated by Octavian at Actium in 31. If the leading families of Asia were embarrassed by their obvious preference for Mark Antony and Cleopatra at this time, they may well have initiated the imperial cult to get back into Octavian's good graces. In 29 BCE Pergamum succeeded in starting an imperial cult dedicated to Octavian, just two years before he took on the title of Augustus. Octavian approved of the cult with the proviso that it also be dedicated to Roma. There was a certain reluctance to approve of emperor cults on the part of the Senate and the emperors themselves were expected to treat the cult delicately: it was a matter of imperial etiquette, even though the occasional emperor lacked this restraint.[64]

In 23 CE, provincial leaders in Asia requested permission from Tiberius to establish another imperial cult. Showing at least some restraint, Tiberius agreed to this as long as Livia and the Senate were included in the honors. This report by Tacitus might be held suspect, since the combination of Tiberius, Livia, and the Senate is an odd one, but it has been confirmed by the discovery of coins depicting these three in Asia Minor. Nevertheless, Tiberius was criticized by the Senate for approving this and he apparently approved of no more during his reign.

Although the approval had been given, it was not yet decided *where* this cult should be established. So in 26 CE, representatives from eleven cities in

---

[63] J. Nelson Kraybill, *Imperial Cult and Commerce in John's Apocalypse*, Journal for the Study of the New Testament Supplement Series, no. 132 (Sheffield: Sheffield Academic Press, 1996), 198, but cf. also 34–38, emphasis mine.

[64] Examples would include Gaius Caligula and Nero, both of whom found their legacies struck down by the Senate through the *damnatio memoriae*. Gaius initiated an imperial cult at Miletus in 40 CE and built a temple there without Senate approval, but this cult quickly dissipated at his death.

Asia went to a hearing in the Senate to argue their case.[65] The imperial cult would not only be a great honor to the locality that was awarded the privilege of hosting it, it would be an economic stimulus for the city as well.[66] Laodicea was quickly eliminated because it was too small and historically insignificant. Sardis almost got it, but Smyrna won out.

Tacitus's account of the establishment of Smyrna's imperial cult shows how cities competed for the honor of having an imperial cult. It also suggests that in the first century CE, the imperial cult was driven more by local, provincial interests than by imperial decrees. And this drive likely had as much or more to do with political and economic benefits than it did with any pious or "theological" commitments to the emperor himself.

Sometime in the early 80s, leaders in Asia won approval from Rome to establish yet a third imperial cult within its borders, even though no other province had more than one. This emperor cult, dedicated generally to the Sebastoi, or the Flavians, would round out the province's cult, since the first two temples were dedicated to Julio-Claudian emperors. The building of the temple took several years. According to Suetonius, Domitian introduced in 86 the demand that he be referred to as *dominus et deus noster* (our lord and God).[67] At this the Senate rebelled and a secret international plot to remove Domitian was instigated. But Domitian soon discovered it and in 87 and 88 executed anyone suspected of being involved. While the temple in Ephesus was being built in 88 CE, Civica Cerealis, the proconsul for Asia, was executed by Domitian on the grounds that he was involved in the treasonous plot threatening the emperor.[68]

---

[65] Tacitus, *The Annals of Imperial Rome*, trans and introd by Michael Grant, Penguin Classics (London and New York: Penguin Books, 1979), 4.55–56.

[66] See Friesen, *Twice Neokoros: Ephesus, Asia and the Cult of the Flavian Imperial Family*, chapt. 6.

[67] See Suetonius, "Domitian," in *The Lives of the Caesars*, Loeb Classical Library (Cambridge and London: Harvard University Press and William Heinemann Ltd, 1929), 13.2; see also Martial, *Epigrammaton liber* 9.56.3; Dio Cassius, *Epitome* 67.14. Some scholars accept the historicity of this claim, but some dispute it. For the arguments of those who dispute it, see, e.g., Leonard L. Thompson, *Book of Revelation*, 105–07; Adela Yarbro Collins, *Crisis and Catharsis*, 71–72; J. Nelson Kraybill, *Imperial Cult and Commerce in John's Apocalypse*, Journal for the Study of the New Testament Supplement Series, no. 132 (Sheffield: Sheffield Academic Press, 1996), 35–36. I consider the arguments against its historicity to be weak. The more important historical issue concerns the scope, significance, and implications of this demand. What is *not* clear historically is that Domitian ever applied this demand systematically or that he used it to impel the emperor cult. It is more likely that the demand was an occasional and idiosyncratic one without serious social repercussions.

[68] Suetonius, *Domitian* 10.2. Cf. also Ethelbert Stauffer, *Christ and the Caesars* (Philadelphia: Westminster, 1955), 160.

While leading families may secretly have supported Cerealis in his "treason," his exposure and execution were no doubt an embarrassment to Asia. Whether in an effort to restore Domitian's favor or out of civic duty or out of economic interests, many of the cities in Asia dedicated and sent statues for the occasion of the opening of this cult in the subsequent years. From his analysis of the inscriptional evidence found in Ephesus, Steve Friesen has discovered that the inscriptions can all be dated to a fairly tight range between 88 and 91 CE, suggesting that the temple was opened for business sometime between September 89 and September 90. Shortly after the establishment of this cult, Ephesus began calling itself *neokoros*, or temple warden. The word quickly became a title of honor adopted by other cities, like Pergamum. All of this shows that the main impetus for the imperial cult came from the provinces, though Domitian likely welcomed it.

Assessing the extent to which the Jewish Christians of the Apocalypse avoided the imperial cult depends in part on knowledge of the sociological location of the Christians at that time and on the religious meaning attached to such contact. J. Nelson Kraybill has recently explored the evidence for the extent to which Christians living in Asia at the end of the first century CE would have been involved in the shipping industry and the trade guilds condemned in Revelation 18.[69] Others have shown that the "divinity" of the emperor in the imperial cult was not really the divinity of a god, but was an honorific nod.[70] In other words, peasants, shippers, philosophers, and historians alike in the Roman world would have agreed implicitly that the language and culture of imperial cult were a social and religious convention that no one took very seriously from an ontological perspective. But John *did* take the cult seriously. He did so not because he did not "get it," but because he was convinced that participation in the cult was insidious, an idolatry no less evil for its seemingly benign character.

John writes as a prophet in the Hebrew tradition of prophecy. Many of the Hebrew prophets wrote in historical situations in which there was no particular social or religious crisis—at least when viewed imperically at the surface level. For instance, the social situation under Jeroboam II when Amos prophesied would not have been understood by most of Amos's contemporaries as a situation of crisis, though perhaps it would have by the people who belonged to the growing class of poor peasants. However, Amos saw his own time as a time of considerable crisis. It is likely that the rhetorical import of John's re-

---

[69] J. Nelson Kraybill, *Imperial Cult and Commerce*.

[70] See, e.g., G. W. Bowersock, "Greek Intellectuals and the Imperial Cult in the Second Century A.D," in *Le Culte des Souverains dans l'Empire Romain: 7 Exposes Suivis de Discussions par Elias Bickerman*, edited by W. den Boer, Entretiens sur l'Antiquité classique, no. 19 (Vandoeuvres-Geneve: Fondation Hardt, 1973), 179–212.

peated emphasis that this is a book of prophecy lay not in his claim to revealed truth as such, but in his understanding that this book was the vehicle through which the "spiritual location" of the seven churches was being revealed.

The important difference between the crisis inscribed in Amos and that inscribed in the Apocalypse is that Amos was convinced that the people of Israel were primarily the guilty ones in danger of God's judgment and that immediate repentance was needed. In the case of the Apocalypse, John was convinced that the Roman Empire and the imperial cult were, under the influence and control of Satan, primarily the guilty ones and that the empire, the cult, and Satan would all bear the brunt of God's judgment. The seven churches were not entirely in the clear, however; rather, they were in danger of being seduced by the imperial cult. The immediate repentance needed was a repentance on the part of God's people; no hope is held out for the empire or its cult. So the crisis inscribed in the Apocalypse is primarily a *spiritual* crisis envisioned by John, but the resolution of that spiritual crisis would ironically induce a very real and dangerous *social* crisis as the churches began faithfully to resist the imperial cult and to face the consequences of their allegiance to Christ.

It is in this context that John develops an ethic of *faithful, nonviolent resistance*—an ethic characterized and impelled by his own unique development of Lamb symbolism. The idea that "resistance" was necessary was not at all obvious to John's hearers; it was itself part of the revelation. It was a resistance whose *goal* was victory, or overcoming; and whose *means* was that of the Lamb. This resistance was not primarily a *defensive* resistance made necessary by an alleged social situation of conflict; we have already seen that such a social situation was historically unlikely. Rather, the resistance called for was an *offensive* maneuver as John tried to unmask the spiritual powers at work behind the churches' compromising involvement in the empire, in its commerce, and in its imperial cult. Some of the churches were already resisting, and John praised them; some of them were not yet resisting—John scolded them. However, John was convinced that as they began or continued to resist faithfully, they, like he himself, would begin to experience the increasing wrath of the beast. In fact, they would begin to lose their lives in this resistance. Like the Lamb, they, too, would be slaughtered.

4. Potential Antecedents in the Old Testament

But here we are again: like *which* lamb? The Graeco-Roman world and the extra-canonical world of Early Judaism produced no convincing model for the Lamb Christology of the Apocalypse. Might there be warrant for reconsidering the lamb traditions of the Hebrew Bible? There are seven main possibilities regarding lamb traditions within the Hebrew Bible upon which John may have drawn. These are: (1) the lambs used for atonement of sins in the sacrificial system (Exod. and Lev.); (2) the paschal lamb of Exodus; (3) Daniel's vision of a ram and a goat; (4) the Suffering Servant Song of Isa 53:7, which refers to the Servant as an ἀμνός (רָחֵל); and (5) the lamb of the Aqedah (Gen 22); (6) the eschatologically victorious lambs of Micah; and (7) the lamb as a symbol of vulnerability in visions of eschatological peace and elsewhere.[71] We will examine each of these suggestions in turn.

4.1 The Lambs of the Sacrificial System

For persons who had witnessed the cultic traditions of the Temple, the perpetual sacrifice of lambs every morning and evening in the Tamid would have created an impressive association of the lamb with cultic sacrifice. In addition to other animals, lambs were offered at the New Moon sacrifices (Exod 29:38–41), the New Year sacrifices (Num 29:1-6), on the Day of Atonement (Num 29:7-11), at the Festival of Booths (Num 29:12-40), the Passover Festival (Num 28:16-25), and at the Festival of Weeks (Num 28:26–31). *Every day* a lamb was to be sacrificed in the morning and another one in the evening (Num 28:1-8), with two additional lambs offered every Sabbath (Num 28:9-10). Would not this perpetual cultic rite have produced a powerful association for the average Jew between the lamb and the sacrificial cult?

Several points can be mustered in favor of this association. First, the lamb in Rev 5:6 is shown as slain (ἐσφαγμένον). Second, his death seems to have some expiatory force, since the hymn that follows the introduction of the Lamb keys in on the death of the Lamb as the key to his worthiness. The phrases ἐν τῷ αἵματι (with the blood) and the verb ἀγοράζω (purchase or redeem) support the idea that the image of the expiatory sacrifice in the Temple is what gives force to the Lamb image in the Apocalypse. Furthermore, this is not the only place that expiation is hinted at in the Apocalypse. The opening hymn of the Apocalypse also uses the phrase ἐν τῷ αἵματι, connecting it with release from sins.[72] Fourth, the Apocalypse is filled with cultic imagery, especially with the

---

[71] Not included in this list is the *Aqedah* of Isaac in Gen 22. In the traditions of rabbinic Judaism this story increasingly came to be seen as a story about the self-sacrificial initiative of Isaac himself—even one in which Isaac came to be seen as a sacrificial lamb—but it appears that this hermeneutical approach post-dates the Apocalypse. For a tracing of the interpretive history of this story, see Mishael Maswari Caspi and Sascha Benjamin Cohen, *The Binding [Aqedah] and Its Transformation in Judaism and Islam: The Lambs of God*, Mellen Biblical Press Series, no. 32 (Lewiston, N.Y./Queenston, Ont./Lampeter, U.K.: Mellen Biblical Press, 1995).

[72] As with most interpreters, I read λύσαντι (one who has freed) in Rev 1:5 as the preferred reading over λούσαντι (one who has washed).

presence of the altar before the throne (6:9; 8:3 [*bis*], 5; 9:13; 11:1; 14:18; 16:7) and of bowls of incense (5:8; 8:3, 4). In light of this impressive evidence, Isbon T. Beckwith has concluded, "the figure is clearly that of the Lamb as an atoning sacrifice."[73]

However, before we pack up our books and go home, we should consider some of the problems with this association. First, the terminology used in the Apocalypse does not fit well with the lambs of the sacrificial system. Ἀγοράζω belongs to the vocabulary of liberation from bondage as much as it does to the vocabulary of sacrifice and atonement. As Sophie Laws and others have pointed out, the Seer consistently uses σφάζω (ἐσφαγμένον) to speak of the Lamb as having been slaughtered, rather than θύω, the more natural verb for sacrifice. This is the terminology of the slaughterhouse, not that of the Temple. While σφάζω is occasionally used in sacrificial contexts,[74] it refers specifically to the slaughter of the animal itself, while θύω is the more general word for offering an animal to God in sacrifice. Θύω does not appear in the Apocalypse. Σφάζω is most often applied to Christ in the Apocalypse (Rev 5:6, 9, 12; 13:8). Once it refers to the murder of others (6:4). One of the heads of the beast was ἐσφαγμένη in 13:3. Twice it refers to the slaughter of the elect in martyrdom (6:9; 18:24). In none of these other cases is the "slaughter" considered expiatory, reducing the possibility that the rhetorical force of the "slaughter" of the Lamb in 5:6 is primarily expiatory.

Furthermore, if the lamb of the sacrificial cult were the main referent here, the absence of other allusions to the sacrificial cult would be puzzling. The word most often used in the Old Testament for the sacrificial lamb is ἀμνός.[75] It does not appear at all in the Apocalypse. On the other hand, ἀρνίον is never applied to the sacrificial lamb in the Old Testament. One of the more important qualifiers used for the lamb in sacrificial contexts is ἄμωμος (faultless or without blemish). Both Jewish and secular sources emphasized that sacrificial victims be inspected and be shown to be without blemish. This adjective *is* used in 1 Peter 1:19, in which the blood of Christ is being compared to that of a sacrificial lamb, an ἀμνὸς ἄμωμος. However, ἄμωμος is not used to modify the Lamb in the Apocalypse; it is used only once, to characterize the 144,000 standing on Mount Zion (Rev 14:5).

Several recent studies of the hymns of the Apocalypse have reaffirmed their composition by the author and their unity with each other as well as with

---

[73] Isbon T. Beckwith, *The Apocalypse of John* (New York: Macmillan, 1919), 315.

[74] See, e.g., Ex 29:16, 20; Lev 1:5, 11.

[75] See Appendix I. Colin Brown concurs: "ἀμνός denoted from the outset a young sheep ... especially as used for sacrifice on numerous cultic occasions. In non-sacrificial contexts, the lamb as an animal for slaughter was called ἀρήν"; Colin Brown, gen. ed., *The New International Dictionary of New Testament Theology* (Grand Rapids, Mich.: Zondervan Publishing House, 1976), 2.410.

the rest of the book.[76] In David Carnegie's view, the only hymn that the author drew from traditional material is the one in Rev 1:5-6—the one hymn in which the expiatory nature of Christ's death seems central.[77] It does not fit in the context as well as the other hymns and its treatment of Christ as the source of redemption (rather than God) is unusual in the Apocalypse. Only in this hymn is redemption from sins mentioned in the Apocalypse. Finally, it is the only hymn in the Apocalypse that appears outside the central section of visions in chapters 4–19. This suggests that while the author of the Apocalypse knew of and affirmed the atonement Christology current in early Christian traditions, that was not his main concern, which lay elsewhere. Although theologians ancient and modern have schooled biblical scholars to understand that the primary role of Christ's death was sacrificial, substitutionary, and perhaps even penal, there is little in the Apocalypse of John to support this understanding of Jesus' death as Atonement.

4.2 The Paschal Lamb of Exodus

The paschal lamb of Exodus represents another potential point of origin for the Lamb Christology. This suggestion benefits from the observation that a Passover Christology was known in early Christian tradition.[78] We know from Rev 1–3 that John wrote the Apocalypse to seven churches located in the province of Asia. The Jewish population of Asia was large and it is not unreasonable to imagine that a christological Passover tradition made its way to Asia through Paul or some other early Christian tradition. It was, in fact, in Sardis where Melito wrote the most extensive homily on Christ as the Passover sacrifice just 75 years later: Περὶ Πάσχα. The allusions to redemption in 1:5 and 5:9 might also suggest this connection.

---

[76] Cf. esp. Klaus-Peter Jörns, *Das hymnische Evangelium: Untersuchungen zu Aufbau, Funktion und Herkunft der hymnischen Stücke in der Johannesoffenbarung*, Studien zum neuen Testament (Gütersloh: Gerd Mohn, 1971); and D. R. Carnegie, "Worthy is the Lamb: The Hymns in Revelation," in *Christ the Lord: Studies in Christology Presented to Donald Guthrie*, edited by Harold H. Rowdon (Downers Grove, Ill.: InterVarsity Press, 1982), 243–56. Although Samuel Läuchli argued that the hymns were an indissoluble unity, he thought they were brought over wholesale from some traditional source; Samuel Läuchli, "Eine Gottesdienststruktur in der Johannesoffenbarung," *Theologische Zeitschrift* 16 (1960), 359–378. On the other hand, John J. O'Rourke believed that he could discover evidence that some of the hymns are based on previous hymns; John J. O'Rourke, "The Hymns of the Apocalypse," *The Catholic Biblical Quarterly* 30, no. 3 (1968): 399–409.

[77] Carnegie, "Worthy is the Lamb," 246–47.

[78] For instance, Christ is explicitly called our πάσχα by Paul in 1Cor 5:7 and allusions to the Passover in the passion narratives play a symbolic role of varying importance in all four Gospels.

The view that the Passover Lamb provides the most plausible source for the Lamb Christology of the Apocalypse is held by such commentators as David E. Aune,[79] Richard Bauckham,[80] Eugenio Corsini,[81] P. A. Harlé,[82] Traugott Holtz,[83] and Jürgen Roloff.[84] Elisabeth Schüssler Fiorenza equivocates on whether Passover Lamb tradition is ultimately compelling as the key to understanding the Lamb Christology of the Apocalypse.[85]

One of the strongest arguments for identifying the Lamb of the Apocalypse with the Passover Lamb is the observation that Christ was often identified with the passover lamb in early Christian tradition. Traugott Holtz and Jürgen Roloff emphasize this preexisting association in their treatments of the Lamb Christology of the Apocalypse. This association begins with 1 Corinthians 5:7: τὸ πάσχα ἡμῶν ἐτύθη Χριστός (Our Passover—Christ—has been sacrificed), written already in the 50s CE. (Note the use of the verb θύω, which, as we saw above, does not appear at all in the Apocalypse.) Holtz believes that 1 Peter 1:18–19 also reflects the passover lamb connection: ἐλυτρώθητε ... τιμίῳ αἵματι ὡς ἀμνοῦ ἀμώμου καὶ ἀσπίλου Χριστοῦ (you were redeemed ... with the precious blood of Christ, like that of an unblemished and spotless lamb). The references to the Passover in John 19:33, 36 provide a clue that John's introduction of Jesus as ἀμνὸς τοῦ θεοῦ in 1:29, 36 should also be associated with the passover lamb/victim.

Also in support of this connection is Revelation 15:3, in which the conquerors (οἱ νικῶντες) on Mount Zion ᾄδουσιν τὴν ᾠδὴν Μωϋσέως τοῦ δούλου τοῦ θεοῦ καὶ τὴν ᾠδὴν τοῦ ἀρνίου (sing the ode of Moses, the servant of God, and the ode of the Lamb). Here the Lamb is explicitly connected with the Exodus traditions. Such a connection cannot be missed, since, as M. Eugene Boring has pointed out, the section from Revelation 15:1–16:21 "represents John's most thorough use of this motif in Revelation."[86] The seven plagues

---

[79] David E. Aune, "Revelation," in *Harper's Bible Commentary*, James L. Mays, gen. ed. (San Francisco: Harper & Row, 1988), 1310.

[80] Richard Bauckham, *The Climax of Prophecy: Studies on the Book of Revelation* (Edinburgh: T. & T. Clark, 1993), 184.

[81] Eugenio Corsini, *The Apocalypse: The Perennial Revelation of Jesus Christ*, translated and edited by Francis J. Moloney, S.D.B., Good News Studies, vol. 5 (Wilmington: Michael Glazier, Inc., 1983), 134.

[82] P[aul] A. Harlé, "L'Agneau de l'Apocalypse et le Nouveau Testament," *Les Etudes Théologiques et Religieuses* 31, no. 2 (1956): 26–35.

[83] Traugott Holtz, *Die Christologie der Apokalypse des Johannes*, 2d ed., reprint, 1962, Texte und Untersuchungen, vol. 85 (Berlin: Akademie, 1971), 44–47.

[84] Jürgen Roloff, *The Revelation of John: A Continental Commentary*, translated by John E. Alsup (Minneapolis: Fortress Press, 1993), 78–79.

[85] Compare Fiorenza, *Revelation*, 60–61; with Fiorenza, *The Book of Revelation: Justice and Judgment*, 95–96.

[86] Boring, *Revelation*, 173.

(πληγή) in 15:1 represent the ten plagues at the Exodus. The sea (θάλασσα) in 15:2 recalls the Red Sea. And the ode of Moses (ἡ ᾠδὴ Μωϋσέως) surely recalls the song that Moses and the children of Israel sang on their safe arrival on the other side of the Red Sea in Exodus 15:1-18.[87]

Some of the specific eschatological woes parallel the Egyptian plagues, such as the plague of sores (Rev 16:2 // the sixth plague, Exod 9:8-12); the sea and rivers turning into blood (Rev 16:3-4 // the first plague, Exod 7:14-25); the plague of darkness (Rev 16:10 // the ninth plague, Exod 10:21-29); the plague of frogs (Rev 16:13 // the second plague, Exod 8:1-15); and the plague of thunder, fire, and hail (Rev 16:18, 21 // the seventh plague, Exod 9:13-35). Elsewhere we see a plague of locusts (Rev 9:3, 7 // Exod 10:1-20) and Rome symbolized as Egypt (Rev 11:8). We might even see in the drying up of bodies of water (Rev 16:12) an allusion to the drying up of the Red Sea (Exod 14:21) and of the Jordan River (Josh 4:23). Thus, "as Israel once stood on the banks of the Red Sea and celebrated God's liberating act of the exodus, the church will stand on the shore of the heavenly sea and sing the ode of Moses and the Lamb."[88]

Certainly, the liberation theme itself is central in the Apocalypse. In a setting in which persecution or expected persecution confronted the believers in the seven churches, the image of the Passover Lamb enabling release from the bondage of Egypt may have been a welcome one. Furthermore, the emphasis on the blood of the lamb (Rev 1:5; 5:9; 7:14; 12:11; 19:13), while appropriate to the Tamid, certain fits the image of the passover victim.

But there are problems with this association as well. First, although we have many allusions to the Exodus in the Apocalypse, we have no explicit references to the Passover, either to the Passover festival or to the Passover victim. The word πάσχα, the proper term for both the Passover festival and the Passover victim, does not even appear in the Apocalypse, which we would expect if the author understands the Lamb as a passover victim, nor does θύω.[89]

Furthermore, as Leon Morris has noted, the Passover victim was not necessarily a lamb. Exodus 12 repeatedly refers to the Passover victim as a שֶׂה, which is a general word that applies equally to sheep or goats. As Exodus 12:5 explicitly states, it could have been a kid (baby goat) as well: the animal may come מִן־הַכְּבָשִׂים וּמִן־הָעִזִּים (from the lambs or from the she-goats). This is hardly a minor point, since the phrase "Passover lamb" is not an ancient one,

---

[87] Cf. also Hab 3:19, where the ode of Habakkuk is seen as a means of "overcoming": "He will put me on the high places to overcome in his song" (ἐπὶ τὰ ὑψηλὰ ἐπιβιβᾷ με τοῦ νικῆσαι ἐν τῇ ᾠδῇ αὐτοῦ; cf. also Ode 4:19).

[88] Boring, *Revelation*, 173.

[89] The word πάσχα does appear, as Appendix I shows, several times in the Septuagint with reference to the passover victim, as well as in 1Cor 5:7.

but a modern one.[90] In New Testament times, Jews simply did not use the word *lamb* when referring to the Passover victim. Furthermore, the word ἀρνίον is never used of the Passover victim in the extant literature. Nowhere is the Lamb portrayed as if it were a passover offering. And the emphasis in the Apocalypse on the Lamb's victory over death and on his royal character does not quite fit the Passover image.

Despite the application of Passover symbolism in the developing Christology of the early Jesus movement, neither specific appeals to this symbolism nor the telltale linguistic markers appear in the Apocalypse. What *appears* to be a linguistic marker—reference to the lamb—turns out to be inappropriate as a designation for the Passover victim. Thus, appeals to the Passover background of the Lamb symbolism of the Apocalypse seem to be mistaken.

4.3 The Suffering Servant Song of Isaiah 53:7

The New Testament literature suggests that the Suffering Servant Song of Isaiah 52:13–53:12 played an important role in the development of Christology in the early church. The song is quoted, for instance, in Acts 8:32-33, in which *lamb* is applied to Jesus. Isaiah 53:7 places lamb (שֶׂה) and sheep (רָחֵל) in parallel position: "Like the *lamb* to the slaughter was led, and like a *sheep* before her shearers is silent, so he opened not his mouth." The Septuagint reverses the words in parallel: "Like a sheep (πρόβατον) to the slaughter was led, and like a lamb (ἀμνός) before its shearer is silent, so he opened not his mouth." Acts 8:32-33 follows the Septuagint of Isa 53:7. In 1 Peter 1:18-19, we read, "You know that you were ransomed ... by the precious blood of Christ, like that of a lamb (ἀμνός) without defect or blemish."

Recall Isaiah 53:7:

> He was oppressed, and he was afflicted,
>   yet he did not open his mouth;
> like a sheep (שֶׂה; πρόβατον) that is led to the slaughter (טֶבַח; σφαγήν),
>   and like a lamb (רָחֵל; ἀμνός) that before its shearers is silent,
>   so he did not open his mouth.

Numerous commentators have found the "suffering servant lamb" of Isaiah 53 helpful as background to the Lamb Christology of the Apocalypse. Although a few scholars, such as Heinrich Kraft and Joseph Comblin,[91] tend to

---

[90] Cf. Leon Morris, *The Gospel According to John*, 2d ed. (Grand Rapids, Mich.: Eerdmans, 1995), 127n48. See also G. Buchanan Gray, *Sacrifice in the Old Testament* (Oxford: Oxford University Press, 1925), 397.

[91] Heinrich Kraft, *Die Offenbarung des Johannes*, Handbuch zum neuen Testament (Tübingen: J.C.B. Mohr, 1974), 109; J. Comblin, *Le Christ dans l'Apocalypse*, Bibliotheque de theologie. Serie 3: Theologie biblique, vol. 6 (Tournai: Desclée, 1965).

see this background as primary, most appeal to Isaiah 53 in combination with other lamb traditions in the Old Testament.

This potential origin has more to commend it, since there are further links with the terminology and thought of the Apocalypse. Here we *do* have the language of the slaughterhouse (טֶבַח; σφαγήν). Furthermore, we are dealing with another widely known element in the development of Christology in the early church.

But here, too, there are problems. In the first place, the word for lamb in the Septuagint of Isa 53:7 is ἀμνός. Second, as Jan Fekkes has pointed out, even though suffering is an important theme in the Apocalypse, the Suffering Servant theme is not taken up or developed in the Apocalypse. Fekkes thus treats the parallel to Isaiah 53:7 as an "unlikely" or "doubtful" parallel according to his classification system.[92] Comblin is aware of this lack of explicit correlation, but claims that the implicit parallels between the Servant texts of Deutero-Isaiah and the Apocalypse are too extensive to be fortuitous. Comblin does not deny that there are Passover echoes here, but claims that the image of the lamb from the Servant passages is superimposed on the Passover victim to form the unique Lamb Christology of the Apocalypse.[93] Exodus traditions dominate Deutero-Isaiah itself. Furthermore, John's appeal to the Servant passages of Isaiah does not derive from the christological traditions of the early church, but on his own fresh and original reading of Isaiah. Thus, John develops a "new" Servant theology in the Apocalypse that draws on the Servant-lamb imagery as well as the eschatological concerns and judgment motifs of Deutero-Isaiah. It is the strong connection between the attributes of the Lamb in the Apocalypse and the eschatological rôle of the Servant that establishes the Servant Lamb as primary.[94]

However, most of the connections cited by Comblin in favor of his thesis draw on themes common to Jewish eschatological texts—most notable are the themes of Israel being a light to the nations, the fulfillment of promises to David, and themes of judgment. While Comblin is able to show intriguing

[92] Jan Fekkes, III, *Isaiah and Prophetic Traditions in the Book of Revelation: Visionary Antecedents and Their Development*, Journal for the Study of the New Testament Supplement Series, no. 93 (Sheffield: JSOT Press, 1994).

[93] "«Comme un agneau conduit à l'abattoir», tel est le Serviteur de Dieu selon *Is.*, LIII, 7. Nous avons bien des raisons de croire que c'est cette comparaison qui est à l'origine de l'Agneau de l'Apocalypse, et que c'est à cet agneau, c'est-à-dire au Serviteur de Dieu, que saint Jean a pensé" J. Comblin, *Le Christ dans l'Apocalypse*, Bibliotheque de theologie. Serie 3: Theologie biblique, vol. 6 (Tournai: Desclée, 1965), 22.

[94] See especially the list of comparisons in J. Comblin, *Le Christ dans l'Apocalypse*, 35–39.

connections to the Servant traditions, it is less clear that these allusions are tied specifically to Lamb Christology of the Apocalypse.

Furthermore, it is imprecise to say that the Suffering Servant is symbolized as a lamb in Isaiah 53:7. The characterization of the Suffering Servant as a lamb is not developed into a symbolism as such. As Wheelwright has maintained, "a symbol has a certain stability which endures beyond one or a few occasions."[95] The symbol for the eschatological figure of Deutero-Isaiah is the Servant, not the Lamb. The *characterization* of the Servant as a Lamb draws on a symbolic tradition already in place in the traditions of the ancient world—namely, the tradition of the vulnerable lamb. Thus the association of the Suffering Servant with the lamb in the biblical tradition is properly an invocation of the broader vulnerable lamb symbolism both within and outside of the biblical tradition. As a result, the passing reference to sheep and lambs in Isaiah 53:7 should not be misconstrued as a source of symbolism separate from that of the vulnerable lamb generally.

4.4 Daniel's Vision of a Ram and a Goat (Dan. 8)

One of the possible sources for the Lamb Christology of the Apocalypse is the Ram Vision of Daniel 8. The passage reads as follows:

> In the third year of the reign of King Belshazzar a vision appeared to me, Daniel, after the one that had appeared to me at first. [2]In the vision I was looking and saw myself in Susa the capital, in the province of Elam, and I was by the river Ulai. [3]I looked up and saw a ram (אַיִל; κριός) standing beside the river. It had two horns. Both horns were long, but one was longer than the other, and the longer one came up second. [4]I saw the ram charging westward and northward and southward. All beasts (חַיּוֹת; θηρία) were powerless to withstand it, and no one could rescue from its power; it did as it pleased and became strong.

> [5]As I was watching, a male goat (צְפִיר־הָעִזִּים; τράγος) appeared from the west, coming across the face of the whole earth without touching the ground. The goat (צָפִיר; τράγος) had a horn between its eyes. [6]It came toward the ram with the two horns that I had seen standing beside the river, and it ran at it with savage force. [7]I saw it approaching the ram. It was enraged against it and struck the ram, breaking its two horns. The ram did not have power to withstand it; it threw the ram down to the ground and trampled upon it, and there was no one who could rescue the ram from its power. [8]Then the male goat grew exceedingly great; but at the height of its power, the great horn was broken, and in its place there came up four prominent horns toward the four winds of heaven.

---

[95] See above; Wheelwright, *The Burning Fountain*, 9–10.

[9]Out of one of them came another horn, a little one, which grew exceedingly great toward the south, toward the east, and toward the beautiful land. [10]It grew as high as the host of heaven. It threw down to the earth some of the host and some of the stars, and trampled on them. [11]Even against the prince of the host it acted arrogantly; it took the regular burnt offering away from him and overthrew the place of his sanctuary. [12]Because of wickedness, the host was given over to it together with the regular burnt offering; it cast truth to the ground, and kept prospering in what it did. [13]Then I heard a holy one speaking, and another holy one said to the one that spoke, "For how long is this vision concerning the regular burnt offering, the transgression that makes desolate, and the giving over of the sanctuary and host to be trampled?" [14]And he answered him, "For two thousand three hundred evenings and mornings; then the sanctuary shall be restored to its rightful state."   NRSV

There are several points of contact between these two apocalypses that make it possible that the imagery of Daniel 8 lies behind the Lamb Christology of the Apocalypse. First, this passage is one of the Old Testament passages in which animals symbolize humans, including "beasts" as adversaries in a conflict of eschatological import. Second, some of the actions of the players in Daniel's vision prefigure those in the Apocalypse. For instance, the little horn that grew as high as heaven—a reference to Antiochus Epiphanes[96]—"threw down to the earth some of the host and some of the stars" (8:10), suggesting Rev 12:4, where the great red dragon's "tail swept down a third of the stars of heaven and threw them to the earth."[97] Third, in both Daniel and the Apocalypse we have a dialogue in heaven initiated by a cry for justice. "How long is this vision ...?" (Dan. 8:13) parallels the Apocalypse: "How long will it be before you judge and avenge our blood ...?" (6:10). Other features common to apocalyptic literature in general appear in both Daniel 8 and the Apocalypse; most significant are a character within the narrative who interprets the vision (Dan 8:15-17 // Rev 7:13-14), the command to seal up the vision (Dan 8:26 // Rev 10:4), and narrative descriptions of the physiological affects of the vision (Dan 8:17, 27 // Rev 1:17; 10:10; 19:10; 22:8). Fortunately, in the case of Daniel, we have a stronger *prima facie* case for establishing literary and conceptual dependence, for at least we know that the author of the Apocalypse knew the Book of Daniel and was deeply influenced by it.

However, although there are certainly broad and deep links between Daniel and the Apocalypse, scholars have wisely avoided interpreting the ram of v. 3 or the goat of v. 5 as a messiah or some other redeemer figure in Early Judaism. In fact, the explanation that follows this vision explicitly identifies the two horns of the ram as the kings of Media and Persia (Dan. 8:20) and the

---

[96] Cf. J. J. Collins, *Daniel*, 331.
[97] Cf. also Rev 6:18; 8:10-12; 9:1.

male goat as the king of Greece (8:21).[98] Thus, if Daniel 8 functions as a source for the Lamb Christology of the Apocalypse, it does so in a very loose and general way as a resource creatively shaped by the author.

4.5 The Aqedah (Gen. 22)

According to Genesis 22, God tested Abraham and told him to take his son Isaac to the land of Moriah to offer him as a burnt sacrifice. As they approached the place of sacrifice, Isaac said to his father, "'Father!' And he [Abraham] said, 'Here I am, my son.' He said, 'The fire and the wood are here, but where is the lamb [or better, sheep: שֶׂה/πρόβατον] for a burnt offering?' Abraham said, 'God himself will provide the lamb [שֶׂה/πρόβατον] for a burnt offering, my son.' So the two of them walked on together" in pregnant silence (Gen 22:7-8, NRSV).

When they arrived at Moriah, Abraham bound Isaac and prepared to kill him on the altar. However, the angel of the Lord stopped Abraham from harming his son. The text continues: "And Abraham looked up and saw a ram [אַיִל/κριός], caught in a thicket by its horns. Abraham went and took the ram [אַיִל/κριός] and offered it up as a burnt offering instead of his son" (Gen 22:13).[99]

The history of this tradition as it developed in Early Judaism and later in rabbinic Judaism is quite complex.[100] The Targums rewrite this story in essentially three ways. First, Abraham tells Isaac that he is to be sacrificed—that Isaac himself is about to be the sacrificial victim. Second, Isaac consents to the sacrifice and both Isaac and Abraham receive a vision of angels. Third, after the angel stops Abraham from harming Isaac, Abraham offers a prayer of thanksgiving.[101]

---

[98] A possible reference to Alexander the Great, if one merges the "great horn" with the he-goat as one (cf. vv. 6, 8, 21). The great horn more clearly represents Alexander; the he-goat may represent kingly or princely power more generally; see John J. Collins, *Daniel: A Commentary on the Book of Daniel* (Hermeneia—A Critical and Historical Commentary on the Bible, Minneapolis: Fortress Press, 1993), 331.

[99] Note the shift in language here from שֶׂה/πρόβατον (sheep) to אַיִל/κριός (ram).

[100] For a tracing of the interpretive history of this story, see Mishael Maswari Caspi and Sascha Benjamin Cohen, *The Binding [Aqedah] and Its Transformation in Judaism and Islam: The Lambs of God*, Mellen Biblical Press Series, no. 32 (Lewiston, N.Y./Queenston, Ont./Lampeter, U.K.: Mellen Biblical Press, 1995). For a careful consideration of the Isaac traditions in the Old Testament, in the texts of Early Judaism, and in the New Testament, see James Swetnam, *Jesus and Isaac: A Study of the Epistle to the Hebrews in the Light of the Aqedah*, Analecta Biblica, no. 94 (Rome: Biblical Institute Press, 1981), 23–85.

[101] Robert Hayward, "The Present State of Research Into the Targumic Account of the Sacrifice of Isaac," *Journal of Jewish Studies* 32 (1981): 127.

The primary issue in tracing the tradition history of the Aqedah is the dating of these developments insofar as this dating suggests the possibility of Aqedah traditions having influenced the writers of the New Testament. The basic lines of debate have been drawn between such scholars as Geza Vermes[102] and Roger Le Déaut[103] on the one hand, who claim that the Aqedah traditions were already developing or had developed in pre-Christian Judaism, and Bruce Chilton and Philip Davies[104] on the other, who claim that the Aqedah traditions developed in the Rabbinic Judaism of the Christian era in polemical response to the Christian doctrine of Jesus' atoning sacrifice.

In the traditions of Rabbinic Judaism this was a story about the self-sacrificial initiative of Isaac himself in which Isaac came to be seen as a sacrificial lamb. In his *Antiquities*, Josephus is at pains to demonstrate that Isaac was fully 25 years old, that Isaac himself fully accepted his father's explanation of what was about to happen joyfully and bravely, and that he actually rushed (ὁρμάω) to the altar and to his own sacrifice (σφαγήν).[105]

The theological and historical issues here are quite complex, involving the theology of expiation, the merits of martyrdom, and the possibility of an anti-Islamic polemic in Pseudo-Jonathan. Within later Rabbinic Judaism, the rewritten Aqedah traditions were invoked to address such diverse issues as the meaning of the Passover, the meaning of the Tamid, and the choice of Mt. Moriah as the place for the Temple. In short, the Aqedah became the battleground site for a whole array of diverse theological disputes in rabbinic Judaism.[106]

It can now be said that the pre-Christian existence of at least some of the Aqedah traditions is without doubt. The reference in Judith 8:25 to the testing of *Isaac* suggests such existence.[107] Though the dating of 4 Maccabees itself is debated, it certainly reflects the development of a martyr theology in which Isaac is lauded as the prototypical martyr (cf. 7:14; 13:12; 16:20).

---

[102] Geza Vermes, *Scripture and Tradition in Judaism* (Leiden: E. J. Brill, 1973), 193–227.

[103] Roger Le Déaut, *La Nuit Pascale: Essai sur la Signification de la Pâque Juive a partir du Targum d'Exode XII 42*, Analecta Biblica, no. 22 (Rome: Institut biblique pontifical, 1963), 131–212.

[104] P. R. Davies and B. D. Chilton, "The Aqedah: A Revised Tradition History," *Catholic Biblical Quarterly* 40 (1978): 514–46.

[105] *Ant* 1.227, 232.

[106] Robert Hayward, "The Present State of Research Into the Targumic Account of the Sacrifice of Isaac," *Journal of Jewish Studies* 32 (1981): 127–28.

[107] Though Swetnam thinks otherwise; cf. James Swetnam, *Jesus and Isaac: A Study of the Epistle to the Hebrews in the Light of the Aqedah*, Analecta Biblica, no. 94 (Rome: Biblical Institute Press, 1981), 35.

More importantly, the Dead Sea Scrolls fragment 4Q225 (4QPseudo-Jubilees[a]) now witnesses to the pre-Christian tradition of Isaac acting as a free agent accepting martyrdom.[108] Although frustratingly fragmentary, two points seem clear: Although in the Hebrew Bible, Isaac does not respond to Abraham's explanation about God providing a lamb in 22:8, in 4Q225 Isaac does respond, as in Targums Pseudo-Jonathan and Neofiti on 22:10. Second, although only one letter of Isaac's response is partially visible, it appears to be the beginning of, "T[ie me well]" (4Q225 2.4), known from the Targums. Thus, 4Q225 is significant evidence in this debate because in this case we can rule out any possible anti-Christian polemic, since the fragment antedates the first century CE.

Is it possible that the Lamb of the Apocalypse is patterned on the Aqedah? Such a suggestion is appealing on several accounts. First, a tradition exists in Rabbinic Judaism that the ram Abraham eventually saw and offered had been prepared from the foundation of the world.[109] Later rabbinic tradition came to see both the daily sacrifice and the Passover as "reminders" of the Aqedah, which itself served as a sort of prototype for the later rites.[110] Although it is presently impossible to demonstrate the antiquity of such a tradition, it is possible that the references to the lamb slain or destined "from the foundation of the world" in both 1 Peter 1:19-20 and Revelation 13:8 reflect the antiquity of a well-developed exegetical tradition.

Second, although Isaac's vulnerability is not presented in the Aqedah traditions as a battle with his father (e.g., as a force of evil), Isaac does represent someone who self-consciously chose the way of vulnerability and whose choice was vindicated. 4Q225 treats the Aqedah as a vindication of both Abraham and Isaac over Mastema, the evil prince of Belial.

Still, there are problems with identifying the Aqedah as the key to the Lamb Christology of the Apocalypse. First, if the Aqedah itself were a significant source of the Lamb Christology of the Apocalypse, one would expect a clear appeal to Abraham or to Isaac in the Apocalypse. Second, it remains unclear how much of the later Aqedah traditions clearly predate the Apocalypse. The clearest pre-Christian traditions are those tied to the honor of martyrdom. While the theme of martyrdom is highly relevant for understanding the Apocalypse—especially a self-chosen martyrdom by a lamb figure—martyrdom

---

[108] See Geza Vermes, "New Light on the Akedah from 4Q225," *Journal of Jewish Studies* 47 (1996): 140–46 for a discussion of this fragment.

[109] Robert Hayward, "The Present State of Research Into the Targumic Account of the Sacrifice of Isaac," *Journal of Jewish Studies* 32 (1981): 141.

[110] LevR 2:11.

itself is a theme readily available from elsewhere in the tradition. [111] At best we are in a position to suggest that the various themes of vulnerability and free agency in the face of impending martyrdom were gaining currency in the two centuries following the Maccabean revolt. The author of the Apocalypse may well have drawn on these developing traditions in such a way as to form a new Gestalt of the Lamb that reflects the author's Christology.

4.6 The Lambs of Micah 5:6 [LXX]

As noted in Appendix I, the word ἀρήν/ἀρνός appears in the LXX in an interesting passage in Micah 5:7(6). It departs significantly from the Hebrew and has no Hebrew antecedent. The NRSV, which follows the Hebrew, reads, "Then the remnant of Jacob, surrounded by many peoples, shall be like dew from the LORD, like showers on the grass which do not depend upon people or wait for any mortal." The Septuagint has, "And the remnant of Jacob will be among the Gentiles in the midst of many peoples, like dew falling from the Lord, and *like lambs in a pasture*, so that no one might ever again be summoned [to battle] nor subjugated among the children of humanity (lit., 'sons of men')" (my translation of καὶ ἔσται τὸ ὑπόλειμμα τοῦ Ιακωβ ἐν τοῖς ἔθνεσιν ἐν μέσῳ λαῶν πολλῶν ὡς δρόσος παρὰ κυρίου πίπτουσα καὶ ὡς ἄρνες ἐπὶ ἄγρωστιν, ὅπως μὴ συναχθῇ μηδεὶς μηδὲ ὑποστῇ ἐν υἱοῖς ἀνθρώπων). This same idea of Israel living as vulnerable lambs among the Gentiles appears in PsSol 8:23, in which ἀρνίον is used. [112]

The parallelism between verses 6 and 7 is more striking in the Septuagint than in the Hebrew:

καὶ ἔσται τὸ ὑπόλειμμα τοῦ Ιακωβ ἐν τοῖς ἔθνεσιν ἐν μέσῳ λαῶν πολλῶν ὡς δρόσος παρὰ κυρίου πίπτουσα καὶ ὡς ἄρνες ἐπὶ ἄγρωστιν, ὅπως μὴ συναχθῇ μηδεὶς μηδὲ ὑποστῇ ἐν υἱοῖς ἀνθρώπων.	καὶ ἔσται τὸ ὑπόλειμμα τοῦ Ιακωβ ἐν τοῖς ἔθνεσιν ἐν μέσῳ λαῶν πολλῶν ὡς λέων ἐν κτήνεσιν ἐν τῷ δρυμῷ καὶ ὡς σκύμνος ἐν ποιμνίοις προβάτων, ὃν τρόπον ὅταν διέλθῃ καὶ διαστείλας ἁρπάσῃ καὶ μὴ ᾖ ὁ ἐξαιρούμενος.
And the remnant of Jacob will be among the Gentiles in the midst of many peoples, like dew falling from the Lord, and like lambs in a pasture, so that no one might ever again be summoned [to battle] nor subjugated among the children of humanity (lit., 'sons of men').	And the remnant of Jacob will be among the Gentiles in the midst of many peoples, like a lion among the animals in the forest, and like a young lion among the flocks of sheep, such that whenever he passes through and attacks, he seizes and there will be no one to rescue.

---

[111] In contrast to 1 Macc., 4 Macc. celebrates the effective atoning death of Israel's martyrs, as does the Testament of Moses; cf. Adela Yarbro Collins, "The Political Perspective of the Revelation to John," *Journal of Biblical Literature* 96 (1977): 241–56.

[112] On whether the Greek represents a misreading of the Hebrew, an intentional departure from it, or simply a different tradition, see further below in Appendix I.

This parallel with the Apocalypse is suggestive and has often been missed. First, this is the only place in the Bible (outside of the Apocalypse) in which lambs and lions are juxtaposed *while representing the same figure:* here, the remnant of Jacob. Second, as in the Apocalypse, the context is clearly eschatological. These verses describe what will be "in the days to come"—בְּאַחֲרִית הַיָּמִים (Micah 4:1; cf. "in that day" in 4:6; 5:10). Third, as with the Apocalypse, the inscribed context is that of conflict in which Israel's existence in the midst of the Gentile nations seems threatened.

Although Leslie Allen does not acknowledge the Septuagintal reading here, he does discuss the "paradoxical" parallelism of these two verses in the Hebrew:

> If the stanzas are structurally symmetrical, they are all the more strikingly diverse in content. The antithetic nature of their parallelism is shown in the use of contrasting imagery: the gentle, refreshing *dew* and the savage, destructive *lion*. In paradoxical fashion the two different roles of the remnant are spelled out: to be channel of divine blessing and agent of divine judgment. [113]

Micah 4 and 5 have long been a focal point for scholars attempting to trace the compositional history of this document. According to Daniel J. Simundson, most scholars attribute "virtually nothing" from these chapters to the eighth-century Micah. [114] These chapters treat the days to come, when the mountain of the Lord's house will be raised higher than all others and the nations shall stream to it, when nations shall beat their swords into plowshares and warfare will cease. This restoration of Israel will entail God's judgment on everything that caused alienation from the Lord, including dependence upon military might (4:3-4; 5:10-11). Finally, an eschatological ruler (whose origin is actually "from of old, from ancient days"; 5:2) will rise up from Bethlehem of Ephrathah. He will stand and feed his flock. He will be "the one of peace" (5:5a), and Israel will finally experience security (5:4).

In the midst of these wonderful visions of the idyllic future in which warfare will cease are equally powerful visions of Israel's defeat of the nations. When Israel is surrounded by hostile nations in 4:11 (possibly, though not necessarily a reference to the invasion of Sennacherib in 701 BCE), Israel is told, "Arise and thresh, O daughter Zion, for I will make your horn iron and your hoofs bronze; you shall beat in pieces many peoples, and [I] shall devote

---

[113] Leslie C. Allen, *The Books of Joel, Obadiah, Jonah and Micah*, The New International Commentary on the Old Testament (Grand Rapids, Mich.: William B. Eerdmans Publishing Company, 1976), 352.

[114] Daniel J. Simundson, "The Book of Micah: Introduction, Commentary, and Reflections," in *The New Interpreter's Bible*, Leander E. Keck, gen. ed. (Nashville: Abingdon Press, 1996), 535.

[הַחֲרַמְתִּי—a technical term in "holy war" texts] their gain to the Lord, their wealth to the Lord of the whole earth."[115] Finally, the remnant of Jacob will pass through the midst of the nations, tear down, and tear (the people?) in pieces like a lion, with no one to deliver (5:8).

What is going on here? Is this a vision of peace through strength, where military might is no longer needed because it was used so decisively? Or do the peace and war traditions ultimately reflect irreconcilable visions, possibly deriving from disparate historical contexts but placed here by some well-meaning by slow-witted redactor? Or did the putative redactor use one of these visions to correct the other in a subtle form of diatribe? Such questions are the lot of anyone seeking to understand and explicate the theological message of Micah.

Leslie Allen suggests that the vision of peace is Micah's own vision and that he "ironically" revives the old war songs in order to expose them as inadequate: "To the chagrin of his audience he chanted the familiar words in a new setting. He took up this enthusiastic expression of Judean confidence, and skillfully wove it into his oracle of the coming king in order to direct his hearers to a sounder source of confidence."[116] James Luther Mays suggests that the later redactor has replaced the earlier motif of destruction into a motif of purging, though the older motif is still present and resists a full transformation.[117] Juan Alfaro thinks that the war traditions represent quotations of the false prophets, which are then corrected by Micah (or the redactor) by means of the peace traditions.[118]

If this reading could be shown to be ancient, or at least pre-Christian, it could suggest that the author of the Apocalypse drew from such a tradition in his own juxtaposition of lamb and lion. However, the fragments of Micah found among the Dead Sea Scrolls suggest that caution is in order. Three mss. apply: one found at Naḥal Ḥever, one at Muraba'at, and one at Qumran. While only one complete word and three partial words from Micah 5:6 survive in 8ḤevXII gr, the reading suggests conformity to a Masoretic-type text, rather

---

[115] This verse (Mic 4:13) is quoted in the Priestly Blessings for the Last Days (1QSb), which interprets the figure as a bull. The passage in question (1QSb 5.20–29) conflates several passages from the Hebrew Bible (e.g., Isa 11:2-5; Mic 4:13; Num 24:17) into a messianic collage.

[116] Leslie C. Allen, *The Books of Joel, Obadiah, Jonah and Micah*, The New International Commentary on the Old Testament (Grand Rapids, Mich.: William B. Eerdmans Publishing Company, 1976), 358.

[117] James Luther Mays, *Micah: A Commentary*, The Old Testament Library (Philadelphia: Westminster Press, 1976), 124–25.

[118] Juan I. Alfaro, *Justice and Loyalty: A Commentary on the Book of Micah*, International Theological Commentary (Grand Rapids and Edinburgh: Wm. B. Eerdmans Publ. Co. and Handsel Press, 1989), 42–61.

than a Septuagint-type text.[119] The crucial word (כרביבים [rain]) is only partially visible in the badly damaged MurXII (Mur88)[120] and not visible at all in 4QXII^g. The words that remain from Micah 5:6 in both MurXII and 4Q82 Frg. 95 (4QXII^g)[121] suggest a high degree of conformity to a Masoretic-type text.

In light of the Septuagintal reading, the Dead Sea Scrolls provide evidence that early in the Christian era, the text of Micah was still fluid. The juxtaposition of visions of peace and war in Micah 4–5 in an eschatological context, with the lion appearing as the symbol for war, may have led an early scribe to insert a lamb figure in order to underscore the visions of peace inscribed there. If such an insertion were pre-Christian, we could have a suggestive candidate for the origin of the lamb figure in the Apocalypse. In any case, the lamb vision and the lion vision represent two distinct theological visions of the future that are not easily resolved, even by the redactors of Micah.

4.7 The Lambs of Eschatological Peace

Lambs play a role in several expressions of hope for eschatological peace in the Old Testament. One of the more striking features of the coming age is that "natural" antipathies will cease. For instance, Isaiah 11:6 reads,

> [6]The wolf (זְאֵב; λύκος) shall live with the lamb (כֶּבֶשׂ; ἀρήν),
>
> the leopard (נָמֵר; πάρδαλις) shall lie down with the kid [or goat] (גְּדִי; ἔριφος),
>
> the calf (עֵגֶל; μοσχάριον) and the lion (כְּפִיר; λέων) and the fatling (מְרִיא; ταῦρος) together,
>
> and a little child (נַעַר קָטֹן; παιδίον μικρὸν) shall lead them.
>
> [7]The cow (פָּרָה; βοῦς) and the bear (דֹּב; ἄρκος) shall graze,
>
> their young shall lie down together;
>
> and the lion (אֲרִי; λέων) shall eat straw like the ox (בָּקָר; βοῦς).

---

[119] The word for rain or lambs is not part of the extant text. The ms. reads [κατα]λοιπον Ιακωβ instead of ὑπόλειμμα Ιακωβ for "remnant of Jacob" and χο[ρτον] instead of ἄγρωστιν for "grass." Furthermore, the editors suggest that on the basis of a letter count, the words ἐν τοῖς ἔθνεσιν (among the Gentiles) and πίπτουσα (fallen) were likely not present in the ms., thus suggesting conformity to an MT-type Greek text. See E. Tov, *The Greek Minor Prophets Scroll from Naḥal Ḥever (8ḤevXIIgr) (The Seiyal Collection I)*, Discoveries in the Judaean Desert, vol. 8 (Oxford: Clarendon Press, 1990), 42, 88. The text is thus, "[And the rem]nant of Jacob [will be in the midst of many peoples] like dew [from the Lord, like showers on the] gr[ass, which do not depend on humans nor do they wait for them]" (my translation). It therefore seems quite unlikely that the "lambs" reading was known to the Qumran community.

[120] P. Benoit, J. T. Milik, and R. Vaux, de, eds., *Les Grottes de Murabba'at*, Discoveries in the Judaean Desert, vol. 2 (Oxford: Clarendon Press, 1961), 195.

[121] See Eugene Ulrich, et. al., *Qumran Cave 4.X: The Prophets*, Discoveries in the Judean Desert, vol. 15 (Oxford: Oxford University Press, 1997), 314.

And in Trito-Isaiah (65:25) we read:

> The wolf (זְאֵב; λύκοι)[122] and the lamb (טָלֶה; ἄρνες) shall feed together,
> the lion (אֲרִי; λέων) shall eat straw like the ox (בָּקָר; βοῦς);
> but the serpent—its food shall be dust!
> They shall not hurt or destroy
> on all my holy mountain,
> says the LORD.[123]

With both of these prophecies, the word used for lamb in the LXX is ἀρήν, although the more common word for lamb in the LXX is ἀμνός.[124] In keeping with the pattern we have seen before, the word ἀρήν is used in this metaphorical context, whereas ἀμνός appears more typically in sacrificial contexts. The word ἀρήν occurs only once in the New Testament: in Luke 10:3, where Jesus says to his disciples, "See, I am sending you out like lambs (ἄρνας; πρόβατα in Mt 10:16) into the midst of wolves (λύκων)." This saying likely derives from Q. More than simply a signal of the danger into which Jesus was sending his disciples, this metaphor likely draws on the eschatological promises of Isaiah 11 and 65. As signals of the eschaton, Jesus' disciples will be like vulnerable lambs bringing peace to the houses that will accept it (Lk 10:5). The eschaton is perceived as the time when vulnerability will no longer be associated with victimization.

There are several problems, however, with identifying the Lamb of the Apocalypse with the lambs of the eschatological peace tradition. First, the vision in the Apocalypse is anything but tranquil. Soon after the Lamb is introduced in Rev 5, we discover in Rev 6 that with the first seal broken by the Lamb, a conquering equestrian was released and he went out conquering. And with the second seal broken, a second equestrian was given authority to "take peace from the earth." Thus, the Lamb in the Apocalypse is not primarily a symbol of tranquility, but the means by which victory is accomplished in the eschatological conflict. This is quite different from the role of the lamb in the Old Testament visions of eschatological peace.

Second, unlike the lambs of eschatological peace, the Lamb of the Apocalypse is a *slaughtered* lamb. This image of a *slaughtered* lamb would seem to destroy the positive imagery of eschatological peace in the Old Testament.

---

[122] The LXX uses the plural forms here.

[123] For an indirectly related example, see Lev 26:6: "And I will grant peace in the land, and you shall lie down, and no one shall make you afraid; I will remove dangerous animals from the land, and no sword shall go through your land"; but see Lev 26:7: "You shall give chase to your enemies, and they shall fall before you by the sword."

[124] Sir 13:17 may reflect an indirect exception here: What does a wolf have in common with a lamb (ἀμνός)? No more has a sinner with the devout.

Unlike the lambs of eschatological peace, which need not fear harm and are *not* harmed, the Lamb of the Apocalypse is a victim of murder, though that victimization has been turned upside-down through his resurrection.

Finally, the stereotypical set of opponents in these visions of eschatological peace are the *wolf* and the lamb, not the *lion* and the lamb.

Thus, although the themes of the eschaton and of the vulnerability of the Lamb seem to connect the lambs of eschatological peace with the Lamb of the Apocalypse, the function of the lamb imagery seems to differ. Furthermore, the function of sheep and lambs in the eschatological texts of the Old Testament are tied primarily to images of dependence and vulnerability. This suggests that the so-called lambs of eschatological peace are simply subsets of the vulnerable lamb tradition we find in the Old Testament and elsewhere (see below).

4.8 The Vulnerable Lamb of the LXX

The word ἀρνίον occurs only five times in the LXX[125]: Jer 11:19 [כֶּבֶשׂ]; 27(50):45 [צָעִיר]; Ps 113(114):4, 6 [בְּנֵי־צֹאן]; and PsSol 8:23. Ἀρνίον translates three different Hebrew words out of its four occurrences in texts with a Hebrew parallel, or four out of five, if one includes Aquila's translation of טְלָאִים in Isa 40:11. Various words for lamb occur nearly 150 times in the Hebrew Bible, along with many more for sheep. כֶּבֶשׂ is the most common word for lamb in the Old Testament.[126] Given this great number of occurrences, it is remarkable that ἀρνίον appears only five or six times and perhaps more remarkable that it "translates" or corresponds to three or four different Hebrew words for lamb. What accounts for the use of ἀρνίον in these selective instances?

Some "Aquila" manuscripts use ἀρνία in Isa 40:11 in place of טְלָאִים (or ἄρνας, LXX). In Isa 40 we have a prophecy of eschatological salvation. The context is the appearance of the Lord with power to deliver and rescue:

See, the Lord God comes with might,
    and his arm rules for him;
his reward is with him,
    and his recompense before him.
He will feed his flock like a shepherd;
    he will gather the lambs (טְלָאִים; ἄρνας[LXX]; ἀρνία[Aq]) in his arms,
and carry them in his bosom,
    and gently lead the mother sheep.[127]

---

[125] An additional appearance of ἀρνίον appears in Aquila's translation of טְלָאִים in Isa 40:11.

[126] According to the Even-Shoshar concordance, it occurs 107 times.

[127] Isa 40:10-11.

Lambs here functions as a metaphor for the weak and vulnerable Israelites, who will experience the compassionate care of a loving and powerful savior.

In Jer 11:19, the prophet laments his status as an unpopular prophet with an unpopular message. He says,

> But I was like a gentle [or innocent; cf. LXX] lamb [כְּכֶבֶשׂ אַלּוּף; ἀρνίον ἄκακον]
> led to the slaughter [לִטְבּוֹחַ; τοῦ θύεσθαι].
> And I did not know it was against me
>   that they devised schemes, saying
> 'Let us destroy the tree with its fruit
>   let us cut him off from the land of the living,
>   so that his name will no longer be remembered!'   —Jer 11:19, NRSV

The use of ἀρνίον at this point to translate כֶּבֶשׂ likely represents the translators' attempts to communicate the position of vulnerability and defenselessness in the face of violent rejection. The Greek adjective ἄκακον underlines the innocence of the lamb, while אַלּוּף underscores its tame or docile (nonviolent) qualities.

In Jeremiah's oracle announcing the fall of Babylon in chap. 50 (LXX 27), the fearsome army from the north will, like a lion (כְּאַרְיֵה), drag defenseless Babylon away: "Surely the little ones of the flock [צְעִירֵי הַצֹּאן; τὰ ἀρνία τῶν προβάτων] shall be dragged away; surely their fold shall be appalled at their fate" (Jer 50:45, NRSV; cf. 49:20, a later editorial revision of the same material that does not appear in the LXX). Here again the theme of defenselessness in the face of physical violence seems to trigger the use of ἀρνίον—the only time ἀρνίον corresponds to צָעִיר in the Old Testament.

Psalm 114 is a hymn of praise with a central theophany recalling the Exodus.[128] Twice there is reference to hills that skip like lambs of the flock [-כִּבְנֵי צֹאן; ὡς ἀρνία προβάτων]. The poetic structure places in parallel the rams (אֵילִים; κριοί) of the first part of the verse with the lambs in the second. Like the mountains that skip like rams, the hills skip like lambs in the presence of the Lord, the God of Jacob, when he led his people out of Exodus as the divine warrior (cf. Exod 15). The skipping is not a skipping of joyful frolic, but a skipping of trembling submission to the awesomeness of God.[129] Just as הַיָּם

---

[128] Westermann classifies it with "the declarative psalm of praises of the people" (Claus Westermann, *Praise and Lament in the Psalms* (Atlanta: John Knox Press, 1981; orig. pub. 1965) 81–83.

[129] Like רָעַד (to quake, tremble), the verb רָקַד (to skip) usually occurs in holy war/theophany contexts (cf. Isa 13:21; Joel 2:5; Nah 3:2; Pss 29:6; 114:4, 6; and 1Chr 15:29; cf. also Wisd 19:9).

In Job 21:11 and Qoh 3:4, however, רָקַד seems to imply simple joyful frivolity. The skipping of lambs and rams is also seen as joyful in the Similitudes, where nearly the same expression is used by the author to describe the joy of the righteous at the resurrection of the dead at the Last Judgment: "In those days, mountains shall dance like (the Sea) bowed in submission to the Lord and divided at the Exodus (Exod 14:21-22), so the mountains and hills skip in ironic submission (cf. Judg 5:4-5). Just as הַיָּם fled when God led Israel out of Egypt (v. 3), so the earth is admonished to tremble in the presence of the Lord (v. 7). As in the Jeremiah references, ἀρνίον communicates a sense of defenseless submission to a superior power.

PsSol 8 is one of the three Psalms that allude most directly to Pompey's capture of Jerusalem in 63 BCE.[130] Here the Psalmist rehearses the terrifying events, prayerfully laments the slaughter, and ponders the justice of God in it. Verses 1–22 consist of the Psalmist's rehearsal of the events. With v. 23, the Psalmist turns to lament, reflection, and supplication. Verse 23 reads:

> God was proven right in his condemnation of the nations of the earth,
> and the devout of God are like innocent lambs [ὡς ἀρνία ἐν ἀκακίᾳ] among
>   them.

The phrase, ἐν ἀκακίᾳ, suggests a parallel with Jer. 11:19, in which Jeremiah says, "I was like a gentle [or innocent] lamb (ἀρνίον ἄκακον)." Again, ἀρνίον seems to communicate something of defenseless vulnerability in the face of a violent, superior power. The vulnerable lamb tradition is certainly known in the New Testament; we have clear references to it in Matt 7:15; 10:16; Luke 10:3; and Acts 20:29.

Thus, in all five [or six] of its appearance in the LXX, ἀρνίον is used symbolically. These ἀρνίον references in the LXX are thus a subset of the larger semantic domain in which *lamb* is used symbolically (see Appendix).

Approximately 10% of the references to lambs in the Old Testament are symbolic. If one removes the Torah from consideration, in which *lamb* is never used symbolically, one sees that in the Prophets and Writings this proportion jumps to nearly half. Most of these references are found in the Latter Prophets and the late wisdom literature.

As we saw at the beginning of this chapter, the symbolism of the Apocalypse is characteristically a tensive symbolism. It is difficult to express in propositional terms the purpose or meaning of any tensive symbol. This difficulty certainly extends to the purpose and meaning of lamb symbolism in the Old Testament. Even when the literal lambs of the sacrificial cult are in view, one cannot deny the presence of symbolic meaning associated with the rite and its victims.

---

rams, and the hills shall leap like kids [or lambs] satiated with milk"; 1En 51:4: Ephraim Isaac, trans. and ed., "1 (Ethiopic Apocalypse of) Enoch," in *Old Testament Pseudepigrapha*, vol. 1, edited by James H. Charlesworth (Garden City, N.Y.: Doubleday, 1983), 51:4. Where Isaac has "kids," Charles has "lambs."

[130] The other two are 2 and 17.

Though further classification and distinction are risky and must remain tentative, the concept of nonviolence or vulnerability seem most capable of characterizing the symbolism expressed in most of these symbolic uses of lamb. In Sirach 47:3 the emphasis may be on the harmlessness of the lamb. In Hosea 4:16; Isaiah 40:11; and possibly 2 Samuel 12:3 the emphasis appears to be on the dependence of the lamb on the tender care of its owner or shepherd (Yahweh, in the first two instances). Vulnerability, nonviolence, or defenseless seem to be at work in the lamb symbolism of 2Sam 12:1-6; Ps 114:4-6; Isa 11:6; 34:6; 53:7; 65:25; Jer 11:19; 50:45; 51:40; Mic 5:7; Sir 13:17;[131] Wis 19:9; and PsSol 8:23.

In Jeremiah, death awaits the ἀρνία; in Psalms, merely submission to the powerful presence and will of Yahweh. In Isaiah, the lambs experience the tender care of the Lord. In the Psalms of Solomon, the lambs represent innocent and vulnerable Israel before the mighty armies of Pompey. In none of the cases does it represent a literal lamb, let alone a sheep or a ram. In none does ἀρνίον represent a substitutionary death, nor is it connected with atonement for sin. Sometimes it implies innocence, but in each of the cases, it symbolizes defenseless vulnerability in the face of violent power.

In a few of these cases, the vulnerability of the lamb is expressed as victimization, where the lamb is one who falls victim (or could easily fall victim) to a superior power. At times this victimization comes at the hands of other people (2Sam 12:1-6; Isa 53:7; PsSol 8:23); at times it comes at the hand of God (Isa 34:6; Jer 50:45; 51:40). But not all vulnerable lambs are victimized in the Old Testament. In fact, vulnerability *without* victimization seems precisely to be the sign of the eschaton: the passages that treat lambs as symbols in the visions of eschatological peace portray vulnerable lambs as safe in the presence of their traditional predators. Thus, while Israel as lamb is always *vulnerable*, Israel as lamb is not always *victim*.

But there are problems with identifying the Lamb of the Apocalypse with the vulnerable lamb tradition in the Old Testament. The most obvious of these is that the Lamb of the Apocalypse hardly seems vulnerable. Certainly the sense of endearment that the diminutive still occasionally expressed in New Testament times[132] cannot be in view. However touching the image of a lamb

---

[131] Note the comment of James L. Crenshaw. In speaking of the denial in Sir 13:17 that a wolf could have "fellowship" with a lamb, he says, "These examples serve to highlight the vulnerable status of poor people in the presence of the rich" (*Harper's Bible Commentary*, James Luther Mays, Harper & Row, and Society of Biblical Literature [San Francisco: Harper & Row, 1988], 846).

[132] See José Berenguer Sánchez, "ἀρνόν en PGurob 22 y el Empleo del Término ἀρνίον en los Papiros Documentales," *Emerita: Revista (Boletin) de Linguística y Filología Clásica* 57, no. 2 (1989): 277–88.

in the arms of God may be, that is not the Lamb of the Apocalypse! The Lamb of the Apocalypse is one who wages war with the sword of his mouth (2:16); from whom kings of the earth and magnates and commanders, the rich and powerful, slave and free, hid in caves and among the rocks of the mountains, saying, "Fall on us and hide us from the presence of the One who sits on the throne and from the wrath of the Lamb" (Rev 6:15). It was, in fact, the obvious fallacy of seeing the Lamb of the Apocalypse as a cute, dear lambkin that propelled Spitta to look for a militant conquering lamb tradition in Early Judaism. Thus, if vulnerability is in view, it can only be a gutsy, costly, and effective kind of vulnerability and an apocalyptic challenge to the usual meaning and value of these nouns and adjectives.

Rather than playing the helpless victim, the Lamb of the Apocalypse is a conquering, *victorious* lamb. In fact, conquering is precisely what makes the Lamb worthy to open the scroll, to break its seals, and to look into it (Rev 5:5, 9). It is to that scene and its definition of victory that we must now turn.

Chapter VI

The Rhetorical Force of the Lamb
Christology in the Apocalypse

This chapter moves beyond the question of the *origins* of the Lamb Christology to ask about John's *use* of it in the Apocalypse. Given the variety of lamb symbolisms available within and without the traditions of Early Judaism, how does the author of the Apocalypse portray the Lamb within the book? How does the Lamb Christology fit with the book's other major themes to propel the rhetoric of the Apocalypse? Does the rhetorical force of the Lamb Christology within the Apocalypse clarify the nature and purpose of the Lamb symbolism?

The answers commentators have given to these questions are surprisingly many. Some contrast the lamb with the lion in terms of appearance and reality. Others divide the images dispensationally, applying the imagery of the *lamb* to Christ's *first* appearance and that of the *lion* to his *second* coming or appearance.[1] Still others refer to the lion and lamb imagery as a "paradox" intended to communicate disparate understandings of the same figure.[2] Others

---

[1] This interpretation is typical among Fundamentalist Evangelicals in North America. For instance, Hal Lindsey says, "When Jesus came to earth the first time He came in humility to offer Himself as the Lamb of God to die for the sins of men. But when He comes again He'll return in the strength and supremacy of a lion" (*There's a New World Coming: A Prophetic Odyssey* [Santa Ana, Cal.: Vision House Publishers, 1973], 94); cf. also George Eldon Ladd: "[The] Messiah has a twofold role to fulfill. First, he must come in humility and meekness to suffer and die; then at the end of the age he must return in power and glory to put all his enemies under his feet. ... The reigning King must be first a crucified Savior" (*A Commentary on the Revelation of John* [Grand Rapids: William B. Eerdmans Publishing Company, 1972], 86–87). Note also the subtitle of the Fisherman Bible Studyguide to John's Apocalypse: *Revelation: The Lamb Who Is the Lion: Thirteen Studies for Individuals or Groups*, Gladys Hunt, rev. ed. (Wheaton, Ill.: Harold Shaw Publishers, 1994 [orig. pub. 1973]).

[2] Cf. e.g., Henry Barclay Swete, *The Apocalypse of St. John: The Greek Text with Introduction, Notes, and Indices*, 3d ed., reprint, 1906 (London: Macmillan and Co., 1909), 78. Bauckham seems close to this approach when he says that "the juxtaposition of more than one image with a single referent is a characteristic of John's visions" (Richard Bauckham, *The Climax of Prophecy: Studies on the Book of Revelation* [Edinburgh: T. & T. Clark, 1993], 179).

claim that John inherited a Lamb tradition from early Christian tradition, but that the divine warrior imagery in the Apocalypse—expressed in part by the figure of "the Lion of the tribe of Judah"—ends up transforming, reinterpreting, or subverting the Lamb Christology.[3] Still others claim that the book's great central image of Christ as the Lamb serves to control and interpret other major themes.[4] The key issues are thus what role the image of Christ as the Lamb plays within the Apocalypse, how the Lamb Christology relates to the other major themes, and how one is to adjudicate these mutually exclusive readings of the lamb Christology.

1. The Christology of the Apocalypse in Political Context

Quite a variety of terms for Christ appears in the Apocalypse, many of which fall into two interrelated categories: terms that emphasize the overcoming of death[5] and terms that have strong political overtones. The latter include "the

---

[3] See Adela Yarbro Collins, "Book of Revelation," *Anchor Bible Dictionary, Volume 5 (O–Sh)*, David Noel Freedman, gen. ed. (New York: Doubleday, 1992), 705.

[4] See, e.g., M. Eugene Boring, *Revelation*, Interpretation: A Bible Commentary for Teaching and Preaching (Louisville: John Knox, 1989), 110–11; George B. Caird, *The Revelation of St. John the Divine*, 2d ed., reprint, 1966, Black's New Testament Commentaries (London: Adam & Charles Black, 1984), 75; Vernard Eller, *The Most Revealing Book of the Bible: Making Sense Out of Revelation* (Grand Rapids, Mich.: William B. Eerdmans Publishing Company, 1974), 79; Ward B. Ewing, *The Power of the Lamb: Revelation's Theology of Liberation for You* (Cambridge, Mass.: Cowley Publications, 1990), *passim*; Ted Grimsrud, *Triumph of the Lamb: A Self-Study Guide to the Book of Revelation*, foreword by Willard M. Swartley (Scottdale, Pa.: Herald Press, 1987), 50–57; Wilfrid J. Harrington, *Revelation*, Sacra Pagina, vol. 16 (Wilmington, Del.: Michael Glazier, 1993), 86–88; Sophie Laws, *In the Light of the Lamb: Imagery, Parody, and Theology in the Apocalypse of John* (Wilmington, Del.: M. Glazier, 1988), 24; Christopher Rowland, *Revelation*, Epworth Commentaries (London: Epworth Press, 1993), 74–80; C. Freeman Sleeper, *The Victorious Christ: A Study of the Book of Revelation* (Louisville, Ky.: Westminster John Knox Press, 1996), 65–66.

We may leave aside the rather strange claim of Frederick Carter that it is not the lamb, but the *dragon* that is the central theme in the Apocalypse. See Frederick Carter, *Symbols of Revelation* (Berwick, Maine: Ibis Press, 2003). Carter suggests that the symbols in the Apocalypse "are manifestly astral images directly connected with the stars of heaven, … mighty cosmic figures, starry symbols of an earlier age, which sought the way of the gods treading skiey paths in dreams of splendour" (Carter, *Symbols of Revelation*, 37). Carter does not pause to argue or demonstrate this claim.

[5] These "titles" include "the firstborn from the dead" (ὁ πρωτότοκος τῶν νεκρῶν; 1:5), "the one who has freed us from our sins in/with his blood" (ὁ λύσας ἡμᾶς ἐκ τῶν ἁμαρτιῶν ἡμῶν ἐν τῷ αἵματι αὐτοῦ; 1:5), "the first and the last" (ὁ πρῶτος καὶ ὁ

ruler of the kings of the earth" (ὁ ἄρχων τῶν βασιλέων τῆς γῆς; 1:5),[6] "messiah" (Χριστός; 11:15, 12:10, 20:4, 6), "the one who is about to shepherd (or rule) all the nations" (ὁ μέλλει ποιμαίνειν πάντα τὰ ἔθνη; 12:5), "lord" (κύριος; 11:8; 14:13; 22:20), "lord of lords and king of kings" (κύριος κυρίων καὶ βασιλεὺς βασιλέων; 17:14; 19:16), "the lion from the tribe of Judah" (ὁ λέων ὁ ἐκ τῆς φυλῆς Ἰούδα; 5:5), "the root of David" (ἡ ῥίζα Δαυίδ; 5:5; 22:16), "the one who has the key of David" (ὁ ἔχων τὴν κλεῖν Δαυίδ; 3:7), the one who sits on the horse (ὁ καθήμενος ἐπὶ τοῦ ἵππου; 19:19,21; cf. also 6:2,4,5,8; 9:17; 19:18 where we have other riders of other horses).

Despite the success Constantinian Christianity has enjoyed in schooling readers to see this language as "spiritual," the political critique inherent in this language could hardly have been missed by first-century readers. The language of kings, kingdoms, and reigning (the βασιλ- word group) abounds in this book, occurring 38 times throughout the Apocalypse.[7] Such language makes most sense in a context where political allegiances were being called into

---

ἔσχατος; 1:17; 2:8; 22:13), "the living one" (ὁ ζῶν; 1:18; cf. 2:8); "the faithful and true witness" (ὁ μάρτυς ὁ πιστὸς καὶ ἀληθινός; 3:14; cf. 1:5; 19:11); "the alpha and the omega" (τὸ ἄλφα καὶ τὸ ὦ; 22:13); "the beginning and the end" (ἡ ἀρχὴ καὶ τὸ τέλος; 22:13).

Also, what does *not appear* may also be worthy of note: *savior* (σωτήρ; but σωτηρία occurs in 7:10; 12:10; 19:1); *teacher* (neither διδάσκαλος nor ῥαββί occurs, but διδάσκω does in 2:14,20, as does διδαχή in 2:14,24); *prophet* (προφήτης; but προφητεία occurs in 1:3; 11:6; 19:10; 22:7,10,18,19; and προφητεύω appears in 10:11; 11:3; προφήτης, referring to people, occurs in 10:7; 11:10,18; 16:6; 18:20,24; and 22:6,9 [cf. προφῆτις, in reference to Jezebel, 2:20]; *master* (δεσπότης, used of God in 6:10); *servant* (παῖς); or *God* (θεός).

[6] The political critique of kingship—or the relativizing of royal authority—inherent in these titles draws on well-established Jewish traditions. The Deuteronomistic historian preserved such a critique in 1Sam 8. And although 1En is itself a diverse collection of writings, one of the most important unifying themes in the collection is its critique of kingship (see 9:4; 12:3; 25:3,5,7; 27:3 [Book I]; 38:4-5; 46:3-5; 53:5; 54:2; 55:3-4; 63:2,4,7 [Book II]; 81:3 [Book III]; 84:2-5 [Book IV]; 91:13 [Book V]).

[7] βασιλεία (reign) occurs in 1:6,9; 5:10; 11:15; 12:10; 16:10; 17:12,17,18; βασιλεύς (king) occurs in 1:5; 6:15; 9:11; 10:11; 15:3; 16:12,14; 17:2,9,12[bis],14[bis],18; 18:3,9; 19:16[bis],18,19; 21:24; βασίλισσα (queen) occurs in 18:7; βασιλεύω (to reign) occurs in 5:10; 11:15,17; 19:6; 20:4,6; 22:5. Those that refer to God or God's messiah are 11:15,17; 12:10; 15:3; 17:14; 19:6,16. Those that refer to the saints as kings or a kingdom or ones who reign are 1:6,9; 5:10[bis]; 20:4,6; 22:5. Those that refer to human subjects generally or to Rome or to human kings as opponents of God include 1:5; 6:15; 10:11; 11:15; 16:12,14; 17:2,9,12 [three times], 14,17,18[bis]; 18:3,7,9; 19:16,18,19; 21:24. Those that refer to the reign of the beasts or of the angel of the bottomless pit include 9:11; 16:10. The count of 38 does not include the use of other words that relate to ruling or reigning, such as ἄρχων (1:5) and ποιμαίνω (2:27; 7:17; 12:5; 19:15).

question. The two pressures in the province of Asia that most adequately explain the presence of such a political critique in the Apocalypse are (a) local pressure to participate in the imperial cult; and (b) the temptation to engage in the sort of commerce and trade that inevitably served the imperial cult. [8]

There is broad agreement that the symbolism of Rev 13, with its parody of the two beasts, is an assault directed at the imperial cult. [9] The first beast rose out of the sea (i.e., from Rome across the sea) and symbolizes the evil of blasphemous Rome and its emperors. It receives its "power and throne and great authority" from the dragon (13:2), previously identified as Satan (12:9). The second beast rose out of the land (i.e., from local, provincial initiatives). "It exercises all the authority of the first beast on its behalf, and it makes the earth and its inhabitants worship the first beast" (13:12). These two beasts thus represent the Roman Empire—or emperors—generally and the priests of the imperial cult—or the imperial cult as such—specifically.

Central to the book's ethical critique is therefore its denunciation of the emperor cult. However, if this were the only concern of the author, one would expect a more consistent or sustained treatment of the emperor cult, especially in Revelation 2 and 3. This we do not have. Although the many participial "titles" of Jesus in Revelation 2 and 3 emphasize his exalted status, it appears that the emperor cult was only one of several examples of compromise with pagan values that concerned our author. For him, such compromise was blasphemy and idolatry.

Many of the titles have to do with the overcoming of death. Although we may more naturally think of overcoming death as a spiritual issue, these titles are political in the sense that the ultimate powerlessness of the governing authorities is celebrated in those titles. The titles that emphasize the overcoming of death may actually be the most political. The Apocalypse is a subversive resistance manual. [10] If the seven churches of Asia were to adopt an ethic of resistance to the empire (including the imperial cult) that would in turn lead to death, then those titles that emphasize the overcoming of death become

---

[8] The word θλῖψις, the semi-technical term in the Apocalypse for "persecution" comes from θλίβω, which means to press or compress. Thus, political "pressure" to compromise with civic imperial cult may have be seen by John as a form of persecution.

[9] See, for example, Elisabeth Schüssler Fiorenza, *Revelation: Vision of a Just World*, Proclamation Commentaries (Minneapolis: Fortress, 1991), 83–87, 119–29; cf. also Steven J. Friesen, *Twice Neokoros: Ephesus, Asia and the Cult of the Flavian Imperial Family*, Religions in the Graeco-Roman World, vol. 116 (Leiden and New York: E.J. Brill, 1993).

[10] Cf. C. Freeman Sleeper, *Victorious Christ*, 56; cf. also Christopher Rowland, "The Apocalypse: Hope, Resistance and the Revelation of Reality," *Ex Auditu* 6 (1990): 129–44.

charged with political import. Resistance to the point of death is a resistance *ethic* in the Apocalypse, not just an ideology of martyrdom (see esp. 12:11). Among the terms or images of Christ used in this way, ἀρνίον is by far the most important.

Even "the faithful witness" (ὁ μάρτυς ὁ πιστός) in 1:5 is a political term. The phrase is a second attributive construction, not a pair of appositional substantives. Although the double μου in ὁ μάρτυς μου ὁ πιστός μου ("my witness, my faithful one") in reference to Antipas in 2:13 makes it clear that the adjectives *there* are appositional substantives, the triadic structure of 1:4-8 makes it probable that the construction here is attributive: "the faithful witness." As Paul Minear has pointed out, five triads appear in 1:4-8. The phrase ὁ μάρτυς ὁ πιστός occurs as one of the three elements of the triad in v. 5a.[11]

Μάρτυς is already on the way toward becoming a technical term in the Apocalypse, but its redefinition was not yet complete.[12] The title ὁ μάρτυς ὁ πιστός likely refers to one who has been brought before the provincial governor and who has not apostasized, as suggested in the Letters of Pliny to Trajan 10.96–97. We will investigate the political implications of the μαρτυ- word group further below.

Elisabeth Schüssler Fiorenza has contrasted the political nature of the book's rhetoric with its liturgical form: While the book's rhetoric "is replete with cultic language and imagery, its social location and theological goal are not liturgical but political."[13] As Jean-Pierre Ruiz has established in several publications,[14] the worship scenes of the Apocalypse are essentially political in their rhetorical force. Specifically, "the mediation of meaning through ritual worked to shape a strategy of resistance."[15]

Even the liturgy of the Apocalypse is essentially political in its rhetorical force. The text itself implies that the function of worship is political. As Adela

---

[11] See Paul S[evier] Minear, *I Saw a New Earth: An Introduction to the Visions of the Apocalypse* (Washington and Cleveland: Corpus Books, 1968), 9–10. Cf. also "the faithful and true witness" (ὁ μάρτυς ὁ πιστὸς καὶ ἀληθινός) in 3:14.

[12] Cf. the analysis of Strathmann in μάρτυς, κτλ., in Gerhard Kittel, ed., *Theological Dictionary of the New Testament*, translated by Geoffrey W. Bromiley (Grand Rapids: Wm. B. Eerdmans Publishing Company, 1964–76), 4:474–514.

[13] Elisabeth Schüssler Fiorenza, *Revelation: Vision of a Just World*, Proclamation Commentaries (Minneapolis: Fortress, 1991), 103.

[14] Jean-Pierre Ruiz, "Betwixt and Between on the Lord's Day: Liturgy and the Apocalypse," in *Society of Biblical Literature 1992 Seminar Papers*, Society of Biblical Literature 1992 seminar papers, no. 31 (Atlanta: Scholars Press, 1992), 654–72; Jean-Pierre Ruiz, "The Politics of Praise: A Reading of Revelation 19:1-10," in *Society of Biblical Literature 1997 Seminar Papers* (Atlanta: Scholars Press, 1997), 374–93. This latter essay was revised as "Praise and Politics in Revelation 19:1-10," in *Studies in the Book of Revelation*, ed. Steve Moyise (Edinburgh: T. & T. Clark, 2001), 69–84.

[15] Jean-Pierre Ruiz, "Praise and Politics in Revelation 19:1-10," 84.

Yarbro Collins has pointed out, "every vision of salvation which *precedes* the depiction of the final battle (19:11–20:3) involves a liturgical element, while those which *follow* do not (20:4-6, 21:1–22:5)."[16] This suggests that the primary function of worship in the Apocalypse is to proclaim and experience salvation proleptically as part of the believing community's resistance to the empire. Once the powers of evil are finally judged, worship and liturgy are no longer needed. There is, in fact, no need for a Temple in the New Jerusalem (21:22). Thus, the rhetorical force of the praise and allegiance expressed in such worship is profoundly political.

2. The Rhetoric of the Apocalypse

The pioneering work in rhetorical readings of the Apocalypse was done by Elisabeth Schüssler Fiorenza.[17] In her 1985 article, "The Followers of the Lamb: Visionary Rhetoric and Social-Political Situation,"[18] Schüssler Fiorenza argued that the Apocalypse is a

> poetic-rhetorical work. It seeks to persuade and motivate by constructing a "symbolic universe" that invites imaginative participation. The strength of its persuasion for action lies ... in the "evocative" power of its symbols as well as in its hortatory, imaginative, emotional language, and dramatic movement, which engage the hearer (reader) by eliciting reactions, emotions, convictions, and identifications.[19]

---

[16] Adela Yarbro Collins, *The Combat Myth in the Book of Revelation*, Harvard Dissertations in Religion, no. 9 (Missoula, Montana: Scholars Press, 1976), 234.

[17] Schüssler Fiorenza built, of course, on the work of others, especially that of Amos N. Wilder. See Amos N. Wilder, "Scholars, Theologians, and Ancient Rhetoric," *Journal of Biblical Literature* 75 (1958): 1–11; Amos N. Wilder, "Rhetoric of Ancient and Modern Apocalyptic," *Interpretation* 25 (October 1971): 436–53; and Amos N. Wilder, "Apocalyptic Rhetorics," chapt. 7 in *Jesus' Parables and the War of Myths: Essays on Imagination in the Scripture*, edited by James Breech, with an introduction by James Breech (Philadelphia: Fortress Press, 1982), 153–68.

[18] Elisabeth Schüssler Fiorenza, "The Followers of the Lamb: Visionary Rhetoric and Social-Political Situation," in *Discipleship in the New Testament*, edited by Fernando Segovia (Philadelphia: Fortress, 1985), 386–403. This article was reprinted as "Visionary Rhetoric and Social-Political Situation" in *The Book of Revelation: Justice and Judgment* (Philadelphia: Fortress, 1985) 181–203; and as "The Followers of the Lamb: Visionary Rhetoric and Social-Political Situation" in *Semeia* 36 (1986): 123–46.

[19] Elisabeth Schüssler Fiorenza, *The Book of Revelation: Justice and Judgment* (Philadelphia: Fortress, 1985), 187.

Schüssler Fiorenza followed up on this essay with her Proclamation Commentaries volume on the Apocalypse in 1991.[20] After an introduction featuring the rationale for and method of rhetorical analysis, Schüssler Fiorenza demonstrates the method in an exegetical section, followed by a section on the "theoethical" implications of such a reading.

Rhetoric should not be misunderstood as having to do primarily with aesthetics. Though it includes aesthetics, its primary concern is with the nature and quality of persuasive discourse. Formally, the Apocalypse exhibits elements of all three types of classical rhetoric: deliberative, forensic, and epideictic, though the epideictic predominates. We need not assume that John's audience was trained in classical rhetoric in order to identify profitably the nature of the rhetoric employed in the Apocalypse.

Signs of deliberative rhetoric include editorial calls to discernment and injunctions to "keep" the words of this prophecy, with which the book begins and ends. The author pronounces "macarisms" or blessings in the first and last chapters of the Apocalypse on those who respond to or "keep" what John writes.[21] He says, "Blessed are ... those who keep the things written in it" (1:3); "Blessed is the one who keeps the words of the prophecy of this book" (22:7).[22] Whatever else we conclude about the book, it was meant to effect a

---

[20] Elisabeth Schüssler Fiorenza, *Revelation: Vision of a Just World*, Proclamation Commentaries (Minneapolis: Fortress, 1991).

[21] All of the "blessings" in the book relate in some way to the resistance ethic of the book; cf. also 14:13; 16:15; 19:9; 20:6; 22:14. Despite Stephen Goranson's efforts to argue to the contrary (Stephen Goranson, "The Text of Revelation 22.14," *New Testament Studies* 43 (1997): 154–57), the reading, πλύνοντες τὰς στολὰς αὐτῶν (those who wash their robes) in 22:14 has better external witnesses and is the more difficult reading when compared to ποιοῦντες τὰς ἐντολὰς αὐτοῦ (those who do his commandments). While "doing his commandments" is certainly an important concern for the author (see the following note), it is more likely that a later scribe was perplexed by a blessing on those who washed their robes (which is nevertheless in keeping with 7:14; cf. also 3:4-5,18; 6:11; 15:6; 16:15; 19:8,14) than by a blessing on those who do his commandments.

[22] Other injunctions to "keep" or "obey" what John has written (or commendations for doing so) appear in 3:3,8,10; 12:17; 14:12; 16:15; 22:9. Partially overlapping these injunctions and commendations is a strong emphasis on the importance of "works"; cf. 2:2,5,6,19,22,23,26; 3:1,2,8,15; 9:20; 14:13; 16:11; 18:6; 20:12,13; 22:12; cf. also 15:3 for God's works. Perhaps the word most characteristic of the author's deliberative rhetoric is his call for (or commendation of) "consistent resistance" (or ὑπομονή): 1:9; 2:2,3,19; 3:10; 13:10; 14:12. While these examples suggest that there was form and content to the kind of response the author envisioned, the rhetorical *form* in which he expressed those interests is primarily epideictic. Thus, we see here a clear example of what Kennedy refers to as the "subtle deliberative purpose" present in epideictic rhetoric (George A. Kennedy, *New Testament Interpretation Through Rhetorical Criticism* [Chapel Hill, N.C./London: University of North Carolina Press, 1984], 74).

faithful response on the part of its hearers. While forensic rhetoric is not as pronounced in the Apocalypse, we see signs of it in the bitter denunciation of Rome, the condemnation of John's opponents in the seven churches, and in the frequent resort to forensic terminology—especially that of the μάρτυς/μαρτυρία word group.

Epideictic rhetoric seeks primarily to shape the readers' identity and values. It does so through specific applications of blame and/or praise on certain actions (primarily in Revelation 2–3), through scenes of worship, and through celebrations over God's judgment on evildoers and over the demise of demonic Rome. The entire narrative structure of the visions in the Apocalypse serves to impel the book's epideictic rhetoric.

Three types of persuasion or "proof" are common in discussions of classical rhetoric: logos, ethos, and pathos. Logos depends on appeals to logic. We see little of this in the Apocalypse. Ethical persuasion depends on establishing the character (ἦθος) of the narrator as trustworthy. Ethical persuasion appears primarily in the opening and closing chapters of the Apocalypse.[23] Pathetical persuasion persuades by exciting the emotions and imagination of the audience.

The Apocalypse is primarily a book of pathetical persuasion, though its persuasive power is not in the logocentric sort of persuasion modern Westerners often associate with the word *persuasion*. The force of its persuasion lies in its attempt to create a frame of reference, an understanding—or *sense*—of the world, of God's work, and of the believing community's faithfulness that is different from that which characterized the seven churches of Asia. As Royalty has noted, it does so by "removing 'common sense' as a guide for perceiving the social order and thereby turning the social order upside down."[24]

It is this pathetical form of persuasion in service of an epideictic rhetoric that we see most clearly at work in the central scene of the Apocalypse. Its rhe-

---

[23] For a good discussion of the ethical persuasion in 1:1-3, see Robert M. Royalty, Jr., "The Rhetoric of Revelation," in *Society of Biblical Literature 1997 Seminar Papers*, Society of Biblical Literature Seminar Papers Series, no. 36 (Atlanta: Scholars Press, 1997), 607–09. To this could be added the humble self-introduction of John in 1:9, where words like ὁ ἀδελφὸς ὑμῶν and συγκοινωνός subtly invite the reader's trust. The command to write, which peppers the Apocalypse (1:11,19; 2:1,8,12,18; 3:1, 7,14; 10:4; 14:13; 19:9; 21:5), adds to the book's "ethical" appeal: the author is simply the trustworthy medium through whom God has given this revelation.

[24] See Robert M. Royalty, Jr., "Rhetoric of Revelation," 600; cf. also Wayne A. Meeks, *The Moral World of the First Christians*, Library of Early Christianity, no. 6 (Philadelphia: Westminster Press, 1986), 143–44. For a similar assessment, see Leonard L. Thompson, "Mooring the Revelation in the Mediterranean," in *Society of Biblical Literature 1992 Seminar Papers*, Society of Biblical Literature 1992 Seminar Papers, no. 31 (Atlanta: Scholars Press, 1992), 651.

torical program makes careful attention to what a text *does* to the reader crucial in interpretation.[25] Thus, a rhetorical approach to understanding the
image of the Lamb in the Apocalypse is necessary.[26]

3. The Central Scene in Revelation 5

As a narrative, the Apocalypse has both characterization and plot.[27] The rhetorical fulcrum of the Apocalypse is the scene in heaven in chapters 4 and 5.[28]
It is here that many of the important themes in the Apocalypse are introduced
for the first time: the throne (though see 1:4; 3:21), the One sitting on the

---

[25] Jörg Frey is especially attentive to what the various images of the Apocalypse
"do" to the reader: "Sie konstituieren eine symbolische Welt, in die die Leserinnen und
Leser eintreten können, so daß in der Lektüre, im Nachvollzug der Visionsbilder des
Werks, ihre eigene Sicht der Welt eine Klärung und fundamentale Neuorientierung er-
fährt." See "Die Bildersprache der Johannesapokalypse," *Zeitschrift für Theologie und
Kirche* 98 (2001): 161–85, esp. 182–83.

[26] The christological investigations of Traugott Holtz, Joseph Comblin, and Nikola
Hohnjec, while helpful, are hindered by their lack of attention to how the Christology
of the Apocalypse *works*, how and what it communicated to the original hearers/read-
ers of the book. As Richard Bauckham has said, "The study of the images of the Apocalypse can usefully proceed only through reconstruction of their resonances in their historical context." The full significance of archetypal images, such as that of the lamb,
"is not appreciable apart from the range of association they were capable of evoking in
the seven churches of Asia in the late first century A.D." (Richard Bauckham, *Climax
of Prophecy*, 179). For a more extended treatment of the role of the Lamb symbolism
within the rhetorical program of the Apocalypse, see Loren L. Johns, "The Lamb in the
Rhetorical Program of the Apocalypse of John," in *Seminar Papers, Part Two* (Atlanta:
Scholars Press, 1998), 762–84. See also the helpful methodological reflections of Jörg
Frey in "Die Bildersprache." Especially helpful is Frey's insistence that the modern interpreter maintain a balanced sense of the role of the individual symbol within the larger "picture book" represented by the Apocalypse: "Der Sinn und die evokative Kraft
des Bildes ergeben sich erst aus dem neuen Ganzen, aber die einzelnen Elemente tra-
gen aus ihrem ursprünglichen Zusammenhang wesentliche Aspekte zu diesem Ganzen
bei" ("Die Bildersprache," 173).

[27] Cf. Thomas Harding, "Take Back the Apocalypse," 29–35; David E. Aune, "The
Apocalypse of John and the Problem of Genre," *Semeia* 36 (1986): 65–96; David L.
Barr, "Using Plot to Discern Structure in John's Apocalypse," in *Proceedings of the
Eastern Great Lakes and Mid-West Biblical Societies* (1995), 23–33.

[28] Cf. Schüssler Fiorenza, *Revelation*, 58. On the importance of Rev 4–5 within the
Apocalypse as a whole, see the new important monograph by Gottfried Schimanowski,
*Die himmlische Liturgie in der Apokalypse des Johannes: Die frühjüdischen Tradition-
en in Offenbarung 4–5 unter Einschluß der Hekhalotliteratur*, Wissenschaftliche Untersuchungen zum neuen Testament, 2.Reihe 154 (Tübingen: Mohr Siebeck, 2002).

throne, the four living creatures, the twenty-four elders, and the Book (or scroll). Though this scene is a unity, it is not independent from the rest of the book.[29]

While the throne vision of chapter 4 is the necessary context, the climax of this scene comes in the fifth chapter. The scene revolves around the question, "Who is worthy to take the scroll?" It is announced that the Lion conqueror is worthy. But what does the seer see? "A lamb standing as slaughtered" (5:6). This scene lies at the theological heart of the Apocalypse. It is specifically designed to communicate the shock, irony, and ethical import of his message that *the Conquering One conquers by being a slain lamb*, not a devouring lion.

The Seer introduces the Lamb in Revelation 5 in such a way as to underscore a central reversal in his apocalypse. At the heart of this reversal is a redefinition of power as perceived in John's theology of the cross. As James H. Charlesworth,[30] Sophie Laws,[31] and others have pointed out, the Apocalypse features a series of reversals, parodies, and redefinitions. What is the nature of the reversal and redefinition intended in the lamb Christology? How does this Christology function in terms of the desired ethical response of the communities to which John was writing?

Nearly all of the commentators on the Apocalypse have rightly recognized the importance of the book's Lamb Christology; many have recognized the structural and theological significance of Rev 4–5 for the book as a whole and the rhetorical force of the introduction of the lamb in this scene. Examples of the latter include Paul Achtemeier, David Barr, Richard Bauckham, M. Eugene Boring, G. B. Caird, Donald Guthrie, and Nikola Hohnjec.[32] Boring

---

[29] Cf. Nikola Hohnjec, *"Das Lamm, τὸ ἀρνίον" in der Offenbarung des Johannes: Eine exegetisch-theologische Untersuchung* (Roma: Herder, 1980), 36.

[30] James H. Charlesworth, "The Apocalypse of John: Its Theology and Impact on Subsequent Apocalypses," in *The New Testament Apocrypha and Pseudepigrapha: A Guide to Publications, with Excursuses on Apocalypses* (Metuchen and London: The American Theological Library Association and Scarecrow Press, 1987), 19–51; see esp. 28–30.

[31] Sophie Laws, *In the Light.*

[32] On Paul J. Achtemeier, see "Revelation 5:1-14," *Interpretation* 40 (1986): 284–85. On David L. Barr, see "The Apocalypse as a Symbolic Transformation of the World: A Literary Analysis," *Interpretation* 38 (January 1984): 39–50. Richard Bauckham says, "The figure of the lamb is introduced in Revelation 5:5-6. The manner of its introduction is very significant." And "the notion of messianic conquest is reinterpreted. ... Precisely by juxtaposing these contrasting images, John forges a symbol of conquest by sacrificial death, which is essentially a new symbol" (Richard Bauckham, *Climax of Prophecy*, 179, 183). On M. Eugene Boring, see especially his section entitled, "The Christological Redefinition of Winning," in M. Eugene Boring, *Revelation*, 108–11. I agree with Boring when he says that the relationship between "lion" and "lamb"

rightly calls this "one of the most mind-wrenching and theologically pregnant transformations of imagery in literature."[33] David Barr says, "A more complete reversal of value would be hard to imagine."[34] In Donald Guthrie's words, "there could hardly be a more striking or unexpected contrast."[35]

Not surprisingly, those who assume the existence of a militaristic redeemer lamb figure in Early Judaism see little or no surprise or contrast here between the lion and the lamb. Josephine Massyngberde Ford:

> Although instead of *arnos*, Greek for "lamb," the diminutive form *arnion*, "little lamb" is used, the strength and maturity of the animal is suggested by its possession of seven horns, the plenitude of strength, and seven eyes, the plenitude of discernment. These features and a study of the background of the image indicate that the character of the Lamb is not sharply contrasted with that of the Lion. Taking into consideration all the information concerning the Lamb which our apocalypse offers, it cannot be doubted that the Lamb is the apocalyptic ram, a synonym for the messiah, a traditional symbol in such literature and quite consonant with the eschatological, fierce preaching of the Baptist.[36]

Even Schimanowski contends that the vulnerability and victimization implied in the "slaughtered" state of the Lamb is entirely in the past for the author of the Apocalypse. There is no redefinition of power at work in this text; the Apocalypse is all about Christ's lordship.[37] While Schimanowski's collection of parallel material is impressive, his methodology is primarily synchronic and his explication of Revelation's symbols is inattentive to the changing shape of symbol in the Second Temple Period.

However, as we established above in chap. 4, the assumption of Ford and others that there was a militaristic lamb redeemer figure in Early Judaism is not supported by the evidence. The fullness of the lamb's strength and discern-

---

"is *crucial* to understanding all of Revelation's theology" (109). On George B. Caird, see *Revelation*, 74–75. On Donald Guthrie, see "The Lamb in the Structure of the Book of Revelation," *Vox Evangelica* 12 (1987) 64–71. On Nikola Hohnjec, see *Das Lamm*, 36–37, 62. In agreement with Van Unnik, Hohnjec says, "So ist Offb 5 nicht nur vom formalen Gesichtspunkt her für die Struktur der Offenbarung des Johannes wichtig, sondern auch betreffs des theologischen Inhalts, vor allem als Ausgangspunkt für das Verständnis ihrer Christologie (p. 63).

[33] M. Eugene Boring, "Narrative Christology in the Apocalypse," *Catholic Biblical Quarterly* 54 (1992) 708.

[34] David L. Barr, "Apocalypse as Symbolic Transformation," 41.

[35] Donald Guthrie, "Lamb in the Structure," 64.

[36] J. Massyngberde Ford, *Revelation*, The Anchor Bible, vol. 38 (Garden City, N.Y.: Doubleday & Company, 1975), 89.

[37] See Schimanowski, *Himmlische Liturgie*, 213.

ment—symbolized by the horns and eyes—shows that the lamb is not simply a symbol of weakness: it really is strong and wise. However, its strength is here being redefined, reconceived. The lamb is strong, but the exhibition of its strength is unconventional: its strength lies in its consistent, nonviolent resistance to evil—a resistance that led to its execution. But the lamb stands triumphant, raised from the dead. Essential to a proper understanding of the book's rhetoric is the recognition that the lamb *has triumphed in* his death and resurrection, not that the lamb *will triumph in the future, subsequent to* his death and resurrection. A close reading of the text supports this important distinction.[38]

Guthrie is right in noting the rhetorical import of the surprising introduction of the lamb, but not in his interpretation of the force of that import. He says, "The slain Lamb is intentionally introduced to focus on the central conviction that the Christian church is a redeemed community and that the Lamb is the representation of redemption as an accomplished act. The agent through whom God will achieve final victory is a symbol of sacrifice."[39] Though this explanation is obscure, Guthrie seems to emphasize the sacrificial connotations associated with the lamb, especially "the ransoming effect of the [lamb's] blood."[40]

The primary ambiguity in Guthrie's explanation lies in his use of the language of sacrifice. While it is certainly true that the slaughter of the lamb is central to the rhetorical force of the image, it is not true that expiation is. In fact, the logic and language of slaughter as expiatory sacrifice are quite rare in the Apocalypse, while the logic and language of slaughter as political resistance and martyrdom are common. Because "sacrificial" language is imprecise and often implies an expiatory force, such language should be avoided with reference to the Apocalypse.[41]

---

[38] Grant Osborne seems to want it both ways: "The direction of the transformation is very important; the final stage is the lamb, not the lion. The paragraph of 5:6-10 tells how the lion of Judah has conquered, not through military power (though that will come) but through paschal sacrifice." While such an interpretation supports a radical redefinition of power in the Apocalypse, on the next page Osborne comments, "The lion is transformed into a lamb that becomes the slain paschal lamb that is again transformed into the conquering ram (the seven horns)! There is even a certain chiasm: lion—lamb—slain lamb—conquering ram"! (Grant R. Osborne, *Revelation* [Baker Exegetical Commentary on the New Testament; Grand Rapids: Baker Books, 2002], 254, 255).

[39] Donald Guthrie, "The Lamb," 65.

[40] Donald Guthrie, "The Lamb," 65.

[41] The Apocalypse of John has traditionally been seen as a problem for a Girardian reading of the New Testament (see, e.g., René Girard, *Things Hidden Since the Foundation of the World*, Jean-Michel Oughourlian and Guy Lefort [Stanford: Stanford University Press, 1987]). The two primary challenges to a Girardian reading of the Apoca-

By the time the lamb is first introduced in chap. 5, some thirty other terms for Christ have been used in the book.[42] The introduction of the lamb in the throne scene in chapter five is handled deliberately and carefully. Although most of the other terms for Christ have already appeared, including even proleptically a picture of Christ on the throne in 3:21, the Seer carefully avoids the word ἀρνίον until the throne room scene in Revelation 5.

The seer's portrayal of Jesus as the lamb is meant to be a surprise. He builds the drama and suspense by introducing an element of *pathos* into the scene.[43] John sees a scroll with writing on both sides in the right hand of the One sitting on the throne. When a powerful angel cries out with a loud voice, "Who is worthy to break the seals" (5:2), the narrator comments that "no one in heaven nor on the earth nor under the earth was able to open the scroll or to look at [inside?] it" (5:3).

Chapter 5 is divided into two scenes, both of which contribute to the centrality of this chapter as the rhetorical fulcrum of the book. The first scene plays out the drama of the scroll in the right hand of the one sitting on the throne. The reader is not told exactly what the scroll represents, but the importance of finding one worthy to break its seals, to open it, and to look inside is

---

lypse lie in its reification of sacrifice through the Lamb Christology and in its notion of divine violence. The first of these challenges is easily overcome, since the Lamb Christology of the Apocalypse, when properly understood, does not support the "generative mimetic scapegoat mechanism." Although Burton Mack defines the word *sacrifice* as referring "ultimately to the structuring mechanism of the hidden level" (Robert Hamerton-Kelly, ed., *Violent Origins: Walter Burkert, René Girard, and Jonathan K. Smith on Ritual Killing and Cultural Formation* [Stanford, Cal.: Stanford University Press, 1987], 10), René Girard now acknowledges that not all sacrifice nor the rhetoric of sacrifice itself necessarily reflects the GMSM. Compare René Girard, *Things Hidden*, 228; and René Girard, *The Scapegoat* (Baltimore: Johns Hopkins University Press, 1986), 200; cf. the comments in Raymund Schwager, "Christ's Death and the Prophetic Critique of Sacrifice," translated by P. Riordan, *Semeia*, no. 33 (1985): 119–20. The second challenge is more serious. Girard unfortunately uses the word *Apocalypse* as a virtual synonym for the logic of violence (René Girard, "The Nonsacrificial Death of Christ," in *The Girard Reader*, edited by James G. Williams, A Crossroad Herder Book [New York: Crossroad, 1996], 185). Nevertheless, Schwager rightly challenges this understanding of the Apocalypse (Raymund Schwager, *Must There Be Scapegoats? Violence and Redemption in the Bible* [San Francisco: Harper & Row, 1987]).

[42] This number includes the many participles in chaps. 2–3, which help to fill out the ingredients of Revelation's Christology. See Appendix II.

[43] See the discussion above on "pathetical" proofs, one of the three standard modes of proof in classical rhetoric. See also Robert M. Royalty, Jr., "Rhetoric of Revelation," 606; George A. Kennedy, *New Testament Interpretation*, 14–19; cf. Aristotle *Rhetoric* 1.2.2–5 [1356a].

clear. A strong angel appears, proclaiming in a loud voice, "Who is worthy to open the scroll and to break its seals?" When no one is found who can do so, John begins to weep uncontrollably.[44] But John's weeping is arrested by an elder who announces that indeed one *has* been found: The lion of the tribe of Judah, the root of David, has conquered [and can thus] open the scroll and its seven seals.

The weeping of John, combined with the loud proclamation of a strong angel and a search that proceeds in heaven, in the earth, and under the earth to find one worthy, adds to the *pathos* of the scene. This is a vitally important matter and has to do with the keys of history, perhaps even the meaning of life or the justice of God.

The Seer does not make clear what the scroll or the breaking of its seals represents. However, the breaking of the seals in Revelation 6–8 associates the scroll in some way with the realization of God's will in history or authority over the course of history.[45] This is not to take a *"weltgeschichtliche"* interpretation of the book, as if Revelation contains a code that, once deciphered, maps out the details of world history. The point is rather that the Lamb represents in some way the key to the working out of God's plan and that God's will for humanity in some way depends upon the victorious success of the Lamb.

But here I think we can say more: the Lamb is, in fact, the revelation of *how* God works in history. The lamb is the "window" through whom God is revealed. If this is true, it would underscore the importance of the claim in 1:1 that the Apocalypse is a revelation of Jesus Christ (objective genitive). This reading is strengthened on the basis of the otherwise inexplicable weeping of John in v. 4.[46] The implication is that the continued progress of history toward its divinely assigned goal would be impeded apart from someone found worthy to open the scroll. But who is worthy (ἄξιος; vv. 2, 4), who has the ability (δύναμαι; v. 3) to open the scroll? Only the one who has *"conquered ... to open the scrolls"* (ἐνίκησεν ... ἀνοῖξαι τὸ βιβλίον καὶ τὰς ἑπτὰ σφραγῖδας αὐτοῦ; v. 5). The requisite worthiness is therefore linked with νικάω (overcome or conquer), an important word for the Seer.

---

[44] The imperfect verb ἔκλαιον with the adjective πολύ strengthens the expression.

[45] Wilfrid J. Harrington calls the lamb's reception of the scroll from the one seated on the throne "a transfer of power" (Wilfrid J. Harrington, *Revelation*, 87). However, the word *transfer* is too strong a word here, since it implies a zero-based sum and there is no hint that the Lamb *replaces* the one seated on the throne; a "conferring of power" would be better.

[46] Weeping and lamentation are a τύπος in the Jeremiah and Baruch traditions (cf. e.g., Jer 3:21; 4:8; 6:26; 7:29; 9:1, 10, 20; 13:17; 16:4-7; 22:10, 18; 25:33; 31:9-21; 34:5; 41:6; 48:5, 32-38; 49:3; 50:4; Bar 1:5; 4:11, 23; 2Bar 10:4-19). Although they function there as a response to the judgments of God, weeping also heightens pathos in one's recognition that injustice is prevailing and God's will is being thwarted.

When one of the elders announces that one *has* conquered and is therefore worthy, he announces the victor as ὁ λέων, ὁ ἐκ τῆς φυλῆς Ἰούδα, and ἡ ῥίζα Δαυίδ. These phrases appear in parallel and are meant to define and explain each other, identifying the redeemer figure with messianic expectations.[47] The mention of "Judah" and "David" obviously recalls traditions and expectations built on ancient Jewish hopes.[48]

3.1 The Lion

The association of the lion with royalty is an ancient one.[49] "From the beginnings of Egypt, [the lion] represented its king, its power, and its immutability."[50] This association was quite literal—the lion was the king and the king was the lion—and structurally deep: "Even the word for 'prince' or 'local ruler' in ancient Egyptian was written with a hieroglyphic ideogram in the form of the forepart of a recumbent and self-composed lion."[51] Later on, in the mid-first-millennium BCE, the lion came to be associated more directly with the god Mihos.[52] .

The royal lions of Egypt are usually portrayed in art as lying down and calmly confident. However, the potential for violence was always inherent in the symbolism. "The very presence of the lion as the Egyptians portrayed him was powerful enough to repel any trespasser."[53] Furthermore, "the Egyptian

---

[47] These phrases derive from Gen 49:9 and Isa 11:1-5 respectively, both of which were classic texts for Jewish restoration hopes in the first century. These titles were already combined in 4QPBless; 1QSb 5.20–29. The "shoot of David" was clearly a common title used for an eschatological redeemer figure in the Dead Sea scrolls; see 4Q285 Frg. 5, lines 3–4; 4QFlor 1.11–12; 4QpIsaᵃ Frg. A; cf. also PsSol 17:24,35–37; 4Ezra 13:10; 1En 49:3; 62:2). See Richard Bauckham, *Climax of Prophecy*, 214; cf. also John J. Collins, *The Scepter and the Star: The Messiahs of the Dead Sea Scrolls and Other Ancient Literature* (New York: Doubleday, 1995), 56–63.

[48] Cf. the judgment of Shemaryahu Talmon that despite the "palpable absence of Messiah-futurism in the Hebrew Scriptures," the concept itself is "deeply rooted in the ancient Israelites' conceptual universe"; Shemaryahu Talmon, "The Concepts of *Māšîaḥ* and Messianism in Early Judaism," in *The Messiah: Developments in Earliest Judaism and Christianity*, edited by James H. Charlesworth (Minneapolis: Fortress Press, 1992), 83.

[49] Cf. Margaret Cool Root, *The King and Kingship in Achaemenid Art* (Acta Iranica 19; Leiden: Brill, 1979).

[50] Arielle P. Kozloff, ed., *Animals in Ancient Art from the Leo Mildenberg Collection*, David Gordon Mitten (Cleveland: Cleveland Museum of Art in cooperation with Indiana University Press, 1981), 58.

[51] Kozloff, *Animals in Ancient Art*, 57.

[52] Kozloff, *Animals in Ancient Art*, 63.

[53] Kozloff, *Animals in Ancient Art*, 57.

king in lion guise attacking a foreigner is a classic Egyptian theme," making clear that violence was at least implicitly part of the symbolism. [54]

Judah, Gad, and Dan were all associated with the lion: "Judah is a lion's (אַרְיֵה; λέων) whelp; from the prey, my son, you have gone up. He crouches down, he stretches out like a lion (אַרְיֵה; λέων), like a lioness (לָבִיא; σκύμνος)—who dares rouse him up?" (Gen 49:9; for Gad, cf. Deut 33:20[55]; for Dan, Deut 33:22). The lion is associated with a victorious and undefeatable people in Numbers 23:24 and 24:9. The strength of Saul and Jonathan is compared to that of lions in 2 Samuel 1:23. In fact, the lion appears to be the quintessential symbol of the warrior and of the warrior's superior power in the Prophets (cf. 2Sam 17:10; Isa 31:4; 38:13; Jer 4:7; 49:19; 50:17,44; Ezek 19:1-6; 22:25-27; Hos 5:14; 13:7-8; Joel 1:6; Mic 5:8). In Jeremiah 51:38, aggressive lions conquer lambs led to the slaughter, and in Ezekiel 38:13 and Nahum 2:13, כְּפִיר [young lion] appears to be a euphemism for warrior. In the Maccabean literature, Judas Maccabeus is specifically called a lion: "He was like a lion in his deeds, like a lion's cub roaring for prey" (1Mac 3:4). In the Eagle Vision of 4 Ezra, the messiah is identified as a lion (see esp. 12:31-32).

As in ancient Near Eastern culture generally, the lion was often associated in the Hebrew Bible with royalty (cf. 1Kgs 7:29,36; 10:19-20; 2Chron 9:18-19; Prov 28:15; 30:30-31; Jer 2:15,30; Ezek 32:2).[56] At times the lion appears to symbolize danger or the power of sheer violence (Deut 19:12; Ps 7:2; 10:9; 17:12; 22:13,21; 35:17; 57:4; 58:6; Prov 20:2; 22:13; 26:13; Prov 28:15; 30:30; Isa 5:29; Jer 12:8; 25:38; Nah 2:11-13). The taming or elimination of the wolf, bear, and lion in the eschaton draws on the traditional association of these animals with aggressive violence (cf. esp. Isa 11:6-7; 35:9; 65:25).

The Qumran covenantors saw the lion primarily as a symbol for aggression and secondarily as a symbol of royalty.[57] Although Gen 49:10 was clearly applied to a messianic figure in the literature at Qumran (cf. 4Q252 Frag. 1 5.1-7), it is not clear that the Qumran covenantors saw the lion as a symbol for the messiah, even though in 1QSb 5.29 the destructiveness of the messiah is *com-*

---

[54] Kozloff, *Animals in Ancient Art*, 66, no. 53.

[55] Deut 33:20 is alluded to in 4QFlor 2.3–4. The context in Florilegium is clearly eschatological, but it is not clear that the lion of Gad in Florilegium (which must be restored from the Hebrew Bible) is considered a messianic character.

[56] This, despite Richard Bauckham's contention to the contrary. See Richard Bauckham, *Climax of Prophecy*, 182n23. Bauckham underestimates the biblical evidence and largely disregards the literary and archaeological evidence in the ancient Near East.

[57] Cf. Geza Vermes, *Scripture and Tradition in Judaism* (Leiden: E. J. Brill, 1973), 40–43.

pared to that of the lion,[58] perhaps drawing on Num 23:24 or Mic 5:8.[59] Nevertheless, the lion in 1QSb 5.29 appears in a passing simile, comparable to the bull in 5.27, and the other texts to which Vermes appeals are all relatively late.

Lions figure prominently in the pesher to Nahum. There the lion of Nahum 2:11b is interpreted as "[Deme]trius, king of Greece, who sought to enter Jerusalem on the counsel of those who seek after smooth things."[60] The "furious lion" in 4QpNah frags. 3–4 1.5–6 probably refers to Alexander Jannaeus, since 1.7 says that he "used to hang men alive," referring approvingly to his crucifixion of 800 Pharisees.[61] However, the commentary treats the lions of Nah 2:13 as the nobles of Jerusalem in 1.11.

Thus, although the lion was a symbol of both power and aggression on the one hand and of royalty on the other, there is no clear evidence in the Dead Sea Scrolls or the Old Testament Pseudepigrapha that the messiah was ever called a lion prior to the first century CE.[62] It would be a mistake to call the lion a symbol of the messiah even in Rev 5, since symbols require a certain stability to qualify as such (see above, chap. 5). The Christ figure is referred to as a lion only in Rev 5:5; the other five occurrences of λεών in the Apocalypse all appear as general, nonmessianic similes, preceded by ὡς (9:8,17; 13:2), ὥς-περ (10:3), or ὅμοιος (4:7). Nevertheless, as a metaphor, the lion of Rev 5—in conjunction with its modifier, "of the tribe of Judah," and the additional title, "root of David"—would quickly and easily have been associated with those eschatological hopes for a political redeemer that emphasized the powerful aggression of Israel toward its Gentile neighbors.

---

[58] Although only the initial א of the word is legible, I follow most interpreters in reconstructing the word as [ריה]א in light of the reference to prey in the following line.

[59] Geza Vermes argues on the basis of 1QSb 5.29; Targum Onkelos on Gen 49:9; 4Ez 12:31-32; and Rev 5:5 that the symbolic representation of the messiah as a lion was "known in all sectors of Palestinian Judaism ... [and] that it represented a tradition familiar to all" (Vermes, *Scripture and Tradition*, 43).

[60] 4QpNah Frgs. 3–4 1.2; Michael Wise, Martin Abegg, and Edward Cook, ed., *The Dead Sea Scrolls: A New Translation* (San Francisco: HarperSanFrancisco, 1996), 217.

[61] Cf. Josephus, *Ant* 13.5.

[62] The "king of peace" who rises from the West in the Apocalypse of Elijah is probably a messianic figure. This figure "will run upon the sea like a roaring lion" (2:7). As O. S. Wintermute has argued, the Apocalypse of Elijah likely postdates the Apocalypse of John and may even be dependent upon it. See James H. Charlesworth, ed., *The Old Testament Pseudepigrapha: Expansions of the "Old Testament" and Legends, Wisdom and Philosophical Literature, Prayers, Psalms, and Odes, Fragments of Lost Judeo-Hellenistic Works*, 2 (Garden City: Doubleday & Company, Inc., 1985), 722–30. However, the use of simile in this statement suggests that even here the author is explaining a characteristic of the messiah, not appealing to a traditional symbol for the messiah.

If neither the lion nor the lamb was a traditional symbol for the messiah, then both the lion and the lamb are new, metaphorical[63] creations of the author that nevertheless draw heavily upon the traditional symbolisms associated with these animals. The author thus chose the lion to represent the powerful aggressive force inherent in one vision of Israel's role in the eschaton and the lamb to represent the vulnerability inherent in another vision of the eschaton.

3.2 The Root

The Greek noun ῥίζα recalls Isaiah 11:1-10 (ῥίζα; שֹׁרֶשׁ). It also recalls 1 Maccabees 1:10, where Antiochus Epiphanes is called "a sinful root" (ῥίζα). It is clear that Isaiah 11:1-10 played an important role in the eschatological expectations of a redeemer figure at Qumran, as did Jeremiah 23:5-6 (cf. 4QpIsa[a] [4Q161] Frag. 8+9+10 lines 15–29). Drawing on Isaiah 11:1 and Jeremiah 23:5-6, the term "branch of David," took on "messianic" significance in the Qumran community.[64] John Collins suggests that the "metaphor of the 'branch' (צמח) is similar to the shoot (נצר, חטר) of Isa 11:1, but not necessarily derived from it."[65] Psalms of Solomon 17 and numerous Dead Sea scrolls independently interpret Isaiah 11 as a messianic text, indicating that "root of David" already played a significant role within the varieties of messianic expectations in first-century Judaism (cf. 4QFlor 3.10–13).[66] Thus, the des-

---

[63] Strictly speaking, the lion of Rev 5:5 is a passing *metaphor* and the lamb is introduced in Rev 5:6 as a metaphor that becomes the leading *symbol* for the messiah in the book. Gottfried Schimanowski claims otherwise. In light of Gen 49, Schimanowski claims that the lion was already easily recognized as a messianic title (cf. Gottfried Schimanowski, *Die himmlische Liturgie in der Apokalypse des Johannes: Die frühjüdischen Traditionen in Offenbarung 4–5 unter Einschluß der Hekhalotliteratur*, Wissenschaftliche Untersuchungen zum neuen Testament, 2.Reihe 154 (Tübingen: Mohr Siebeck, 2002), see esp. 199.

[64] John J. Collins, *The Scepter and the Star*, 25. I am using the word *messianic* here in a broad sense, not as a technical term for a well-defined eschatology. For a discussion of the problematics of this term, see James H. Charlesworth, "From Messianology to Christology: Problems and Prospects," chapt. 1 in *The Messiah: Developments in Earliest Judaism and Christianity*, edited by James H. Charlesworth, in collaboration with J. Brownson, M. T. Davis, S. J. Kraftchick, and A. F. Segal (Minneapolis: Fortress Press, 1992), 3–35.

[65] Collins, *The Scepter and the Star*, 26. The "Branch of David" appellation is common in the Dead Sea Scrolls, appearing in 4Q161 (4QpIsa[a]), 4Q285 (the 'Dying Messiah' fragment), 4Q174 (Florilegium), and 4Q252 (4QpGen, the Patriarchal Blessings). In 4Q252 5.3 the "branch of David" is specifically equated with the "righteous messiah."

[66] For helpful discussions of the evidence, see James H. Charlesworth, ed., *The Messiah*; and John J. Collins, *The Scepter and the Star*.

ignations of Christ in v. 5 recall and build on the political aspirations of the Jewish people for their messiah.

This first scene, which extends to v. 7, is seemingly self-contained and appears to be resolved when it is announced that the lion of the tribe of Judah, the root of David, has conquered. The language of conquering and the traditional appeals to "the tribe of Judah" and "root of David" suggest the onset of the messianic redemption long awaited. The lion-like powerful messianic ruler, the royal descendant of David, is about take his reign and destroy the Gentiles. All that remains is for the lion to take the scroll and begin his reign.

3.3 The Lamb

But wait! What John sees is a *lamb*, standing slaughtered,[67] with seven horns and seven eyes! This is a powerful and mind-wrenching switch of images for which the reader is unprepared. Despite the reader's encounter already in chapters one through five with dozens of christological appellations celebrating Jesus' power and authority, the reader has had no hint that he would be followed throughout the rest of the book primarily as *lamb*. At the heart of this switch is the author's conviction that Jesus' death and resurrection represent not only the key to the redemption of God's people, but also the key to God's victory over evil within history. Theologically, the switch suggests that the crucial role of the messiah in history—whether speaking of his first or second coming—looks less like that of a lion and more like that of a lamb. As John looks on, the lamb goes and takes the scroll from the right hand of the one sitting on the throne.

3.4 The Praise

The second scene is filled with praise. In three outwardly expanding concentric waves of praise, the reader sees and hears a crescendo of praise and worship that eventually envelopes the whole universe. In the first circle, the four living creatures and the 24 elders fall before the lamb and sing a "new song."[68]

---

[67] The phrase ἑστηκὸς ὡς ἐσφαγμένον (standing as slaughtered) is an odd one that no doubt refers to the death and resurrection of Jesus. Rev 11:11 supports the implicit connection with standing and resurrection (cf. also 20:12; Ezek 37:10). For a treatment of the variety of the ways in which the author uses ὡς in the Apocalypse, see above.

[68] "New song" is, according to Bauckham, "holy war terminology for a hymn in praise of a fresh victory of the divine Warrior over his foes (Pss 98:1-3; 144:9; Isa 42:10-13; Jdt 16:2-3)." See also Exod 15:1-21; Judg 11:34; Pss 33:3; 40:3; 96:1; 149:1,6-9; Isa 24:14-16; 1QM 14.2; Rev 14:3. See Richard Bauckham, *Climax of Prophecy*, 230; Tremper Longman III, "The Divine Warrior: The New Testament Use of an Old Testament Motif," *Westminster Theological Journal* 44, no. 2 (Fall 1982): 300–02.

In the second circle, myriads and myriads and thousands and thousands of angels surround the throne and the living creatures and the elders, and they say
with a loud voice that the Lamb is worthy. Finally, in the third circle, the
whole universe gets involved: every creature in heaven and on earth and under
the earth and in the sea, and—lest any have been missed—"all the things in
them," ascribe blessing and honor and glory and power forever and ever to the
one seated on the throne and to the Lamb.

The expanding crescendo of praise, which eventually envelopes every person and creature in the universe, provides a powerful climax to chapter 5 and
rhetorically impels the reader to join in recognizing the Lamb's victory. The
content of the praise further clarifies the author's Christology. The first two
circles of praise begin with the adjective ἄξιος (worthy) and are directed to the
Lamb. The third circle is directed to both God and the Lamb. The first circle
of praise is connected most directly with the first scene through the appearance
of common keywords λαβεῖν (to take), βιβλίον (scroll), ἀνοίξαι (to open), τὰς
σφραγίδας αὐτοῦ (its seals), and σφαζεῖν (to slaughter).

Significantly, the reason for Jesus' worthiness, identified previously only
through the verb νικάω (to conquer), is identified here through a ὅτι clause
with his slaughter: ἄξιος εἶ ... ὅτι ἐσφάγης: You are worthy ... *because* you
were slaughtered (5:9). In John's theology, it is Jesus' cross and resurrection
that make him worthy of taking the scroll and revealing history's outcome, *not*
the integrity of the life he led, as Unnik argued.[69] Although the second circle
of praise does not include a ὅτι clause, the participial modifier in second
attributive position—ἄξιόν ἐστιν τὸ ἀρνίον τὸ ἐσφαγμένον (worthy is the lamb
that was slaughtered)—again connects the *worthiness* of the lamb to the
slaughter of the lamb.

The words for slaughter, σφάζω and its cognates, are used in the Septuagint both for the slaughter of animals and the murder of humans. In the
New Testament the word is used only for the murder of humans. In 1 John
3:12 it refers to Cain's murder of Abel. In Revelation 6:4 it refers to the murder of people by other people. In 6:9 it refers to the execution of believers "on
account of the word of God and the testimony they had given." In Revelation
13:3 it refers to the murder of one of the heads of the beast. In 18:24 it refers
to the murder of prophets, saints, and all those who had been martyred. In
Revelation 5:6,9,12; and 13:8 it refers to the murder of Jesus. This is violent
imagery born of conflict. Jesus' death is consistently tied to the language of
witness and of victory in the Apocalypse. Atonement for sins is not in view.[70]

---

[69] W. C. van Unnik, "'Worthy is the Lamb': The Background of Apoc 5," in
Mélanges Bibliques en Hommage Au R. P. Béda Rigaux, edited by Albert Descamps
and A. de Halleux (Gembloux: Duculot, 1970), 445–61.

[70] I would not argue that the Apocalypse is a polemic against the Pauline theology
of the cross or against Pauline soteriology. Rev 1:5 seems designed to "connect" John's

The tenses in these scenes of praise are significant. The three verbs that provide the content of the ὅτι clause in v. 9b are ἐσφάγης, ἠγόρασας, and ἐποίησας (you were slaughtered, you purchased, and you made).[71] These are not proleptic visions of the victory the lamb will enjoy when he conquers evil; rather they are celebrations of the victory the lamb has already accomplished in his victory over evil, though it takes a revelation from God to see what he has accomplished and how he has accomplished it.

By introducing the Lamb as he does in chap. 5, the author underscores a central reversal in his apocalypse. Rhetorically, the author's strategy in the first scene is to build tension through underscoring both the importance of history's resolution and the tragedy that proceeds from the lack of such a resolution. The weeping in the first part of the chapter becomes praise and celebration in the second half of the chapter. But before this tension is fully resolved, the reader is introduced to yet another shock: the shock of the switch from lion to lamb—from the symbol of power and domination to the symbol of vulnerability and nonviolence. Implicit in the introduction of the victor is the identification of *who* has the keys to history; implicit in the switch from lion to lamb is the answer to the unspoken question of *how* he gained that victory.

But is this really a redefinition of victory as nonviolent resistance to the point of death? Is there truly a connection in the Apocalypse between Christ's death on the cross and the manner in which the readers are invited to resist? If so, one would expect corroborating evidence of some kind. Such corroborating evidence does indeed exist. In the paragraphs that follow, we will consider the

---

theology of the cross with the atonement theology he inherited in the tradition. John's use of the "slaughter" of Jesus, however, has a much different function. Interestingly, the hymn in Rev 1:5-6 that expresses a more traditional theology of the cross is the one hymn that Carnegie thinks was pre-Johannine and that John composed the rest himself. See p. 130 above. Beale imports too many ideas from classical Orthodox theology in his comments on Rev 5:6 when he says that Christ "willingly submitted to the unjust penalty of death, which was imposed on him ultimately by the devil. As an innocent victim he became a representative penal substitute for the sins of his people" (G.K. Beale, *The Book of Revelation*, 353). As David Aune notes, even if the Lamb symbol in the Apocalypse refers to the Passover lamb, which was a type of peace offering, none of the peace offerings of the Old Testament had anything to do with atonement for sins (cf. David E. Aune, *Revelation 1–5*, Word Biblical Commentary, no. 52a [Dallas: Word Books, 1997], 372).

[71] The tense of the third person plural form of βασιλεύω in v. 10b is another matter. The question here is how and when the believers will participate in the Lamb's victory. The majority of texts have βασιλεύσουσιν, the future (they will reign). A few have βασιλούουσιν, the present tense (they are reigning); while a few others have the first person plural future, βασιλούσομεν (we will reign). While the resolution of this matter is important for understanding the book's ethic, it is less important for understanding the book's Christology.

manner in which Jesus' death is treated as paradigmatic for human ethical response.

4. Christology and Ethics in the Apocalypse

There is a close relationship between Christology and ethics in the Apocalypse. Some scholars, such as Wayne Meeks, argue that it is inappropriate to apply the word *ethics* to much of the New Testament, including the Apocalypse, because the word points to "a reflective, second-order activity."[72] Meeks prefers to speak of *moral implications* within the New Testament documents, rather than of *ethical systems*. Meeks claims that "'morality' ... names a dimension of life, a pervasive and, often, only partly conscious set of value-laden dispositions, inclinations, attitudes, and habits."[73] If we were to accept Meeks' definition of these terms, we would aim to research the "moral" message of the Apocalypse.

One may quickly grant that in the Apocalypse there is none of the logocentric, system-oriented, "reflective, second-order" kind of deliberation Meeks defines as "ethics." However, the problem with such tight definitions of ethics and morality is that they leave little room for describing the shape, or the concrete expressions, of the faithfulness the Apocalypse seeks to engender. I am using the language of *ethics* here to describe the shape of the readers' response to the revelation that John as author imagined and desired.

The author's desired response is broad and multi-faceted. It is more than just adopting the proper set of moral decisions over against an improper set; it includes seeing the world in a different way, recognizing Rome and the emperor cult for the beasts they are, saying no to the seductive compromises offered by the competing voices in the churches, and putting one's life on the line in doing so. As Leonard Thompson has pointed out, the Apocalypse should not be read simply as an exercise in imaginative thinking. Rather, the author "is sending a message which intends to create a certain way of living in and seeing the world."[74] It thus requires (and exhibits) a rhetorical strategy that is not primarily logo-centric in its force.

---

[72] Wayne A. Meeks, *The Origins of Christian Morality* (New Haven, Conn.: Yale University Press, 1993), 4. Not all scholars are willing to adopt such a narrow definition of ethics. See, e.g., David L. Barr, "Towards an Ethical Reading of the Apocalypse: Reflections on John's Use of Power, Violence, and Misogyny," in *Society of Biblical Literature 1997 Seminar Papers*, Society of Biblical Literature Seminar Papers Series, no. 36 (Atlanta: Scholars Press, 1997), 358–73.

[73] Wayne A. Meeks, *Origins of Christian Morality*, 4.

[74] Leonard L. Thompson, "Mooring the Revelation," 635.

The ethics of the Apocalypse is thus ethics writ large—ethics that touch the expanse of how believers are to understand life itself and how they are to live in an idolatrous and compromising society. Just as Jesus conquered through his faithful witness, so the author expected the believers to conquer through their faithful witness. The theological program of the author is rhetorically propelled by a Lamb Christology that is closely associated to an ethic of faithful witness. Because this theology is not argued logocentrically or developed systematically, it is essential that the interpreter pay close attention to the rhetorical poetics of the book. Any pericope-by-pericope exegesis of the book that does not do so will therefore be lacking.[75]

4.1 "Witness" in the Apocalypse

One way to examine the extent to which the author connects his Christology with his ethics is through paying close attention to his use of the νικάω and μαρτυρέω word groups. In Revelation 1:5 Jesus is introduced as the faithful witness, the firstborn from the dead, and the ruler of the kings of the earth. The epithets here are significant, for all three underscore the political nature of the rhetoric of the Apocalypse and the close relationship between Christology and ethics within it.

Jesus is the faithful witness (ὁ μάρτυς ὁ πιστός; 1:5; 3:14), just as Antipas was the faithful witness (ὁ μάρτυς μου ὁ πιστός μου; 2:13). Just as Jesus died for *his* witness, so did Antipas. But as firstborn from the dead, Jesus also has the keys of death and of Hades (1:18), the key of David (3:7), and the key to the abyss (9:1; 20:1). In other words, Jesus' death and resurrection show his victory over the evil that put him to death. And if there is any question about Jesus' authority in relation to that of the earthly rulers of the believers in Asia, Jesus is also the ruler of the kings of the earth. Jesus is thus introduced with language that is explicitly political, which serves to invite the reader into Jesus' realm of victory and authority, while undercutting civil religion as allegiance to the empire.

John suggests that Jesus' own faithful witness led to his execution, but that that execution itself proved to be Jesus' victory over the powers of death. Furthermore, Jesus' own suffering-reigning-resisting victory turns out to be *a way of being in the world*—a model for believers. John's self-introduction to his readers establishes empathy (ἦθος) with his readers through his use of such words as "your brother" (ὁ ἀδελφὸς ὑμῶν) and "partner" (συγκοινωνός). He is

---

[75] Although Nikola Hohnjec's analysis of the individual lamb pericopes in the book is well-done and systematic, his lack of attention to the book's rhetorical force and his use of traditional theological categories limit the study's usefulness. See Nikola Hohnjec, *Das Lamm*.

also beginning to establish a world view, a way of being in the world that he himself is experiencing and is inviting his readers to experience also.

Discussions about μαρτυρία Ἰησοῦ in the Apocalypse often founder on the debate about whether the genitive is objective or subjective—whether the witness is a witness *to* Jesus, or whether John is speaking of Jesus' *own* witness.[76] The phrase is certainly important in the rhetoric of the book. It occurs six times, at key junctures in the book: in 1:2,9; 12:17; 19:10 [*bis*]; and 20:4, besides the occurrences of the nouns μαρτυρία (6:9; 11:7; 12:11), μάρτυς (1:5; 2:13; 3:14; 11:3; 17:6), and μαρτύριον (15:5), and the verb μαρτυρέω (1:2; 22:16,18,20).

There can be no doubt that both the objective and the subjective are envisioned in the book. The emphasis on the faithfulness of Jesus himself as a witness (1:5; 3:14) makes clear that the witness he gave was his *own* (subjective genitive). However, Antipas is commended as ὁ μάρτυς μου ὁ πιστός μου (my witness, my faithful one), and John was on Patmos on account of τὴν μαρτυρίαν Ἰησοῦ (the [his] witness to Jesus). These uses of the word require that the witness Antipas and John gave was *to* Christ (objective genitive). We thus see behind this witness language the degree to which John's Christology is connected to his ethics.

Μαρτυρία and μάρτυς are both closely linked to martyrdom in this book, though not entirely synonymous with it. The word μάρτυς in the Apocalypse was on its way to becoming a technical term for martyr, but its transformation was not yet complete. Although the "witness of Jesus" for which John was banished to Patmos (1:9) may eventually have been *sealed* with his martyrdom, it is not *synonymous* with his martyrdom.

Can we say more about the nature of this witness? What does it mean to be a faithful witness? Revelation 1:5 suggests that Jesus' own witness resulted in his martyrdom on the cross. The "faithful witness" of Antipas also resulted in his martyrdom (he "was killed"; ἀπεκτάνθη—2:13). Likewise, those who were under the altar in 6:10 had been slaughtered on account of the word of God and the *testimony* they had. The 144,000 "follow the Lamb wherever he goes" (14:4) and stand victorious with the Lamb on Mt. Zion. This suggests that the faithful are those who "follow" (i.e., emulate) the Lamb both in his faithful witness and in his triumphant rule.

According to Revelation 1:9, John shares in that witness even though he has not himself yet been killed. This point is important because it shows that the "witness" envisioned in the Apocalypse is not just a "passive acceptance of

---

[76] See, e.g., the exchange between Petros Vassiliadis and Fred Mazzaferri: Petros Vassiliadis, "The Translation of *Martyria Iēsou* in Revelation," *Bible Translator* 36, no. 1 (January 1985): 129–34; Fred[erick] Mazzaferri, "*Martyria Iēsou* Revisited," *Bible Translator* 39 (January 1988): 114–22.

suffering," as Adela Yarbro Collins has maintained,[77] but rather the sort of nonviolent resistance to evil in which both Jesus and John engaged. This sort of witness may—indeed, probably will—result in the believer's execution. John's "partnership" with his readers lies in τῇ θλίψει καὶ βασιλείᾳ καὶ ὑπομονῇ ἐν Ἰησοῦ (the suffering, the kingdom, and the consistent resistance that is in Jesus; 1:9).

> The striking character of the image used [the lamb in Rev 5] should not lead us to suppose that passivity is all that is encouraged thereby. ... The Lamb goes to its death not with a fatalistic acceptance of its lot. Nor is its death all that is important about it. Jesus is after all the 'faithful witness' (1.5; 3.14). He has had an active role in life, and, like the two witnesses in ch. 11, that activity in pursuance of the witness to God led to death. That task of witness ... [is] no mere acceptance of death. It is testimony before the nations of that other way, the way of truth. That is what true messiahship consists of.[78]

Just as Jesus was slaughtered for his witness, so are the saints murdered (σφάζω) for the testimony (μαρτυρία) that they have given (6:10). Similarly, the testimony (μαρτυρία, 11:7) of the two witnesses (μάρτυσιν, 11:3) lead to their death in 11:7. In 12:11, the word of the testimony (μαρτυρία) of "our brothers" seems connected to the fact that they were willing to give up their lives: οὐκ ἠγάπησαν τὴν ψυχὴν αὐτῶν ἄχρι θανάτου. In 17:6 the Great Whore is drunk from the blood (i.e., martyrdom) of the saints and[79] from the blood of the witnesses to Jesus (τῶν μαρτύρων Ἰησοῦ). In 20:4 John saw the souls of those who had been beheaded on account of their *testimony* to Jesus and on account of the word of God.

In Revelation 19:10 we read the enigmatic statement, ἡ γὰρ μαρτυρία Ἰησοῦ ἐστιν τὸ πνεῦμα τῆς προφητείας: "For the testimony of/to/from Jesus is the spirit of prophecy." Boring suggests that since prophecy is bound indissolubly to the testimony Jesus himself gave on earth; and since the testimony is *from* the risen Lord, also identified as the word of God; and since the testimony must also be a testimony *to* the crucified Jesus—the genitive inscribed in Ἰησοῦ must be an objective genitive, a subjective genitive, and a genitive of origin rolled into one.[80] However, because the context of this statement is a refusal statement—where the angel warns John not to worship him, but to worship God—there is also the suggestion in this verse that the testimony to Jesus consists of refusing to participate in the emperor cult.[81] Thus, just as Jesus was

---

[77] Adela Yarbro Collins, "The Political Perspective of the Revelation to John," *Journal of Biblical Literature* 96 (1977): 247.

[78] Christopher Rowland, *Revelation*, 78.

[79] Or "namely" or "that is," if the καί of 17:6 is epexegetical.

[80] M. Eugene Boring, *Revelation*, 194.

[81] Elisabeth Schüssler Fiorenza, *Revelation*, 102–03.

faithful in *his* witness, *his* consistent resistance, which led to *his* death, so are the believers in Asia to be faithful in *their* witness, *their* consistent resistance, which, the author believes, will lead to *their* death.

John can summarize his entire book as a matter of *testifying to* (ἐμαρτύρη-σεν) the word of God and the *witness* of Jesus Christ (τὸν λόγον τοῦ θεοῦ καὶ τὴν μαρτυρίαν Ἰησοῦ Χριστοῦ—1:2). Indeed faithful testimony is what binds the characters of this book together: from Jesus the faithful witness (1:5,9; 3:14; 21:20) to John, the author (1:2,9; 21:18), to the mediating angel (21:16), and finally to Antipas (2:13) and all the other saints who remain faithful to the end (12:11; 17:6; 19:10), especially the prophets (11:3,7; 19:10). This link is especially apparent in the final chapter, where the mediating angel (21:16), the author (21:18), and Jesus himself (21:20) all testify (μαρτυρέω) to "these things."

Witness in the Apocalypse thus connects the work of the Lamb with the faithful response of the readers/hearers. The ones who will stand with the Lamb on Mt. Zion are those "who follow the Lamb wherever he goes" (14:4). A lifestyle that rejects the authority (and divinity) of the emperor may well lead to a situation in which one will be dragged before the governor in order to "testify" there. And if Pliny's correspondence with Trajan is to be taken into account, such a "witness" may in turn lead to one's "witness" in martyrdom. Thus, the victory of the Lamb in its slaughter serves to effect and empower the believers' victory through their own faithful witness.

4.2 "Triumph" in the Apocalypse

Near the heart of the rhetorical pulse of the Apocalypse is its redefinition of triumph.[82] By means of the rhetorical form of apocalyptic literature, the message of John's Apocalypse is that Christ has conquered the powers of evil through his faithful witness, which eventuated in his death on the cross, and its ethical message and promise are that the saints will conquer in the same way. The high point in the struggle between good and evil will not be reached in the eschatological messianic war; it has already been reached in the death and resurrection of Christ.[83]

But if one's faithful witness ends in death, does not that death signify the futility of that witness? If vulnerability *without* victimization is at the heart of the eschatological vision (Isa 11:6-7; 17:2; Hos 2:18; Zeph 3:13), is not the

---

[82] One of the more extensive studies of the theme of triumph in the Apocalypse is that of Ragnar Leivestad, which remains valuable for its insights. See Ragnar Leivestad, *Christ the Conqueror: Ideas of Conflict and Victory in the New Testament* (London: S.P.C.K., 1954), 212–38.

[83] Cf. William Klassen, "Vengeance in the Apocalypse of John," *Catholic Biblical Quarterly* 28 (1966): 305.

death of the vulnerable the ultimate tragedy? Not according to the Apocalypse. As we have already seen, the lamb is deemed worthy precisely because he overcame (ἐνίκησεν). He conquered. He proved victorious. And he did so by dying, by being slaughtered, by redeeming people from every tribe and tongue and people and nation with his blood, and by making them a kingdom and priests (5:9-10).

To be sure, some victimization is implied. The dark reality of evil on this side of the fullness of God's reign means that those who wish to follow the Lamb will suffer some victimization. Nevertheless, the message of the Apocalypse is that such victimization is being redefined. The "second death" will have no power over those who suffer in this way (2:11; 20:6,14; 21:8). That is, the hope of resurrection and a final judgment relativizes the victimization experienced in such murders. Although this sort of reasoning sometimes is employed to support an escapist ethic, the active nonviolent resistance ethic of the Apocalypse eschews such a quietistic fatalism.

If the Apocalypse understands Jesus' death as faithful, consistent, nonviolent resistance to the point of death, and if it intends to connect such resistance with the faithful martyrdom of the believers, one would expect to see a clear connection between the language of victory (νίκη) won by Christ through his death and the language of victory won by believers in their own faithful, consistent, nonviolent resistance to the point of death. Evidence for such a connection abounds in the Apocalypse.

Modern commentators should be cautious about interpreting separate sections of the Apocalypse in isolation from the rest lest one miss the careful inter-connectedness crucial for apprehending its rhetorical force. Although chapters 4–5 represent the rhetorical fulcrum for the Christology of the Apocalypse, chapters 2–3 prepare the way for those chapters. In Revelation 2–3, the author addresses the churches most directly.

The political form and function of the so-called letters to the seven churches are unmistakable. Although the specific calls to action are relatively few and vague,[84] the oracles' rhetorical force—that of reforming or recreating the audience's symbolic universe—is clear enough. Formally and structurally, these oracles are strongly similar to ancient royal and imperial edicts.[85] Rhetorically, they invite the reader/hearer to assume a stance of resistance toward unfaithful neighbors.

---

[84] See, e.g., Robert M. Royalty, Jr., "Rhetoric of Revelation," 602.

[85] David E. Aune, "The Form and Function of the Proclamations to the Seven Churches (Revelation 2–3)," *New Testament Studies* 36 (April 1990): 182–204. "The primary literary genre to which the seven proclamations belong is that of the *royal* or *imperial edict*" (see David E. Aune, *Revelation 1–5*. Word Commentary Series, vol. 52 [Dallas: Word Books, 1997], 119; emphasis Aune's).

As commentators have noted, there is a strong formal consistency in these so-called letters, or prophetic oracles. They share (a) the command to write to the angel of the church of ... (2:1,8,12,18; 3:1,7,14); (b) the introduction, "These are the words of ..." (2:1,8,12,18; 3:1,7,14); followed by (c) a christological appellation (2:1,8,12,18; 3:1,7,14); (d) the words, "I know ..." (2:2,9, 13,19; 3:1,8,15); (e) words of commendation (2:2-3,9,13,19; 3:8-10);[86] (f) words of condemnation (2:4,14-15,20-21; 3:1,15,17);[87] (g) a direct imperative (2:5,10,16,24-25; 3:2-3,11,18-20); (h) a warning or word of judgment if the church does not heed the oracle (2:5b,16b,22-23; 3:3b,16);[88] (i) a promise to the one who "conquers" or "overcomes" (2:7b,11b,17b,26-28; 3:5,12,21); and (j) a call to discernment ["Let anyone who has an ear listen to what the Spirit is saying to the churches" (2:7,11,17,29; 3:6,13,22)].

The Apocalypse is full of negative sobriquets (e.g., Nicolaitans [2:6,15], Jezebel [2:20], Balaamites [2:14]) and references to people who "call themselves" one thing (2:2,9,20) but "are not" (2:2,9), to the blasphemy of those who consider themselves part of the believing community (2:9), to the synagogue of Satan (2:9; 3:9), to liars (2:2), and to evildoers *among the people of God* (2:2).[89] These references suggest that the author does not share his readers' assessment of the current situation.[90] The command to repent is given to the churches of Ephesus (2:5), Pergamum (2:16), Sardis (3:3), and Laodicea (3:19). At Thyatira, Jezebel was given the chance to repent, but it was too late for her (2:21). Three of the congregations are told, "I have this [or a few things] against you" (Ephesus, 2:4; Pergamum, 2:14; and Thyatira, 2:20). Sardis is told specifically to wake up (3:2-3; cf. 16:15, where one of the macarisms is for those who stay awake).

With the exception of the oracles to Smyrna and Philadelphia, these are not the words one would expect from a pastor who is writing to comfort the afflicted. Rather, these words are intended to goad the comfortable, to call for renewed commitment to the gospel, to call for resistance—a costly resistance

---

[86] Only the oracles to the churches of Sardis and Laodicea lack these words of commendation, about which there seems little to praise.

[87] Only the oracles to the churches of Smyrna and Philadelphia lack these words of condemnation, about which there seems little to condemn.

[88] These words of warning are lacking in the oracles to Smyrna and Philadelphia—the same churches for which there were no words of condemnation. Two of the oracles add an additional commendation after the condemnation and before the call to discernment: Ephesus (2:6) and Sardis (3:4).

[89] For an excellent analysis of the central role of "naming" in the rhetorical strategy of the Seer, see Edith M. Humphrey, "On Visions, Arguments and Naming: The Rhetoric of Specificity and Mystery in the Apocalypse," presentation at the Society of Biblical Literature (San Francisco, 1997).

[90] Cf. Leonard L. Thompson, "Mooring the Revelation," 648.

that the author was convinced would cost them their lives. The implied problem behind these prophetic oracles was the temptation to compromise one's witness, given the subtle (or overt) pressures and opportunities in Graeco-Roman society in Asia. It was a compromise the author equated with idolatry.

Each of these oracles ends with a promise "to the one who conquers" and a call to discernment. Rhetorically, the effect of a vision of Christ addressing each church individually would have been powerful. The implicit prophetic claims of the oracles add to their rhetorical force, from the prototypical, "Thus says the LORD,"[91] to the prophetic invitation to hear (see below). The concluding promise to "the one who conquers" rhetorically places the faithful reader in a stance of conflict, a stance of resistance.

The connection between Christology and ethics goes further: believers are to share with the Lamb the functions of lordship normally reserved for the messiah. The epexegetical καί in the promise to the conquerer in Thyatira suggests that conquering is essentially equivalent to keeping Christ's works to the end (2:26). To such a person, Christ promises authority over the nations! (2:26). Furthermore, the traditional messianic text from Psalm 2—"and he will rule them with an iron rod as when ceramic pots are shattered"[92]—is here attributed not to the messiah, but to the conquering believers! We see the same phenomenon in 20:4,6, where the beheaded are given thrones and share in the messiah's task of reigning. The ruling of the believers is linked to the Lamb's triumph in 5:10: καὶ βασιλεύσουσιν ἐπὶ τῆς γῆς (and they will reign on the earth). Finally, the concluding clause of the visions (prior to the epilogue in 22:6-21) is, καὶ βασιλεύσουσιν εἰς τοὺς αἰῶνας τῶν αἰώνων: and they (the servants of God) will reign forever and ever. Thus, just as the saints "follow" the Lamb wherever he goes in his faithful witness and martyr death, so also do they follow the Lamb in his victory and his messianic prerogative to rule.

The "letters" to the seven churches rise to a climax with the final oracle in which Christ is portrayed as "the Amen, the faithful and true witness, the beginning of God's creation" (3:14). Like the promise to the conquerer in Thyatira, the promise to the conquerer in Laodicea explicitly connects the victory of Christ with the victory of the saints. Like the others, this oracle concludes with a promise "to the one who conquers" and a call to discernment. In Revelation 3:21, the promise is that Christ will grant to the one who overcomes the right to sit with Christ on his throne. This conquering and the rights that come with it represent yet another explicit linking of Christology

---

[91] Here the authoritative voice of the Lord is really the authoritative voice of the messiah, "the one who ...."

[92] Messianic allusions to Psalm 2 also appear in PsSol 17:23-24; Mat 3:17; Lk 3:22; Acts 4:25-26; 13:33; Heb 1:5; 5:5; 4Ez 13:33-38; 4QFlor (4Q174) 3.18–19; and in Rev 12:5; 19:15,19.

and ethics in the Apocalypse: "To the one who conquers I will give the right to sit with me on my throne, *just as I myself conquered and sat with my Father on his throne*" (3:21). Thus, 2:26 and 3:21 provide a clear indication that the believers share in Christ's eschatological rule, just as they share in Christ's faithful witness unto death.

The victory hymn of the heavenly court in 12:10-12 contains one of the more remarkable explanations of the cause for rejoicing. It is announced that the great accuser of "our brothers and sisters" has been thrown down from heaven and they (our brothers and sisters) have "triumphed over him [the accuser] on account of the blood of the lamb and on account of the word of their testimony, and they did not struggle to preserve their own lives" (12:11). Here again we see the close connection between Christology and ethics in the Apocalypse. Just as Christ remained a faithful witness and triumphed through his death, so the believers' willingness to maintain their testimony to the point of death constitutes their victory over the accuser.

The willingness both on the part of Jesus and on the part of the Asian believers to maintain their witness faithfully unto death is crucial here. It not only recalls the scene in the throne room, where the Lamb is said to have over-come *because* he was slaughtered; it also suggests that the Lamb Christology of the Apocalypse is related to defiant martyrdom. Jeremiah, too, was main-taining a faithful witness—a prophetic denunciation of Judah—in the face of hostile denunciation. The hostility of his own people of Anatoth grew so se-vere that they plotted to murder him. According to Jeremiah 11, Jeremiah himself was not aware of their hostility until it was revealed to him by God (11:18). Then Jeremiah says, "But I was like a gentle lamb (ἀρνίον ἄκακον) led to the slaughter (τοῦ θύεσθαι)" (11:19).

While the author of the Apocalypse is redefining the meaning and nature of *conquest* here, he is not claiming that white is black or up is down. It is not as if "conquering" has become a code word for a narrowly conceived spiritual triumph that is won through dying. Losing is not paradoxically winning, nor winning losing. When the first seal was broken, a rider on a white horse appeared and he went out "conquering and in order to conquer" (νικῶν καὶ ἵνα νικήσῃ; 6:2). Most commentators agree that this rider is not a figure for Christ, but a counter figure, a "victorious warrior who in his form embodies aggression and conquest."[93] When the two witnesses complete their testimony, the beast will make war with them and "will conquer" (νικήσει) them and kill them (11:7). The second beast was allowed to make war on the saints and "to conquer" (νικῆσαι) them (13:7).

---

[93] Jürgen Roloff, *The Revelation of John: A Continental Commentary*, translated by John E. Alsup (Minneapolis: Fortress Press, 1993), 86.

Nevertheless, the means by which the saints prove victorious is through their witness and their martyr deaths. They can even be called "the ones who conquered" (νικῶντας, 15:2). In Revelation 17:14 the kings of the earth "will make war with the lamb and the lamb will conquer (νικήσει) them, because he is lord of lords and king of kings, and the ones with him are called and chosen and faithful." In chapter 21, when John sees the new heaven and new earth, and the new holy city Jerusalem coming down out of heaven, the eschatological promises are given to "the one who conquers" (ὁ νικῶν; 21:7).

The author's ambiguous use of the νικη- word group suggests that victory is a matter of spiritual discernment. What may *seem* to be victory through violent aggression and forceful subjugation, may actually be defeat. What may *seem* to be defeat—through experiencing violent aggression, forceful subjugation, or even death—may actually be victory. The most significant battle in the Apocalypse is therefore a battle for *perception* fought on the rhetorical battlefield.

4.3 The Prophetic Calls to Discernment

Further evidence for such a battle lies in the direct editorial appeals to the reader. One such appeal surfaces in the refrain, "Let the one who has an ear hear what the Spirit is saying to the churches," ὁ ἔχων οὖς ἀκουσάτω τί τὸ πνεῦμα λέγει ταῖς ἐκκλησίαις, which is repeated verbatim near the end of each of the seven letters to the churches of the Apocalypse in 2:7,11,17,29; 3:6,13,22. Another appearance of this saying, worded similarly, is in 13:9: "If anyone has an ear, let him [or her] hear!" (εἴ τις ἔχει οὖς ἀκουσάτω).

The invitation to hear is common in the Old Testament, especially in the Prophets (cf. Deut 29:4; 32:1; Judg 5:3; 1Kgs 22:19; 2Kgs 19:16; Pss 17:1,6; 39:12; 49:1; 115:6; 135:17; Prov 22:17; Isa 32:3; 33:15; 42:20; 48:8; 64:4; Jer 6:10; 13:15; 17:23; 42:15; Amos 7:16; Zech 7:11). But the specific implication that one can have ears and still not hear draws on a well-established tradition in the Prophets about the nature of spiritual perception. For instance, in Isaiah 6:10 the prophet connects "closed" (lit., "uncircumcised") ears with the refusal to acknowledge or respond to the warning of God. Refusing to hear with one's ears is a symbol for remaining unrepentant. Often this "inability" to hear is treated as God's doing (see, e.g., Isa 29:9-12; Deut 29:4). In Isaiah 29:11 the stupor that identifies blind unresponsiveness is compared to the inability to read the words of a sealed document: "The vision of all this has become for you like the words of a sealed document. If it is given to those who can read, with the command, 'Read this,' they say, 'We cannot, for it is sealed.'" In Ezek 12:2 having ears to hear, but not hearing, is treated as a matter of rebellion.

This prophetic tradition is picked up in Mark 4:9,23 (cf. Mt 11:15; 13:9, 43; 15:10; Lk 8:18). For instance, in Mark 4:9, Jesus says, "Let the one who has ears to hear, listen!" (ὃς ἔχει ὦτα ἀκούειν ἀκουέτω). Whether this tradition goes back to Jesus or is redactional is not our concern here. Our point is that in inviting the reader who has ears to listen, the author is (1) identifying with the prophetic tradition as such;[94] (2) challenging the reader to perceive spiritually—that is, to go beyond surface interpretation or what seems obvious to the senses; and (3) warning the reader that failure to perceive spiritually is tantamount to rebellion against God. Just as the seven oracles challenge the hearers/readers to perceive reality on a different level, so do the visions that follow. The specific invitation to hear what the Spirit is saying to the churches thus connects the explicit ethical instructions of Rev 2–3 with the visions of 4–22.

Closely related to the above editorial comment is the phrase, "Let the one who has a mind ...." For instance, in Rev 13:18 we read, "Ὧδε ἡ σοφία ἐστίν· ὁ ἔχων νοῦν ...." In Rev 17:9 we see a similar saying, "ὧδε ὁ νοῦς ὁ ἔχων σοφίαν." Both of these function as clues to the reader that what follows has special revelatory significance and that this significance is available only to the one who has opened the mind to wisdom.

This redefinition of conquering is similar to the redefinition of conquering in the Maccabean literature, especially in 4 Maccabees. In 4 Maccabees, panegyric takes center stage as the stories of ancient heroes demonstrate the superiority of reason (understood primarily as the power of purposeful, wise decision) over rash, unreflective, and foolish emotion. And like the Seer of the Apocalypse, the author of 4 Maccabees sees life as a conflict, with faithfulness requiring a resistance ethic. Through faithful suffering, including martyrdom, the faithful "conquer" their enemies.

More than half of the occurrences of νικάω in the LXX are in 4 Maccabees.[95] Eleazar and the seven brothers were able to "conquer" the tyrant and to purify the land from tyranny because of their courage and endurance (ὑπομονή), even though they resisted nonviolently and died in the process (1:11). Even as old Eleazar was being beaten, bathed in sweat and gasping for breath,

---

[94] The author's repeated insistence that his book is a divinely commissioned work of prophecy (1:3; 10:11; 22:7,9,10,18,19) underscores not its interest in prediction, though that may be a peripheral concern of the book. Rather, it underscores the classical tradition of prophecy in the Hebrew Bible that emphasized "prophetic *discernment* of the true nature of the historical situation and a prophetic *demand* for an appropriate response." See Richard Bauckham, "Approaching the Apocalypse," in *Decide for Peace: Evangelicals and the Bomb*, edited by Dana Mills-Powell (Basingstoke: Marshall Pickering, 1986), 94.

[95] 4Mac 1:11; 3:17; 6:10,33; 7:4,11; 8:2; 9:6,30; 11:20; 13:2,7; 16:14; 17:15,24.

he conquered (ἐνίκα) his torturers by means of his courageous spirit (6:10; cf. 7:4; 8:2; 9:6). The means of this triumph is conceived of as ὑπομονή (endurance or consistent resistance) διὰ τὴν εὐσέβειαν (on religious grounds; 9:30). In other words, an ethic of consistent, nonviolent resistance, born of a commitment to God, is the means to victory over evil. Indeed, "religious knowledge" (ἡ εὐσεβὴς ἐπιστήμη), understood as nonviolent resistance unto death, is "invincible" (ἀνίκητος; 11:21). Similarly, the mother of the seven sons "conquered" (ἐνίκησας) the tyrant through her own steadfastness and was thus found to be more powerful than a man (16:14).

As in the Apocalypse, although *conquering* is redefined in 4 Maccabees, it is not *reversed* in meaning. At the end of the book, Antiochus Epiphanes is so impressed by the courage and endurance of the faithful Hebrews that he uses their courage and endurance as a means for motivating his own troops, making *them* brave and courageous for infantry battle and siege. "And he ravaged and conquered (ἐνίκησεν) all his enemies" (17:24). This concluding comment shows that the main concern of the author of 4 Maccabees is with the superior power of courage and single-minded purpose, not with the superiority of non-violent means of resistance over violent means of resistance. The author of 4 Maccabees can thus express this superior power of courage and single-minded purpose either through resolute and fearless martyrdom or through courage and bravery on the battlefield.

4.4 The Lamb as Divine Warrior

The promise of blessing in the Apocalypse on those who "conquer" assumes, of course, a conflict. As we have suggested above, this conflict is part of the revelation, part of the rhetorical strategy of the author, not necessarily an obvious component in the social situation of the seven churches. But conflict is not only part of the rhetorical framework of the Apocalypse; it is also *narrated* in the visions of the book. The elements that form the building blocks of this conflict are heavily dependent on the "combat myth" that had already existed for millennia in various forms in the ancient Near East.[96]

In the Hebrew Bible, the Exodus was the paradigmatic holy war—or better, "Yahweh war"—in which God alone fought to free the Israelites from Egypt (Exod 14:13-14). This monergism is seen again in God's salvation of Hezekiah from Sennecharib and in God's salvation of Jehoshaphat from the Moabites and Ammonites. But we also see in the tradition of holy war a synergistic

---

[96] Adela Yarbro Collins' dissertation remains the most helpful analysis of the dependence of the Apocalypse on those traditional elements. See Adela Yarbro Collins, *Combat Myth*.

model in which the Israelites fought *along with* God, sometimes in a dysfunctional way.[97]

One of the more insightful analyses of the theological import of the combat myth in the Apocalypse is that of Richard Bauckham in chapter 8 of his book, *The Climax of Prophecy: Studies on the Book of Revelation*.[98] Bauckham maintains that the monergistic ideal formed the model for the proto-apocalyptic visions of holy war in which "God fights alone (Isa 59:16; 63:3) or with his heavenly army (Joel 3:11b; Zech 14:5b)."[99] It is not until we come to the Jewish literature written *after* the first century CE that we find a truly violent messiah who leads the troops of Israel in a holy war against her enemies.[100] Central to the Lamb Christology of the Apocalypse is the forging of a new understanding of the means by which one conquers: that of a consistent, nonviolent resistance born of clear allegiance to God that may well result in death.

The battle scenes in the Apocalypse are indeed strange. Just when one appears to be on the verge of a real battle, it turns out that it is already over. In Revelation 7, the 144,000 appear to be soldiers mustered for war. But they are robed in white (7:13-14), and have made their robes white in the blood of the Lamb (7:14), suggesting that their victory comes by way of their own deaths.

---

[97] For an excellent, accessible discussion of monergism and synergism in the holy war traditions of the Old Testament, see Albert Curry Winn, *Ain't Gonna Study War No More: Biblical Ambiguity and the Abolition of War* (Louisville: Westminster/John Knox, 1993). See also John H. Yoder, "Ethics and Eschatology," *Ex Auditu* 6 (1990): 119–28.

[98] Richard Bauckham, "The Apocalypse as a Christian War Scroll," chapt. 8 in *The Climax of Prophecy: Studies on the Book of Revelation* (Edinburgh: T. & T. Clark, 1993), 210–37. This is a revised version of the previously published R[ichard] Bauckham, "The Book of Revelation as a Christian War Scroll," *Neotestamentica* 22 (1988): 17–40. For other treatments of the holy war motif in the Apocalypse, see Devon Harvey Wiens, *Holy War Theology in the New Testament and Its Relationship to the Eschatological Day of the Lord Tradition*, Ph.D. dissertation, reprint, 1967 (Ann Arbor, Mich.: University Microfilms International, 1982); Charles Homer Giblin, "The Cohesive Thematic of God's Holy War of Liberation," appendix in *The Book of Revelation: The Open Book of Prophecy*, Good News Studies, no. 34 (Collegeville, Minn.: Liturgical Press, 1991), 222–31; Tremper Longman III, "Divine Warrior," 290–307.

[99] Richard Bauckham, "The Apocalypse as a Christian War Scroll," 211.

[100] This is true of PsSol 17 despite John J. Collins' claims to the contrary. Compare John J. Collins, *The Scepter and the Star*, 55, with William Klassen, "Jesus and the Messianic War," in *Early Jewish and Christian Exegesis: Studies in Memory of W. H. Brownlee*, eds C. A. Evans and W. F. Stinespring (Atlanta: Scholars Press, 1987), 159–60. Bauckham sees the contrast of the peaceable multitude with the warlike multitude of the nations in 4 Ezra 13 as evidence of "a polemic against apocalyptic militarism" (Richard Bauckham, "The Apocalypse as a Christian War Scroll," 219–20).

They have not defiled themselves with women (14:4), suggesting that their "victory" is won in a holy war.[101]

The war that does exist in the Apocalypse is strangely nonconventional. In Rev 2:16, Christ warns the people of Pergamum about the Nicolaitans among them. He says, πολεμήσω μετ' αὐτῶν ἐν τῇ ῥομφαίᾳ τοῦ στόματός μου (I will make war with them with the sword of my mouth). In 12:7 there is war in heaven as Michael and his angels fight the dragon and his angels. In 13:4 the whole earth worships the beast and questions whether anyone can resist (i.e., "make war on") the beast. In 17:14 the ten kings make war on the Lamb and the Lamb conquers them "because he is Lord of lords and King of kings and the ones with him are called and chosen and faithful." Thus the Lamb and his followers gain the victory because of their righteous deeds *off* the battlefield, not because of their skill in physical combat.

The closest we get to a battle scene in the Apocalypse is in chapter 19. There we read that John saw heaven opened[102] and, behold, a white horse, and the one seated on it was faithful, called, and true (cf. 1:5; 3:14), and he judges and "makes war" (πολεμεῖ) in righteousness. The rider approaches the battle dressed in a robe dipped in blood (19:13)—his own blood of witness/martyrdom. In keeping with the pivotal scene in Rev 5 and the message of the book as a whole (cf. esp. the references to blood in 1:5; 7:14; 12:11), the blood here is the blood of martyrdom. This contrasts with Isa 63:1-3, the source of this imagery, where the blood is the blood of the enemies of the divine warrior.[103] John is, in fact, challenging the reader to look more carefully at his language and to reinterpret Isaiah 63 in the light of the Lamb. The warrior himself is called "the word of God" (19:13) and his only weapon is the sword that comes out of his mouth (19:15; cf. 1:16; 2:12). So even here, no real battle scene is

---

[101] Refrainment from sexual intercourse is a traditional element in the holy war motif. See 1Sam 21:4-5; cf. also Deut 20:1-9; 23:9-10; Philo, *De Cherubim* 49–50. See esp. the comments of Charles Homer Giblin in, Charles Homer Giblin, "God's Holy War of Liberation," 226.

[102] Though ἀνοίγω is an important verb in the Apocalypse, occurring 27 times, this is the first time since 4:1 that we have explicitly seen *heaven* opened (though cf. 11:19; 15:5, where the *Temple* of God in heaven is opened).

[103] Cf. esp. M. Eugene Boring, *Revelation*, 196–97; and Wilfrid J. Harrington, *Revelation*, 192–94; cf. also John Sweet, *Revelation*, reprint, 1979 (Philadelphia: Trinity Press International, 1990), 282–83; Pablo Richard, *Apocalypse: A People's Commentary on the Book of Revelation*, The Bible & Liberation Series (Maryknoll, N.Y.: Orbis Books, 1995), 147; Gerhard A. Krodel, *Revelation*, Augsburg Commentary on the New Testament (Minneapolis: Augsburg Publishing House, 1989), 323. G. B. Caird argues that the blood on the Rider's garments is neither his own nor that of his enemies, but that of the martyr saints (George B. Caird, *Revelation*, 243).

narrated. In fact, no battle story is possible, since the decisive battle is long over.[104]

That is also why he can already ride the white horse. His victory is consistently portrayed in terms of his death and resurrection. The ones with him are not human warriors eager to take vengeance on the nations, but "armies of heaven, wearing fine linen, white and pure" (19:14). We have just been informed that the wearing of fine linen is granted by God and that it refers to τὰ δικαιώματα τῶν ἁγίων (the righteous deeds of the saints; 19:8).

Thus no conventional battles at all are narrated in the Apocalypse—eschatological or otherwise. The only battles in the central section of the Apocalypse are the same battles that the saints are enjoined to engage in the prophetic oracles in Revelation 2–3. Unlike the War Scroll of Qumran, the Apocalypse does not invite the saints to join in the final eschatological battle. The reason the author nowhere narrates an extended conflict or battle between the Lamb and the dragon or beasts is because the only real conflicts envisioned in the Apocalypse are first, the one that has already occurred in the death and resurrection of Christ; and second, the ones in which the saints are already engaged through consistent nonviolent resistance.

4.5 But is the Vision Really Ethical?

Debate about the Apocalypse's ethical vision shows no sign of waning. Many commentators have concluded that its ethical vision ultimately fails. For instance, although Tina Pippin was originally attracted to its liberationist ethic, she concluded that its deep misogyny ultimately destroys its ethical vision.[105] In a similar vein, Jack Sanders says, "It is its retreat from the ethical dimension that is the basic evil of the Apocalypse." "It is unfortunate that we are

---

[104] Cf. Ted Grimsrud, "Peace Theology and the Justice of God in the Book of Revelation," in *Essays on Peace Theology and Witness*, edited by Willard M. Swartley, *Occasional Papers*, no. 12 (Elkhart, Ind.: Institute of Mennonite Studies, 1988), 145; Vernard Eller, *Most Revealing*, 176–79.

[105] Tina Pippin, *Death and Desire: The Rhetoric of Gender in the Apocalypse of John*, Literary Currents in Biblical Interpretation (Louisville: Westminster/John Knox Press, 1992), 47; cf. also Tina Pippin, "Eros and the End: Reading for Gender in the Apocalypse of John," *Semeia*, no. 59 (1992): 193–217; Tina Pippin, "The Heroine and the Whore: Fantasy and the Female in the Apocalypse of John," *Semeia*, no. 60 (1992): 67–82. For similar critiques, see Susan R. Garrett, "Revelation," in *The Women's Bible Commentary*, edited by Carol A. Newsom and Sharon H. Ringe (Louisville: Westminster/John Knox Press, 1992), 377; Adela Yarbro Collins, "Feminine Symbolism in the Book of Revelation," *Biblical Interpretation* 1, no. 1 (1993): 27; M[arla] J. Selvidge, "Powerful and Powerless Women in the Apocalypse," *Neostamentica* 26, no. 1 (1992): 157–67.

today experiencing a revival of just the kind of Christianity found in Revelation."[106]

A careful response to Tina Pippin's argument is not possible here. However, since we have maintained that attention to what a text *does* through rhetorical criticism is crucial for understanding the message of the Apocalypse, her argument is relevant. The misogyny of the Apocalypse runs deep, according to Pippin. It silences women. It marginalizes them. It destroys women as women. It rapes women and it objectifies women through its own stereotyping. Worse yet, "the Apocalypse is blind to its own mechanism of scapegoating."[107] Although the Lamb ostensibly becomes the scapegoat that exposes and disempowers the generative mimetic scapegoat mechanism, that mechanism is reified not only in the beasts and the dragon, but especially in the women with seductive power (i.e., Jezebel, the Woman Clothed with the Sun, and the Whore). Thus women are the double victims in this narrative. The violent destruction of Whore Rome is admittedly cathartic, but the subtlety with which the misogyny is inscribed in this catharsis makes it all the more frightening.

Schüssler Fiorenza agrees that the text is androcentric but maintains that focusing on its androcentrism is not helpful, and ultimately not a faithful reading of the Apocalypse. Although she allows that Pippin's ideological reading of the Apocalypse is legitimate, it does not go far enough. That is, one must investigate the rhetorical strategy of the Apocalypse more broadly in order to determine whether or how much it shares in the discourses of domination and dehumanization. Thus, to read *only* for gender codes apart from examining the larger rhetorical strategy is to impose a modern ideology on the text that ironically reinscribes androcentrism in the text in a reductionistic way![108]

The Apocalypse of John is arguably the most dangerous book in the history of Christendom in terms of the history of its effects. Even if its vision is ultimately ethical and nonviolent, we must unfortunately admit it has not been very successful in terms of the history of its effects. So even if John *intended* a nonviolent ethic—elusive as authorial intent is—does that ethic come through in our reading? Does the Apocalypse reward patient readers who are attentive to the subtleties of its rhetoric and its repeated calls for discernment on their part? Does the Apocalypse create a symbolic universe that reforms and reshapes a community's world view in positive and life-giving ways?

I would suggest that the book's relative lack of success in terms of its history of effects is due in part to the "success" readers from the second century to

---

[106] Jack T. Sanders, *Ethics in the New Testament: Change and Development* (Philadelphia: Fortress Press, 1975), 114–15.

[107] Tina Pippin, *Death and Desire*, 84; cf. also 47.

[108] See Fiorenza, *Revelation*, 12–15, for a summary of Fiorenza's feminist reading strategy in comparison with other feminist reading strategies on the Apocalypse.

today have enjoyed in ignoring the book's rhetorical force within its original historical setting.[109] The more closely the symbolism of the book is read in light of actual first-century people and events, the more clearly does the book empower readers—ancient and modern alike—to adopt an ethic of nonviolent, faithful witness.

Because John's vision of renewal entails both a new earth and a new heaven, some have seen this felt need for renewal as indicative of a deep pessimism in John's ethic. There *is* a pessimism inherent in that vision. It is a pessimism that grows out of a deep sense of disappointment in the failures of humanity to realize God's glory on earth. The vision of a new heaven and a new earth derives from Trito-Isaiah's similar disappointment as he experienced a restoration of Judah that was much less glorious than that envisioned by Deutero-Isaiah.

The author calls for a courageous and active "resistance" (ὑπομονή) to the evils of Greco-Roman culture and religion. It is a clear "No" to the possibility of humanity's bringing in the fullness of God's reign, and a joyful and confident "Yes" to the way of Christ, demonstrated most poignantly in his faithful witness—a witness that led to his death on the cross. So the politics of John's Apocalypse are radically anti-establishmentarian. But is its political ethic essentially nonviolent? Does the lamb replace and redefine the lion ... or does the lion ultimately co-opt and subvert the lamb? Is there a lion in that lamb's clothing?

And what about the terrible violence of the book? The Apocalypse virtually seethes with images of blood and violence. To make matters worse, God and the Lamb are often envisioned as the source of the violence, sometimes to the accompaniment of cries of vengeance on the part of the saints. Is this an ethical vision? Does Revelation's great central image of Christ as the Lamb serve to control and interpret the other major themes, including the divine warrior and judgment imagery? Or does the divine warrior tradition ends up transforming, reinterpreting, or subverting the Lamb Christology? To use Steve Moyise's language, does the lion lie down with the lamb in Revelation?[110]

---

[109] See Wes Howard-Brook and Anthony Gwyther, *Unveiling Empire: Reading Revelation Then and Now*, foreword by Elizabeth McAlister (Orbis Books, 1999), esp. xxiv.

[110] See Steve Moyise, "Does the Lion Lie Down with the Lamb?" in *Studies in the Book of Revelation*, 181–94. The question itself is a tad misleading on a couple of levels, since it seems to imply that the lion and lamb imagery in Revelation may be designed to communicate a vision of eschatological peace, as suggested by Isaiah 11:6, where the "wolf" (זְאֵב; λύκος) lies down with the lamb (כֶּבֶשׂ; ἀρήν/ἀρνός). However, we do not see *lions* lying down with lambs *either* in the Hebrew Bible's visions of eschatological peace *or* in Revelation. In Rev 5, the lamb *replaces* the lion rather than coexists with it. Moyise denies in the next-to-last sentence of his book that the "Lamb

In speaking of the Bible in general and Revelation in particular, the nineteenth-century American philosopher C.S. Pierce responds to what he sees as a fundamental *lack* of ethical virtue in the rhetoric of the Apocalypse:

> Little by little the bitterness increases until in the last book of the New Testament, its poor distracted author represents that all the time Christ was talking about having come to save the world, the secret design was to catch the entire human race, with the exception of a paltry 144,000, and souse them all in brimstone lake, and as the smoke of their torment went up for ever and ever, to turn and remark, "There is no curse any more." Would it be an insensible smirk or a fiendish grin that should accompany such an utterance? I wish I could believe St. John did not write it.[111]

Along a similar line, Michael Grosso considers the author of Revelation triumphalistic and to exhibit a self-righteous indifference toward the fate of others. According to Grosso, the author exhibits such pleasure in the torments of others that he can only be thought of as sadistic and barbaric.[112]

Are these charges valid? Revelation has certainly offended many readers—both ancient and modern—at a basic level. What should the modern reader who wishes to read and interpret ethically do with such a vision?

One of the early attempts to deal with this offense was by William Klassen in his 1966 article, "Vengeance in the Apocalypse of John."[113] For Klassen the mitigating factors are these: (1) The followers of the Lamb do not participate in the battles of the Lamb—only in the Lamb's victory; (2) God is never described as going out to war, and when the Lamb makes war ($\pi o\lambda \varepsilon \mu \acute{\varepsilon} \omega$), the battle is fought not with literal weapons, but with the sword of the Word of God; (3) we never see the saints as enjoying forever the torture of their enemies; (4) although the concept of the wrath of God may seem unsettling or unwelcome to us, we must get "accustomed to seeing [it] as central to the

---

simply replaces the Lion" (p. 194), and he is right in one sense. Although the Lamb *does* replace the Lion on the surface of the narrative—rather than remain in juxtaposition with it—it does not seem to do so on the *rhetorical* level. Moyise is skeptical that any one reading can legitimately control or interpret other readings on this point.

[111] Charles S. Pierce, "Evolutionary Love," *The Essential Pierce: Selected Philosophical Writings*, vol. 1 (1867–1893), ed. Nathan House and Christian Koesel (Indiana University Press, 1992) 365–366. I am grateful to David L. Barr for bringing Pierce to my attention. See David L. Barr, "Towards an Ethical Reading of the Apocalypse: Reflections on John's Use of Power, Violence, and Misogyny," *Society of Biblical Literature 1997 Seminar Papers* (Atlanta: Scholars Press, 1997), 358.

[112] See Michael Grosso, *The Millennium Myth: Love and Death at the End of Time* (Wheaton, Ill.: Quest Books, 1995); see esp. 24–25, 36–39.

[113] William Klassen, "Vengeance in the Apocalypse of John," *Catholic Biblical Quarterly* 28 (1966): 300–11.

Christian faith"[114]; (5) the imprecations in the Apocalypse are not substantially different from the imprecations of the Psalms; and (6) the literary motif that unifies the Apocalypse is the seven-fold blessing (1:3; 14:13; 16:15; 19:9; 20:6; 22:7; 22:14), not a series of curses; (7) in the Old Testament God judged by inflicting suffering, but in the Apocalypse he judges by accepting suffering; (8) the destiny of the world will be determined not by the violence of humanity, but by the lamb who refused to choose between pacifism or militarism, but overcame violence by his own sacrificial death.[115]

Although I have some trouble with the third and fourth points above, I agree that these points "mitigate" the offense of violence in the Apocalypse. The last two points are crucial for understanding the ethics of the Apocalypse. However, the mitigation provided by these observations is only partial. We are left with the language of violence on the surface of the text and a lingering suspicion that there is something violent at work in the very argumentation of the book.

In his 1988 article, "Peace Theology and the Justice of God in the Book of Revelation," Ted Grimsrud argues that the plague visions and the outpouring of God's wrath are somehow part of God's justice.[116] God is just in this vision because (1) the ultimate result of God's work is the New Jerusalem; (2) the controlling metaphor in the book is the slain Lamb; (3) punishment is (primarily) of evil powers, not people as such; and (4) the saints are called to follow the Lamb wherever he goes by conquering as he conquered—conquering as redefined by remaining faithful throughout their lives, not, as some other apocalypses have it, by participating in a literal eschatological messianic war.

Grimsrud's explication suggests that because God is God and not human, we cannot and should not expect God to act "ethically" as defined by Christian human ethics. Because eschatological judgment belongs to God alone, it belongs to God in a way that it could never belong to humans. Therefore, we cannot and should not expect God to be "ethical," even if at some level God is "just." In good biblical fashion, Grimsrud allows the sovereignty of God to lie behind and somehow support the outworkings of human history, including even the evil within history. If evil seems to have the upper hand, it is only because at some level God has allowed it. But we should not mistake God's "allowing" of evil and violence for God's intentional "willing" of evil and vio-

---

[114] Klassen, "Vengeance in the Apocalypse," 310.

[115] Klassen, "Vengeance in the Apocalypse," 310.

[116] Ted Grimsrud, "Peace Theology and the Justice of God in the Book of Revelation," *Essays on Peace Theology and Witness*, ed. Willard M. Swartley (Occasional Papers, No. 12; Elkhart, Ind.: Institute of Mennonite Studies, 1988), 154–78; see esp. 142.

lence.[117] So even if God is sovereign over the outworking of the evil of violence in this world, God's purposeful presence in such allowance is a matter of mystery and a second-level willing.

Grimsrud says nothing about the rhetorical or reader-response *effect* of such a violent revelation on the reader of the first-century or twenty-first century. His treatment of the theological problem of Revelation's violence depends instead on a rational explanation about how such a violent vision can undergird an ethic of nonviolence. Furthermore, Grimsrud's appeal to the New Jerusalem as the "ultimate result of God's work" suggests that a nonviolent or just end justifies a violent or unjust means. Nevertheless, his insistence that the symbol of the lamb controls the other metaphors in the book and his contention that the saints are invited to conquer as the Lamb conquered are both correct readings of the Apocalypse, in my opinion, and significant for dealing with the violence of the book as a theological problem.

In his helpful excursus on this problem,[118] M. Eugene Boring identifies four considerations that mitigate the theological offense of the book's violent imagery. First, one must acknowledge the "givenness" of John's situation of suffering. Second, John is appropriating and adapting elements within his tradition, such as the combat myth, not creating them from scratch. Third, the violence and blood in the Apocalypse are features of John's visionary and metaphorical language. They function not primarily to make objective statements about the fate of the unredeemed, but to sustain the believing community's resistance from within a faith perspective. Fourth, John's theology ultimately controls and qualifies the violent imagery. John refuses to underestimate the reality of evil and injustice in the world. Nevertheless, the apocalyptic terror is transformed through John's Christology. Christ conquers by being a lamb, not by being a lion. The saints conquer by emulating the Lamb, not the lion. Finally, there are hints that despite the destruction, John expected *all* of creation to experience God's redemption. In the end, it is Death and Hades that are cast into the lake of fire, not their victims (20:14).

For the most part, I accept Boring's statements. As Boring suggests, the believing community's discomfort with the violence of the Apocalypse is not unlike its discomfort with the imprecatory Psalms. Like Grimsrud, Boring

---

[117] Cf. Pablo Richard: "the plagues of the trumpets and bowls in Revelation refer not to 'natural' disasters, but to the agonies of history that the empire itself causes and suffers; they are agonies of the beast caused by its very idolatry and lawlessness. Today the plagues of Revelation are rather the disastrous results of ecological destruction, the arms race, irrational consumerism, the idolatrous logic of the market, and the irrational use of technology and of natural resources" (Pablo Richard, *Apocalypse*, 86).

[118] "Interpreting Revelation's Violent Imagery," in M. Eugene Boring, *Revelation*, 112–19.

would say that existential catharsis is not on the same level morally as direct action in personal revenge. To call for God's vengeance itself requires acknowledging that vengeance belongs to God, *not* to the believing community. To bless those who metaphorically dash the babies of one's enemies against the rock—while morally questionably—is still morally superior than to grasp God's prerogative and do so oneself (cf. Ps 137:9). Furthermore, the calls for justice in the Apocalypse never reach the blood-thirsty heights achieved in the War Scroll or the Thanksgiving Scrolls at Qumran or those achieved in the Apocalypse of Peter.

Whatever the socio-political situation of the addressees of the book, it is clear that the author is writing from a situation of personal suffering (1:9). It is too easy to blame the victim for a "lack of love." It is disingenuous for people in positions of power and privilege to score the oppressed for not being dispassionate or "loving" in their calls for justice. Evil and injustice are not "nice." Although the author's strong theology of the sovereignty of God seems to highlight God's active role in retributive justice, there are clues in the text that the "wrath" of God and of the Lamb is really the impersonal working out, within history, of the results of evil's own self-destruction.[119]

Boring's second point is important, especially in light of Pippin's strategy of reading. The faithful reader must take into account the differences between an ahistorical modern reaction to the text and the way in which a first-century reader would have reacted to the text. Doing so requires all of the historical work of the historical-critical method as well as the sensitivities of rhetorical criticism. The ethics of reading demands patient attention to the content of the message, to its historical and literary context, and to the nature and force of its rhetorical presentation.

Boring missteps a bit when he assumes that the Lion was part of the tradition inherited by John. The Lion does not appear to have been a traditional symbol for the messiah. Literarily, the so-called juxtaposition of lion and lamb in Rev 5 quickly falls apart: it is not sustained throughout the book. Rather, the lion immediately disappears from view never to be heard from again and the lamb becomes the controlling image. This suggests that the images of the lion and the lamb were created specifically to address competing visions of how the messiah wields power. The triumph of the Lamb through his faithful

---

[119] The classic theological study on the wrath of God in the Apocalypse is that of A. T. Hanson: Anthony Tyrrell Hanson, *The Wrath of the Lamb* (London: SPCK, 1957), esp. 159–201; cf. also Ted Grimsrud, "Peace Theology," 135–53; William Klassen, "Vengeance in the Apocalypse," 300–11. For an example of "wrath" used as an impersonal expression of unfortunate or difficult circumstances without any implication that God's own displeasure lay behind it, see 1Macc 1:64: καὶ ἐγένετο ὀργὴ μεγάλη ἐπὶ Ἰς-ραηλ σφόδρα.

witness unto death does not immediately eventuate in a utopian peace. The whole creation does not suddenly become "nice," as we might wish. Rather, the revelation of the Lamb's triumph *unmasks* the evil of violence. The Lamb does not *unleash* these horrors on the earth; rather, he *reveals* the horrific depth of evil for what it is as well as the just deeds of God (15:4).

In a posthumously published book, *Vision and Violence*, Arthur Mendel explores the relationship between apocalyptic thinking and violence. [120] He investigates the roots of what he calls "apocalyptic thinking," surveys its manifestations throughout the history of the last two millennia, and attempts to describe its "ultimate meaning." He concludes that apocalyptic thought per se represents a tendency toward violence. He worries about modern fundamentalist movements and their fascination with apocalypticism, concluding that what we need today is a more modest and human philosophy that is committed to the repair of the world. In Mendel's view, apocalypticism and violence go hand-in-hand. The world could afford such cooperation until the advent of nuclear weapons and the prospect of universal devastation. Today, however, we must put away apocalypticism and put a check on the rising fundamentalism that typically wreaks havoc with apocalyptic thought.

In his book, *Arguing the Apocalypse: A Theory of Millennial Rhetoric*, Stephen O'Leary takes much the same approach as Arthur P. Mendel, except that instead of surveying the history of apocalyptic thought over the centuries, O'Leary investigates the rhetorical strategies that have characterized apocalypticism and apocalyptic writings. [121] Neither Mendel nor O'Leary is a biblical scholar. Both define "apocalyptic" with broad and imprecise strokes, using the historical sweep of the last 2,000 in their attempt to get at the "deep structure" of apocalypticism, whether that deep structure is to be found in a certain "mind set" or a certain "rhetoric." O'Leary looks at how apocalyptic argument has worked over the last 2,000 years and reads Revelation in light of that history. His book is a map to the so-called millennial consciousness.

I object to this approach because in both cases, supposed characteristics of "apocalypticism" as such are used as lenses through which to interpret Revelation. I would argue for a rhetorical approach to biblical interpretation that is more historical. Attention to historical context need not ultimately distance the reader from the text, as Moyise claims, [122] but can actually make the text more

---

[120] Arthur P. Mendel, *Vision and Violence* (Ann Arbor, Mich.: University of Michigan Press, 1992).

[121] Stephen D. O'Leary, *Arguing the Apocalypse: A Theory of Millennial Rhetoric* (New York: Oxford University Press, 1994).

[122] See Moyise, *Studies in the Book of Revelation*, ix–x. A historically alert rhetorical criticism can avoid the methodological dichotomy Moyise establishes in the introduction of this book even if Greg Carey is right that the Revelation's rhetoric is unstable because its ethoi are contradictory. For Carey's argument, see pp. 194, 199 below.

available to contemporary communities of faith that are struggling with similar questions about the theological implications of political allegiances. As Elisabeth Schüssler Fiorenza puts it, since the Apocalypse is

> a partial theological response in a particular socio-historical situation, the Apocalypse's narrative symbolization calls for critical assessment and theo-ethical evaluation in a contemporary rhetorical situation. Such a critical ideo-logical evaluation is necessary because the symbolic world of the Apocalypse is not only a theo-ethical model *of* its own socio-political world but also a theo-ethical model *for* socio-political life today.[123]

I do not hold to some anthropological or psychological "deep structure" that allows us to take an essentially ahistorical or nonhistorical approach to understanding the book. While the study of historical theology is important and useful, we must never confuse it with biblical interpretation. The Apocalypse of John should always be free to critique and correct later interpretations and uses of it by the church.[124]

In an important article on ethical readings of the Apocalypse, David L. Barr addresses the problematic violent rhetoric of the Apocalypse.[125] He argues that a proper reading of Revelation turns the popular American understanding of the Apocalypse on its head. In the popular imagination, God conquers by power and the violence of holy war. This is presumably justified be-

---

[123] Elisabeth Schüssler Fiorenza, "The Words of Prophecy: Reading the Apocalypse Theologically," in *Studies in the Book of Revelation*, ed. Steve Moyise (Edinburgh: T & T Clark, 2001), 1–19; see p. 11. This article was first published as "Die Worte der Prophetie: Die Apokalypse des Johannes theologisch lesen," *Jahrbuch für Biblische Theologie: Prophetie und Charisma* 14 (1999): 71–94.

[124] In his 110-page article on "War and Peace in the New Testament" in *Aufstieg und Niedergang der römischen Welt*, Willard Swartley dedicates five pages to the Apocalypse. Swartley claims that Revelation makes four distinctive contributions toward a New Testament peace theology: (1) It poses starkly the relationship between war and peace to the worship of God and God's fight against evil. (2) The earthly powers are expressions of evil spiritual power. (3) The role of believers is to trust God for the warfare and the victory through resistance that is both passive and active. (4) The model of the Lamb is paradigmatic and normative for believers. Although I think Swartley is largely correct with each of these claims, he does not address the violent *rhetoric* of the Apocalypse as a theological problem. See Willard M. Swartley, "War and Peace in the New Testament," *Aufstieg und Niedergang der römischen Welt*, Teil II, Principat; Band 26.3 (Berlin: de Gruyter, 1996), 2297–408.

[125] David L. Barr, "Towards an Ethical Reading of the Apocalypse: Reflections on John's Use of Power, Violence, and Misogyny," *Society of Biblical Literature 1997 Seminar Papers*, no. 36 (Atlanta: Scholars Press, 1997), 358–73. Also available on the Internet at http://www.wright.edu/~dbarr/moral.htm.

cause it leads to a good end. Nevertheless, the Apocalypse does not support such a reading for the following reasons:

First, God does not overcome evil by superior power. Revelation does not support the morality of domination. In this story, evil only appears to be conquered by power. In this story, evil is conquered by the death of the lamb.

Second, the apparent delay in judgment of the wicked is due not to divine indifference, but to John's basic understanding that human acts cause human downfall.

Third, in using the conventional apocalyptic imagery of his day, John did not write an immoral story. While we rightly shrink from the scenes of violence in Revelation, honesty requires that we acknowledge that ancient sensibilities are not the same as modern ones. While the book's *image* of violence is problematic, its *understanding* of violence is not.

Fourth, wars and disasters are not the means to the coming of the new heaven and new earth, but rather human endeavors to avoid God's new world. Renewal comes *after* violence, but not *through* violence.

Fifth, while God's reign is spiritual, it is not *only* spiritual; it has clear sociological and political implications. The spiritual vision of the Apocalypse does not *free* Christians from the real world of economic and political pressures, but rather it *prepares* them through a major paradigm shift in world view (a shift that the author calls "revelation" or "apocalypse") for real *engagement* with that world. Evil is real and is embodied in the empire. Therefore, the faithful witness to which the author calls his readers is not "just" a spiritual one, but one with difficult and challenging moral and political obligations. The author is calling his readers to resist the powers of domination in the specific social and economic circumstances of Roman Asia Minor. According to Barr, John's story stands firmly against violence and domination and calls the audience to active resistance to the powers of Rome.

These are significant claims by Barr. If he is right, then the offense we feel toward the rhetoric of violence employed by the author of the Apocalypse is largely mitigated. But Barr is not content simply to say or imply that we should not be offended. Commenting on John's personification of Babylon as a whore, Barr says, "It is dangerous that John used a human image here. We must challenge the text at this point (as we must challenge its comfort with violence generally). The question is how to challenge it."[126]

However, Greg Carey is largely unconvinced by the arguments of Barr and others that these factors mitigate the offense inherent in Revelation's rhetoric.[127] For all of its admitted egalitarianism, the Apocalypse demands the sub-

---

[126] David L. Barr, "Twoards an Ethical Reading of the Apocalypse," 360.

[127] For Carey's discussion of these attempts, see "Appropriating John's Ethos: Possible Mitigating Factors," in *Elusive Apocalypse*, 176–81.

mission of its readers. And if the author holds that suffering conquers evil, he also revels in the suffering about to come on his opponents. His authority alone can be trusted. We are left with the irony that all readings of the Apocalypse, whether of liberationists or premillennial dispensationalists, implicitly adopt the author's authoritarian ethos. So how can we escape this ironic situation? We cannot, Carey concludes. As such, Carey laments that even his own reading as a postmodern critic shares in the power and domination he had hoped to escape from the beginning.[128]

In his 2001 collection of essays on Revelation, Steve Moyise concludes with his own essay, "Does the Lion Lie Down with the Lamb?"[129] Are we supposed to reinterpret the apocalyptic violence, with its note of vengeance and gloating, as symbolic of Christ's self-sacrifice? he asks. Or is this just Christian wishful thinking? In answer to his own question, Moyise draws on deconstruction to argue that the text resists a firm answer to this question. He agrees with David Aune that although a theology of the cross is a central theological emphasis in Rev. 5, it is a marginal conception elsewhere in the book.[130] In the end, he concludes, it will not do to eliminate all interpretations other than one's own. We have an ethical obligation to resist certain interpretations, whether or not there are good exegetical grounds on which to do so.

> The Lion/Lamb juxtaposition is not so stable that readers are *forced* to reinterpret the apocalyptic violence in non-violent ways. It is imperative that they do so (for the good of humanity), but it is also imperative that they realize the precarious instability of such a position. Thus in answer to this chapter's title, I do not think the Lion does lie down with the Lamb. The juxtaposition *allows* a non-violent interpretation but it also reveals a fundamental danger, namely, that the weapons of resistance can end up supporting the very values being resisted. It does not do justice to the book of Revelation to advocate a position where Lamb simply replaces Lion. Evil is much more complex than that.[131]

As I noted above,[132] Moyise's way of phrasing the issue introduces several questionable assumptions: first, that the lion *ever* lay down with the lamb in biblical eschatology, and second, that the symbols of lion and lamb in Revelation are juxtaposed. As I have demonstrated above, the lamb does not *coexist* with the lion in some ongoing peaceful juxtaposition. Rather, the lamb *replaces* the lion as a symbol of the nature of Christ's victory despite his murder.

---

[128] Carey, *Elusive Apocalypse*, 184–85.

[129] Steve Moyise, "Does the Lion Lie Down with the Lamb?" *Studies in the Book of Revelation*, ed. Steve Moyise (Edinburgh: T & T Clark, 2001), 181–94.

[130] Moyise, "Does the Lion Lie Down with the Lamb?" 184.

[131] Moyise, "Does the Lion Lie Down with the Lamb?" 194.

[132] See note 110 above.

Moyise is well aware of the multitude of commentators who argue that a redefinition of power and of victory is at the heart of the Apocalypse. He is also aware that there exists in "certain strands of modern theology" the idea that the crucifixion of Jesus demonstrates that God's power is found in weakness, not strength.[133] He denies, however, that the Apocalypse witnesses to such a theology or that the Lamb symbolizes self-sacrifice and vulnerability. Because he wants to be an ethical reader, he wishes that it were so, but he thinks honesty compels him to conclude otherwise.

One of the problems here is that Moyise seems to imagine peace theology to be primarily a vision of peace *as absence of conflict*, even as the Apocalypse is full of both conflict and violence. But the Apocalypse of John advocates a theology of peace in its conception of how God deals with violence—through faithful, nonviolent witness to the point of death—and how God's people are to deal with violence—by following the Lamb wherever he goes, which means exhibiting the same faithful, nonviolent witness to the point of death.

In what follows, Moyise reviews the old evidence for a militaristic, apocalyptic lamb-redeemer figure that C.H. Dodd, Raymond Brown, and Josephine Massyngberde Ford, among others, cited in dependence upon Friedrich Spitta—evidence that has now been shown to be invalid and which must be discounted. Moyise concludes that Harold Bloom and Josephine Massynberde Ford may actually be "more honest" and "less biased" in their reading of the Apocalypse. Moyise then cites the failure of the (mostly irrelevant) Domitianic persecution hypothesis, the advent of deconstruction, literary theory, and the demise of "authorial intent" as a valid criterion in his attempt to demonstrate that the Apocalypse resists ecclesiastical and canonical-critical attempts to tame or control its interpretation. Moyise concludes that the Book of Revelation is not best served when modern interpreters find ways to eliminate all interpretations other than their own. Moyise is left in a rather strange position. Ethically, he feels impelled to exercise a responsible hermeneutic that unfortunately, he thinks, cannot be justified exegetically or methodologically.

Moyise raises more issues in this suggestive essay than can be dealt with briefly here. But several observations may be in order. First, the appeal to a supposed lamb-redeemer figure in apocalyptic Judaism is now shown to be invalid. Extant literature from Second Temple Judaism simply does not bear witness to such a figure.

Second, while ideological readings of the Apocalypse are legitimate, I have argued that the modern reader has an obligation to read this ancient text as a means of communication within the author's sociopolitical situation. Although biblical studies in the modernist historical-critical mode has clearly needed the

---

[133] Moyise cites Jürgen Moltmann's reading of the Apostle Paul as an example. "Does the Lion Lie Down with the Lamb?" 182.

chastening of deconstruction and of literary theory, ideological readings that ignore the complex rhetoric of the book within its own sociopolitical context are just as unethical as Fundamentalist and dispensational readings that do so. What is needed is not an ahistorical reader-response analysis, but the sort of reader-response analysis *in historical context* that rhetorical criticism provides. To be sure, the hard, objective controls that modernists schooled in the historical-critical method once thought were there simply are not. But responsible reading communities can weigh arguments and be convinced along various lines ... and be more or less faithful along the way.

Finally, in his argument that no scholar can or should claim that his or her reading of the Apocalypse is better than another reading, he fails to consider that he is making such an argument himself! While Carey is right to focus on the problematic nature of the author's conception of authority for any liberationist reading of the Apocalypse,[134] Moyise seems to imply that any argument at all is a claim to authority! That need not be so, depending on how, explicitly or implicitly, scholars claim authority in their argumentation.

Mitchell Reddish denies that the idea of the sovereignty of God necessarily fosters patriarchal domination, violence, and abuse of power. "A careful reading of the Apocalypse," he says, "reveals that, for John, God's control over the universe is exemplified in the sacrificial, suffering work of the Lamb, not in coercive domination."[135] While I agree that a careful reading of the Apocalypse supports the radical redefinition of power Reddish is identifying here, I believe that we must take special care to recognize the coerciveness of theologies of sovereignty in the real history of the church.

In any case, Reddish has learned from feminist critique of the violent rhetoric of the Apocalypse:

> The concerns about misogynist and violent imagery are legitimate concerns. They are not simply an attempt to be 'politically correct' or to split linguistic or theological hairs. Language is important. It is more than simply the vehicle for one's message. The language itself becomes a part of the message. For some readers, in the case of Revelation 17, the medium prevents them from hearing the message of the text.[136]

Despite the "militaristic and even violent imagery in the book itself," Reddish says, "one must distinguish between texts that use language and imagery to encourage or endorse violence and those that use traditional imagery to subvert violence. The Apocalypse belongs in the latter category."[137] Throughout

---

[134] See p. 199 below.

[135] Mitchell G. Reddish, *Revelation* (Smyth & Helwys Bible Commentary; Macon, Ga.: Smyth & Helwys, 2001), 22.

[136] Reddish, *Revelation*, 337.

[137] Reddish, *Revelation*, 25.

his commentary, Reddish counsels his reader about how best to teach, preach on, or present the text of the Apocalypse so as to minimize its violent rhetoric. The closest Reddish comes to *Sachkritik* is when he suggests that "in certain settings and with certain groups, this text is perhaps best left unheard, particularly if the situation does not allow critical comment or discussion."[138]

The Lamb of Revelation is manifestly no cute, little nonviolent Lamb. It is a powerful and courageous Lamb who, through his consistent nonviolent and faithful witness, conquered evil. He did not deny the reality of evil or the reality of violence or "lie down with the lion" in some utopian idealism. The author of the Apocalypse would agree with Moyise that evil is much too complex for that. Rather, the Lamb overcame evil by refusing to adopt its methods and its rules and bearing its brunt. And he serves in the Apocalypse as a consistent and trustworthy model for believers facing the harsh realities of civic pressures to conform to the expectations of Graeco-Roman society.

So if a nonviolent redefinition of power really is at the heart of the Apocalypse, why has the book been so distrastrously unsuccessful in the history of its interpretation? Why did the author fail so miserably in terms of the actual history of the reading of the Apocalypse? Such questions deserve considered responses by persons familiar with both Second Temple Judaism and the historical contextualization of "Christian"-Jewish theology in Graeco-Roman culture.[139] Certainly the second century already provides ample evidence of serious misunderstandings and misreadings by early church fathers. I noted the irony in chapter one[140] that the Apocalypse may have been "saved" for the canon by early church leaders who forced an ahistorical, allegorizing interpretation on it. Walter Wink is probably right that we have been schooled so thoroughly in the myth of the efficacy of violence—what he calls the "domination system"—that we have found it easy to interpret what the author "must" be intending to say in light of how we "know" the world works. Steven Friesen says that "Revelation's assessment of power is so contrary to normal human practice that most churches throughout history have not agreed with John either."[141]

However, it will not do to say simply that although the ethical message of the Apocalypse is consistent and nonviolent, most subsequent readers misun-

---

[138] Reddish, *Revelation*, 338.

[139] Some of the theological contextualization that took place in the first couple of centuries CE and which was set in stone by the early church leaders can and should be rethought, despite the two-millennium tradition that it was done right and cannot or should not be rethought.

[140] Above, p. 2, note 5.

[141] Steven J. Friesen, *Imperial Cults and the Apocalypse of John: Reading Revelation in the Ruins* (Oxford: Oxford University Press, 2001), 216.

derstood that message. Although John's message may have been one of non-violence, there is in the rhetoric of the Apocalypse an unescapable and problematic violence that weakens and subverts that message. That violence lies both on the surface of the message and inherent in the rhetoric itself. As author, John assumes the authority not only of a prophet but of Godself in his condemnation of his opponents. Instead of engaging his opponents or their views, he vilifies his opponents. Although a more historical rhetorical approach might mitigate the offense of this approach, it might also actually deepen such offense.

When readers—ancient and modern alike—attempt to interpret its symbolism within a world view "marked" by the domination system of the beast, the results can be (and historically have been) disastrous. But the book's relative *lack* of success in terms of its history of effects is due in part to the violent nature of the book's own rhetoric.

Greg Carey's rhetorical-critical analysis is distinctive in his insistence that careful attention be paid to the role and importance of personal authority in any rhetorical-critical study of the Apocalypse. Carey is correct when he says, "however one negotiates Revelation's violence, liberationist interpretations are left with a difficult moral ethos, which is inclusive in that it takes the side of the marginalized but is also exclusivist in identifying persons, groups, and structures with oppression."[142] The ethos of Revelation is therefore unstable in that it is torn between egalitarian and authoritarian impulses. "The problem *within Revelation's rhetoric* is that it cannot sustain its own vision—that of a priestly dominion in which John is a partner under God's rule (1:9)."[143] Because Revelation is at the same time egalitarian and authoritarian, inviting and exclusivist, it is an "elusive" apocalypse.[144] The problem is that even though "Revelation subverts imperial authority ... it contributes to the foundations of a new discourse of domination."[145]

---

[142] Greg Carey, "The Apocalypse and Its Ambiguous Ethos," in *Studies in the Book of Revelation*, edited by Steve Moyise (Edinburgh: T & T Clark, 2001), 163–80.

[143] Greg Carey, *Elusive Apocalypse: Reading Authority in the Revelation to John*, Studies in American Biblical Hermeneutics, no. 15 (Macon, Ga.: Mercer University Press, 1999), 173. Emphasis original.

[144] See Greg Carey, "The Apocalypse and Its Ambiguous Ethos," 164. Carey admits that the problem of authority in biblical theology is by no means limited to the rhetoric of the Apocalypse, since any confession of divine authority implies a judgment on the authority of other individuals and institutions (see p. 180; see also p. 176 in *Elusive Apocalypse*). Thus, the "offense" in the rhetoric of the Apocalypse may be related to the "offense" of any confession of Jesus as Lord. There is a significant difference, however, between the imperialistic "Jesus is Lord" of Christendom and the confessional "Jesus is Lord" of the pre- or post-Christendom church.

[145] Greg Carey, *Elusive Apocalypse*, 175.

Elisabeth Schüssler Fiorenza likewise considers the problematic nature of this rhetoric:

> The Apocalypse's symbolic universe and prophetic world of vision is without question violent. One could point to the violence unleashed from the throne of G*d against all of humanity in general and against Jezebel in particular. While one could argue, as I have done, that the basic theological paradigm of the Apocalypse is not holy war and destruction but justice and judgment, not prediction of certain events but exhortation and threat, it is nevertheless necessary to engage in theological ideology critique and to assess critically the violence proclaimed by the Apocalypse in the name of G*d. To learn how to engage in such a critical theological adjudication is especially important for those who proclaim Scripture as the Word of G*d if they are not to continue promulgating G*d as a G*d legitimating dehumanizing oppression and vindictive destruction.[146]

Although I believe that Schüssler Fiorenza is mostly right here, the Apocalypse can still reward patient readers who are attentive to its repeated calls for discernment on their part *if* they also critically resist its rhetoric on some levels. When properly apprehended, the Apocalypse challenges readers—ancient and modern alike—to critique civil religion, to resist its blasphemous idolatry, and to maintain a faithful witness nonviolently, even to the point of death.

Do the ironies and parodies in the Apocalypse ultimately destabilize its vision or do they simply replace one oppression with another? This question is taken up by Harry Maier in his book, *Apocalypse Recalled*. Like Carey's "elusive" Apocalypse, Maier says that "John's final vision ... reveals the Apocalypse situated precariously amid unstable ironies."[147] The key to the instability of Revelation's rhetoric is its theology of the cross. It is not that its theology of the cross can sustain a utopian political vision, for it cannot. If the theology of Revelation is neither systematic nor coherent, it is because it was meant to be primarily deconstructive. The unlikely figure of the victorious slain lamb returns again and again to destabilize the politics of imperial domination. [148]

> The Book of Revelation entertains its listeners with many wars and battles, but military victory in the Apocalypse always return to the death of the Lamb. His defeat is what delivers victory and thereby contests what we might mean

---

[146] Fiorenza, "The Words of Prophecy," 19.

[147] Harry O. Maier, *Apocalypse Recalled: The Book of Revelation after Christendom* (Minneapolis: Fortress Press, 2002), 191.

[148] In a similar manner, Leonard L. Thompson appears to experience no real offense at the rhetoric of the Apocalypse. Why? Because the apocalyptic genre was known to its first-century readers and because the vision is ultimately destabilizing of the social order (see Leonard L. Thompson, *Revelation*; Abingdon New Testament Commentaries [Nashville: Abingdon Press, 1998], 32).

when we speak of winners and losers. The Apocalypse does not build heavenly Jerusalem on the foundation of glorious military might, but on a glorious defat, both of the Lamb and of those witnesses faithful unto death (21:14; see also 3:12). John's Revelation ends by keeping the promise that 'Jesus Christ is the faithful witness, the firstborn of the dead, and the ruler of the kings of the earth' (1:5). But it does so through an ironizing parody of the politics of domination. It inscribes a deeply destabilizing irony into notions of power and might dominant among John's contemporaries. ...

[John's] vision leaves us with instability on all sides, save this—the promise of life through faithful testimony to the slain Lamb, and the power that conquers through dying.[149]

According to Maier, Revelation leaves us with a "cruciform irony," while the Lamb's followers recognize "how often in Christendom's history 'awakenings' have led to the supplanting of the ironical power of the slain Lamb and to the supplanting of costly testimony to him with the power of Caesar's sword and the translation of the gospel into political organizations, moral orders, and institutional arrangements."[150]

Since John's vision of renewal entails both a new earth and a new heaven, some have seen this "need" as indicative of a deep pessimism in John's ethic. There *is* a pessimism inherent in that vision. It is a pessimism that grows out of a deep sense of disappointment in the failures of humanity to realize God's glory on earth. The vision of a new heaven and a new earth derives from Trito-Isaiah's similar disappointment as he experienced a restoration of Judah that was much less glorious than that envisioned by Deutero-Isaiah. The renewal of both heaven and earth is thus a prophetic legacy drawn from Isaiah 65:17 and 66:22, a prophetic hope reflected also in 2 Peter 3:13.

But there is also a vibrant optimism in the Apocalypse: the power of the believing community lies in the power of the Lamb, the power of faithful witness. The "endurance" the author calls for is no hands-wringing, pietistic ὑπομονή. Rather, he calls for a courageous and active "resistance" (ὑπομονή) to the evils of Graeco-Roman culture and religion. It is a clear "No" to the possibility of humanity's bringing in the fullness of God's reign, and a joyful and confident "Yes" to the way of Christ, demonstrated most poignantly in his faithful witness—a witness that led to his death on the cross.

Although the politics of John's Apocalypse are radically antiestablishmentarian, its political *ethic* is essentially nonviolent. The lamb Christology communicates the nonviolence of this ethic without undermining the radical resistance nature of its political ethic. As demonstrated above, there is little in the

---

[149] Maier, *Apocalypse Recalled*, 196, 197.
[150] Maier, *Apocalypse Recalled*, 205.

Apocalypse of John to support an understanding of Jesus' death as "sacrificial" in the substitutionary or penal sense.

In 2 Clement (c. 150 CE) the tradition of the vulnerable lamb is specifically tied to the theme of martyrdom in an expansion based on Luke 10:3:

> For the Lord says, 'You will be like lambs in the midst of wolves.' And Peter answered and said to him, 'If the wolves then tear the lambs apart?' Jesus answered Peter, 'Let the lambs not fear the wolves after their death, and you—do not fear those who kill you but cannot do anything else to you; rather, fear the One who, after you die, has the authority to throw your soul and body into the hell of fire.[151]

In each of these places, Clement of Alexandria uses the word ἀρνίον rather than the ἀρήν/ἀρνός of Luke 10:3.

According to Papias, Jesus taught that the amazing growth of the kingdom of God would result in a time when "all animals, feeding then only on the productions of the earth, would become peaceable and harmonious, and be in perfect subjection to man" and that this would be in fulfillment of Isaiah's prophecy, "The wolf shall lie down with the lamb."[152]

5. Conclusion

Our analysis has led us to conclude that the strategy of the Seer is to introduce the Lamb in chap. 5 in such a way as to underscore a central reversal in his apocalypse—a reversal in the conventional wisdom about the nature and function of power in the world. This reversal is set up with symbols clearly tied to the messiah, symbols like one from the tribe of Judah and the root of David. But there is a redefining of the nature and method of the messiah's victory. In the Apocalypse, the author draws from a multi-faceted mine of associations to the lamb in order to create a powerful new christological statement pregnant with ethical implications. Specifically, the power and authority, or worthiness, to unfold God's will for humanity are located in the readiness to die a witness's death. At the heart of this reversal lies an ethical intent; at the surface lies a Lamb Christology.

---

[151] My translation of the Greek text from Kirsopp Lake, trans., *The Apostolic Fathers, Volume 1*, Loeb Classical Library (Cambridge and London: Harvard University Press and William Heinemann Ltd, 1935), 2Clem 5.2–4.

[152] Alexander Roberts and James Donaldson, eds., "The Fragments of Papias," in *The Ante-Nicene Fathers: Translations of the Writings of the Fathers Down to A.D. 325*, A. Cleveland Coxe, gen. ed., The Ante-Nicene Fathers, vol. 1 (New York: Charles Scribner's Sons, 1925), 154. This fragment is known from Irenaeus's *Against Heresies* 5.32.

The Lamb Christology predominates in this vision precisely because it expresses best the author's own understanding of the nature and importance of the death and resurrection of Christ for the question of how believers in the province of Asia are to express *their* resistance to evil. The theology of the Apocalypse can even be characterized as a theology of peace if *peace* is defined not as absence of conflict, but as an ethic of nonviolent resistance to evil. This ethic requires assurance that the death of faithful testimony is really a symbol of victory—both for the Lamb and for believers who follow him.

There is no lack of evidence for the fact that the lamb today continues to symbolize vulnerability in the face of violence or perceived violence. William Mulready's 1820 painting, *The Wolf and the Lamb*, is one clear witness. In that painting a menacing bully (the wolf) intimidates a cowering classmate (the lamb) on the way home from school. In its December 20, 1890, issue, *Punch* magazine featured a parody of Mulready's painting in which a Russian cossack took the place of the bully and a Jew the place of the cowering child. The caption read, "The Russian Wolf and the Hebrew Lamb."[153]

People seldom act on the basis of reality. Rather, they act on the basis of their *perception* of reality. This has been true throughout history, both before and after the Enlightenment. However, with the Enlightenment came a new confidence about humanity's ability to see reality "as it is" and thus to discount the value of dreams and visions. The same can be said about the value of symbol and the power of icons to inspire, motivate, and see beyond the material.

It is at the level of the power of perceptions that the Apocalypse has both its greatest danger and its greatest potential for creating a new world today. Interestingly, it is when people act on the basis of their *perception* of reality (whether objectively "accurate" or not) that they create new realities. So the perception of a new or different reality is not just a mind game or an exercise in aesthetics; it is *the gateway to* that new or different reality.

Here also is the critical key to a faithful reading of the Apocalypse. If one sees the lamb standing as slain as the decisive act of God in history, then that Christology will lead to an ethic that embraces a committed, nonviolent resistance to evil. A much different ethic emerges if one sees Jesus' death simply as the required interlude necessary for the forgiveness of sins but essentially irrelevant for the working out of God's will in history. Here is the real danger of readings of the Apocalypse that ignore or deny the redefining going on within the vision. Hope—if it derives from a clear, empowering vision of God's reality—is itself *an effective action* insofar as persons in community act on the basis of a new understanding or interpretation of reality. That is what Amos

---

[153] See the fascinating article by Linda Rozmovits, "*The Wolf and the Lamb*: An Image and Its Afterlife," *Art History* 18, no. 1 (March 1995): 97–111.

Wilder was getting at when he said that dreams, visions, and utopias are more than just aesthetics: they *engage* us.[154]

What is at stake in this issue? Is Christ a symbol of vulnerability or of force? If Malina is right, it is the latter. According to Malina, the purpose of portraying Christ as a cosmic lamb becomes apparent when one realizes that the cosmic lamb is really the powerful and violent ram of Aries. "All the imagery associated with the Lamb is that of power, force, control, and conquest."[155] It was his *power* that was significant to John, and "power means the ability to control others based on an implied sanction of force."[156] Although the readers of the Apocalypse were suffering no persecution, according to Malina, such a message would have been welcome "in a culture that submitted to nature and its forces" and would have provided a "renewed zest for living."[157]

But Malina is quite wrong. The Seer does not represent Christ as lamb in order to suggest his "ability to control others based on an implied sanction of force"; rather, he represents Christ as lamb in order to represent the vulnerability that inevitably accompanies faithful witness. Such a faithful and vulnerable witness is what enables the believers to share in Christ's victory (3:21). Such vulnerability is no weakness; instead, it proves triumphant over the powers of evil and exposes the weakness of violence. This significance is admittedly not obvious; it is itself part of the revelation given to John, hence his repeated calls to hear what the Spirit is saying to the churches.

John saw the cosmic significance of the cross of Jesus in the present course of human history. John's is a *theologia crucis* as profound and as worthy of Christian theology as any in the New Testament, though it develops in directions different from Paul's or the Fourth Evangelist's. For John saw that the answer to idolatry is not complacent capitulation or assimilation, nor is it violent resistance. Rather, it is an active resistance motivated and modeled by the nonviolent resistance of Jesus—a resistance that has as its inspiration Jesus' own yes to God and no to human violence—a resistance that is symbolized in the Apocalypse by the figure of the Lamb and in Christian iconography by the cross.

From our perspective today we might well criticize John for not being more systematic in his presentation of Jesus' death on the cross or for recognizing the implications of his theology for his own rhetoric or how Jesus' death might judge his own vituperative spirit. Nevertheless, he saw something of the cosmic significance of the death of Jesus—not just as a means of salvation from

---

[154] Cf. Amos N. Wilder, "Apocalyptic Rhetorics," esp. 168.

[155] Bruce J. Malina, *On the Genre and Message of Revelation: Star Visions and Sky Journeys* (Peabody, Mass: Hendrickson Publishers, 1995), 101.

[156] Malina, *Genre and Message*, 263.

[157] Malina, *Genre and Message*, 263.

sins, but as the revelation of God's will for dealing with violent evil and the means of unfolding God's plan. Only Jesus is worthy of opening the scroll. The new reality envisioned by John is a reality in which all creatures, whether on land or sea, or *in* the sea, whether in heaven, on earth, or under the earth, will unite in recognizing the cross of Christ as the ultimate victory over the evil that seeks to control and dominate humanity to its own demise.

The ethics of the Apocalypse is thus not one that eschews responsibility in the world, but one that embraces the cross as the key to how that responsibility is expressed. The vision of faithfulness to the witness of Jesus includes the witness *about* Jesus, the witness that *leads to* suffering and death, and the witness *of* suffering and death. Through its epideictic rhetoric, the Apocalypse challenges the hearing/reading community to enter that vision. It is not a vision designed to make the community passive or to disempower it or to encourage it to withdraw in a cloistered existence. It is a vision designed to empower the community, to enter the fray with a courageous nonviolent resistance that may well lead to martyrdom. This sort of resistance is as active as any physical warfare. "While rejecting the apocalyptic militancy that called for literal holy war against Rome, John's message is not, 'Do not resist!' It is, 'Resist!—but by witness and martyrdom, not by violence.'"[158]

The violence implicit in the rhetoric employed by John is to be lamented, especially with regard to his invectives against his opponents and his debasing of them. At this level, a broader biblical theology would counsel resistance to John and his message. It would "identify the destructive poison as well as the nourishing bread" contained in John's Apocalypse.[159] However, to suggest that John's vision ultimately fails because it lacks a fully coherent ethic or theology begs the questions of genre and purpose. Evil *is* complex. Sometimes all we can do is weep and lament, while "victory" seems elusive. Ultimately, John's purpose was more deconstructive than constructive, and the Apocalypse more of a "revelation" or an expose than a cogent argument.

Nevertheless, critical appreciation and appropriation of John's message requires active involvement in the world—an involvement marked not by compromise or a quiet "hanging on," but by a roaring "No!" to the idolatry of business as usual within the Empire, and a consistent nonviolent resistance to those forces of evil. The hearing/reading community is empowered to engage in such resistance because the Lamb has already won the victory.

To God and to the Lamb I will sing.

---

[158] Richard Bauckham, *The Theology of the Book of Revelation*, New Testament Theology (Cambridge and New York: Cambridge University Press, 1993), 92.

[159] Fiorenza, "The Words of Prophecy," 19.

Appendix I

The Semantic Domain of "Lamb" in the Old Testament

In the following charts or tables I have organized visually the correspondences between the Hebrew and Greek words for lamb by individual passage. The first chart represents the entire domain. The second one only those passages that refer to lambs in the general (i.e., nonsacrificial, nonsymbolic) sense. Most of these passages refer to lambs in their utilitarian use for food or wool.

The third chart shows which words are used of the sacrificial lamb; that is, the lamb as a burnt offering. The fourth chart treats the Passover lamb, and the fifth chart treats the uses of lamb as a symbol in the Hebrew Bible and Septuagint. Most of these occurrences communicate vulnerability, though it is difficult to be propositionally precise about this symbolism.

	כֶּבֶשׂ	כֶּשֶׂב	כִּבְשָׂה כַּבְשָׂה	כִּשְׂבָּה	שֶׂה¹ שֶׂה
ἀμνός[5]	Ex 29:38, 39 [*bis*], 40, 41; Lev 9: 3; 12:6; 14:10, 12, 13, 21, 24, 25; 23: 18, 19, 20; Num 6:12, 14; 7:15, 21, 27, 33, 39, 45, 51, 57, 63, 69, 75, 81, 87; 15:5; 28:3, 4 [*bis*], 7, 8, 9, 11, 13, 14, 19, 21 [*bis*], 27, 29 [*bis*]; 29: 2, 4 [*bis*], 8, 10 [*bis*], 13, 15 [*bis*], 17, 18, 20, 21, 23, 24, 26, 27, 29, 30, 32, 33, 36, 37; 2Chr 29:21, 22, 32; 35: 7; Ezra 8:35; Job 31:20; Ezek 46:4, 5, 6, 7, 11, 13, 15; Hos 4:16; Sir 13:17	Ge 30:40			Lev 12:8; Num 15:11; Deut 14:4
ἀμνάς[6]	Num 7:17, 23, 29, 35, 41, 47, 53, 59, 65, 71, 77, 83, 88		Gen 21: 28, 29, 30; Num 6:14; 2Sam 12: 3, 4, 6	Lev 5:6	
ἀρήν [ἀρνός][7]	Ex 12:5; 1Chr 29:21; Isa 1:11; 5:17; 11:6	Gen 30:32, 33, 35; Lev 1:10; 3:7			Gen 30:32
ἀρνίον	Jer 11:19				
πρόβα- τον[8]	Lev 4:32; 23:12; Num 15:11; Prov 27:26	Lev 4:35; 7:23; 17:3; 22:19, 27; Num 18:17; Deut 14:4		Lev 14:10	Gen 22:7, 8; Ex 12:3 [*bis*], 4 [*bis*], 5; Ex 13:13; 34:20; Lev 22:23; 1Sam 17:34; Isa 53:7
πάσχα[9]					
φασεκ					
φασεχ					

	כַּר²	צְעִירֵי הַצּאן	צאן³ בְּנֵי־צאן	רָחֵל	טָלֶה	פֶּסַח	[no Hebrew equivalent]⁴
ἀμνός⁵	Ezek 27:21		Gen 30:40 [bis]	Isa 53:7			WisSol 19:9; Odes 14:17
ἀμνάς⁶							
ἀρήν [ἀρνός]⁷	Deut 32:14; 2Kgs 3:4; Isa 34:6; Jer 51(28):40				1Sam 7:9 [// Sir 46:16]; Isa 40:11; 65:25		Dan 3:39; Mic 5:7 (6)7; 1Esdr 1:7; 6:29 (28); 7:7; 8:14, 66 (63); Sir 46:16; 47:3;10 Pr of Az 17 [=Dan 3:39]; Odes 2:14 [=Deut 32:14]; 7:39 [=Dan 3:39]
ἀρνίον		Jer 50 (27):45¹¹	Ps 114:4, 6¹²	Isa 40:11^Aq			PsSol 8:23
πρόβα-τον⁸	Ps 65 (64):13 (14)		Gen 30:40; 31:38; Ex 12:21; Deut 32:14; Ezek 45:15	Gen 31:38; 32:14 (15)			
πάσχα⁹						Ex 12: 21; Ezra 6:20	1Esdr 1:1, 6, 12; 7:12
φασεκ						2Chr 30:15,17	
φασεχ						2Chr 35:1, 6, 9, 11, 13	

Notes to pp. 208–209

[1] There is no Septuagintal equivalent to שֶׂה in Isa 66:3. The שֶׂה in Josh 6:21 is "translated" ὑποζύγιον (donkey) in the LXX. The שֶׂה in Judg 6:4 and Zeph 2:6 is translated ποίμνιον (flock) in the LXX. Like πρόβατον (see below), שֶׂה is a common and general word for sheep or flock and appears more often than what this chart reflects. The appearances in which it is translated by πρόβατον are given only when they are translated "lamb" in the New Revised Standard Version.

[2] ἀμπελώνων (from ἄμπελος [vine]) is the "substitution" for כַּר in 1Sam 15:9; and ἑρπετόν is substituted for כַּר in Isa 16:1. It is not translated in Ezek 39:18. ἔριφος is the "translation" or substitution for כַּר in Amos 6:4. Places where כַּר clearly means "pasture," "battering ram," or "saddlebag" are not included here.

[3] Like שֶׂה above, צֹאן (flock) is a common word in the Hebrew Bible, occurring over 200 times and referring generally to small, four-footed animals. However, the expression בְּנֵי־צֹאן occurs only in Ps 114:4 and 6 and in Jer 31:12, where the word κτηνῶν from κτῆνος (flock or possession) is substituted for it in the Septuagint (cf. also Jer 38:12, a passage of eschatological peace).

[4] Song of Solomon 6:6 has ἀγέλη (herd) for רָחֵל.

[5] In the Jacob and Laban story, ἀμνός is a form of wages promised by Laban to Jacob. It may also be a synonym for "times," as if δέκα ἀμνάς were equivalent to δεκάκις. It is substituted for קְשִׂיטָה (an unknown unit of measurement) in Gen 33:19. Each of the three times קְשִׂיטָה appears in the Hebrew Bible, it is translated in the LXX by ἀμνός (Gen 33:19) or ἀμνάς (Josh 24:32 and Job 42:11).

Not included in the chart are the passages where ἀμνός is the translation of the Aramaic אִמַּר (Ezra 6:9, 17; 7:17). ἀμνός is without Hebrew equivalent in Gen 31:7. It is the translation of (or substitution for) אֶלֶף in 2Chr 35:8 and for עַתּוּד in Zech 10:3.

[6] Like ἀμνός (see above), ἀμνάς appears also to be a unit of money.

[7] ἀρήν translates גְּדִי (kid) in Ex 23:19; 34:26; and Deut 14:21. ἀρήν also translates מְרִיא (fatling) in 2Sam 6:13 and 1Kgs 1:9, 19, 25 but it has no Hebrew equivalent in Prov 27:26. ἀρήν also appears in an interesting passage in Micah 5:7(6), where it departs significantly from the Hebrew and has no Hebrew antecedent. The NRSV, which follows the Hebrew, reads, "Then the remnant of Jacob, surrounded by many peoples, shall be like dew from the Lord, like showers on the grass which do not depend upon people or wait for any mortal." The LXX has, "And the remnant of Jacob will be among the Gentiles in the midst of many peoples, like dew falling from the Lord, and like lambs in a pasture, so that no one might ever again be summoned [to battle] nor subjugated among the children of humanity (lit., 'sons of men')" (my translation of "καὶ ἔσται τὸ ὑπόλειμμα τοῦ Ιακωβ ἐν τοῖς ἔθνεσιν ἐν μέσῳ λαῶν πολλῶν ὡς δρόσος παρὰ κυρίου πίπτουσα καὶ ὡς ἄρνες ἐπὶ ἄγρωστιν ὅπως μὴ συναχθῇ μηδεὶς μηδὲ ὑποστῇ ἐν υἱοῖς ἀνθρώπων"). This same idea of Israel living as vulnerable lambs among the Gentiles appears in PsSol 8:23, where ἀρνίον is used. The suggestion of Lust that

ἄρνες in Micah 5:7 (6) represents a misreading of the Hebrew כ/רביב (like dewdrops) as כ/כרי (like lambs) is unlikely—an unnecessary emendation—in view of the parallel expression in PsSol 8:23 and the tradition of the lambs of eschatological peace known elsewhere (cf. J. Lust, ed. *A Greek-English Lexicon of the Septuagint: Part 1: A-I.* Stuttgart: Deutsche Bibelgesellschaft, 1992, p. 61). Furthermore, the additional phrase, ὅπως μὴ συναχθῇ μηδεὶς μηδὲ ὑποστῇ ἐν υἱοῖς ἀνθρώπων suggests that ἄρνες is more than simply a misreading of כ/רביב.

[8] πρόβατον also appears in 2Chr 35:9, where כֶּבֶשׂ is assumed. It is substituted for בָּקָר in 2Chr 35:8 and Jer 31(38):12. Like שֶׂה (see above), πρόβατον is a common and general word for sheep or flock, appearing over 300 times in the Septuagint, according to Hatch and Redpath. The appearances in which it translates שֶׂה are given only when they are translated "lamb" in the New Revised Standard Version.

[9] פֶסַח also corresponds to πάσχα at Ex 12:11, 27, 43, 48; 34:25; Lev 23:5; Num 9:2, 4, 6, 10, 12, 13, 14 [bis]; 28:16; 33:3; Deut 16:1, 2, 5, 6; Josh^B 5:10; 2Kgs 23:21, 22, 23; Ezra 6:19; and Ezek 45:21, where it likely refers to the Passover Festival as a whole, rather than to the Passover Lamb specifically. פֶסַח also appears where πάσχα is assumed at Num 9:5 and Josh^B 5:11 and where φασεχ is assumed in 2Chr 35:19. πάσχα appears where פֶסַח is assumed at Ezra 6:21. πάσχα appears without Hebrew equivalent, referring to the Passover Festival as a whole, rather than to the Passover Lamb specifically, at 1Esdras 1:1, 6, 8, 9, 13, 16, 17, 18, 19, 20; and 7:10. πάσχα is a transliteration of the Aramaic פַסְחָא whereas φασεκ and φασεχ are transliterations of פֶסַח; Josephus also uses φάσκα in *Ant* 9.271. Apart from Jer 31(38):8, which has φασεκ/פֶסַח, the use of φασεκ and φασεχ is limited to 2 Chronicles. For a discussion of the etymology and phonological history of this word, see *Vom alten zum neuen Pascha: Geschichte und Theologie des Osterfestes*, by Herbert Haag (Stuttgarter Bibelstudien, 49; Stuttgart: KBW Verlag, 1971), 22–28.

[10] The expression here is actually ἄρνασι προβάτων.

[11] The expression here is actually צְעִירֵי הַצֹּאן. This same expression can also be found in Jer 49:20, in a similar indictment against Edom, where the LXX (30:14) has ἐλάχιστα τῶν προβάτων.

[12] The expression translating בְּנֵי־צֹאן in both of these verses is actually ἀρνία προβάτων.

Appendix I

General Uses of "Lamb" (Nonsacrificial, Nonsymbolic

	כֶּבֶשׂ	כֶּשֶׂב	כִּבְשָׂה כַּבְשָׂה	כִּשְׂבָּה	שֶׂה שֶׂה	כַּר	צְעִירֵי הַצֹּאן	צֹאן בְּנֵי־ צֹאן	רָחֵל	טָלֶה	פֶּסַח	[no Hebrew equiv.]
ἀμνός	Job 31:20	Gen 30:40			Deut 14:4	Ezek 27:21		Gen 30:40 [*bis*]				
ἀμνάς			Gen 21: 28, 29, 30									
ἀρήν- ἀρνός		Gen 30: 32, 33, 35			Gen 30:32	Deut 32: 14; 2Kgs 3:4						
ἀρνίον												
πρόβα- τον	Prov 27:26	Deut 14:4			1Sam 17: 34	Ps 65 (64): 13 (14)		Gen 30:40; 31:38; Deut 32:14	Gen 31:38; 32:14 (15)			
πάσχα												
φασεκ												
φασεχ												

The Sacrificial Lamb in the Hebrew Bible and Septuagint

	כֶּבֶשׂ	כֶּשֶׂב	כִּבְשָׂה כַּבְשָׂה	כִּשְׂבָּה	שֶׂה שֶׂה	כַּר	צְעִירֵי הַצֹּאן	צֹאן בְּנֵי־צֹאן	רָחֵל	טָלֶה	פֶּסַח	[no Hebrew equiv.]
ἀμνός	Exod 29:38, 39 [bis], 40, 41; Lev. 9: 3; 12:6; 14:10, 12, 13, 21, 24, 25; 23: 18, 19, 20; Num 6:12, 14; 7:15, 21, 27, 33, 39, 45, 51, 57, 63, 69, 75, 81, 87; 15:5; 28:3, 4 [bis], 7, 8, 9, 11, 13, 14, 19, 21 [bis], 27, 29 [bis]; 29: 2, 4 [bis], 8, 10 [bis], 13, 15 [bis], 17, 18, 20, 21, 23, 24, 26, 27, 29, 30, 32, 33, 36, 37; 2 Chron 29:21, 22, 32; 35: 7; Ezra 8:35; Ezek 46:4, 5, 6, 7, 11, 13, 15				Lev 12:8; Num 15:11							Odes 14:17
ἀμνάς	Num 7:17, 23, 29, 35, 41, 47, 53, 59, 65, 71, 77, 83, 88		Num 6:14	Lev 5:6								
ἀρήν [ἀρνός]	1Chron 29:21; Isa 1:11	Lev 1:10; 3:7								1Sam 7:9		Dan 3:39; 1Es1:7; 7:7; 8:14, 66 (63); Sir 46:16; Pr of Az 17; Odes 2:14; 7:39
ἀρνίον												
πρόβατον	Lev 4:32; 23:12; Num 15:11	Lev 4:35; 7:23; 17:3; 22:19, 27; Num 18:17		Lev 14:10	Gen 22:7, 8; Ex 13:13; 34:20; Lev 22:23			Ezek 45:15				
πάσχα												
φασεκ												
φασεχ												

"Lamb" as Symbol in the Hebrew Bible and Septuagint

	כֶּבֶשׂ	כֶּשֶׂב	כִּבְשָׂה כַּבְשָׂה	כִּשְׂבָּה	שֶׂה שֶׂה	כַּר	צְעִירֵי הַצֹּאן	צֹאן בְּנֵי־צֹאן	רָחֵל	טָלֶה	פֶּסַח	[no Hebrew equiv.]
ἀμνός	Hos 4:16; Sir 13:17								Isa 53:7			Wisd 19:9
ἀμνάς			2Sam 12:3, 4, 6									
ἀρήν [ἀρνός]	Isa 5:17; 11:6					Isa 34:6; Jer 51 (28):40				Isa 40:11; 65:25		Mic 5:7 (6); Sir 47:3
ἀρνίον	Jer 11:19						Jer 50 (27):45	Ps 114:4, 6	Isa 40:11[Aq]			PsSol 8:23
πρόβατον					Isa 53:7							
πάσχα												
φασεκ												
φασεχ												

The Passover Lamb in the Hebrew Bible and the Septuagint

	כֶּבֶשׂ	כֶּשֶׂב	כִּבְשָׂה כַּבְשָׂה	כִּשְׂבָּה	שֶׂה שֵׂה	כַּר	צְעִירֵי הַצֹּאן	צֹאן בְּנֵי־ צֹאן	רָחֵל	טָלֶה	פֶּסַח	[no Hebrew equiv.]
ἀμνός												
ἀμνάς												
ἀρήν [ἀρνός]	Exod 12:5											1Esdr 6:29 (28)
ἀρνίον												
πρόβα-τον					Ex 12:3 [bis], 4 [bis], 5			Ex 12:21				
πάσχα											Ex 12:21; Ezra 6:20	1Esdr 1:1, 6, 12; 7:12
φασεκ											2Chron 30:15, 17	
φασεχ											2Chron 35:1, 6, 9, 11, 13	

Appendix II

"Titles" Used for Jesus in the Apocalypse

The pages that follow contain an exhaustive listing of the titles used of Jesus in the Apocalypse of John. It should be noted that I use the word *titles* here in quite a broad sense to include symbols, metaphors, similes, and participial constructions. Technically, ἀρνίον is not a title; it is the controlling metaphor or symbol used by the author to express his conception of who Jesus is and what is the significance of his death for the community of faith in Asia.

Titular approaches to the study of the Christologies of the New Testament tend to be reductionistic in assuming that the weight of an author's Christology can be and is carried in the titles used by that author. I do not make that assumption here. If we understand *title* in its narrower sense, then most of the "titles" represented here are not really titles at all, and none can be seen as a key to the Christology of the Apocalypse.

The author attributes many titles to Christ in the Apocalypse as part of a rhetorical device used extensively by the author—the device of naming. While titles for God and for Christ abound, so do names for Satan, for the beast— indeed for anyone, mythological or historical, who opposes the will of God.

The preponderance of participial constructions indicates that the author has a dynamic understanding of Christ and of his work. Even traditionally weighty titles as "Son of God" and "Son of Man" are used so infrequently and inconsequentially here as to suggest their relative unimportance.[1] The key to appropriating the author's Christology lies in responding to the prophetic word, recognizing the power of Christ's presence in the worshipping community, and understanding both the power and the relevance of his death and resurrection for lives of faith in the first century CE.

The titles are presented here roughly in order of their appearance in the Apocalypse. My English translation of the words and phrases appears first, followed by

---

[1] For a careful investigation of the "Son of Man" "title" in the Apocalypse, see Adela Yarbro Collins, "The 'Son of Man' Tradition and the Book of Revelation," in *The Messiah: Developments in Earliest Judaism and Christianity*, edited by James H. Charlesworth, in collaboration with J. Brownson, M. T. Davis, S. J. Kraftchick, and A. F. Segal (Minneapolis: Fortress Press, 1992), 536–68. See esp. p. 568: "The use of the quasi-titular definite form of the phrase is apparently unknown to the author of Revelation."

the Greek. Note here that many of the titles are prefaced by ὡς. Two important exceptions to this are ἀρνίον (throughout) and λόγος τοῦ θεοῦ (19:13).

Titles in Revelation 1

Jesus Christ (Ἰησοῦ Χριστοῦ) • 1:1, 2, 5

the faithful witness (ὁ μάρτυς ὁ πιστός) • 1:5 — See also 3:14 below. Compare with μάρτυς, used of witnesses to Jesus (i.e., believer-martyrs[?]) in 11:3 and 17:6. Conversely, this could be "the witness, the faithful one" (ὁ μάρτυς, ὁ πιστός), taking the substantives as appositional. The RSV translates it, "the faithful witness," but the editors of the 27th edition of the Nestle-Aland text have put a comma between μάρτυς and ὁ in the Greek, indicating that they should be understood as separate (appositional) substantives. The repetition of the μου in the description of Antipas as "my witness, my faithful one" (ὁ μάρτυς μου ὁ πιστός μου) in 2:13 (see 2:10 and 17:6) makes it clear that the similar phrase there is appositional. However, the author's predilection for "triadic formulas" elsewhere in the salutation[2] suggests that what we have here is a second attributive construction, since the three phrases in apposition to Ἰησοῦ Χριστοῦ would then be: (1) ὁ μάρτυς ὁ πιστός; (2) ὁ πρωτότοκος τῶν νεκρῶν; and (3) ὁ ἄρχων τῶν βασιλέων τῆς γῆς. See also 19:11 below. Also "these words" are faithful, or trustworthy, in 21:5 and 22:6.

the firstborn from the dead (ὁ πρωτότοκος τῶν νεκρῶν) • 1:5

the ruler of the kings of the earth (ὁ ἄρχων τῶν βασιλέων τῆς γῆς) • 1:5 — This should probably be interpreted over against the woman who is "the great city which has dominion [kingship] over the kings of the earth" (ἡ πόλις ἡ μεγάλη ἡ ἔχουσα βασιλείαν ἐπὶ τῶν βασιλέων τῆς γῆς)

the one who continually loves us (ὁ ἀγαπῶν ἡμᾶς) • 1:5; cf. also 3:9

the one who has freed us from our sins in/with his blood (ὁ λύσας ἡμᾶς ἐκ τῶν ἁμαρτιῶν ἡμῶν ἐν τῷ αἵματι αὐτοῦ). Λύω also is used of *breaking* the seals (5:2), *letting loose* the four angels bound at the Euphrates (9:14), and *letting* Satan *out* of prison (20:3, 7) • 1:5

[He is coming with the clouds and every eye will see him, including whoever pierced him, and all the tribes of the earth will wail over him. Yes! Amen! quoting Dan 7:13; Zech 12:10ff (according to the translation of Aquila and Theodotion [instead of LXX]); Gen 12:3; and 28:14] • [1:7]

Jesus (Ἰησοῦς) • 1:9 [*bis*]; 12:17; 14:12; 17:6; 19:10 [*bis*]; 20:4; 22:16

the voice (ἡ φωνή) • 1:12 — φωνή occurs 55 times in the book (1:10, 12, 15 [*bis*], 3:20; 4:1, 5; 5:2, 11, 12; 6:1, 6, 7, 10; 7:2, 10; 8:5, 13 [*bis*]; 9:9 [*bis*], 13; 10:3 [*bis*], 4, 7, 8,; 11:12, 15, 19; 12:10; 14:2 [4 times], 7, 9, 13, 15, 18; 16:1, 17, 18; 18:2, 4, 22 [*bis*], 23; 19:1, 5, 6 [3 times], 17; 21:3. This is the only one that seems to suggest a hypostatic being, but cf. 3:20; 4:1; 6:6; 10:8.[3]

---

[2] Cf. Paul S[evier] Minear, *I Saw a New Earth: An Introduction to the Visions of the Apocalypse*, with a foreword by Myles M. Bourke (Washington and Cleveland: Corpus Books, 1968), 9–10.

[3] Cf. J. H. Charlesworth, "The Jewish Roots of Christology: The Discovery of the Hypostatic Voice," *Scottish Journal of Theology* 39, no. 1 (1986): 19–41.

one like a son of man [or one like the Son of Man] (ὅμοις υἱὸς ἀνθρώπου) · 1:13; 14:14; cf. Dan 7:13; Ez 1:26. The Apocalypse is notable for its *rare* use of this "title."[4] The decision of the translators of the New Revised Standard Version to treat this as a formal title, to capitalize "Son" and "Man," and to supply the definite article in English where it is lacking in the Greek is an unfortunate one.[5] [See also the detailed Christophany in 1:12-16.][6]

the first and the last (ὁ πρῶτος καὶ ὁ ἔσχατος) · 1:17; 2:8 [to Smyrna]; 22:13

the living one (ὁ ζῶν) · 1:18

[I was dead and behold I am living into the ages of the ages (ἐγενόμην νεκρὸς καὶ ἰδοὺ ζῶν εἰμι εἰς τοὺς αἰῶνας τῶν αἰώνων). Compare this with the reference to *God* as "the God who lives into the ages of the ages" in 15:7 (ὁ θεὸς ὁ ζῶν εἰς τοὺς αἰῶνας τῶν αἰώνων).] · [1:18; with some variation, 2:8 (to Smyrna)]

[I have the keys of Death and Hades (ἔχω τὰς κλεῖς τοῦ θανάτου καὶ τοῦ ᾅδου) · [1:18]

Titles in the Letters to the Seven Churches

the one who holds the seven stars in his right hand (ὁ κρατῶν τοὺς ἑπτὰ ἀστέρας ἐν τῇ δεξιᾷ αὐτοῦ) · 2:1 [to Ephesus]; cf. 3:1

the one who walks in the midst of the seven golden lampstands (ὁ περιπατῶν ἐν μέσῳ τῶν ἑπτὰ λυχνιῶν τῶν χρυσῶν) · 2:1 [to Ephesus]

the one who has the sharp, two-edged sword (ὁ ἔχων τὴν ῥομφαίαν τὴν δίστομον τὴν ὀξεῖαν) · 2:12 [to Pergamum]

Son of God (υἱὸς τοῦ θεοῦ).[7] · 2:18 [to Thyatira]

the one having his eyes like a flame of fire (ὁ ἔχων τοὺς ὀφθαλμοὺς αὐτοῦ ὡς φλόγα πυρὸς) · 2:18 [to Thyatira]

[the one] whose feet [are] like burnished bronze (οἱ πόδες αὐτοῦ ὅμοιοι χαλκολιβάνῳ) · 2:18 [to Thyatira]

---

[4] See Dwight Marion Beck, "The Christology of the Apocalypse of John," in *New Testament Studies: Critical Essays in New Testament Interpretation, with Special Reference to the Meaning and Worth of Jesus*, edited by Edwin Prince Booth (New York and Nashville: Abingdon-Cokesbury Press, 1942), 276.

[5] See Adela Yarbro Collins, "The 'Son of Man' Tradition and the Book of Revelation," in *The Messiah*, 536–68.

[6] James D. G. Dunn thinks that the fact that this Christophany incorporates features from Daniel's Ancient of Days (Dan. 7) and from the angel of Dan. 10 and from the sound of the glory of the God of Israel's coming like the sound of many waters (Ezek. 43:2) shows that Israel's monotheism is here being compromised. See James D. G. Dunn, "Was Christianity a Monotheistic Faith from the Beginning?" *Scottish Journal of Theology* 35 (1982): 326. However, Loren Stuckenbruck has convincingly shown that the author has taken care to maintain a monotheistic framework. See Loren T. Stuckenbruck, *Angel Veneration and Christology: A Study in Early Judaism and in the Christology of the Apocalypse of John*. WUNT 2/70 (Tubingen: Mohr-Siebeck, 1995), esp. 261–65.

[7] See Dwight Marion Beck, "The Christology of the Apocalypse of John," 276.

the one who searches mind and heart (ὁ ἐραυνῶν νεφροὺς καὶ καρδίας) • 2:23 [to Thyatira]

the one who has the seven spirits of God and the seven stars (ὁ ἔχων τὰ ἑπτὰ πνεύματα τοῦ θεοῦ καὶ τοὺς ἑπτὰ ἀστέρας) • 3:1 [to Sardis]; cf. 2:1

the holy one (ὁ ἅγιος) • 3:7 [to Philadelphia]

the true one (ὁ ἀληθινός) • 3:7 [to Philadelphia]

the one who has the key of David (ὁ ἔχων τὴν κλεῖν Δαυίδ) • 3:7 [to Philadelphia]

the one who opens and no one will lock (ὁ ἀνοίγων καὶ οὐδεὶς κλείσει) • 3:7 [to Philadelphia]

the one who locks and no one opens (ὁ κλείων καὶ οὐδεὶς ἀνοίγει) • 3:7 [to Philadelphia]

the Amen (ὁ ἀμήν) • 3:14 [to Laodicea]

the faithful and true witness (ὁ μάρτυς ὁ πιστὸς καὶ ἀληθινός) • 3:14 [to Laodicea]; cf. also 1:5 above: ὁ μάρτυς[,] ὁ πιστός; cf. also 19:11, "[one] [called] faithful and true" ([καλούμενος] πιστὸς καὶ ἀληθινός)

the beginning of God's creation (ἡ ἀρχὴ τῆς κτίσεως τοῦ θεοῦ) • 3:14 [to Laodicea]

Titles in Revelation 4 and Following

the lion from the tribe of Judah (ὁ λέων ὁ ἐκ τῆς φυλῆς Ἰούδα) • 5:5

the root of David (ἡ ῥίζα Δαυίδ) • 5:5; 22:16 is similar but adds one element: "the root and offspring of David" (ἡ ῥίζα καὶ τὸ γένος Δαυίδ)

lamb (ἀρνίον) — 29 times (including those in the next listing below), 28 or 29 of which are references to Jesus • 5:6, 8, 12, 13; 6:1, 16; 7:9, 10, 14, 17; 12:11; 13:8; 14:1, 4 [*bis*], 10; 15:3; 17:14 [*bis*]; 19:7, 9; 21:9, 14, 22, 23, 27; 22:1, 3. Ἀρνίον in 13:11 refers to another beast who "had two horns like a lamb." R. H. Charles includes this one as also being a reference to Jesus, emending it to read τῷ ἀρνίῳ.[8]

the lamb that was slain (τὸ ἀρνίον τὸ ἐσφαγμένον) • (5:6 — ἀρνίον ἑστηκὸς ὡς ἐσφαγμένον); 5:12; 13:8. Cf. 5:9. Σφάζω is also used of people who were killed for their testimony in 6:9 and 18:24; for murder in general in 6:4; for political assassination in 13:3 (μίαν ἐκ τῶν κεφαλῶν αὐτοῦ ὡς ἐσφαγμένην εἰς θάνατον).

messiah (Χριστός) • 11:15, 12:10, 20:4, 6 — The first two of these references are to *his* Christ (αὐτοῦ); i.e., *God's* messiah.

child (τὸ τέκνον)[9] • 12:4

a male son (υἱὸς ἄρσεν) • 12:5 — Note the problem of the neuter adjective (ἄρσεν instead of ἄρσην) modifying the masculine υἱός. In 12:13 we have "the male [child]" (ὁ ἄρσην), where the adjective is used substantively.

the one who is going to (or is about to) rule/shepherd all the nations (ὁ μέλλει ποιμαίνειν πάντα τὰ ἔθνη) • 12:5

---

[8] R. H. Charles, *A Critical and Exegetical Commentary on the Revelation of St. John*, Vol. 2, The International Critical Commentary (Edinburgh: T. & T. Clark, 1920), 452.

[9] Although there is some question whether τὸ τέκνον in 12:4 and υἱὸς ἄρσεν and ὁ μέλλει ποιμαίνειν πάντα τὰ ἔθνη in 12:5 refer to Christ, I follow here the majority of commentators who hold that they do.

lord of lords and king of kings (κύριος κυρίων καὶ βασιλεὺς βασιλέων) • 17:14;
19:16 reverses it: βασιλεὺς βασιλέων καὶ κύριος κυρίων — Beale thinks this derives from Daniel 4:37 (LXX).[10] This is possible, but one should also note that
this title had long been used for monarchs in Eastern courts and was even used
for God in Maccabean writings. See, e.g., 3 Macc. 5:35 [NRSV]: "Then the
Jews, on hearing what the king had said, praised the manifest Lord God, King of
kings, since this also was his aid that they had received" (οἵ τε Ιουδαῖοι τὰ παρὰ
τοῦ βασιλέως ἀκούσαντες τὸν ἐπιφανῆ θεὸν κύριον βασιλέα τῶν βασιλέων
ἤνουν καὶ τῆσδε τῆς βοηθείας αὐτοῦ τετευχότες).

lord (κύριος) • 11:8; 14:13?; 22:20 — Regarding 14:13, Beck says, "Probably 'Lord'
here refers to Jesus, but John usually reserves the term for God. This forms
another instance of his remarkable reluctance to use one of the most popular
terms for Jesus known in early Christianity."[11]

[he has a name no one knows but himself (ἔχων ὄνομα γεγραμμένον ὃ οὐδεὶς οἶδεν εἰ
μὴ αὐτός). Cf. also 3:12: "my own new name" (τὸ ὄνομά μου τὸ καινόν)] •
[19:12]

the one who sits on the cloud (ὁ καθήμενος ἐπὶ τῆς νεφέλης) • 14:15, 16; see also
14:14

[a shepherd. I hesitate to include this, since this is not a substantive, but a verb: ποι
μανεῖ. Nevertheless, it communicates the ironic picture of a lamb who is also a
shepherd.] • [7:17]

the word of God (ὁ λόγος τοῦ θεοῦ) • 9:13

[See the detailed Christophany in 19:11-16, somewhat analogous to the Christophany
in 1:12-16.]

the one who sits on the horse (ὁ καθήμενος ἐπὶ τοῦ ἵππου) • 19:19, 21; but cf. also
6:2, 4, 5, 8; 9:17; 19:18 where we have other "sitters" (i.e., other riders of other
horses. These horses are white, red, black, pale, cavalry horses, and general [or
army?] horses).

the alpha and the omega (τὸ ἄλφα καὶ τὸ ὦ) • 22:13 — This must be interpreted as an
intentional juxtaposition with 1:8 and 21:6 where the same phrase is used for
God.

the beginning and the end (ἡ ἀρχὴ καὶ τὸ τέλος) • 22:13 — This must also be interpreted as an intentional juxtaposition with 21:6, where the same phrase is used
for God. Between this phrase and the above one, within 22:13, we have "the first
and the last" (ὁ πρῶτος καὶ ὁ ἔσχατος). In 1:8 ἡ ἀρχὴ καὶ τὸ τέλος is the reading
of a minority of manuscripts, including the original hand of Codex Sinaiticus and
several others.

the bright morning star (ὁ ἀστὴρ ὁ λαμπρὸς ὁ πρωϊνός) • 22:16; cf. also 2:28

Lord Jesus (in vocative: κύριε Ἰησοῦ) • 22:20, 21

Having noted what words *are* used in relation to Jesus, it is also important to note
what does *not* appear. See above, 152, note 5.

---

[10] Gregory K. Beale, "The Origin of the Title 'King of Kings' and 'Lord of Lords'
in Revelation 17:14," *New Testament Studies* 31 (1985): 618–20.

[11] Dwight Marion Beck, "The Christology of the Apocalypse of John," 273.

Bibliography

Abaecherli, A. "Imperial Symbols on Certain Coins." *Classical Philology* 30 (1935): 131–40.

Abrams, M. H. "Apocalypse: Theme and Romantic Variations." In *The Revelation of Saint John the Divine*, edited by Harold Bloom. Modern Critical Interpretations, 7–33. New York, New Haven, and Philadelphia: Chelsea House Publishers, 1988.

Achtemeier, Paul J. "Revelation 5:1-14." *Interpretation* 40 (1986): 283–88.

Adkins, Lesley, and Roy A. Adkins. *Dictionary of Roman Religion*. New York: Facts on File, Inc., 1996.

Aelian, Claudius. *On the Characteristics of Animals*. Alwyn Faber Scholfield. Loeb Classical Library, no. 446. Cambridge, Mass.: Harvard University Press, 1958–59.

Agourides, Savas. "The Character of the Early Persecutions of the Church." In *Orthodox Theology and Diakonia*, edited by D. Constantelos, 117–43. Brookline, Mass.: Hellenic College Press, 1981.

Alfaro, Juan I. *Justice and Loyalty: A Commentary on the Book of Micah*. International Theological Commentary. Grand Rapids and Edinburgh: Wm. B. Eerdmans Publ. Co. and Handsel Press, 1989.

Allen, Leslie C. *The Books of Joel, Obadiah, Jonah and Micah*. The New International Commentary on the Old Testament. Grand Rapids, Mich.: William B. Eerdmans Publishing Company, 1976.

Aristophanes. *The Frogs*. Translated and edited by Richmond Alexander Lattimore. The Complete Greek Comedy. Ann Arbor, Mich.: University of Michigan Press, 1962.

Attridge, Harold W. "Greek and Latin Apocalypses." *Semeia*, no. 14 (1979): 159–86.

Augustine. *The City of God*. Translated by Marcus Dods, with an introduction by Thomas Merton. The Modern Library. New York: The Modern Library, 1950.

Aune, David E. "The Apocalypse of John and the Problem of Genre." *Semeia*, no. 36 (1986): 65–96.

———. "The Form and Function of the Proclamations to the Seven Churches (Revelation 2–3)." *New Testament Studies* 36 (April 1990): 182–204.

———. "Revelation." In *Harper's Bible Commentary*, James L. Mays, gen. ed., 1300–19. San Francisco: Harper & Row, 1988.

———. *Revelation 1–5*. Word Biblical Commentary, vol. 52A. Dallas: Word Books, 1997.

———. *Revelation 6–16*. Word Biblical Commentary, vol. 52B. Dallas: Word Books, 1998.

——. *Revelation 17–22*. Word Biblical Commentary, vol. 52C. Dallas: Word Books, 1998.

Barnard, L. W. "Clement of Rome and the Persecution of Domitian." *New Testament Studies* 10 (1964): 251–60.

Barr, David L. "The Apocalypse as a Symbolic Transformation of the World: A Literary Analysis." *Interpretation* 38 (January 1984): 39–50.

——. *Tales of the End: A Narrative Commentary on the Book of Revealtion*. Santa Rosa, Cal.: Polebridge Press, 1998.

——. "Towards an Ethical Reading of the Apocalypse: Reflections on John's Use of Power, Violence, and Misogyny." In *Society of Biblical Literature 1997 Seminar Papers*. Society of Biblical Literature Seminar Papers Series, no. 36, 358–73. Atlanta: Scholars Press, 1997. See also http:// www.wright.edu/~dbarr/moral.htm.

——. "Using Plot to Discern Structure in John's Apocalypse." In *Proceedings of the Eastern Great Lakes and Mid-West Biblical Societies*, 23–33, 1995.

——. "Waiting for the End that Never Comes: The Narrative Logic of John's Story." In *Studies in the Book of Revelation*, edited by Steve Moyise, 101–12. Edinburgh: T & T Clark, 2001.

Barrett, C[harles] K[ingsley]. *The New Testament Background: Writings from Ancient Greece and the Roman Empire That Illuminate Christian Origins*. Rev. ed. San Francisco: HarperSanFrancisco, 1995.

Bauckham, Richard. "The Apocalypse as a Christian War Scroll." Chapt. 8 in *The Climax of Prophecy: Studies on the Book of Revelation*, 210–37. Edinburgh: T. & T. Clark, 1993.

——. "Approaching the Apocalypse." In *Decide for Peace: Evangelicals and the Bomb*, edited by Dana Mills-Powell, 88–98. Basingstoke: Marshall Pickering, 1986.

——. "The Book of Revelation as a Christian War Scroll." *Neotestamentica* 22 (1988): 17–40.

——. *The Climax of Prophecy: Studies on the Book of Revelation*. Edinburgh: T. & T. Clark, 1993.

——. "The Delay of the Parousia." *Tyndale Bulletin* 31 (1980): 3–36.

——. "The Fallen City: Revelation 18." Chapt. 6 in *The Bible in Politics: How to Read the Bible Politically*, by Richard Bauckham, 85–102. Louisville, Ky.: Westminster/John Knox Press, 1989.

——. *The Theology of the Book of Revelation*. New Testament Theology. Cambridge and New York: Cambridge University Press, 1993.

Bauer, Walter. *A Greek-English Lexicon of the New Testament and Other Early Christian Literature: A Translation and Adaptation of Walter Bauer's Griechisch-Deutsches Wörterbuch zu den Schriften des neuen Testaments und der übrigen urchristlichen Literatur*. 2d ed. Trans and ed. William F. Arndt and F. Wilbur Gingrich, ed. Frederick W. Danker. 1957. Chicago: University of Chicago, 1979.

Beale, Gregory K. *The Book of Revelation: A Commentary on the Greek Text*. New International Greek Testament Commentary. Grand Rapids: Eerdmans, 1999.

——. "The Origin of the Title 'King of Kings' and 'Lord of Lords' in Revelation 17:14." *New Testament Studies* 31 (1985): 618–20.

Beasley-Murray, G. R. *The Book of Revelation*. 2d ed. 1974. New Century Bible Commentary. Grand Rapids, Mich.: Wm. B. Eerdmans Publishing Co., 1978.

————. "How Christian is the Book of Revelation?" In *Reconciliation and Hope: New Testament Essays on Atonement and Eschatology Presented to L. L. Morris on His 60th Birthday*, edited by Robert J. Banks, 275–84. Grand Rapids: William B. Eerdmans Publishing Company, 1974.

Beck, Dwight Marion. "The Christology of the Apocalypse of John." In *New Testament Studies: Critical Essays in New Testament Interpretation, with Special Reference to the Meaning and Worth of Jesus*, edited by Edwin Prince Booth. New York and Nashville: Abingdon-Cokesbury Press, 1942.

Beckwith, Isbon T. *The Apocalypse of John*. New York: Macmillan, 1919.

Bell, Robert E. *Dictionary of Classical Mythology: Symbols, Attributes, and Associations*. Oxford and Santa Barbara, Cal.: ABC CLIO, 1982.

Benoit, P., J. T. Milik, and R. Vaux, de, eds. *Les Grottes de Murabba'at*. Discoveries in the Judaean Desert, vol. 2. Oxford: Clarendon Press, 1961.

Berenguer Sánchez, José. "ἀρνόν en PGurob 22 y el Empleo del Término ἀρνίον en los Papiros Documentales." *Emerita: Revista (Boletin) de Lingüística y Filología Clásica* 57, no. 2 (1989): 277–88.

Bialik, Hayim Nahman, ed. *The Book of Legends [Sefer Ha-Aggadah]: Legends from the Talmud and Midrash*. Edited by Yehoshua Hana Ravnitzky. Translated by William G. Braude, with an introduction by David Stern. New York: Schocken Books, 1992.

Black, Matthew. *The Book of Enoch or I Enoch: A New English Edition with Commentary and Textual Notes*. James C. Vanderkam and O[tto] Neugebauer. Studia in Veteris Testamenti Pseudepigrapha, vol. 7. Leiden: E.J. Brill, 1985.

Blount, Brian K. *Cultural Interpretation; Reorienting New Testament Criticism*. Minneapolis: Fortress Press, 1995.

Boesak, Allan A. *Comfort and Protest: Reflections on the Apocalypse of John of Patmos*. Philadelphia: Westminster Press, 1987.

Boll, Franz. *Aus der Offenbarung Johannis: Hellenistische Studien zum Weltbild der Apokalypse*. Stoicheia: Studien zur Geschichte des antiken Weltbildes und der griechischen Wissenschaft, vol. 1. Leipzig/Berlin: B.G. Teubner, 1914.

Bonnefoy, Yves, comp. *Greek and Egyptian Mythologies*. Edited by Wendy Doniger. Chicago: University of Chicago Press, 1992.

Boring, M. Eugene. "Narrative Christology in the Apocalypse." *The Catholic Biblical Quarterly* 54, no. 4 (October 1992): 702–23.

————. "Revelation 19–21: End Without Closure." *Princeton Seminary Bulletin* (1994). Supplementary Issue, no. 3.

————. *Revelation*. Interpretation: A Bible Commentary for Teaching and Preaching. Louisville: John Knox, 1989.

Bowersock, G. W. "Greek Intellectuals and the Imperial Cult in the Second Century A.D." In *Le Culte des Souverains dans l'Empire Romain: 7 Exposes Suivis de Discussions par Elias Bickerman*, edited by W. den Boer. Entretiens sur l'Antiquite classique, no. 19, 179–212. Vandoeuvres-Geneve: Fondation Hardt, 1973.

Brown, Colin, gen. ed. *The New International Dictionary of New Testament Theology*. Grand Rapids, Mich.: Zondervan Publishing House, 1976.

Brown, Francis, ed. *The New Brown, Driver, and Briggs Hebrew and English Lexicon of the Old Testament.* By William Gesenius, translated by Edward Robinson, in collaboration with S[amuel] R[olles] Driver and Charles A[ugustus] Briggs. 1907. Lafayette, Ind.: Associated Publishers and Authors, 1981.

Brown, Raymond E. *The Gospel According to John, I–XII: A New Translation with Introduction and Commentary.* 2d ed. 1966. The Anchor Bible, vol. 29. Garden City, New York: Doubleday & Co., 1981.

Brown, Robert, Jr. *Researches Into the Origin of the Primitive Constellations of the Greeks, Phoenicians and Babylonians.* London: Williams and Norgate, 1899–1900.

Bryan, David. *Cosmos, Chaos and Kosher Mentality.* Journal for the Study of the Pseudepigrapha Supplement Series, no. 12. England: Sheffield Academic Press, 1995.

Buchanan, George Wesley. *The Book of Revelation: Its Introduction and Prophecy.* New Testament Series, vol. 22. Lewston/Queenston/Lampeter: Mellen Biblical Press, 1993.

Burchard, C. "Das Lamm in der Waagschale: Herkunft und Hintergrund eines haggadischen Midraschs zu Ex 1:15-22." *Zeitschrift für die neutestamentliche Wissenschaft* 57 (1966): 219–28.

Burney, Charles Fox. *The Aramaic Origin of the Fourth Gospel.* Oxford: Clarendon Press, 1922.

Caird, George B. *The Revelation of St. John the Divine.* 2d ed. 1966. Black's New Testament Commentaries. London: Adam & Charles Black, 1984.

Campbell, Joseph. *The Mythic Image.* In collaboration with M. J. Abadie. Princeton, N.J.: Princeton University Press, 1984.

——. *The Way of the Animal Powers.* Historical atlas of world mythology, vol. 1. San Francisco: Harper & Row, 1983.

Carnegie, D. R. "Worthy is the Lamb: The Hymns in Revelation." In *Christ the Lord: Studies in Christology Presented to Donald Guthrie,* edited by Harold H. Rowdon, 243–56. Downers Grove, Ill.: InterVarsity Press, 1982.

Carey, Greg. "The Apocalypse and Its Ambiguous Ethos." In *Studies in the Book of Revelation,* edited by Steve Moyise, 163–180. Edinburgh: T & T Clark, 2001.

——. *Elusive Apocalypse: Reading Authority in the Revelation to John.* Macon, Ga.: Mercer University Press, 1999.

Carter, Frederick. *Symbols of Revelation.* Berwick, Me.: Ibis Press, 2003.

Caspi, Mishael Maswari, and Sascha Benjamin Cohen. *The Binding [Aqedah] and Its Transformation in Judaism and Islam: The Lambs of God.* Mellen Biblical Press Series, no. 32. Lewiston, N.Y./Queenston, Ont./Lampeter, U.K.: Mellen Biblical Press, 1995. Vi, 175 pp.

Charles, R. H., ed. *The Greek Versions of the Testaments of the Twelve Patriarchs: Edited from Nine MSS. Together with the Variants of the Armenian and Slavonic Versions and Some Hebrew Fragments.* Oxford: Clarendon Press, 1908.

——. *The Book of Enoch.* 2d ed. 1893. Oxford: Clarendon Press, 1912.

——. *A Critical and Exegetical Commentary on the Revelation of St. John.* Vol. 1. The International Critical Commentary. Edinburgh: T. & T. Clark, 1920.

——. *A Critical and Exegetical Commentary on the Revelation of St. John.* Vol. 2. The International Critical Commentary. Edinburgh: T. & T. Clark, 1920.

——. *Studies in the Apocalypse.* Edinburgh: T. & T. Clark, 1913.

Charlesworth, James H. "The Jewish Roots of Christology: The Discovery of the Hypostatic Voice." *Scottish Journal of Theology* 39, no. 1 (1986): 19–41.

———, trans. and ed. "More Psalms of David." In collaboration with James A. Sanders. In *Old Testament Pseudepigrapha, Volume 2*, James H. Charlesworth, gen. ed., 608–24. Garden City, N.Y.: Doubleday, 1983.

———, ed. *The Messiah: Developments in Earliest Judaism and Christianity*. In collaboration with J. Brownson, M. T. Davis, S. J. Kraftchick, and A. F. Segal. Minneapolis: Fortress Press, 1992.

———, ed. *The Old Testament Pseudepigrapha: Expansions of the "Old Testament" and Legends, Wisdom and Philosophical Literature, Prayers, Psalms, and Odes, Fragments of Lost Judeo-Hellenistic Works*. 2. Garden City: Doubleday & Company, Inc., 1985.

———. "The Apocalypse of John: Its Theology and Impact on Subsequent Apocalypses." Pt. 2 in *The New Testament Apocrypha and Pseudepigrapha: A Guide to Publications, with Excursuses on Apocalypses*, edited by James H. Charlesworth, 19–51. Metuchen and London: The American Theological Library Association and Scarecrow Press, 1987.

———. "Folk Traditions in Jewish Apocalyptic Literature." In *Mysteries and Revelations: Apocalyptic Studies Since the Uppsala Colloquium*, edited by John J. Collins and James H. Charlesworth. Journal for the Study of the Pseudepigrapha Supplement Series, no. 9, 91–113. Sheffield: JSOT Press, 1991.

———. "From Messianology to Christology: Problems and Prospects." Chapt. 1 in *The Messiah: Developments in Earliest Judaism and Christianity*, edited by James H. Charlesworth, in collaboration with J. Brownson, M. T. Davis, S. J. Kraftchick, and A. F. Segal, 3–35. Minneapolis: Fortress Press, 1992.

———. "The Historical Jesus in Light of Writings Contemporaneous with Him," edited by W. Haase. Aufstieg und Niedergang der Römischen Welt: Principat, no. 25, 451–76, 1982.

———. "Jewish Interest in Astrology During the Hellenistic and Roman Period." *Aufstieg und Niedergang der römischen Welt: II, Principat* 20.2 (1987): 926–56.

———. *The Odes of Solomon*. Pseudepigrapha Series, vol. 7. Chico: Scholars Press, 1977.

———. *The Old Testament Pseudepigrapha and the New Testament: Prolegomena for the Study of Christian Origins*. Society for New Testament Studies Monograph Series, no. 54. Cambridge: Cambridge University Press, 1985.

Chesterton, G. K. *Orthodoxy*. New York: John Lane Co., 1908.

Chevalier, Jacques M. *A Postmodern Revelation: Signs of Astrology and the Apocalypse*. Toronto: University of Toronto Press, 1997.

Coenen, Lothar, gen. ed. *Theologisches Begriffslexikon zum neuen Testament*, coedited by Erich Beyreuther and Hans Bietenhard, Band II/1 (Wuppertal: Theologischer Verlag Rolf Brockhaus).

Cohn, Norman. *Cosmos, Chaos, and the World to Come: The Ancient Roots of Apocalyptic Faith*. New Haven and London: Yale University Press, 1993.

———. *The Pursuit of the Millennium: Revolutionary Millenarians and Mystical Anarchists of the Middle Ages*. 2d ed. 1957. New York: Oxford University Press, 1970.

Collins, Adela Yarbro. "Book of Revelation." In *Anchor Bible Dictionary, Volume 5 (O–Sh)*, David Noel Freedman, gen. ed., 694–708. New York: Doubleday, 1992.
———. *The Combat Myth in the Book of Revelation*. Harvard Dissertations in Religion, no. 9. Missoula, Montana: Scholars Press, 1976.
———. *Crisis and Catharsis: The Power of the Apocalypse*. Philadelphia: Westminster Press, 1984.
———. "Dating the Apocalypse of John." *Biblical Research* 26 (1981): 33–45.
———. "Feminine Symbolism in the Book of Revelation." *Biblical Interpretation* 1, no. 1.
———. "The Political Perspective of the Revelation to John." *Journal of Biblical Literature* 96 (1977): 241–56.
———. "Reading the Book of Revelation in the Twentieth Century." *Interpretation* 40, no. 3 (July 1986): 229–42.
———. "The 'Son of Man' Tradition and the Book of Revelation." In *The Messiah: Developments in Earliest Judaism and Christianity*, edited by James H. Charlesworth, in collaboration with J. Brownson, M. T. Davis, S. J. Kraftchick, and A. F. Segal, 536–68. Minneapolis: Fortress Press, 1992.
Collins, John J. *Daniel: A Commentary on the Book of Daniel*. Hermeneia—A Critical and Historical Commentary on the Bible. Minneapolis: Fortress Press, 1993.
———. *The Scepter and the Star: The Messiahs of the Dead Sea Scrolls and Other Ancient Literature*. New York: Doubleday, 1995.
Comblin, J. *Le Christ dans l'Apocalypse*. Bibliotheque de theologie. Serie 3: Theologie biblique, vol. 6. Tournai: Desclée, 1965.
Corsini, Eugenio. *The Apocalypse: The Perennial Revelation of Jesus Christ*. Translated and edited by Francis J. Moloney, S.D.B. Good News Studies, vol. 5. Wilmington: Michael Glazier, Inc., 1983.
Cross, F. L., and E. A. Livingstone, eds. *The Oxford Dictionary of the Christian Church*. 2d ed. 1957. Oxford: Oxford University Press, 1983.
Danby, Herbert, ed. *The Mishnah*. Oxford: Clarendon, 1933.
Darmon, Jean-Pierre. "The Powers of War: Ares and Athena in Greek Mythology." Translated by Danielle Beauvais. In *Greek and Egyptian Mythologies*, edited by Wendy Doniger, compiled by Yves Bonnefoy, 114–15. Chicago: University of Chicago Press, 1992.
———. "The Semantic Value of Animals in Greek Mythology." Translated by Danielle Beauvais. In *Greek and Egyptian Mythologies*, edited by Wendy Doniger, compiled by Yves Bonnefoy, 128–33. Chicago: University of Chicago Press, 1992.
Daube, David. *Ancient Hebrew Fables: The Inaugural Lecture of the Oxford Centre for Postgraduate Hebrew Studies*. Oxford: Oxford Centre for Postgraduate Hebrew Studies, 1973.
Davies, P. R., and B. D. Chilton. "The Aqedah: A Revised Tradition History." *Catholic Biblical Quarterly* 40 (1978): 514–46.
Derchain, Phillipe. "The Divine and the Gods in Ancient Egypt." Translated by David White. In *Greek and Egyptian Mythologies*, edited by Wendy Doniger, compiled by Yves Bonnefoy, 224–29. Chicago: University of Chicago Press, 1992.
Dietrich, Walter. "Gott als König: Zur Frage nach der theologischen und politischen Legitimät religiöser Begriffsbildung." *Zeitschrift für Theologie und Kirche* 77 (1980): 251–68.

Diogenes Laertius. *Diogenes Laertius I.* Translated and edited by R. D. Hicks. Loeb Classical Library. Cambridge, Mass.: Harvard University Press, 1925.

Dodd, C. H. *The Apostolic Preaching and Its Developments.* 2d ed. 1936. London: Hodder and Stoughton, 1944.

———. *The Authority of the Bible.* London, 1960.

———. *The Interpretation of the Fourth Gospel.* Cambridge, England: Cambridge University Press, 1953.

Dohmen. "כֶּבֶשׂ [Kebes]." In *Theological Dictionary of the Old Testament,* 43–52. Grand Rapids, Mich.: Eerdmans.

Drummond, Sir William. *The Oedipus Judaicus.* With an introduction by James P. Carley. 1811. Kent: Research Into Lost Knowledge Organisation, 1986.

Dughi, Thomas Arthur. *The Breath of Christ's Mouth: Apocalypse and Prophecy in Early Reformation Ideology.* Ph.D. Diss. Johns Hopkins University, 1990.

Dunn, James D. G. "Was Christianity a Monotheistic Faith from the Beginning?" *Scottish Journal of Theology* 35 (1982): 303–36.

Dupuis, Charles-François. *The Origin of All Religious Worship.* 1872. New York: Garland Publishing, 1984.

Eco, Umberto. *The Name of the Rose.* Translated by William Weaver. 1980. New York: Warner Books, 1984.

Ehrman, Bart D. *The Orthodox Corruption of Scripture: The Effect of Early Christological Controversies on the Text of the New Testament.* Oxford: Oxford University Press, 1993.

Eller, Vernard. *The Most Revealing Book of the Bible: Making Sense Out of Revelation.* Grand Rapids, Mich.: William B. Eerdmans Publishing Company, 1974.

Emmerson, Richard K., and Ronald B. Herzman. *The Apocalyptic Imagination in Medieval Literature.* Philadelphia, 1992.

Emmerson, Richard Kenneth. *Antichrist in the Middle Ages: A Study of Medieval Apocalypticism, Art, and Literature.* Seattle: University of Washington Press, 1981.

———, and Bernard McGinn, eds. *The Apocalypse in the Middle Ages.* Ithaca and London: Cornell University Press, 1992.

Etheridge, J. W. *The Targums of Onkelos and Jonathan Ben Uzziel on the Pentateuch with the Fragments of the Jerusalem Targum, from the Chaldee.* 1862. New York: Ktav Publishing House, 1968.

Eusebius. *The Ecclesiastical History, Volume 1.* Translated and edited by Kirsopp Lake. Loeb Classical Library. Cambridge, Mass.: Harvard University Press, 1980.

Ewing, Ward B. *The Power of the Lamb: Revelation's Theology of Liberation for You.* Cambridge, Mass.: Cowley Publications, 1990.

Fauré, Paul. "Crete and Mycenae: Problems of Mythology and Religious History." Translated by David White. In *Greek and Egyptian Mythologies,* edited by Wendy Doniger, compiled by Yves Bonnefoy, 30–40. Chicago: University of Chicago Press, 1992.

Fekkes, Jan, III. *Isaiah and Prophetic Traditions in the Book of Revelation: Visionary Antecedents and Their Development.* Ph.D. Diss. Journal for the Study of the New Testament Supplement Series, no. 93. Sheffield: JSOT Press, 1994.

230   *Bibliography*

Feldman, Louis H. *Josephus and Modern Scholarship (1937–1980)*. Berlin and New York: Walter de Gruyter, 1984.

Ferguson, Everett. *Backgrounds of Early Christianity*. Grand Rapids, Mich.: William B. Eerdmans Publishing Company, 1987.

Ferguson, John. *The Religions of the Roman Empire*. Aspects of Greek and Roman Life. Ithaca, N.Y.: Cornell University Press, 1970.

Fiorenza, Elisabeth Schüssler. *The Book of Revelation: Justice and Judgment*. Philadelphia: Fortress, 1985.

——. "The Followers of the Lamb: Visionary Rhetoric and Social-Political Situation." In *Discipleship in the New Testament*, edited by Fernando Segovia, 386–403. Philadelphia: Fortress, 1985.

——. *Revelation: Vision of a Just World*. Proclamation Commentaries. Minneapolis: Fortress, 1991.

——. "Visionary Rhetoric and Social-Political Situation." Chapt. 7 in *The Book of Revelation: Justice and Judgment*, 181–203. Philadelphia: Fortress Press, 1985.

——. "The Words of Prophecy: Reading the Apocalypse Theologically." In *Studies in the Book of Revelation*, edited by Steve Moyise, 1–19. Edinburgh: T & T Clark, 2001.

——. "Die Worte der Prophetie. Die Apokalypse des Johannes theologisch lesen." *Jahrbuch für Biblische Theologie: Prophetie und Charisma* 14 (1999): 71–94.

Fischer, Karl Martin. "Die Christlichkeit der Offenbarung Johannes." *Theologische Literaturzeitung* 106, no. 3 (1981): 165–72.

Fish, Stanley. *Is There a Text in This Class?: The Authority of Interpretive Communities*. Cambridge: Harvard University Press, 1980.

Fishwick, Duncan. *The Imperial Cult in the Latin West: Studies in the Ruler Cult of the Western Provinces of the Roman Empire*. Etudes preliminaires aux religions orientales dans l'Empire romain, no. 108. Leiden and New York: E. J. Brill, 1987–92.

Fletcher, Angus. *Allegory: The Theory of a Symbolic Mode*. Ithaca, N.Y.: Cornell Paperbacks, 1970.

Flusser, David. "Aesop's Miser and the Parable of the Talents." In *Parable and Story in Judaism and Christianity*, edited by Clemens Thoma and Michael Wyschogrod. Studies in Judaism and Christianity: Exploration of Issues in the Contemporary Dialogue Between Christians and Jews, 9–25. New York: Paulist Press, 1989.

——. "Ursprung und Vorgeschichte der Jüdischen Gleichnisse." Chapt. 6 in *Die Rabbinischen Gleichnisse und der Gleichniserzähler Jesus*. Judaica et Christiana, 141–60. Bern: Peter Lang.

——. "Vision of Seventy Shepherds." In *Encyclopaedia Judaica*, vol. 14. Jerusalem and New York: Encyclopaedia Judaica and Macmillan, 1971–72.

Ford, J. Massyngberde. *Revelation*. The Anchor Bible, vol. 38. Garden City, N.Y.: Doubleday & Company, 1975.

Freedman, David Noel, editor-in-chief. *Anchor Bible Dictionary*. Associate editors Gary A. Herion, David F. Graf, and John David Pleins, managing editor Astrid B. Beck. New York, N.Y.: Doubleday, 1992.

Friesen, Steven J. *Imperial Cults and the Apocalypse of John: Reading Revelation in the Ruins*. Oxford: Oxford University Press, 2001.

———. *Twice Neokoros: Ephesus, Asia and the Cult of the Flavian Imperial Family.* Religions in the Graeco-Roman World, vol. 116. Leiden and New York: E.J. Brill, 1993.

Fröhlich, Ida. "The Symbolical Language of the Animal Apocalypse of Enoch (1 Enoch 85–90)." *Revue de Qumran* 14 (April 1990): 629–36.

Frye, Northrop. *Anatomy of Criticism: Four Essays.* Princeton: Princeton University Press, 1971.

———. *Words with Power: Being a Second Study of "the Bible and Literature."* San Diego: Harcourt Brace Jovanovich, 1990.

Funk, Robert W. "Myth and Literal Non-Literal." In *Parables and Presence*, 111–38. Philadelphia: Fortress Press, 1982.

Gantz, Timothy. *Early Greek Myth: A Guide to Literary & Artistic Sources.* 2 volume set. John Hopkins.

Garrett, Susan R. "Revelation." In *The Women's Bible Commentary*, edited by Carol A. Newsom and Sharon H. Ringe. Louisville: Westminster/John Knox Press, 1992.

Gentry, Jr., Kenneth L. *Before Jerusalem Fell: Dating the Book of Revelation: An Exegetical and Historical Argument for a Pre-A.D. 70 Composition.* Tyler, Texas: Institute for Christian Economics, 1989.

Giblin, Charles Homer. "The Cohesive Thematic of God's Holy War of Liberation." Appendix in *The Book of Revelation: The Open Book of Prophecy.* Good News Studies, no. 34, 222–31. Collegeville, Minn.: Liturgical Press, 1991.

Girard, René. "The Nonsacrificial Death of Christ." In *The Girard Reader*, edited by James G. Williams. A Crossroad Herder Book, 177–88. New York: Crossroad, 1996.

———. *The Scapegoat.* Baltimore: Johns Hopkins University Press, 1986.

———. *Things Hidden Since the Foundation of the World.* Jean-Michel Oughourlian and Guy Lefort. Stanford: Stanford University Press, 1987.

Golan, Ariel. "The Sacred Ram." In *Myth and Symbol: Symbolism in Prehistoric Religions*, translated by Rita Schneider-Teteruk, 79–92. Jerusalem: Ariel Golan, 1991.

Goodenough, Erwin Ramsdell. *Jewish Symbols in the Greco-Roman Period.* Ed & comp Jacob Neusner. Bollingen Series. Princeton, N.J.: Princeton University Press, 1988.

Goranson, Stephen. "The Text of Revelation 22.14." *New Testament Studies* 43 (1997): 154–57.

Gordon, Edmund I. "Sumerian Animal Proverbs and Fables: 'Collection Five'." *Journal of Cuneiform Studies* 12, no. 1 (1958): 1–21.

———. "Sumerian Animal Proverbs and Fables: 'Collection Five' (Conclusion)." *Journal of Cuneiform Studies* 12, no. 2 (1958): 43–75.

Grant, Michael, and John Hazel. *Who's Who in Classical Mythology.* 1973. New York: Oxford University Press, 1993.

Gray, G. Buchanan. *Sacrifice in the Old Testament.* Oxford: Oxford University Press, 1925.

Greenfield, Jonas C. "An Astrological Text from Qumran (4Q318) and Reflections on Some Zodiacal Names." Coauthor Michael Sokoloff. *Revue de Qumran* 16, no. 64 (December 1995): 507–25.

Gressmann, Hugo. *Der Messias.* Forschungen zur Religion und Literature des alten und neuen Testaments, vol. 26. Göttingen: Vandenhoeck & Ruprecht, 1929.

Griffiths, J. Gwyn. "Apocalyptic in the Hellenistic Era." In *Apocalypticism in the Mediterranean World,* edited by David Hellholm, 273–93.

Grimal, Nicolas-Christophe. *A History of Ancient Egypt.* Translated by Ian Shaw. Oxford and Cambridge, Mass.: Blackwell, 1994.

Grimsrud, Ted. "Peace Theology and the Justice of God in the Book of Revelation." In *Essays on Peace Theology and Witness,* edited by Willard M. Swartley. Occasional Papers, no. 12, 135–53. Elkhart, Ind.: Institute of Mennonite Studies, 1988.

———. *Triumph of the Lamb: A Self-Study Guide to the Book of Revelation.* With a foreword by Willard M. Swartley. Scottdale, Pa.: Herald Press, 1987.

Guthrie, Donald. "The Lamb in the Structure of the Book of Revelation." *Vox Evangelica* 12 (1987): 64–71.

———. *The Relevance of John's Apocalypse.* Grand Rapids, Mich.: William B. Eerdmans Publishing Company, 1987.

Grosso, Michael. *The Millennium Myth: Love and Death at the End of Time.* Wheaton, Ill.: Quest Books, 1995.

Gwyn, Douglas. *Apocalypse of the Word: The Life and Message of George Fox (1624–1691).* Richmond, Ind.: Friends United Press, 1986.

Hamerton-Kelly, Robert, ed. *Violent Origins: Walter Burkert, René Girard, and Jonathan K. Smith on Ritual Killing and Cultural Formation.* With an introduction by Burton Mack, commentary by Renato Rosaldo, Walter Burkert, et al. Stanford, Cal.: Stanford University Press, 1987.

Hanson, Anthony Tyrrell. *The Wrath of the Lamb.* London: SPCK, 1957.

Hanson, Paul D. *The Dawn of Apocalyptic: The Historical and Sociological Roots of Jewish Apocalyptic Eschatology.* 2d ed. 1975. Philadelphia: Fortress Press, 1979.

Harding, Thomas. "Take Back the Apocalypse." *Touchstone* 3, no. 1 (January 1985): 29–35.

Harlé, P[aul]. *La Bible d'Alexandrie.* Vol. 3, *Le LéVitique.* D[idier] Pralon. Paris: Cerf, 1988.

———. "L'Agneau de l'Apocalypse et le Nouveau Testament." *Les Etudes Théologiques et Religieuses* 31, no. 2 (1956): 26–35.

Harrington, Wilfrid J. *Revelation.* Sacra Pagina, vol. 16. Wilmington, Del.: Michael Glazier, 1993.

Hatch, Edwin. *A Concordance to the Septuagint and the Other Greek Versions of the Old Testament (Including the Apocryphal Books).* By Henry A[deney] Redpath. 1897–1906. Grand Rapids, Mich.: Baker Book House, 1983.

Hayward, Robert. "The Present State of Research Into the Targumic Account of the Sacrifice of Isaac." *Journal of Jewish Studies* 32 (1981): 127–50.

Hellholm, D., ed. *Apocalypticism in the Mediterranean World and the Near East: Proceedings of the International Colloquium on Apocalypticism. Uppsala, August 12–17, 1979.* Tübingen: J. C. B. Mohr (Paul Siebeck), 1983.

Herodotus. *Herodotus.* Edited and translated by A. D. Godley. Loeb Classical Library. Cambridge, Mass.: Harvard University Press, 1981.

Hofius, Otfried. "'Αρνίον – Widder oder Lamm? Erwägungen zur Bedeutung des Wortes in der Johannesapokalypse." *Zeitschrift für die Neutestamentlichen Wissenschaft* 89 (1998): 272–281.

Hofmann, H.-U. *Luther und die Johannes Apocalypse.* Tübingen: Siebeck, 1982.

Hohnjec, Nikola. *"Das Lamm, τὸ ἀρνίον in der Offenbarung des Johannes: eine exegetisch-theologische Untersuchung.* Roma: Herder, 1980.

Holtz, Traugott. *Die Christologie der Apokalypse des Johannes.* 2d ed. 1962. Texte und Untersuchungen, vol. 85. Berlin: Akademie, 1971.

Homer. *The Iliad.* Edited and translated by A. T. Murray. Loeb Classical Library. Cambridge, Mass.: Harvard University Press, 1978.

Hornung, Erik. *Conceptions of God in Ancient Egypt: The One and the Many.* Translated by John Baines. Ithaca, N.Y.: Cornell University Press, 1982.

——. "Names and Combinations of Gods." Chapt. 3 in *Conceptions of God in Ancient Egypt: The One and the Many*, translated by John Baines, 66–99. Ithaca, N.Y.: Cornell University Press, 1982.

Horst, Pieter W. van der. "Lamb." In *Dictionary of Deities and Demons in the Bible*, edited by Karel van der Toorn, Bob Becking, and Pieter W. van der Horst, 938–41. Leiden/New York/Köln: E.J. Brill, 1995.

Howard-Brook, Wes, and Anthony Gwyther. *Unveiling Empire: Reading Revelation Then and Now.* Foreword by Elizabeth McAlister. The Bible & Liberation Series. Maryknoll, N.Y.: Orbis Books, 1999.

Humphrey, Edith M. "On Visions, Arguments and Naming: The Rhetoric of Specificity and Mystery in the Apocalypse." San Francisco, 1997. Also available on the Internet at: http://www.wright.edu/academics/faculty/dbarr/humphrey.htm.

Isaac, Ephraim, trans. and ed. "1 (Ethiopic Apocalypse of) Enoch." In *Old Testament Pseudepigrapha*, vol. 1, edited by James H. Charlesworth, 5–89. Garden City, N.Y.: Doubleday, 1983.

Janssen, Jozef M. A. "Over Farao Bokchoris." In *Varia Historica, Aangeboden Aan Professor Doctor A. W. Byvanck Ter Gelegenheid Van Zijn Zeventigste Verjaardag*, 17–29. Assen: Van Gorcum, 1954.

Jeremias, Joachim. "Das Lamm, das aus der Jungfrau hervorging (Test. Jos. 19,8)." *Zeitschrift für die Neutestamentliche Wissenschaft* 57 (1966): 216–19.

——. "ἀμνός, ἀρήν, ἀρνίον." In *Theological dictionary of the New Testament*, edited by Gerhard Kittel, trans and ed Geoffrey W. Bromiley, 338–41. Grand Rapids: Wm. B. Eerdmans Publishing Company, 1964.

Jonge, Martinus de. *The Testaments of the Twelve Patriarchs: A Study of Their Text, Composition, and Origin.* Leiden: Brill, 1953.

Jörns, Klaus-Peter. *Das Hymnische Evangelium: Untersuchungen zu Aufbau, Funktion und Herkunft der Hymnischen Stücke in der Johannesoffenbarung.* Studien zum Neuen Testament. Gütersloh: Gerd Mohn, 1971.

Juvenalis, Decimus Junius. *Juvenal and Persius.* English translation by G.G. Ramsay. Harvard University Press: London, 1971.

Kákosy, L. "Prophecies of Ram Gods." *Acta Orientalia (Hungary)* 19, no. 3 (1966): 341–58.

Kahn-Lyotard, Laurence. "Hermes." Translated by Danielle Beauvais. In *Greek and Egyptian Mythologies*, edited by Wendy Doniger, compiled by Yves Bonnefoy, 185–89. Chicago: University of Chicago Press, 1992.

Katz, Peter. *Philo's Bible: The Aberrant Text of Bible Quotations in Some Philonic Writings and Its Place in the Textual History of the Greek Bible*. Cambridge: Cambridge University Press, 1950.

Kennedy, George A. *New Testament Interpretation Through Rhetorical Criticism*. Chapel Hill, N.C./London: University of North Carolina Press, 1984.

Kittel, Gerhard, ed. *Theological Dictionary of the New Testament*. Translated by Geoffrey W. Bromiley. Grand Rapids: Wm. B. Eerdmans Publishing Company, 1964–76.

Klassen, William. "Jesus and the Messianic War." In *Early Jewish and Christian Exegesis: Studies in Memory of W. H. Brownlee*, eds C. A. Evans and W. F. Stinespring, 155–75. Atlanta: Scholars Press, 1987.

———. "Vengeance in the Apocalypse of John." *Catholic Biblical Quarterly* 28 (1966): 300–11.

Knibb, Michael A[nthony]. *The Ethiopic Book of Enoch: A New Edition in the Light of the Aramaic Dead Sea Fragments*. In collaboration with Edward Ullendorff. John Rylands University Library of Manchester. Manuscript. Ethiopic 23. Oxford and New York: Clarendon Press and Oxford University Press, 1978.

Koch, Klaus. "Das Lamm, das Ägypten vernichtet: Ein Fragment aus Jannes und Jambres und sein geschichtlicher Hintergrund." *Zeitschrift für die neutestamentliche Wissenschaft* 57 (1966): 79–93.

———. *The Rediscovery of Apocalyptic: A Polemical Work on a Neglected Area of Biblical Studies and Its Damaging Effects on Theology and Philosophy*. Translated by Margaret Kohl. Studies in Biblical Theology. London: S.C.M. Press, 1972.

Kocsis, Elemer. "Apokalyptik und politisches Interesse im Spätjudentum." *Judaica* 27 (1971): 71–89.

Koester, Helmut, author & trans. *Introduction to the New Testament*. Vol. 1, *History, Culture, and Religion of the Hellenistic Age*. Hermeneia: Foundations and Facets. Philadelphia: Fortress Press, 1982.

Koresh, David. "The Decoded Message of the Seven Seals of the Book of Revelation." Unpublished paper. With a preface by Phillip Arnold, compiled by James D. Taylor. Houston: Reunion Institute, 1994.

Kozloff, Arielle P., ed. *Animals in Ancient Art from the Leo Mildenberg Collection*. David Gordon Mitten. Cleveland: Cleveland Museum of Art in cooperation with Indiana University Press, 1981.

Kraeling, Carl H. *The Synagogue*. 1956. Excavations at Dura-Europos: Final Report, vol. 8. New York: KTAV Publishing House, 1979.

Kraft, Heinrich. *Die Offenbarung des Johannes*. Handbuch zum neuen Testament. Tübingen: J. C. B. Mohr, 1974.

Kraybill, J. Nelson. *Imperial Cult and Commerce in John's Apocalypse*. Journal for the Study of the New Testament Supplement Series, no. 132. Sheffield: Sheffield Academic Press, 1996.

Kretschmar, G. *Die Offenbarung des Johannes: Die Geschichte ihrer Auslegung im 1. Jahrtausend*. Calwer Theologische Monographien. Stuttgart: Calwer Verlag, 1985.

Krodel, Gerhard A. *Revelation*. Augsburg Commentary on the New Testament. Minneapolis: Augsburg Publishing House, 1989.

Ladd, George Eldon. *A Commentary on the Revelation of John*. Grand Rapids: William
B. Eerdmans Publishing Company, 1972.

Lake, Kirsopp, trans. *The Apostolic Fathers, Volume 1*. Loeb Classical Library. Cambridge and London: Harvard University Press and William Heinemann Ltd, 1935.

Laurin, R. B. "The Problem of Two Messiahs in the Qumran Scrolls." *Revue de Qumran* 4 (1963–64): 39–52.

Läuchli, Samuel. "Eine Gottesdienststruktur in der Johannesoffenbarung." *Theologische Zeitschrift* 16 (1960). 359–378.

Lawrence, David Herbert, 1885–1930. *Apocalypse*. With an introduction by Richard
Aldington, 1892–1962. 1931. Penguin Twentieth-Century Classics. Harmondsworth: Penguin Books, 1974.

Laws, Sophie. *In the Light of the Lamb: Imagery, Parody, and Theology in the Apocalypse of John*. Wilmington, Del.: M. Glazier, 1988.

Le Déaut, Roger. *La Nuit Pascale: Essai sur la Signification de la Pâque Juive a Partir du Targum d'Exode XII 42*. Analecta Biblica, no. 22. Rome: Institut biblique
pontifical, 1963. 423 pp.

Leclant, J. "The Cults of Isis Among the Greeks and in the Roman Empire." Translated
by Danielle Beauvais. In *Greek and Egyptian Mythologies*, edited by Wendy Doniger, compiled by Yves Bonnefoy, 245–51. Chicago: University of Chicago Press,
1992.

Lehrman, S. M., trans. and ed. *Exodus*. H. Freedman, gen. ed. Midrash Rabbah. London and New York: Soncino Press, 1983.

Leivestad, Ragnar. *Christ the Conqueror: Ideas of Conflict and Victory in the New
Testament*. London: S.P.C.K., 1954.

Leroi-Gourhan, André. "Prehistoric Religion." Translated by Gerald Honigsblum. In
Greek and Egyptian Mythologies, edited by Wendy Doniger, compiled by Yves
Bonnefoy, 10–20. Chicago: University of Chicago Press, 1992.

Levine, Lee I. *Ancient Synagogues Revealed*. Jerusalem and Detroit: The Israel Exploration Society and Wayne State University Press, 1982.

Liddell, Henry George, comp. *A Greek-English Lexicon: With a Supplement*. A new
ed., rev. and augm. throughout by Henry Stuart Jones, with the assistance of Roderick McKenzie, and with the cooperation of many scholars. In collaboration with
Robert Scott and Henry Stuart Jones. 1951. Oxford: Clarendon Press, 1968.

Lind, Millard C. "Hosea 5:8–6:6." Expository article. *Interpretation: A Journal of
Bible and Theology* 38, no. 4 (October 1984): 398–403.

Lindars, Barnabas. "A Bull, a Lamb and a Word: 1 Enoch 90:38." *New Testament Studies* 22 (1975–76): 483–86.

Lindsey, Hal. *There's a New World Coming: A Prophetic Odyssey*. Santa Ana, Cal.:
Vision House Publishers, 1973.

Litvinskii, B. "Sheep and Goats." In *The Encyclopedia of Religion*, vol. 13, edited by
Mircea Eliade. New York: Macmillan, 1987.

Liver, J. "The Doctrine of the Two Messiahs in Sectarian Literature in the Time of the
Second Commonwealth." *Harvard Theological Review* 52 (1959): 156–63.

Lohmeyer, Ernst. *Die Offenbarung des Johannes*. 6th ed. 1926. Handbuch zum Neuen Testament, no. 16. Tübingen: J.C.B. Mohr, 1953.

Longman, Tremper, III. "The Divine Warrior: The New Testament Use of an Old Testament Motif." *Westminster Theological Journal* 44, no. 2 (Fall 1982): 290–307.

Louw, Johannes P., and Eugene A. Nida, eds. *Greek-English Lexicon of the New Testament Based on Semantic Domains; Volume 1: Introductions & Domains*. In collaboration with Rondal B. Smith and Karen A. Munson. New York: United Bible Societies, 1988.

Maher, Michael. "Targum Pseudo-Jonathan: Exodus." In *Targum Neofiti 1: Exodus; and Targum Pseudo-Jonathan: Exodus*, Martin McNamara, gen. ed. The Aramaic Bible: The Targums. Collegeville, Minn.: Liturgical Press, 1987.

Maier, Harry O. *Apocalypse Recalled: The Book of Revelation after Christendom*. Minneapolis: Fortress Press, 2002.

Malina, Bruce J. *On the Genre and Message of Revelation: Star Visions and Sky Journeys*. Peabody, Mass: Hendrickson Publishers, 1995.

Manilius, Marcus. *Astronomica*. Translated and edited by G. P. Goold. Loeb Classical Library, no. 469. Cambridge, Mass.: Harvard University Press, 1977.

Martin, Thomas R. *Ancient Greece: From Prehistoric to Hellenistic Times*. New Haven, Conn., and London: Yale University Press, 1996.

Mauser, Ulrich. "Historical Criticism: Liberator or Foe of Biblical Theology?" Chapt. 5 in *The Promise and Practice of Biblical Theology*, edited by John H. P. Reumann, with a preface by John W. Vannorsdall, 99–113. Minneapolis: Fortress, 1991.

Mays, James Luther, ed. *Harper's Bible Commentary*. Harper & Row, and Society of Biblical Literature. San Francisco: Harper & Row, 1988.

———. *Micah: A Commentary*. The Old Testament Library. Philadelphia: Westminster Press, 1976. Xii, 169 pp.

Mazar, Benjamin, ed. *Views of the Biblical World*. 5 vols. Translated by M. Dagut, in collaboration with Michael Avi-Yonah and Abraham Malamat. Chicago: Jordan Publications, 1959.

Mazzaferri, Fred[erick]. "Martyria Iesou Revisited." *Bible Translator* 39 (January 1988): 114–22.

McCown, C. C. "Hebrew and Egyptian Apocalyptic Literature." *Harvard Theological Review* 18 (1925): 357–411.

McFayden, Donald. "The Occasion of the Domitianic Persecution." *The American Journal of Theology* 24 (1920): 46–66.

McGaughy, Lane C. "Pagan Hellenistic Literature: The Babrian Fables." In *Society of Biblical Literature 1977 Seminar Papers*. Society of Biblical Literature Seminar Papers Series, 205–14. Missoula, Mont.: Scholars Press, 1978.

McGinn, Bernard. "The Calabrian Abbot: Joachim of Fiore in the History of Western Thought." New York/London: Macmillan/Collier Macmillan, 1985.

———. *Visions of the End: Apocalyptic Traditions in the Middle Ages*. New York: Columbia University Press, 1979.

Meeks, Wayne A. *The Moral World of the First Christians*. Library of Early Christianity, no. 6. Philadelphia: Westminster Press, 1986.

———. *The Origins of Christian Morality*. New Haven, Conn.: Yale University Press, 1993.

Mellaart, James. *Catal Huyuk: A Neolithic Town in Anatolia.* New York: McGraw-Hill, 1967.

Mendel, Arthur. *Vision and Violence.* Ann Arbor, Mich.: University of Michigan Press, 1992.

Mercer, Calvin R. *Norman Perrin's Interpretation of the New Testament: From "Exegetical Method" to "Hermeneutical Process."* Studies in American Biblical Hermeneutics, no. 2. Macon, Ga.: Mercer University Press, 1986.

Meyer, Eduard. "Ein neues Bruchstück Manethos über das Lamm des Bokchoris." *Zeitschrift für Ägyptische Sprache und Altertumskunde* 46 (1909–10): 135–36.

Milburn, R. L. P. "The Persecution of Domitian." *Church Quarterly Review* 278 (January–March 1945): 154–64.

Milgrom, Jacob. "Further on the Expiatory Sacrifices." *Journal of Biblical Literature* 115, no. 3 (Fall 1996): 511–14.

———. *Leviticus 1–16: A New Translation with Introduction and Commentary.* Anchor Bible, vol. 3. New York: Doubleday, 1991.

———. *Studies in Cultic Theology and Terminology.* Studies in Judaism in late antiquity, vol. 36. Leiden: E. J. Brill, 1983.

Milik, J. T. *The Books of Enoch.* M. Black. Oxford: Oxford University Press, 1976.

Millar, Fergus. "The Imperial Cult and the Persecutions." In *Le Culte des Souverains dans l'Empire Romain,* edited by W. den Boer. Foundation Hardt pour l'Étude de l'Antiquité Classique, 145–75. Geneva: Vandoeuvres, 1972.

Miller, Patrick D. "Animal Names as Designations in Ugaritic and Hebrew." *Ugarit-Forschung* 2 (1970): 177–86.

Minear, Paul S[evier]. *I Saw a New Earth: An Introduction to the Visions of the Apocalypse.* With a foreword by Myles M. Bourke. Washington and Cleveland: Corpus Books, 1968.

Moor, J. C. de, and E. van Staalduine-Sulman. "The Aramaic Song of the Lamb." *Journal for the Study of Judaism* 24, no. 2 (1993): 266–79.

Moore, Stephen D. *Literary Criticism and the Gospels: The Theoretical Challenge.* New Haven and London: Yale University Press, 1989.

Moorhead, James H. *American Apocalypse: Yankee Protestants and the Civil War, 1860–1869.* New Haven: Yale University Press, 1978.

Morenz, Siegfried. "Ägypten und die Bibel." In *Die Religion in Geschichte und Gegenwart,* vol. 1, Kurt Galling, gen. ed., edited by Hans Campenhausen, Freiherr von. Tübingen: J.C.B. Mohr, 1957.

Morris, Leon. *The Gospel According to John.* 2d ed. Grand Rapids, Mich.: Eerdmans, 1995.

Mounce, Robert H. *The Book of Revelation.* New International Commentary on the New Testament. Grand Rapids: Eerdmans, 1977.

———. "Christology of the Apocalypse." *Foundations* 11 (January–March 1968): 42–51.

Moyise, Steve, ed. *Studies in the Book of Revelation.* Edinburgh: T & T Clark, 2001.

Münchow, Christoph. *Ethik und Eschatologie: Ein Beitrag zum verständnis der frühjüdischen Apokalyptik mit einem Ausblick auf das neue Testament.* Göttingen: Vandenhoeck & Ruprecht, 1981.

Murmelstein, B. "Das Lamm in Test. Jos. 19:8." *Zeitschrift für die neutestamentliche Wissenschaft* 59 (1968): 273–79.

Mussies, G. "The Greek of the Book of Revelation." In *L'Apocalypse Johannique et l'Apocalyptique dans le Nouveau Testament*, edited by Jan Lambrecht. Bibliotheca Ephemeridum Theologicarum Lovaniensium, no. 53, 167–77. Leuven: Leuven University Press, 1980.

Ness, Lester John. *Astrology and Judaism in Late Antiquity*. Ph.D. Diss. 1990. University Microfilms International. Ann Arbor, Mich., 1997.

Newman, Barclay. "The Fallacy of the Domitian Hypothesis: A Critique of the Irenaeus Source as a Witness for the Contemporary Historical Approach to the Interpretation of the Apocalypse." *New Testament Studies* 10, no. 1 (1963): 133–39.

O'Donovan, Oliver. "The Political Thought of the Book of Revelation." *Tyndale Bulletin* 37 (1986): 61–94.

O'Leary, Stephen D. *Arguing the Apocalypse: A Theory of Millennial Rhetoric*. New York: Oxford University Press, 1994.

O'Neill, John C. "The Lamb of God in the Testaments of the Twelve Patriarchs." In *New Testament Backgrounds: A Sheffield Reader*, edited by Craig A. Evans and Stanley E. Porter. The Biblical Seminar, vol. 43, 46–66. Sheffield: Sheffield Academic Press, 1997.

O'Rourke, John J. "The Hymns of the Apocalypse." *The Catholic Biblical Quarterly* 30, no. 3 (1968): 399–409.

Osborne, Grant R. *Revelation*. Baker Exegetical Commentary on the New Testament. Grand Rapids: Baker Books, 2002.

Parker, Robert C. T. "Sacrifice, Greek." In *Oxford Classical Dictionary*, 3d ed., edited by Simon Hornblower and Antony Spawforth. Oxford: Oxford University Press, 1996.

Patrides, C. A., and Joseph Wittreich, eds. *The Apocalypse in English Renaissance Thought and Literature*. Ithaca, N.Y.: Cornell University Press, 1984.

Paul, Ian. "The Book of Revelation: Image, Symbol and Metaphor." In *Studies in the Book of Revelation*, edited by Steve Moyise, 131–47. Edinburgh: T & T Clark, 2001.

Pausanias. *Description of Greece*. Translated by W.H.S. Jones. Cambridge, Mass.: Harvard University Press, 1918.

Perrin, Norman. "Eschatology and Hermeneutics: Reflections on Method in the Interpretation of the New Testament." *Journal of Biblical Literature* 93 (March 1974): 3–14.

———. "The Interpretation of a Biblical Symbol." *Journal of Religion* 55 (1975): 348–70.

———. *Jesus and the Language of the Kingdom: Symbol and Metaphor in New Testament Interpretation*. Philadelphia: Fortress, 1976.

Perry, Ben Edwin, ed. and trans. *Babrius and Phaedrus*. Loeb Classical Library. Cambridge, Mass.: Harvard University Press, 1965.

Philo. *Loeb Classical Library*. Translated by J. W. Earp. 10. Cambridge and London: Harvard University Press and William Heinemann Ltd, 1921.

———. *The Works of Philo: Complete and Unabridged*. Translated by C. D. Yonge, with an introduction by David M. Scholer. Peabody, Mass.: Hendrickson Publishers, 1993.

Pietersma, Alfred, and R. T. Lutz, trans. and eds. "Jannes and Jambres." In *Old Testament Pseudepigrapha, Volume 2*, James H. Charlesworth, gen. ed., 426–42. Garden City, N.Y.: Doubleday, 1983.

Pinney, Roy. *The Animals in the Bible: The Identity and Natural History of All the Animals Mentioned in the Bible*. Philadelphia and New York: Chilton Books, 1964.

Pippin, Tina. *Death and Desire: The Rhetoric of Gender in the Apocalypse of John*. Literary Currents in Biblical Interpretation. Louisville: Westminster/John Knox Press, 1992.

———. "Eros and the End: Reading for Gender in the Apocalypse of John." *Semeia*, no. 59 (1992): 193–217.

———. "The Heroine and the Whore: Fantasy and the Female in the Apocalypse of John." *Semeia*, no. 60 (1992): 67–82.

Porter, Paul A. *Metaphors and Monsters: A Literary-Critical Study of Daniel 7 and 8*. Coniectanea biblica, Old Testament, no. 20. Uppsala: Gleerup, 1983.

Price, Simon R. F. *Rituals and Power: The Roman Imperial Cult in Asia Minor*. New York and Cambridge: Cambridge University Press, 1984.

Priest, John. "Thomas and Aesop." Chapt. 8 in *New Perspectives on Ancient Judaism*. Vol. 2, *Religion, Literature, and Society in Ancient Israel, Formative Christianity and Judaism*, edited by Jacob Neusner, et al. Studies in Judaism, 115–32. Lanham, Md.: University Press of America, 1987.

Prigent, Pierre. *L'Apocalyptique*. Edited by F. Raphaël. Études d'Histoire des Religions, no. 3. Paris: Librairie Orientaliste Paul Geuthner.

———. "Au Temps de l'Apocalypse, 1: Domitien (A Suivre)." *Revue d'Histoire et de Philosophie Religieuses* 54, no. 4 (1974): 455–83.

———. *L'Image dans le Judaisme: Du IIe Au VIe Siècle*. Le Monde de la Bible, no. 24. Geneva: Labor et Fides, 1991.

Rand, J. A. du. "An Apocalyptic Text, Different Contexts and an Applicable Ethos." *Journal of Theology in South Africa* 78 (1992): 75–83.

Rapp, F. "Apocalypse et Mouvements Populaires Au Moyen Age." In *Apocalyptique*, edited by Freddy Raphael. Études d'Histoire des Religions, no. 3. Paris: Librairie Orientaliste Paul Geuthner, 1977.

Reddish, Mitchell G. *Revelation*. Smyth & Helwys Bible Commentary. Macon, Ga.: Smyth & Helwys, 2001.

Richard, Pablo. *Apocalypse: A People's Commentary on the Book of Revelation*. The Bible & Liberation Series. Maryknoll, N.Y.: Orbis Books, 1995.

Ricoeur, Paul. "The Decline of Rhetoric: Tropology." Chapt. 2 in *The Rule of Metaphor*, by Paul Ricoeur. 1975, 44–64. Toronto: University of Toronto Press, 1977.

———. *The Rule of Metaphor: Multi-Disciplinary Studies of the Creation of Meaning in Language*. Translated by Robert Czerny, Kathleen McLaughlin, and John Costello. University of Toronto Romance Series, no. 37. Toronto: University of Toronto Press, 1977.

———. *The Symbolism of Evil*. Translated by Emerson Buchanan. Boston: Beacon Press, 1969.

Rist, Martin. "The Revelation of St. John the Divine." In *Interpreter's Bible, Volume 12*, George Arthur Buttrick, gen. ed., 345–613. New York: Abingdon Press, 1957.

Roberts, Alexander, and James Donaldson, eds. "The Fragments of Papias." In *The Ante-Nicene Fathers: Translations of the Writings of the Fathers Down to A.D. 325*, A. Cleveland Coxe, gen. ed. The Ante-Nicene Fathers, vol. 1, 153–55. New York: Charles Scribner's Sons, 1925.

Robertson, J. M., ed. *Religious Systems of the World: A Contribution to the Study of Comparative Religion, a Collection of Addresses Delivered at South Place Institute, Now Revised and in Some Cases Rewritten by the Authors, Together with Some Others Specially Written for This Volume*. 10th ed. London: G. Allen, 1911.

Roloff, Jürgen. *The Revelation of John: A Continental Commentary*. Translated by John E. Alsup. Minneapolis: Fortress Press, 1993.

Rosivach, Vincent J. *The System of Public Sacrifice in Fourth-Century Athens*. Atlanta: Scholars Press, 1994.

Rowland, Christopher. "The Apocalypse: Hope, Resistance and the Revelation of Reality." *Ex Auditu* 6 (1990): 129–44.

———. *The Open Heaven: A Study of Apocalyptic in Judaism and Early Christianity*. New York: Crossroad, 1982.

———. *Revelation*. Epworth Commentaries. London: Epworth Press, 1993.

Royalty, Robert M., Jr. "The Rhetoric of Revelation." In *Society of Biblical Literature 1997 Seminar Papers*. Society of Biblical Literature Seminar Papers Series, no. 36, 596–617. Atlanta: Scholars Press, 1997.

Rozmovits, Linda. "*The Wolf and the Lamb*: an Image and Its Afterlife." *Art History* 18, no. 1 (March 1995): 97–111.

Ruiz, Jean-Pierre. "Betwixt and Between on the Lord's Day: Liturgy and the Apocalypse." In *Society of Biblical Literature 1992 Seminar Papers*. Society of Biblical Literature 1992 seminar papers, no. 31, 654–72. Atlanta: Scholars Press, 1992.

———. "The Politics of Praise: A Reading of Revelation 19:1-10." In *Society of Biblical Literature 1997 Seminar Papers*, 374–93. Atlanta: Scholars Press, 1997.

———. "Praise and Politics in Revelation 19:1-10." In *Studies in the Book of Revelation*, edited by Steve Moyise, 69–84. Edinburgh: T & T Clark, 2001.

Sanders, Jack T. *Ethics in the New Testament: Change and Development*. Philadelphia: Fortress Press, 1975.

Sanders, James A. "Non-Massoretic Psalms." In *Angelic Liturgy, Prayers, and Psalms*, James H. Charlesworth, gen. ed., edited by Henry W. L. Rietz. The Dead Sea Scrolls: Hebrew, Aramaic and Greek texts with English translations, vol. 4. Tübingen and Louisville, Ky.: J.C.B. Mohr (Siebeck) and Westminster John Knox Press, 1997.

Schimanowski, Gottfried. *Die himmlische Liturgie in der Apokalypse des Johannes: Die frühjüdischen Traditionen in Offenbarung 4–5 unter Einschluß der Hekhalot-literatur*. Wissenschaftliche Untersuchungen zum neuen Testament, 2.Reihe 154. Tübingen: Mohr Siebeck, 2002.

Schnapp-Gourbeillon, Annie. "The Animal as Agent." In *Greek and Egyptian Mythologies*, edited by Wendy Doniger, compiled by Yves Bonnefoy, 130–31. Chicago: University of Chicago Press, 1992.

———. "The Heroic Bestiary." In *Greek and Egyptian Mythologies*, edited by Wendy Doniger, compiled by Yves Bonnefoy, 128–30. Chicago: University of Chicago Press, 1992.

Schürmann, Heinz. *Studien zur neutestamentlichen Ethik.* In collaboration with Thomas Söding. Stuttgarter Biblische Aufsatzbände. Stuttgart: Verlag Katholisches Bibelwerk, 1990.

Schwager, Raymond. "Christ's Death and the Prophetic Critique of Sacrifice." Translated by P. Riordan. *Semeia,* no. 33 (1985): 109–23.

——. *Must There Be Scapegoats? Violence and Redemption in the Bible.* San Francisco: Harper & Row, 1987.

Schwarzbaum, Haim. "Talmudic-Midrashic Affinities of Some Aesopic Fables." In *Essays in Graeco-Roman and Related Talmudic Literature,* edited by Henry A. Fischel. The Library of Biblical Studies, 425–42. New York: KTAV Publishing House, 1977.

Seebass, Gottfried. "The Importance of Apocalyptic for the History of Protestantism." *Colloquium* 13, no. 1 (October 1980): 24–35.

Selvidge, M[arla] J. "Powerful and Powerless Women in the Apocalypse." *Neotestamentica* 26, no. 1 (1992): 157–67.

Shaw, George Bernard. *The Adventures of the Black Girl in Her Search for God.* New York: Dodd, Mead & Company, 1933.

Shaw, Ian, ed. *British Museum Dictionary of Ancient Egypt.* Edited by Paul Nicholson. London: The British Museum, 1995.

Silva, David A. de. "On the Genre and Message of Revelation: Star Visions and Sky Journeys." Review. *Journal of Biblical Literature* 116, no. 3 (Fall 1997).

Simundson, Daniel J. "The Book of Micah: Introduction, Commentary, and Reflections." In *The New Interpreter's Bible,* Leander E. Keck, gen. ed., 531–89. Nashville: Abingdon Press, 1996.

Sleeper, C. Freeman. *The Victorious Christ: A Study of the Book of Revelation.* Louisville, Ky.: Westminster John Knox Press, 1996.

Slingerland, H. Dixon. *The Testaments of the Twelve Patriarchs: A Critical History of Research.* Society of Biblical Literature Monograph Series, vol. 21. Missoula, Montana: Scholars Press, 1977.

Smallwood, E. Mary. "Domitian's Attitude Toward the Jews and Judaism." *Classical Philology* 51 (1956): 1–13.

Smelik, K., and E. Hemelrijk. "'Who Knows not What Monsters Demented Egypt Worships': Opinions on Egyptian Animal Worship in Antiquity as Part of the Ancient Conception of Egypt." In *Aufstieg und Niedergang der Römischen Welt, 2.* Vol. 8, *Principat 17-4: Heidentum: Römische Götterkulte, Orientalische Kulte in der Römischen Welt,* edited by Wolfgang Haase, 1852–2000. Berlin: Walter de Gruyter, 1984.

Sparks, H. F. D., ed. *The Apocryphal Old Testament.* Oxford: Oxford University Press, 1984.

Spitta, Friedrich. *Streitfragen der Geschichte Jesu.* Göttingen: Vandenhoeck und Ruprecht, 1907.

Stauffer, Ethelbert. *Christ and the Caesars.* Philadelphia: Westminster, 1955.

Steinfels, Peter. "Bible's Book of Revelation Was Key to Waco Cult." *New York Times* 142 (1993): 16.

Steinsaltz, Adin. *The Talmud: The Steinsaltz Edition, a Reference Guide.* New York: Random House, 1989.

Stone, Michael A., ed. *The Literature of the Jewish People in the Period of the Second Temple and the Talmud*. Compendia Rerum Iudaicarum ad Novum Testamentum. Assen and Philadelphia: Van Gorcum and Fortress Press, 1984.

Stonehouse, Ned Bernard. *The Apocalypse in the Ancient Church: A Study in the History of the New Testament Canon*. Goes, Netherlands: Oosterbaan & Le Cointre, 1929.

Straten, F. T. van. *Hiera Kala: Images of Animal Sacrifice in Archaic and Classical Greece*. Religions in the Graeco-Roman world, vol. 127. Leiden: E.J. Brill, 1995.

Stuckenbruck, Loren T. *Angel Veneration and Christology: A Study in Early Judaism and in the Christology of the Apocalypse of John*. WUNT 2/70. Tübingen: Mohr-Siebeck, 1995.

Suetonius. "Domitian." In *The Lives of the Caesars*. Loeb Classical Library. Cambridge and London: Harvard University Press and William Heinemann Ltd, 1929.

Sweet, John. *Revelation*. 1979. Philadelphia: Trinity Press International, 1990.

Swete, Henry Barclay. *The Apocalypse of St. John: The Greek Text with Introduction, Notes, and Indices*. 3d ed. 1906. London: Macmillan and Co., 1909.

Swetnam, James. *Jesus and Isaac: A Study of the Epistle to the Hebrews in the Light of the Aqedah*. Analecta Biblica, no. 94. Rome: Biblical Institute Press, 1981.

Tabor, James D. *Why Waco? Cults and the Battle for Religious Freedom in America*. Coauthor Eugene V. Gallagher. Berkeley: University of California Press, 1995.

Tacitus. *The Annals of Imperial Rome*. Trans and introd by Michael Grant. Penguin Classics. London and New York: Penguin Books, 1979.

Talbert, Charles H. *The Apocalypse: A Reading of the Revelation of John*. Louisville: Westminster John Knox Press, 1994.

Talmon, S[hemaryahu]. "The Concepts of *Māšîaḥ* and Messianism in Early Judaism." In *The Messiah: Developments in Earliest Judaism and Christianity*, edited by James H. Charlesworth, 79–115. Minneapolis: Fortress Press, 1992.

Taylor, Lily Ross. *The Divinity of the Roman Emperor*. 1931. American Philological Association Monograph Series, no. 1. Atlanta: Scholars Press, 1975.

Tertullian. *The Five Books Against Marcion*. Eds Alexander Roberts and James Donaldson. The Ante-Nicene fathers: translations of the writings of the fathers down to A.D. 325, vol. 3. New York: Charles Scribner's Sons, 1925.

Thompson, Leonard L. *The Book of Revelation: Apocalypse and Empire*. New York, Oxford: Oxford University Press, 1990.

———. "Mooring the Revelation in the Mediterranean." In *Society of Biblical Literature 1992 Seminar Papers*. Society of Biblical Literature 1992 seminar papers, no. 31, 635–53. Atlanta: Scholars Press, 1992.

Tiller, Patrick A. *A Commentary on the Animal Apocalypse of I Enoch*. Early Judaism and Its Literature, no. 4. Atlanta, Ga.: Scholars Press, 1993.

Tillich, Paul. *Dynamics of Faith*. New York: Harper & Brothers, 1957.

Toperoff, Shlomo Pesach. *The Animal Kingdom in Jewish Thought*. Northvale, N.J.: J. Aronson, 1995.

Touilleux, Paul. *L'Apocalypse et les Cultes de Domitien et de Cybele*. Paris: Libraire Orientaliste Paul Geunther, 1935.

Tov, E. *The Greek Minor Prophets Scroll from Nahal Hever (8HevXIIgr) (The Seiyal Collection I)*. Discoveries in the Judaean Desert, vol. 8. Oxford: Clarendon Press, 1990.

Trocmé, Etienne. "Lamb of God." In *The Oxford Companion to the Bible*, edited by Bruce M. Metzger and Michael D. Coogan, 418–19. New York and Oxford: Oxford University Press, 1993.

Ulrich, Eugene, et. al. *Qumran Cave 4.X: The Prophets*. Discoveries in the Judean Desert, vol. 15. Oxford: Oxford University Press, 1997.

Unnik, W. C. van. "'Worthy is the Lamb': The Background of Apoc 5." In *Mélanges Bibliques en Hommage Au R. P. BéDa Rigaux*, edited by Albert Descamps and A. de Halleux, 445–61. Gembloux: Duculot, 1970.

VanderKam, James C. *Enoch and the Growth of an Apocalyptic Tradition*. The Catholic Biblical Quarterly Monograph Series, no. 16. Washington, D.C.: The Catholic Biblical Association of America, 1984.

Vassiliadis, Petros. "The Translation of Martyria Iesou in Revelation." *Bible Translator* 36, no. 1 (January 1985): 129–34.

Vermes, Geza. "New Light on the Akedah from 4Q225." *Journal of Jewish Studies* 47 (1996): 140–46.

——. *Scripture and Tradition in Judaism*. Leiden: E. J. Brill, 1973.

Vielhauer, Philip. "Apocalypses and Related Subjects: Introduction." Revised by Georg Strecker. In *New Testament Apocrypha*, edited by Wilhelm Schneemelcher and Edgar Hennecke, translated by Robert McL. Wilson. 1965, 542–602. Louisville, Ky.: Westminster/John Knox Press, 1992.

Virgil. *Works*. Translated and edited by H[enry] Rushton Fairclough. Loeb Classical Library. Cambridge, Mass.: Harvard University Press, 1986.

Vogel, Winfried. "The Eschatological Theology of Martin Luther; Part II: Luther's Exposition of Daniel and Revelation." *Andrews University Seminary Studies* 25, no. 2 (Summer 1987): 183–99.

Wainwright, Arthur W. *Mysterious Apocalypse: Interpreting the Book of Revelation*. Nashville: Abingdon Press, 1993.

Walters, P. *The Text of the Septuagint: Its Corruptions and Their Emendation*. Cambridge: Cambridge University Press, 1973.

Warden, Preston Duane. *Alienation and Community in 1 Peter (Asia Minor, Anatolia)*. Ph.D. dissertation. Duke University, 1986.

Weitzmann, Kurt. *The Frescoes of the Dura Synagogue and Christian Art*. Coauthor Herbert L. Kessler. Washington, D.C.: Dumbarton Oaks Research Library and Collection, 1990.

Wengst, Klaus. "Babylon the Great and the New Jerusalem: The Visionary View of Political Reality in the Revelation of John." In *Politics and Theopolitics in the Bible and Postbiblical Literature*, edited by Henning Graf Reventlow, Yair Hoffman, and Benjamin Uffenheimer. Journal for the Study of the Old Testament Supplement Series, no. 171, 189–202. Sheffield: JSOT Press, 1994.

——. *The Pax Romana and the Peace of Jesus Christ*. Translated by John Bowden. 1986. Philadelphia: Fortress Press, 1987.

West, David R. *Some Cults of Greek Goddesses and Female Daemons of Oriental Origin*. Alter Orient und Altes Testament. Kevelaer/Neukirchen-Vluyn: Butzon & Bercker/Neukirchener Verlag, 1995.

Whale, Peter. "The Lamb of John: Some Myths About the Vocabulary of the Johannine Literature." *Journal of Biblical Literature* 106 (1987): 289–95.

Wheelwright, Philip. *The Burning Fountain: A Study in the Language of Symbolism.* 2d ed. 1954. Bloomington, Ind.: University of Indiana Press, 1968.

Wheelwright, Philip. *Metaphor and Reality.* 6th ed. 1962. Bloomington, Ind.: University of Indiana Press, 1975.

Whittaker, Molly. *Jews and Christians: Graeco-Roman Views.* Cambridge Commentaries on Writings of the Jewish and Christian world, 200 B.C. to A.D. 200, vol. 6. Cambridge and New York: Cambridge University Press, 1984.

Wiens, Devon Harvey. *Holy War Theology in the New Testament and Its Relationship to the Eschatological Day of the Lord Tradition.* Ph.D. dissertation. 1967. Ann Arbor, Mich.: University Microfilms International, 1982.

Wilder, Amos N. "Apocalyptic Rhetorics." Chapt. 7 in *Jesus' Parables and the War of Myths: Essays on Imagination in the Scripture*, edited by James Breech, with an introduction by James Breech, 153–68. Philadelphia: Fortress Press, 1982.

———. "Rhetoric of Ancient and Modern Apocalyptic." *Interpretation* 25 (October 1971): 436–53.

———. "Scholars, Theologians, and Ancient Rhetoric." *Journal of Biblical Literature* 75 (1958): 1–11.

Williams, George Huntston, and Angel M. Mergal, eds. *Spiritual and Anabaptist Writers.* The Library of Christian Classics, vol. 25. Philadelphia: Westminster Press, 1957.

Wilson, J. Christian. "The Problem of the Domitianic Date of Revelation." *New Testament Studies* 39 (1993): 587–605.

Wink, Walter. *Engaging the Powers: Discernment and Resistance in a World of Domination.* The Powers, vol. 3. Philadelphia: Fortress, 1992.

Winn, Albert Curry. *Ain't Gonna Study War No More: Biblical Ambiguity and the Abolition of War.* Louisville: Westminster/John Knox, 1993.

Wischnitzer, R. "The Beth Alpha Mosaic: A New Interpretation." *Jewish Social Studies* 17 (1955): 133–44.

Wise, Michael Owen. *Thunder in Gemini: And Other Essays on the History, Language and Literature of Second Temple Palestine.* Journal for the Study of the Pseudepigrapha Supplement Series, no. 15. Sheffield: JSOT Press, 1994.

———, Martin Abegg, and Edward Cook, eds. *The Dead Sea Scrolls: A New Translation.* San Francisco: HarperSanFrancisco, 1996.

Yoder, John H. "Ethics and Eschatology." *Ex Auditu* 6 (1990): 119–28.

Index of Ancient Sources

The ancient sources are indexed here in the following order and arrangement: (1) Old Testament; (2) New Testament; (3) Apocrypha; (4) Old Testament Pseudepigrapha; (5) Josephus; (6) Philo; (7) Dead Sea Scrolls; (8) Greek and Latin Authors; (9) Apostolic Literature and Christian Apocrypha; (10) Rabbinic Literature; and (11) Documentary Papyri.

1. Old Testament

Genesis

12:3	218
21:28	29, 31, 208, 212
21:29	29, 31, 208, 212
21:30	29, 31, 208, 212
22	128, 137–140
22:7	208, 213
22:7-8	137
22:8	139, 208, 213
22:13	137
28:14	218
30:32	29, 208, 212
30:33	29, 208, 212
30:35	29, 208, 212
30:40	29, 208–209, 212
31:7	210
31:38	31, 209, 212
32:14(15)	31, 212
33:19	210
49	167
49:9	164–165
49:10	165

Exodus

2:11-15	103
5:21	99
7:5	79
7:14-25	132
8:1-15	132
8:26	99
9:8-12	132
9:13-35	132
10:1-20	132
10:21-29	132
12	132
12:3	208, 215
12:4	208, 215
12:5	29–30, 132, 208, 215
12:11	211
12:21	100, 209, 215
12:27	211
12:43	211
12:48	211
13:13	208, 213
14:21	132
14:21-22	147
15	146
15:1-18	132
15:1-21	168
15:15	80
23:19	35, 210
29:16	129
29:20	129
29:38-41	33, 128
29:38	208, 213
29:39	208, 213
29:40	208, 213
29:41	208, 213
32	71
34:20	208, 213
34:25	211
34:26	210

Leviticus

1–16	30
1:3-13	35
1:5	129
1:10	37, 208, 213

2. New Testament

3. Apocrypha

4. Old Testament Pseudepigrapha

11. Documentary Papyri

Index of Modern Authors

Subject Index

Attic period pottery 62
Attis 66, 68
Augustine 2–3
Augustus 65, 124
Authorial intent 16–17, 119, 171, 186, 196, 202
Avenge: see "Vengeance"
Azzai, Ben 23

Baal Zephon 72
Babrius 52–54
Babylon 10, 48–49, 52, 71, 117, 194
Bagōsēs 34
Bakenranef 47
Balaamites 177
Banebdjedet 43
Bara 71
Beast 20, 26, 41, 55, 59, 82, 89, 91, 97, 104, 115, 117–118, 127, 129, 135–136, 152–153, 169, 171, 179, 184–186, 190, 199, 217
Belial 139
Beliar 88
Beth Alpha synagogue 72
Bethlehem 141
Birket Karun 48
Bocchoris 42, 47–51, 75, 100, 103
Branch Davidians 5
Bride 68
Bubastis 49
Bull 30–31, 40, 51, 59, 64, 67–68, 71–72, 80–81, 83–85, 90, 92, 96–98, 109

Cain 169
Caligula: see "Gaius"
Catal Huyuk 43
Christology 11, 17–19, 22, 27
Circe 68
Civica Cerealis 125–126
Civil disobedience 1
Civil war, American 6
Claudius 68
Clement of Alexandria 123
Cleopatra 124
Colchis 61

Colophon 58
Combat myth: see "divine warrior tradition"
Conquering: see "Victory"
Consistent resistance (ὑπομονή) 122–123, 156, 161, 174–175, 182, 185, 187, 201
Constans, Emperor 67
Crete 56
Criobolium 67–68
Crusades 1–2
Cybele 60, 66–68

Damnatio memoriae 124
Dante 7
Date of Revelation's composition 123
David 78, 89, 96–97, 104–106, 135
David, Root of: see "Root of David"
Dead Sea Scrolls 36, 69–70, 84, 91, 105, 139, 142–143, 164, 166–167
(see also "Qumran")
Decoding: see "referentialism"
Delay of the Parousia 119, 150
Deliberative rhetoric: see "Rhetoric, deliberative"
Delphi 58
Demetrius 166
Didyma 58
Dindymus, Mt. 66
Dionysius of Alexandria 2
Dionysos 59–60
Dispensationalism 115, 150, 195
Divine warrior tradition 19–20, 87, 103, 111, 142, 146, 151, 155, 168, 182–184, 189, 193, 200, 205
Diwya 56
Djebel Bes Seba 43
Domination system 9, 18, 53, 116, 170, 186, 194–195, 197–201, 203, 205
Dominus et deus noster 125
Domitian 58, 66, 120–126
Domitianic persecution 120–124, 196
Dragon 20, 41, 60, 136, 151, 153, 184–186
Dura-Europos 72

Pshenhor 49
Ptolemies 90
Pu'ah 102
Pylos 55

Quaker tradition 7
Qumran 36, 70, 72–73, 84, 90, 142–143,
 165, 167, 185, 191
(see also "Dead Sea Scrolls")

Rabelais 7
Ram 22–26, 30–31, 35, 41–47, 49, 51,
 57–62, 64–68, 70–73, 75, 78–80, 83,
 89–90, 93, 96–97, 99–101, 106, 108–
 109, 135–140, 146, 161
Rashi 99
Red Sea 132
Referentialism 111–119, 163
Renaissance 6
Resistance literature 9–11, 18, 20, 51,
 65–66, 95, 100, 116, 119, 127, 153–
 155, 172, 174–175, 203–204
Revenge: see "Vengeance"
Rhea 66–67
Rhetoric and rhetorical method 5–7, 10,
 12–16, 18, 20–21, 27–28, 39, 74, 109,
 111, 116–117, 119–121, 123, 126,
 129, 150, 154–158, 160–162, 169–
 173, 175–178, 180, 182, 185–188,
 190, 192, 194, 197–200, 204–205, 217
Rhetoric, deliberative 156
Rhetoric, epideictic 156–157, 205
Rhetoric, forensic 156–157
Roma 124
Roman Empire 126, 153
Rome 45, 49, 51–52, 66, 99, 117, 120,
 124–125, 132, 152–153, 157, 171,
 186, 194, 205
Root of David 64, 78, 152, 163–164,
 166–168, 202, 220

Sacrifice 1, 23, 26, 29–39, 43–44, 47, 54,
 57, 59–65, 68, 75, 78, 98–101, 108–
 109, 128–131, 133, 137–140, 144,
 147, 159, 161–162, 189, 195–197,
 202, 207

Samuel 105
Sardis 65, 69, 121, 125, 130, 177, 220
Saul 89, 165
Scroll 5, 13, 51–52
Sebennytus 49
Sefer HaRazim 72
Seleucids 89–90, 114
Sennacherib 141, 182
Senate 124–125
Septuagint (LXX) 25–29, 32, 34–39, 79–
 80, 97, 108, 132–134, 140–143, 169,
 181, 207, 210–211, 218, 221
Seven wonders of the world 66
Shabako 47
Shallum, Rabbi 99
Shammai 28
Shifra 102
Shu 47
Slaughter 2, 25, 31, 38, 68, 97–98, 111,
 127–129, 133–134, 144, 146–147,
 159–161, 165, 168–170, 173–176,
 179, 220
Smyrna 66, 125, 177, 219
Soba 44
Social ethics 6–9, 11
Sokhnopaiou Nesos 48
Sophocles 58
Suetonius 125
Suffering servant 11, 108, 128, 133–135
Sumerian fables 52–53, 55, 59
Susanna 99
Symbolism and symbol analysis 14, 15,
 18–20, 31, 38, 40–76, 80, 82, 90–91,
 98–99, 101, 108–120, 127–128, 130,
 132–133, 135–136, 143–144, 147–148,
 150–151, 153, 155, 158–161, 164–
 167, 170, 176, 180, 185–187, 190–
 191, 193, 195–196, 199–200, 202–
 204, 207, 217
Symbols, "steno" 111–116
Symbols, "tensive" 111–114, 116, 147
Syria 50–51, 89
Syriac 106

Tacitus 42, 100, 125
Taharqo 44

Wissenschaftliche Untersuchungen zum Neuen Testament

Alphabetical Index of the First and Second Series

Bosman, Philip: Conscience in Philo and Paul. 2003. *Volume II/166.*

Brocke, Christoph vom: Thessaloniki – Stadt des Kassander und Gemeinde des Paulus. 2001. *Volume II/125.*

Brunson, Andrew: Psalm 118 in the Gospel of John. 2003. *Volume II/158.*

Büchli, Jörg: Der Poimandres – ein paganisiertes Evangelium. 1987. *Volume II/27.*

Bühner, Jan A.: Der Gesandte und sein Weg im 4. Evangelium. 1977. *Volume II/2.*

Burchard, Christoph: Untersuchungen zu Joseph und Aseneth. 1965. *Volume 8.*

– Studien zur Theologie, Sprache und Umwelt des Neuen Testaments. Ed. von D. Sänger. 1998. *Volume 107.*

Burnett, Richard: Karl Barth's Theological Exegesis. 2001. *Volume II/145.*

Byron, John: Slavery Metaphors in Early Judaism and Pauline Christianity. 2003. *Volume II/162.*

Byrskog, Samuel: Story as History – History as Story. 2000. *Volume 123.*

Cancik, Hubert (Ed.): Markus-Philologie. 1984. *Volume 33.*

Capes, David B.: Old Testament Yaweh Texts in Paul's Christology. 1992. *Volume II/47.*

Caragounis, Chrys C.: The Son of Man. 1986. *Volume 38.*

– see *Fridrichsen, Anton.*

Carleton Paget, James: The Epistle of Barnabas. 1994. *Volume II/64.*

Carson, D.A., O'Brien, Peter T. and *Mark Seifrid* (Ed.): Justification and Variegated Nomism: A Fresh Appraisal of Paul and Second Temple Judaism. Volume 1: The Complexities of Second Temple Judaism. *Volume II/140.*

Ciampa, Roy E.: The Presence and Function of Scripture in Galatians 1 and 2. 1998. *Volume II/102.*

Classen, Carl Joachim: Rhetorical Criticsm of the New Testament. 2000. *Volume 128.*

Colpe, Carsten: Iranier – Aramäer – Hebräer – Hellenen. 2003. *Volume 154.*

Crump, David: Jesus the Intercessor. 1992. *Volume II/49.*

Dahl, Nils Alstrup: Studies in Ephesians. 2000. *Volume 131.*

Deines, Roland: Jüdische Steingefäße und pharisäische Frömmigkeit. 1993. *Volume II/52.*

– Die Pharisäer. 1997. *Volume 101.*

Dettwiler, Andreas and *Jean Zumstein (Ed.):* Kreuzestheologie im Neuen Testament. 2002. *Volume 151.*

Dickson, John P.: Mission-Commitment in Ancient Judaism and in the Pauline Communities. 2003. *Volume II/159.*

Dietzfelbinger, Christian: Der Abschied des Kommenden. 1997. *Volume 95.*

Dobbeler, Axel von: Glaube als Teilhabe. 1987. *Volume II/22.*

Du Toit, David S.: Theios Anthropos. 1997. *Volume II/91*

Dunn, James D.G. (Ed.): Jews and Christians. 1992. *Volume 66.*

– Paul and the Mosaic Law. 1996. *Volume 89.*

Dunn, James D.G., Hans Klein, Ulrich Luz and *Vasile Mihoc* (Ed.)*:* Auslegung der Bibel in orthodoxer und westlicher Perspektive. 2000. *Volume 130.*

Ebertz, Michael N.: Das Charisma des Gekreuzigten. 1987. *Volume 45.*

Eckstein, Hans-Joachim: Der Begriff Syneidesis bei Paulus. 1983. *Volume II/10.*

– Verheißung und Gesetz. 1996. *Volume 86.*

Ego, Beate: Im Himmel wie auf Erden. 1989. *Volume II/34*

Ego, Beate and *Lange, Armin* with *Pilhofer, Peter (Ed.):* Gemeinde ohne Tempel – Community without Temple. 1999. *Volume 118.*

Eisen, Ute E.: see *Paulsen, Henning.*

Ellis, E. Earle: Prophecy and Hermeneutic in Early Christianity. 1978. *Volume 18.*

– The Old Testament in Early Christianity. 1991. *Volume 54.*

Endo, Masanobu: Creation and Christology. 2002. *Volume 149.*

Ennulat, Andreas: Die 'Minor Agreements'. 1994. *Volume II/62.*

Ensor, Peter W.: Jesus and His 'Works'. 1996. *Volume II/85.*

Eskola, Timo: Messiah and the Throne. 2001. *Volume II/142.*

– Theodicy and Predestination in Pauline Soteriology. 1998. *Volume II/100.*

Fatehi, Mehrdad: The Spirit's Relation to the Risen Lord in Paul. 2000. *Volume II/128.*

Feldmeier, Reinhard: Die Krisis des Gottessohnes. 1987. *Volume II/21.*

– Die Christen als Fremde. 1992. *Volume 64.*

Feldmeier, Reinhard and *Ulrich Heckel* (Ed.): Die Heiden. 1994. *Volume 70.*

Fletcher-Louis, Crispin H.T.: Luke-Acts: Angels, Christology and Soteriology. 1997. *Volume II/94.*

Förster, Niclas: Marcus Magus. 1999. *Volume 114.*

Forbes, Christopher Brian: Prophecy and Inspired Speech in Early Christianity and its Hellenistic Environment. 1995. *Volume II/75.*

Fornberg, Tord: see *Fridrichsen, Anton.*

Fossum, Jarl E.: The Name of God and the Angel of the Lord. 1985. *Volume 36.*

Fotopoulos, John: Food Offered to Idols in Roman Corinth. 2003. *Volume II/151.*

Frenschkowski, Marco: Offenbarung und Epiphanie. Volume 1 1995. *Volume II/79 –* Volume 2 1997. *Volume II/80.*

Frey, Jörg: Eugen Drewermann und die biblische Exegese. 1995. *Volume II/71.*
– Die johanneische Eschatologie. Volume I. 1997. *Volume 96.* – Volume II. 1998. *Volume 110.*
– Volume III. 2000. *Volume 117.*

Freyne, Sean: Galilee and Gospel. 2000. *Volume 125.*

Fridrichsen, Anton: Exegetical Writings. Edited by C.C. Caragounis and T. Fornberg. 1994. *Volume 76.*

Garlington, Don B.: 'The Obedience of Faith'. 1991. *Volume II/38.*
– Faith, Obedience, and Perseverance. 1994. *Volume 79.*

Garnet, Paul: Salvation and Atonement in the Qumran Scrolls. 1977. *Volume II/3.*

Gese, Michael: Das Vermächtnis des Apostels. 1997. *Volume II/99.*

Gheorghita, Radu: The Role of the Septuagint in Hebrews. 2003. *Volume II/160.*

Gräbe, Petrus J.: The Power of God in Paul's Letters. 2000. *Volume II/123.*

Gräßer, Erich: Der Alte Bund im Neuen. 1985. *Volume 35.*
– Forschungen zur Apostelgeschichte. 2001. *Volume 137.*

Green, Joel B.: The Death of Jesus. 1988. *Volume II/33.*

Gregory, Anthony: The Reception of Luke and Acts in the Period before Irenaeus. 2003. *Volume II/169.*

Gundry Volf, Judith M.: Paul and Perseverance. 1990. *Volume II/37.*

Hafemann, Scott J.: Suffering and the Spirit. 1986. *Volume II/19.*
– Paul, Moses, and the History of Israel. 1995. *Volume 81.*

Hahn, Johannes (Ed.): Zerstörungen des Jerusalemer Tempels. 2002. *Volume 147.*

Hannah, Darrel D.: Michael and Christ. 1999. *Volume II/109.*

Hamid-Khani, Saeed: Relevation and Concealment of Christ. 2000. *Volume II/120.*

Hartman, Lars: Text-Centered New Testament Studies. Ed. von D. Hellholm. 1997. *Volume 102.*

Hartog, Paul: Polycarp and the New Testament. 2001. *Volume II/134.*

Heckel, Theo K.: Der Innere Mensch. 1993. *Volume II/53.*
– Vom Evangelium des Markus zum viergestaltigen Evangelium. 1999. *Volume 120.*

Heckel, Ulrich: Kraft in Schwachheit. 1993. *Volume II/56.*
– Der Segen im Neuen Testament. 2002. *Volume 150.*
– see *Feldmeier, Reinhard.*
– see *Hengel, Martin.*

Heiligenthal, Roman: Werke als Zeichen. 1983. *Volume II/9.*

Hellholm, D.: see *Hartman, Lars.*

Hemer, Colin J.: The Book of Acts in the Setting of Hellenistic History. 1989. *Volume 49.*

Hengel, Martin: Judentum und Hellenismus. 1969, ³1988. *Volume 10.*
– Die johanneische Frage. 1993. *Volume 67.*
– Judaica et Hellenistica. Kleine Schriften I. 1996. *Volume 90.*
– Judaica, Hellenistica et Christiana. Kleine Schriften II. 1999. *Volume 109.*
– Paulus und Jakobus. Kleine Schriften III. 2002. *Volume 141.*

Hengel, Martin and *Ulrich Heckel* (Ed.): Paulus und das antike Judentum. 1991. *Volume 58.*

Hengel, Martin and *Hermut Löhr* (Ed.): Schriftauslegung im antiken Judentum und im Urchristentum. 1994. *Volume 73.*

Hengel, Martin and *Anna Maria Schwemer:* Paulus zwischen Damaskus und Antiochien. 1998. *Volume 108.*
– Der messianische Anspruch Jesu und die Anfänge der Christologie. 2001. *Volume 138.*

Hengel, Martin and *Anna Maria Schwemer* (Ed.): Königsherrschaft Gottes und himmlischer Kult. 1991. *Volume 55.*
– Die Septuaginta. 1994. *Volume 72.*

Hengel, Martin; Siegfried Mittmann and *Anna Maria Schwemer* (Ed.): La Cité de Dieu / Die Stadt Gottes. 2000. *Volume 129.*

Herrenbrück, Fritz: Jesus und die Zöllner. 1990. *Volume II/41.*

Herzer, Jens: Paulus oder Petrus? 1998. *Volume 103.*

Hoegen-Rohls, Christina: Der nachösterliche Johannes. 1996. *Volume II/84.*

Hofius, Otfried: Katapausis. 1970. *Volume 11.*
– Der Vorhang vor dem Thron Gottes. 1972. *Volume 14.*
– Der Christushymnus Philipper 2,6-11. 1976, ²1991. *Volume 17.*
– Paulusstudien. 1989, ²1994. *Volume 51.*

– Neutestamentliche Studien. 2000. *Volume 132.*
– Paulusstudien II. 2002. *Volume 143.*
Hofius, Otfried and *Hans-Christian Kammler:* Johannesstudien. 1996. *Volume 88.*
Holtz, Traugott: Geschichte und Theologie des Urchristentums. 1991. *Volume 57.*
Hommel, Hildebrecht: Sebasmata. Volume 1 1983. *Volume 31* – Volume 2 1984. *Volume 32.*
Hvalvik, Reidar: The Struggle for Scripture and Covenant. 1996. *Volume II/82.*
Johns, Loren L.: The Lamb Christology of the Apocalypse of John. 2003. *Volume II/167.*
Joubert, Stephan: Paul as Benefactor. 2000. *Volume II/124.*
Jungbauer, Harry: „Ehre Vater und Mutter". 2002. *Volume II/146.*
Kähler, Christoph: Jesu Gleichnisse als Poesie und Therapie. 1995. *Volume 78.*
Kamlah, Ehrhard: Die Form der katalogischen Paränese im Neuen Testament. 1964. *Volume 7.*
Kammler, Hans-Christian: Christologie und Eschatologie. 2000. *Volume 126.*
– Kreuz und Weisheit. 2003. *Volume 159.*
– see *Hofius, Otfried.*
Kelhoffer, James A.: Miracle and Mission. 1999. *Volume II/112.*
Kieffer, René and *Jan Bergman (Ed.):* La Main de Dieu / Die Hand Gottes. 1997. *Volume 94.*
Kim, Seyoon: The Origin of Paul's Gospel. 1981, [2]1984. *Volume II/4.*
– "The 'Son of Man'" as the Son of God. 1983. *Volume 30.*
Klauck, Hans-Josef: Religion und Gesellschaft im frühen Christentum. 2003. *Volume 152.*
Klein, Hans: see *Dunn, James D.G..*
Kleinknecht, Karl Th.: Der leidende Gerechtfertigte. 1984, [2]1988. *Volume II/13.*
Klinghardt, Matthias: Gesetz und Volk Gottes. 1988. *Volume II/32.*
Köhler, Wolf-Dietrich: Rezeption des Matthäusevangeliums in der Zeit vor Irenäus. 1987. *Volume II/24.*
Kooten, George H. van: Cosmic Christology in Paul and the Pauline School. 2003. *Volume II/171.*
Korn, Manfred: Die Geschichte Jesu in veränderter Zeit. 1993. *Volume II/51.*
Koskenniemi, Erkki: Apollonios von Tyana in der neutestamentlichen Exegese. 1994. *Volume II/61.*
Kraus, Thomas J.: Sprache, Stil und historischer Ort des zweiten Petrusbriefes. 2001. *Volume II/136.*
Kraus, Wolfgang: Das Volk Gottes. 1996. *Volume 85.*

– and *Karl-Wilhelm Niebuhr* (Ed.): Frühjudentum und Neues Testament im Horizont Biblischer Theologie. 2003. *Volume 162.*
– see *Walter, Nikolaus.*
Kreplin, Matthias: Das Selbstverständnis Jesu. 2001. *Volume II/141.*
Kuhn, Karl G.: Achtzehngebet und Vaterunser und der Reim. 1950. *Volume 1.*
Kvalbein, Hans: see *Ådna, Jostein.*
Laansma, Jon: I Will Give You Rest. 1997. *Volume II/98.*
Labahn, Michael: Offenbarung in Zeichen und Wort. 2000. *Volume II/117.*
Lambers-Petry, Doris: see *Tomson, Peter J.*
Lange, Armin: see *Ego, Beate.*
Lampe, Peter: Die stadtrömischen Christen in den ersten beiden Jahrhunderten. 1987, [2]1989. *Volume II/18.*
Landmesser, Christof: Wahrheit als Grundbegriff neutestamentlicher Wissenschaft. 1999. *Volume 113.*
– Jüngerberufung und Zuwendung zu Gott. 2000. *Volume 133.*
Lau, Andrew: Manifest in Flesh. 1996. *Volume II/86.*
Lawrence, Louise: An Ethnography of the Gospel of Matthew. 2003. *Volume II/165.*
Lee, Pilchan: The New Jerusalem in the Book of Relevation. 2000. *Volume II/129.*
Lichtenberger, Hermann: see *Avemarie, Friedrich.*
Lieu, Samuel N.C.: Manichaeism in the Later Roman Empire and Medieval China. [2]1992. *Volume 63.*
Loader, William R.G.: Jesus' Attitude Towards the Law. 1997. *Volume II/97.*
Löhr, Gebhard: Verherrlichung Gottes durch Philosophie. 1997. *Volume 97.*
Löhr, Hermut: Studien zum frühchristlichen und frühjüdischen Gebet. 2003. *Volume160.*
– : see *Hengel, Martin.*
Löhr, Winrich Alfried: Basilides und seine Schule. 1995. *Volume 83.*
Luomanen, Petri: Entering the Kingdom of Heaven. 1998. *Volume II/101.*
Luz, Ulrich: see *Dunn, James D.G.*
Maier, Gerhard: Mensch und freier Wille. 1971. *Volume 12.*
– Die Johannesoffenbarung und die Kirche. 1981. *Volume 25.*
Markschies, Christoph: Valentinus Gnosticus? 1992. *Volume 65.*
Marshall, Peter: Enmity in Corinth: Social Conventions in Paul's Relations with the Corinthians. 1987. *Volume II/23.*

Mayer, Annemarie: Sprache der Einheit im Epheserbrief und in der Ökumene. 2002. *Volume II/150.*

McDonough, Sean M.: YHWH at Patmos: Rev. 1:4 in its Hellenistic and Early Jewish Setting. 1999. *Volume II/107.*

McGlynn, Moyna: Divine Judgement and Divine Benevolence in the Book of Wisdom. 2001. *Volume II/139.*

Meade, David G.: Pseudonymity and Canon. 1986. *Volume 39.*

Meadors, Edward P.: Jesus the Messianic Herald of Salvation. 1995. *Volume II/72.*

Meißner, Stefan: Die Heimholung des Ketzers. 1996. *Volume II/87.*

Mell, Ulrich: Die „anderen" Winzer. 1994. *Volume 77.*

Mengel, Berthold: Studien zum Philipperbrief. 1982. *Volume II/8.*

Merkel, Helmut: Die Widersprüche zwischen den Evangelien. 1971. *Volume 13.*

Merklein, Helmut: Studien zu Jesus und Paulus. Volume 1 1987. *Volume 43.* – Volume 2 1998. *Volume 105.*

Metzdorf, Christina: Die Tempelaktion Jesu. 2003. *Volume II/168.*

Metzler, Karin: Der griechische Begriff des Verzeihens. 1991. *Volume II/44.*

Metzner, Rainer: Die Rezeption des Matthäusevangeliums im 1. Petrusbrief. 1995. *Volume II/74.*

– Das Verständnis der Sünde im Johannesevangelium. 2000. *Volume 122.*

Mihoc, Vasile: see *Dunn, James D.G..*

Mineshige, Kiyoshi: Besitzverzicht und Almosen bei Lukas. 2003. *Volume II/163.*

Mittmann, Siegfried: see *Hengel, Martin.*

Mittmann-Richert, Ulrike: Magnifikat und Benediktus. *1996. Volume II/90.*

Mußner, Franz: Jesus von Nazareth im Umfeld Israels und der Urkirche. Ed. von M. Theobald. 1998. *Volume 111.*

Niebuhr, Karl-Wilhelm: Gesetz und Paränese. 1987. *Volume II/28.*

– Heidenapostel aus Israel. 1992. *Volume 62.*

– see *Kraus, Wolfgang*

Nielsen, Anders E.: "Until it is Fullfilled". 2000. *Volume II/126.*

Nissen, Andreas: Gott und der Nächste im antiken Judentum. 1974. *Volume 15.*

Noack, Christian: Gottesbewußtsein. 2000. *Volume II/116.*

Noormann, Rolf: Irenäus als Paulusinterpret. 1994. *Volume II/66.*

Novakovic, Lidija: Messiah, the Healer of the Sick. 2003. *Volume II/170.*

Obermann, Andreas: Die christologische Erfüllung der Schrift im Johannesevangelium. 1996. *Volume II/83.*

Öhler, Markus: Barnabas. 2003. *Volume 156.*

Okure, Teresa: The Johannine Approach to Mission. 1988. *Volume II/31.*

Oropeza, B. J.: Paul and Apostasy. 2000. *Volume II/115.*

Ostmeyer, Karl-Heinrich: Taufe und Typos. 2000. *Volume II/118.*

Paulsen, Henning: Studien zur Literatur und Geschichte des frühen Christentums. Ed. von Ute E. Eisen. 1997. *Volume 99.*

Pao, David W.: Acts and the Isaianic New Exodus. 2000. *Volume II/130.*

Park, Eung Chun: The Mission Discourse in Matthew's Interpretation. 1995. *Volume II/81.*

Park, Joseph S.: Conceptions of Afterlife in Jewish Insriptions. 2000. *Volume II/121.*

Pate, C. Marvin: The Reverse of the Curse. 2000. *Volume II/114.*

Peres, Imre: Griechische Grabinschriften und neutestamentliche Eschatologie. 2003. *Volume 157.*

Philonenko, Marc (Ed.): Le Trône de Dieu. 1993. *Volume 69.*

Pilhofer, Peter: Presbyteron Kreitton. 1990. *Volume II/39.*

– Philippi. Volume 1 1995. *Volume 87.* – Volume 2 2000. *Volume 119.*

– Die frühen Christen und ihre Welt. 2002. *Volume 145.*

– see *Ego, Beate.*

Pöhlmann, Wolfgang: Der Verlorene Sohn und das Haus. 1993. *Volume 68.*

Pokorný, Petr and *Josef B. Souček:* Bibelauslegung als Theologie. 1997. *Volume 100.*

Pokorný, Petr and *Jan Roskovec (Ed.):* Philosophical Hermeneutics and Biblical Exegesis. 2002. *Volume 153.*

Porter, Stanley E.: The Paul of Acts. 1999. *Volume 115.*

Prieur, Alexander: Die Verkündigung der Gottesherrschaft. 1996. *Volume II/89.*

Probst, Hermann: Paulus und der Brief. 1991. *Volume II/45.*

Räisänen, Heikki: Paul and the Law. 1983, ²1987. *Volume 29.*

Rehkopf, Friedrich: Die lukanische Sonderquelle. 1959. *Volume 5.*

Rein, Matthias: Die Heilung des Blindgeborenen (Joh 9). 1995. *Volume II/73.*

Reinmuth, Eckart: Pseudo-Philo und Lukas. 1994. *Volume 74.*

Reiser, Marius: Syntax und Stil des Markus-
evangeliums. 1984. *Volume II/11.*
Richards, E. Randolph: The Secretary in the
Letters of Paul. 1991. *Volume II/42.*
Riesner, Rainer: Jesus als Lehrer. 1981, ³1988.
Volume II/7.
– Die Frühzeit des Apostels Paulus. 1994.
Volume 71.
Rissi, Mathias: Die Theologie des Hebräerbriefs.
1987. *Volume 41.*
Roskovec, Jan: see *Pokorný, Petr.*
Röhser, Günter: Metaphorik und Personifikation
der Sünde. 1987. *Volume II/25.*
Rose, Christian: Die Wolke der Zeugen. 1994.
Volume II/60.
Rüegger, Hans-Ulrich: Verstehen, was Markus
erzählt. 2002. *Volume II/155.*
Rüger, Hans Peter: Die Weisheitsschrift aus der
Kairoer Geniza. 1991. *Volume 53.*
Sänger, Dieter: Antikes Judentum und die
Mysterien. 1980. *Volume II/5.*
– Die Verkündigung des Gekreuzigten und
Israel. 1994. *Volume 75.*
– see *Burchard, Christoph*
Salzmann, Jorg Christian: Lehren und
Ermahnen. 1994. *Volume II/59.*
Sandnes, Karl Olav: Paul – One of the
Prophets? 1991. *Volume II/43.*
Sato, Migaku: Q und Prophetie. 1988.
Volume II/29.
Schaper, Joachim: Eschatology in the Greek
Psalter. 1995. *Volume II/76.*
Schimanowski, Gottfried: Die himmlische
Liturgie in der Apokalypse des Johannes.
2002. *Volume II/154.*
– Weisheit und Messias. 1985. *Volume II/17.*
Schlichting, Günter: Ein jüdisches Leben Jesu.
1982. *Volume 24.*
Schnabel, Eckhard J.: Law and Wisdom from
Ben Sira to Paul. 1985. *Volume II/16.*
Schutter, William L.: Hermeneutic and
Composition in I Peter. 1989. *Volume II/30.*
Schwartz, Daniel R.: Studies in the Jewish
Background of Christianity. 1992.
Volume 60.
Schwemer, Anna Maria: see *Hengel, Martin*
Scott, James M.: Adoption as Sons of God.
1992. *Volume II/48.*
– Paul and the Nations. 1995. *Volume 84.*
Shum, Shiu-Lun: Paul's Use of Isaiah in
Romans. 2002. *Volume II/156.*
Siegert, Folker: Drei hellenistisch-jüdische
Predigten. Teil I 1980. *Volume 20* – Teil II
1992. *Volume 61.*
– Nag-Hammadi-Register. 1982. *Volume 26.*

– Argumentation bei Paulus. 1985. *Volume 34.*
– Philon von Alexandrien. 1988. *Volume 46.*
Simon, Marcel: Le christianisme antique et son
contexte religieux I/II. 1981. *Volume 23.*
Snodgrass, Klyne: The Parable of the Wicked
Tenants. 1983. *Volume 27.*
Söding, Thomas: Das Wort vom Kreuz. 1997.
Volume 93.
– see *Thüsing, Wilhelm.*
Sommer, Urs: Die Passionsgeschichte des
Markusevangeliums. 1993. *Volume II/58.*
Souček, Josef B.: see *Pokorný, Petr.*
Spangenberg, Volker: Herrlichkeit des Neuen
Bundes. 1993. *Volume II/55.*
Spanje, T.E. van: Inconsistency in Paul? 1999.
Volume II/110.
Speyer, Wolfgang: Frühes Christentum im
antiken Strahlungsfeld. Volume I: 1989.
Volume 50.
– Volume II: 1999. *Volume 116.*
Stadelmann, Helge: Ben Sira als Schriftgelehr-
ter. 1980. *Volume II/6.*
Stenschke, Christoph W.: Luke's Portrait of
Gentiles Prior to Their Coming to Faith.
Volume II/108.
Stettler, Christian: Der Kolosserhymnus. 2000.
Volume II/131.
Stettler, Hanna: Die Christologie der Pastoral-
briefe. 1998. *Volume II/105.*
Stökl Ben Ezra, Daniel: The Impact of
Yom Kippur on Early Christianity. 2003.
Volume 163.
Strobel, August: Die Stunde der Wahrheit. 1980.
Volume 21.
Stroumsa, Guy G.: Barbarian Philosophy. 1999.
Volume 112.
Stuckenbruck, Loren T.: Angel Veneration and
Christology. 1995. *Volume II/70.*
Stuhlmacher, Peter (Ed.): Das Evangelium und
die Evangelien. 1983. *Volume 28.*
– Biblische Theologie und Evangelium. 2002.
Volume 146.
Sung, Chong-Hyon: Vergebung der Sünden.
1993. *Volume II/57.*
Tajra, Harry W.: The Trial of St. Paul. 1989.
Volume II/35.
– The Martyrdom of St.Paul. 1994.
Volume II/67.
Theißen, Gerd: Studien zur Soziologie des
Urchristentums. 1979, ³1989. *Volume 19.*
Theobald, Michael: Studien zum Römerbrief.
2001. *Volume 136.*
Theobald, Michael: see *Mußner, Franz.*
Thornton, Claus-Jürgen: Der Zeuge des
Zeugen. 1991. *Volume 56.*

Thüsing, Wilhelm: Studien zur neutestamentlichen Theologie. Ed. von Thomas Söding. 1995. *Volume 82.*

Thurén, Lauri: Derhethorizing Paul. 2000. *Volume 124.*

Tomson, Peter J. and *Doris Lambers-Petry* (Ed.): The Image of the Judaeo-Christians in Ancient Jewish and Christian Literature. 2003. *Volume 158.*

Treloar, Geoffrey R.: Lightfoot the Historian. 1998. *Volume II/103.*

Tsuji, Manabu: Glaube zwischen Vollkommenheit und Verweltlichung. 1997. *Volume II/93.*

Twelftree, Graham H.: Jesus the Exorcist. 1993. *Volume II/54.*

Urban, Christina: Das Menschenbild nach dem Johannesevangelium. 2001. *Volume II/137.*

Visotzky, Burton L.: Fathers of the World. 1995. *Volume 80.*

Vollenweider, Samuel: Horizonte neutestamentlicher Christologie. 2002. *Volume 144.*

Vos, Johan S.: Die Kunst der Argumentation bei Paulus. 2002. *Volume 149.*

Wagener, Ulrike: Die Ordnung des „Hauses Gottes". 1994. *Volume II/65.*

Walker, Donald D.: Paul's Offer of Leniency (2 Cor 10:1). 2002. *Volume II/152.*

Walter, Nikolaus: Praeparatio Evangelica. Ed. von Wolfgang Kraus und Florian Wilk. 1997. *Volume 98.*

Wander, Bernd: Gottesfürchtige und Sympathisanten. 1998. *Volume 104.*

Watts, Rikki: Isaiah's New Exodus and Mark. 1997. *Volume II/88.*

Wedderburn, A.J.M.: Baptism and Resurrection. 1987. *Volume 44.*

Wegner, Uwe: Der Hauptmann von Kafarnaum. 1985. *Volume II/14.*

Weissenrieder, Annette: Images of Illness in the Gospel of Luke. 2003. Volume II/164.

Welck, Christian: Erzählte ‚Zeichen'. 1994. *Volume II/69.*

Wiarda, Timothy: Peter in the Gospels . 2000. *Volume II/127.*

Wilk, Florian: see *Walter, Nikolaus.*

Williams, Catrin H.: I am He. 2000. *Volume II/113.*

Wilson, Walter T.: Love without Pretense. 1991. *Volume II/46.*

Wisdom, Jeffrey: Blessing for the Nations and the Curse of the Law. 2001. *Volume II/133.*

Wucherpfennig, Ansgar: Heracleon Philologus. 2002. *Volume 142.*

Yeung, Maureen: Faith in Jesus and Paul. 2002. *Volume II/147.*

Zimmermann, Alfred E.: Die urchristlichen Lehrer. 1984, ²1988. *Volume II/12.*

Zimmermann, Johannes: Messianische Texte aus Qumran. 1998. *Volume II/104.*

Zimmermann, Ruben: Geschlechtermetaphorik und Gottesverhältnis. 2001. *Volume II/122.*

Zumstein, Jean: see *Dettwiler, Andreas*

For a complete catalogue please write to the publisher
Mohr Siebeck • P.O. Box 2030 • D–72010 Tübingen/Germany
Up-to-date information on the internet at www.mohr.de